The 1st Amendment in the Classroom Series, Number 2

RELIGION

Freedom of

EDITED BY HAIG A. BOSMAJIAN

NEAL-SCHUMAN PUBLISHERS, INC.
NEW YORK   LONDON

THE FIRST AMENDMENT IN THE CLASSROOM SERIES
Edited by Haig A. Bosmajian

The Freedom to Read Books, Films and Plays. The First Amendment in the Classroom Series, No. 1. Foreword by Ken Donelson. ISBN 1-55570-001-2.

Freedom of Religion. The First Amendment in the Classroom Series, No. 2. ISBN 1-55570-002-0.

Freedom of Expression. The First Amendment in the Classroom Series, No. 3. ISBN 1-55570-003-9.

Academic Freedom. The First Amendment in the Classroom Series, No. 4. ISBN 1-55570-004-7.

The Freedom to Publish. The First Amendment in the Classroom Series, No. 5. ISBN 1-55570-005-5.

Published by Neal-Schuman Publishers, Inc.
23 Leonard Street
New York, New York 10013

Printed and bound in the United States of America.

Library of Congress Cataloging-in-Publication Data

Freedom of religion.

   (The First Amendment in the classroom series; no. 2)
   Includes index.
   1. Religion in the public schools—Law and legis-
lation—United States—Cases. I. Bosmajian, Haig A.
II. Series.
KF4162.A7F74 1987   344.73'0796   86-33317
ISBN 1-55570-002-0   347.304796

Contents

Preface

THE *First Amendment in the Classroom Series* responds to the need for teachers, students, parents, and school board members to become more aware of how First Amendment rights apply to the classrooms of a free society. Those cherished rights, if they have any meaning, are directly relevant and essential to our schools. What is especially needed is a wider familiarity with and understanding of the arguments and reasoning used to reach judgments regarding First Amendment issues, so often controversial and divisive, affecting what goes on in the classroom. To be unfamiliar with those arguments is to be unprepared to defend the First Amendment rights of students and teachers. Those arguments will be found in this series devoted to (1) the banning of books, plays, and films; (2) religion and prayer in the classroom; (3) symbolic speech; (4) teaching methods and teachers' classroom behavior; and (5) school publications and underground newspapers. My earlier volume, *Censorship, Libraries, and the Law,* covers cases of school library censorship.

When United States District Judge Hugh Bownes declared unconstitutional a Portsmouth, New Hampshire, Board of Education rule forbidding "distribution of non-school sponsored written materials within the Portsmouth schools and on school grounds for a distance of 200 feet from school entrances," he declared in the order of the court that "this opinion and Order is to be posted on the school bulletin board in a prominent place, and copies of this opinion and Order are to be made available to the students in the school library."[1]

This was a reminder to students, teachers, and school board members—but especially to the students—that First Amendment rights applied to them. As the United States Supreme Court had put it exactly thirty years earlier in *Barnette,* the First Amendment rights need to be practiced in our schools "if we are not to strangle the free mind at its source and teach youth to discount important principles of our government as mere platitudes."[2]

While the actual decisions in the cases involving the First Amendment rights of students and teachers in the classroom are crucial, the arguments and reasoning in the opinions are equally important. *Why* did the court decide that students could not be prohibited from distributing their literature? *Why* did the court decide that students could not be compelled to salute the flag? *Why* could the teacher not be dismissed for using books containing "offensive" language? *Why* could not the school board dismiss the teacher for using "unorthodox" teaching methods? *Why* could not parents have sex education banned from the school? *Why* did the court decide that prayer in the classroom was unconstitutional? Understanding the "whys" leads to an understanding of the workings of a democratic society.

In 1937, when throughout the world democratic institutions were being threatened and some were being destroyed, John Dewey observed that wherever political democracy has fallen, "it was too exclusively political in nature. It had not become part of the bone and blood of the people in daily conduct of life. Democratic forms were limited to Parliament, elections, and combats between parties. What is happening proves conclusively, I think, that unless democratic habits of thought and action are part of the fibre of a people, political democracy is insecure. It cannot stand in isolation. It must be buttressed by the presence of democratic methods in all social relationships."[3]

When the students, teachers, school boards, and parents involved in these cases insisted on exercising their First Amendment freedoms, they learned that the principles of our democracy are not "mere platitudes." For the students especially, the cases helped demonstrate that the Bill of Rights and "democratic habits of thought and action are part of the fibre of a people." These cases show political democracy "buttressed by the presence of democratic methods" in one realm of our society—the classroom.

It has been clearly established at several levels of our judicial system that protecting the First Amendment freedoms of teachers and students is crucial in a free society. In *Barnette,* the United States Supreme Court declared: "The Fourteenth Amendment, as now applied to the States, protects the citizen against the State itself and all of its creatures—Boards of Education not excepted. These have, of course, important, delicate, and highly discretionary functions, but none that they may not perform within the limits of the Bill of Rights.That they are educating the young for citizenship is reason for scrupulous protection of Constitutional freedoms of the individual, if we are not to to strangle the free mind at its source and teach youth to discount important principles of our government as mere platitudes."

In giving First Amendment protection to junior and senior high school students who had worn black armbands to school to protest U.S. involvement in the Vietnam War, the United States Supreme Court spoke most clearly in *Tinker* on the issue of the First Amendment rights of teachers and students. Justice Abe Fortas, delivering the opinion of the Court, said in 1969: "First Amendment rights, applied in light of the special characteristics of the school environment, are available to teachers and students. It can hardly be argued that either students or teachers shed their constitutional rights to freedom of speech or expression at the schoolhouse gate. This has been the unmistakable holding of this Court for almost 50 years."[4]

When in 1978 United States District Court Judge Joseph Tauro ordered school authorities to return to the high school library a book which had been removed because it contained a "dirty, filthy" poem, he reiterated in his own words what had been declared in *Tinker:* ". . . the First Amendment is not merely a mantle which students and faculty doff when they take their places in the classroom."[5]

On these pages are the stories of students and teachers who risked much to fight for their First Amendment rights in the classroom, who did not "shed their constitutional rights to freedom of speech or expression at the schoolhouse gate" and did not see the First Amendment as "merely a mantle which students and teachers doff when they take their places in the classroom." What is encouraging is that in almost all the cases appearing in this series, students and teachers have been given First Amendment protection by the courts.

The reasons given in the opinions on these pages are applicable to many of those First Amendment controversies which may never reach the courts. Edward Jenkinson, who has done much research and writing on censorship in the schools and who chaired the National Council of Teachers of English Committee Against Censorship has reported: "During the early seventies, approximately one hundred censorship incidents were reported to the ALA [American Library Association]'s Office for Intellectual Freedom each year. By 1976, the number had risen to slightly less than two hundred and climbed to nearly three hundred in 1977." Shortly after the 1980 Presidential election, Judith Krug of the American Library Association estimated a threefold increase in reported censorship incidents, "which would mean roughly nine hundred reported incidents a year." But as Jenkinson points out, the reported incidents "are only a small part of the censorship attempts each year. . . . After talking with teachers, librarians and administrators in meetings in 33 states, I believe that for every reported incident of censorship at least fifty go unreported."[6]

The First Amendment in the Classroom makes available the many substantial arguments that can be used by students, teachers, and parents involved in First Amendment controversies surrounding teachers and students in the classroom. The reasons given by the judges on these pages are there for students, teachers, and parents to use in their efforts to persuade school boards and others that the First Amendment applies to the school environment and that the "Fourteenth Amendment, as now applied to the States, protects the citizen against the State itself and all of its creatures—Boards of Education not excepted."

In his discussion of the nature and function of the judicial court opinion, legal scholar Piero Calamandrei has observed that "the most important and most typical indication of the rationality of the judicial function is the reasoned opinion." Of the need for the judge to present the reasoned opinion, Calamandrei says that

> "ever since justice descended from heaven to earth and the idea gained ground that the judge is a human being and not a supernatural and infallible oracle to be adored, whose authority is beyond question, man has felt the need of a rational explanation to give validity to the word of the judge." [The major function of the reasoned opinion, explains Calamandrei,] "is an explanatory or, one might say, a pedagogical one. No longer content merely to command, to proclaim a *sic volo, sic iubeo* [So I wish, so I command] from his high bench, the judge descends to the level of the parties, and although still commanding, seeks to impress them with the reasonableness of the command. The reasoned opinion is above all the justification of the decision and as such it attempts to be as persuasive as it can."[7]

Like the judge, neither supernatural nor infallible, we are asked for rational explanations to justify our decisions. The judicial opinions on these pages provide useful and persuasive reasons.

I hope that readers of the books in this series—students, teachers, school board members, parents, and others—will develop their appreciation for and commitment to the First Amendment rights of students and teachers in the classroom and will recognize the variety of arguments available to counter those who would not have the First Amendment apply to teachers and students. The First Amendment freedoms were put into the Bill of Rights to be used; the court opinions in this book demonstrate that teachers and students usually get First Amendment protection from the courts. We must recognize, however, that freedoms not exercised by the citizenry lose their vitality. Teachers and students, said Chief Justice Earl Warren, "must always remain free to inquire, to study and to evaluate, to gain new maturity and understanding; otherwise our civilization will stagnate and die."[8]

NOTES

1. *Vail* v. *Bd. of Ed. of Portsmouth School Dist.,* 354 F. Supp. 592 (1973).
2. *West Virginia State Bd. of Ed.* v. *Barnette,* 319 U.S. 624 (1943).
3. John Dewey, "Democracy and Educational Administration," *School and Society,* 45(April 3, 1937), p. 462.
4. *Tinker* v. *Des Moines School Dist.,* 393 U.S. 503 (1969).
5. *Right to Read Defense Committee* v. *School Committee, Etc.,* 454 F. Supp. 703 (1978).
6. Edward Jenkinson, "Protecting Holden Caulfield and His Friends from the Censors," *English Journal,* 74(January 1985), p. 74.
7. Piero Calamandrei, *Procedure and Democracy,* trans. John C. Adams and Helen Adams (New York: New York University Press, 1956), p. 53.
8. *Sweezy* v. *New Hampshire,* 354 U.S. 234 (1957).

Constitutional Amendments

ARTICLE I

Congress shall make no law respecting an establishment of religion, or prohibiting the free exercise thereof; or abridging the freedom of speech, or of the press; or the right of the people peaceably to assemble, and to petition the government for a redress of grievances.

ARTICLE XIV

All persons born or naturalized in the United States, and subject to the jurisdiction thereof, are citizens of the United States and of the State wherein they reside. No State shall make or enforce any law which shall abridge the privileges or immunities of citizens of the United States; nor shall any State deprive any person of life, liberty or property, without due process of law; nor deny to any person within its jurisdiction the equal protection of the law.

Judicial Circuits

Circuits	Composition
District of Columbia	District of Columbia
First	Maine, Massachusetts, New Hampshire, Puerto Rico, Rhode Island
Second	Connecticut, New York, Vermont
Third	Delaware, New Jersey, Pennsylvania, Virgin Islands
Fourth	Maryland, North Carolina, South Carolina, Virginia, West Virginia
Fifth	Louisiana, Mississippi, Texas
Sixth	Kentucky, Michigan, Ohio, Tennessee
Seventh	Illinois, Indiana, Wisconsin
Eighth	Arkansas, Iowa, Minnesota, Missouri, Nebraska, North Dakota, South Dakota
Ninth	Alaska, Arizona, California, Idaho, Montana, Nevada, Oregon, Washington, Guam, Hawaii, Northern Marianna Islands
Tenth	Colorado, Kansas, New Mexico, Oklahoma, Utah, Wyoming
Eleventh	Alabama, Georgia, Florida

Foreword

by Albert J. Menendez

Reading the cases and the admirable synopses preceding them in this very necessary and helpful volume, I was taken back in time to my days as a student growing up in northern Florida during the 1940s and 1950s.

What occurred in the schools of my youth seems amazing in retrospect. I can vividly recall the daily prayers, Bible readings, religious devotions, and evangelistic services conducted by jocks who encouraged us to score a touchdown for Jesus, religious clubs, and full-fledged holiday observances. And I mean full-fledged.

I think it was the fall of 1952 when, as a fifth-grader with a mellifluous voice, I was selected to play the role of a Puritan father in the annual Thanksgiving pageant. Came the time, and I, bedecked in suitable attire, delivered a sermon worthy of the finest Puritan divines of old. (It was written by a teacher. I did not ad lib, thank God.) The service concluded with several fine old Protestant hymns traditionally associated with the season.

A few weeks later we had a Christmas pageant that would have rivaled any good High Episcopal service, complete with processional, choir robes, a creche, and triumphant carol singing. As I recall, we sang "Come All Ye Faithful" in Latin, much to the delight of our music teacher. The whole community was involved. Parents and faculty thought it was delightful. Looking back, I wonder how they got away with it. No one suggested that this was an inappropriate activity for a public school. The religious homogeneity of my community—almost all were conservative Protestants—was undoubtedly a factor in keeping Lake Forest School on the side of religious conformity.

But even in a large urban high school—Jacksonville's Robert E. Lee, with its 2,000 students—the religious emphasis was no less intense. Daily prayers were read over the loud speaker during home room. Bible readings were assigned to each student. (Fortunately, no one read the more lurid passages from the Old Testament.) We even had denominational student clubs, in addition to Young Life and Youth for Christ. Once or twice a year, required student assemblies included harangues from local evangelists and religious workers assigned to public school "ministries."

None of these mandated activities seemed to have elicited much positive response by my fellow students. Some looked out the window, studied or daydreamed during the religious devotions. Most seemed indifferent to it all.

At graduation time we were all required to attend a Baccalaureate service at a local church. This time I put my foot down. I felt that to compel a student to attend a service in order to graduate was an unfair imposition. I requested that my

---

Albert J. Menendez is Director of Research at Americans United for Separation of Church and State.

parents write a respectful letter asking that I be excused. It was not because of any hostility toward religion; I attended church faithfully in those days. I was too young to say that this requirement was unconstitutional or constituted a probable violation of the Establishment Clause. But I knew it was wrong. After numerous appeals, the principal relented, and about thirty of the 540 graduates opted out for reasons of conscience. We were immediately labeled irreligious troublemakers by conformist students who themselves rarely if ever attended church.

I recall earlier incidents from my past: my third-grade teacher, a Miss Tidd, lectured the class one Monday on Armageddon, the Second Coming, and the certain damnation of all who rejected fundamentalist Protestantism. A ninth grade teacher, a Baptist from South Carolina, made insulting and ignorant remarks about Catholics and Jews several times during the year 1956. All of these experiences left permanent marks, and undoubtedly shaped my views on religious liberty, the voluntary character of true religion, and the importance of preserving separation of church and state.

Fortunately, conditions like this began to change after the Supreme Court ruled against mandated prayer and devotional Bible reading in 1962 and 1963. But many southern communities remain recalcitrant, even in 1987.

This is why this admirably up to date and complete volume of relevant court cases involving religious activities in the classroom is so important: The problem persists everywhere in this nation.

Since certain fundamentalist groups have given notice that they consider American public schools legitimate targets for evangelization—and in some southern states have been encouraged by local authorities to do so—we can be certain of frequent legal battles over the constitutionally proper place of religion in the classroom and in the curriculum. Recent efforts to legitimate the teaching of creationism in public school science classes is evidence of this.

There are many strengths in *Freedom of Religion* which should commend it to prospective readers. Not only does it contain important U.S. Supreme Court decisions, but relevant Appeals Court, District Court, and state Supreme Court decisions are also included. While these latter do not always have the same precedential value as the High Court rulings, they are useful in understanding how courts have tried to resolve the complex issues surrounding religion in the classroom. The thrust of these decisions is strongly against state sponsorship of religious activities.

Those who need to be informed about the legal context of this vital topic will find essential information in Professor Bosmajian's clear and precise volume. *Freedom of Religion* will be of great value to law students and professors, scholars, teachers, school personnel, school board members and attorneys—indeed to anyone interested in the subject.

Introduction

W HEN in 1962 the United States Supreme Court declared unconstitutional New York's school prayer statute in *Engel* v. *Vitale,* the Court's decision was lauded by some, but many condemned it as "asinine," the eight-man majority was referred to as "eight silly old men," and the decision was characterized as constituting another "major triumph for the forces of secularism and atheism." In *The Wall Between Church and State,* Philip Kurland wrote: "The reaction was an unenlightened one in the sense that the spokesmen for the various groups in the community committed themselves without reading and weighing what the Court said. They were all prepared to speak out on the basis of fragmentary news stories and statements of the Court's conclusion" [Dallin Oaks, ed., *The Wall Between Church and State,*1963, p. 148].

The twenty-one opinions in *Freedom of Religion* appear in their entirety and have been made available so that we can speak out, not on the basis of fragmentary stories and statements, but on the basis of having read and weighed what the courts have said about religion in our public school classrooms. The cases represent major Supreme Court and lower court rulings made over the past forty years. They address classroom prayer, periods of silence, Bible readings in the classroom, and other issues surrounding the First and Fourteenth Amendments. Each case is preceded by a brief introduction encapsulating the reasoning behind the decisions. In the cases of *McCollum, Engel, Schempp,* and *Jaffree* reprinted here, the opinions of the Court appear but the concurring and dissenting opinions do not because the latter opinions comprise over two hundred twenty-five pages in the United States Reports.

The United States Supreme Court has consistently applied the First Amendment to attempts to bring prayer and religion into the classroom; with few exceptions, the lower courts too have decided to keep religious practices out of public school classrooms. In only two of the cases compiled here did the courts decide to allow "religion" into the classroom. In one case (*Florey,* 1980), the United States Court of Appeals, Eighth Circuit, did not find unconstitutional a school's use of religious music, art, and history as part of classroom lessons on religious holidays. In the other case (*Gaines,* 1976), a United States District Court in Massachusetts upheld the constitutionality of a Massachusetts statute which provided that, at the beginning of the school day, there was to be a period of silence for meditation and prayer in each class, a statute similar to others struck down by various courts, including one declared unconstitutional by the United States Supreme Court (*Wallace* v. *Jaffree,* 1985). However, as the cases in this volume clearly reveal, the courts at all levels have been generally consistent in keeping prayer and religious activities out of our nation's public schools.

"Congress shall make no law respecting an establishment of religion, or prohibiting the free exercise thereof. . . . " The First Amendment protects the citizenry against federal abridgment of religious freedom; the Fourteenth Amendment, through its "life and liberty" provision, protects it against abridgment by the states. The Establishment Clause ensures that the government—federal or state—will not impose religion or any religious tests on anyone through its agencies, statutes, and practices. It is the Establishment Clause that prohibits the State from requiring as a condition of employment that individuals assert a belief in God; it is the Establishment Clause which prohibits the State from requiring that state composed prayers or any other kind of prayers be recited in public school classrooms; it is the Establishment Clause which prohibits taxpayers' money from being used to support religious proselytizing in our classrooms. The Free Exercise Clause in the First Amendment ensures that we can worship as we please and hold whatever religious beliefs we wish. In the words of the Supreme Court over a century ago in *Watson* v. *Jones* (1872): "In this country the full and free right to entertain any religious belief, to practice any religious principle, and to teach any religious doctrine which does not violate the laws of morality and property, and which does not infringe personal rights, is conceded to all. The law knows no heresy, and is committed to the support of no dogma, the establishment of no sect."

Over the years, attempts to bring religion into the classroom have taken a variety of forms. In 1940, several religious groups in Champaign, Illinois, as reported by the Supreme Court in *McCollum* v. *Board of Education,* "obtained permission from the Board of Education to offer classes in religious instruction to public school pupils in grades four to nine inclusive. Classes were made up of pupils whose parents signed printed cards requesting that their children be permitted to attend; they were held weekly, thirty minutes for the lower grades, forty-five minutes for the higher." Religious teachers were brought into the schools to teach the classes which "were conducted in the regular classrooms of the school building. Students who did not choose to take the religious instruction were not released from public school duties; they were required to leave their classrooms and go to some other place in the school building for pursuit of their secular studies."

In 1944, ten-year-old James Terry McCollum did not participate in this religious instruction and on one occasion was ordered to sit at a desk in the hallway where students passing by teased him, thinking that he was being punished. In effect, young McCollum, by being required to leave the classroom and go to some other place in the school building, was compelled by the state to reveal his religious inclinations and beliefs; the child's religious preference, an otherwise private matter, had been made public. Parent Vashti McCollum went to the Illinois courts seeking to prohibit the public schools from teaching religious education during regular school hours.

The Illinois Supreme Court decided against McCollum in 1947. One year later, the United States Supreme Court declared the Champaign, Illinois, religious instruction program unconstitutional. Justice Black, delivering the opinion of the Court, said: "Pupils compelled by law to go to school for secular education are released in part from their legal duty upon the condition that they attend religious classes. This is beyond all question a utilization of the tax-established and tax-supported public school system to aid religious groups to spread their faith. And it falls squarely under the ban of the First Amendment." Citing from *Everson* v. *Bd. of Education,* 330 U.S. 1 (1947), Black wrote: "In the words of Jefferson, the clause against establishment of religion by law was intended to erect 'a wall of separation between church and state.'" At the end of his opinion, Black restated this metaphor: " . . . as we said in the *Everson* case, the First Amendment has erected a wall between Church and State which must be kept high and impregnable. Here not only are the State's tax-supported public school buildings used for the dissemination of religious doctrines. The State also affords sectarian groups an invaluable aid in that it helps to provide pupils for their religious classes through use of the State's compulsory public school machinery. This is not separation of Church and State."

In *Engel* v. *Vitale* (1962), Justice Black, again delivering the opinion of the Court, declared unconstitutional New York's state composed prayer for school children. Justice Black wrote: "There can be no doubt that New York's state prayer program officially establishes the religious beliefs embodied in the Regents' prayer. The respondents' [New York] argument to the contrary, which is largely based upon the contention that the Regents' prayer is 'non-denominational' and the fact that the program, as modified and approved by state courts, does not require all pupils to recite the prayer but permits those who wish to do so to remain silent or be excused from the room, ignores the essential nature of the program's constitutional defects. Neither the fact that the prayer may be denominationally neutral nor the fact that its observance on the part of the students is voluntary can serve to free it from the limitations of the Establishment Clause, as it might from the Free Exercise Clause, of the First Amendment, both of which are operative against the States by virtue of the Fourteenth Amendment.''

One year later, the United States Supreme Court, in *Abington* v. *Schempp*, declared unconstitutional a Pennsylvania statute requiring Bible readings at the opening of each school day, and a Baltimore school board rule providing for Bible readings or the recitation of the Lord's Prayer in its classrooms. "The conclusion follows," said the Court, "that in both cases the laws require religious exercises and such exercises are being conducted in direct violation of the rights of the appellees and petitioners. Nor are these required exercises mitigated by the fact that individual students may absent themselves upon parental request, for that fact furnishes no defense to a claim of unconstitutionality under the Establishment Clause. . . . Further, it is no defense to urge that the religious practices here may be relatively minor encroachments on the First Amendment. The breach of neutrality that is today a trickling stream may all too soon become a raging torrent and, in the words of Madison, 'it is proper to take alarm at the first experiment on our liberties.'''

While the Court declared unconstitutional the recitation by public school students of the state composed prayer, the Bible readings, and recitation of the Lord's Prayer, other types of religious activities were still being brought into the classroom. In 1964, a DeKalb, Illinois, kindergarten teacher required the children in her class to recite, prior to the morning snack, the following verse:

> We thank you for the flowers so sweet;
> We thank you for the food we eat;
> We thank you for the birds that sing;
> We thank you for everything.

Before some parents expressed complaints, the teacher had required her students to end the above verse with "We thank you, God, for everything." The parents of five-year-old Laura DeSpain brought action to enjoin school district officials from requiring their child to recite the prayer during regular school hours. After the United States District Court ruled in *DeSpain* v. *DeKalb County Community School Dist. 428* (1966) that the above verse was not a prayer or religious activity within the meaning of the Constitution, the United States Court of Appeals, Seventh Circuit, reversed, stating in *DeSpain* (1967) that "the so-called secular purposes of the verse were merely adjunctive and supplemental to its basic and primary purpose, which was the religious act of praising and thanking the Deity." The District Court judge had asserted that this is "a case *de minimis.* Despite the theologians' characterization of this verse as a prayer, the court believes that set in the framework of the whole school day, its purpose was not to pray but to instill in the children an appreciation of and gratefulness for the world around them— the birds, the flowers, the food, and everything. They asked no blessing; they sought no divine assistance." The U.S. Court of Appeals, however, saw it differently: "Certainly this verse was as innocuous as could be insofar as constituting an imposition of religious tenets upon nonbelievers. We are reminded, however, of what the Supreme Court said in *Schempp*: '[I]t is no defense to urge that the religious practices here may be relatively minor encroachments on the First Amendment.'''

A different kind of attempt to bring religion into the classroom was made in

1978, when the state of Kentucky passed legislation which required that a copy of the Ten Commandments be posted on the wall of each public classroom in the state. The Kentucky Supreme Court in *Stone* v. *Graham* (1980) decided that the statute did not violate the First Amendment. The United States Supreme Court disagreed, and in deciding that posting the Commandments on the classroom walls was a violation of the Establishment Clause, the Court said in *Stone* v. *Graham:* "The pre-eminent purpose for posting the Ten Commandments is plainly religious in nature. The Ten Commandments are undeniably a sacred text in the Jewish and Christian faiths, and no legislative recitation of a supposed secular purpose can blind us to that fact. The Commandments do not confine themselves to arguably secular matters, such as honoring one's parents, killing or murder, adultery, stealing, false witness, and covetousness. . . . Rather, the first part of the Commandments concerns the religious duties of believers: worshipping the Lord God alone, avoiding idolatry, not using the Lord's name in vain, and observing the Sabbath Day."

In the 1980s, the courts at various levels have had to rule on more subtle attempts to bring religion into the public schools, such as statutes requiring a period of voluntary prayer or meditation. For example, the Massachusetts legislature was considering an act which provided: "At the commencement of the first class of each day in all grades in all public schools the teacher in charge of the room in which each class is held shall announce that a period of voluntary prayer or meditation may be offered by a student volunteer, not to exceed one minute in duration." In *Opinions of the Justices to the House of Representatives, Mass.* (1982) the Massachusetts Justices concluded that the bill "if enacted, could violate the First and Fourteenth Amendments to the Constitution."

The same year, a United States District Court in Tennessee declared unconstitutional Tennessee's statute which stated: "At the commencement of the first class of each day in all grades in all public schools, the teacher in charge of the room in which such class is held shall announce that a period of silence not to exceed one minute in duration shall be observed for meditation or prayer or personal beliefs and during any such period, silence shall be maintained." In *Beck* v. *McElrath* the court rejected the state's contention that "the statute merely provides for enforcement of a moment of silence in public schools. . . . As all terms in the statute are viewed together and accorded reasonable meaning, it is difficult to escape the conclusion that the legislative purpose was advancement of religious exercises in the classroom."

New Jersey took a different approach, not mentioning in its statute "prayer" or "meditation" or "personal beliefs"; instead, the New Jersey statute required that public school principals and teachers "shall permit students to observe one minute of silence to be used solely at the discretion of the individual students, before the opening exercises of each day for quiet and private contemplation or introspection." Declaring the statute unconstitutional, a United States District Court concluded in *May* v. *Cooperman* (1983) that, in response to public sentiment, New Jersey legislators had introduced "one bill after another in an attempt to reintroduce prayer in the public schools notwithstanding the Supreme Court's ruling." The statute was a guise to bring prayer into the classroom; the court declared that "the purpose of Bill 1064 was to mandate a period at the start of each school day when all students would have an opportunity to engage in prayer." The purpose of the New Jersey statute, said Judge Debevoise, "is religious, not secular."

In 1985, the United States Supreme Court declared unconstitutional an Alabama statute which read: "At the commencement of the first class of each day in all grades in all public schools the teacher in charge of the room in which each class is held may announce that a period of silence not to exceed one minute in duration shall be observed for meditation or voluntary prayer, and during any such period no other activities shall be engaged in." Justice Stevens, delivering the opinion of the Court in *Wallace* v. *Jaffree,* asserted that the record in this case revealed that the enactment of the statute "was not motivated by any clearly secular purpose—indeed, the statute had *no* secular purpose."

Again and again, the courts have invoked the metaphoric "wall of separation" between church and state in declaring these numerous statutes unconstitutional, whether the activities required in classrooms took the form of a state composed prayer, verses read from the Bible, recitation of the Lord's prayer, a "period of voluntary prayer or meditation," or a minute for "quiet and private contemplation or introspection." The "wall of separation" has stood as a strong argument against bringing religious practices into our public schools. In 1985, a United States District Court in West Virginia, in declaring unconstitutional a West Virginia "prayer amendment," relied in *Walter* v. *West Virginia Bd. of Education* on the "wall" metaphor as applied by Supreme Court Justice Black in *Everson*:

> The "establishment of religion" clause of the First Amendment means at least this: Neither a state nor the Federal Government can set up a church. Neither can pass laws which aid one religion, aid all religions, or prefer one religion over another. Neither can force nor influence a person to go to or to remain away from church against his will or force him to profess a belief or disbelief in any religion. . . . No tax in any amount, large or small, can be levied to support any religious activities or institutions, whatever they may be called, or whatever form they may adopt to teach or practice religion. Neither a state nor the Federal Government can, openly or secretly, participate in the affairs of any religious organizations or groups and vice versa. In the words of Jefferson, the clause against establishment of religion by law was intended to erect "a wall of separation between Church and State."

While the "prayer" cases predominate in this volume, the courts have had to deal with other classroom-religion issues. For example, the New York Supreme Court decided in *La Rocca* v. *Board of Ed. of Rye City Sch. Dist.* (1978) against a teacher who had used the classroom for religious proselytizing; the United States Court of Appeals decided in *Nartowicz* v. *Stripling* (1984) against a Georgia county school district which had permitted the schools' public address systems to be used for announcements of church-sponsored activities; a United States District Court held in *Malnak* v. *Yogi* (1977) that teaching the course "Science of Creative Intelligence/Transcendental Meditation" in the New Jersey public high schools violated the Establishment Clause.

The courts have been consistent in their decisions to keep religious practices and proselytizing out of the classroom, recognizing that at times the arguments that these practices are "secular" and hence not violations of the Establishment Clause are a guise. When, in 1985, a United States District Court declared in *Walter* (1985) that West Virginia's "prayer amendment" was unconstitutional, District Court Judge Hallanan rejected the Board of Education's argument that the prayer amendment had "the primary purpose and effect of promoting not religion, but religious freedom. The promotion of religious freedom is a legitimate secular purpose, consonant with the purpose of the Free Exercise Clause of the First Amendment." The District Court did not find this argument persuasive, condemning the manner in which the citizenry had been misled: "This Court cannot refrain from observing that in its opinion a *hoax* conceived in political expediency has been perpetrated upon those sincere citizens of West Virginia who voted for this amendment to the West Virginia Constitution in the belief that even if it violated the United States Constitution 'majority rule' would prevail. There is no such provision in the Constitution." [italics added].

Deception and pretext on the part of legislators and school board members came under attack two years earlier when a United States District Court in New Mexico in *Duffy* v. *Las Cruces Public Schools* (1983) declared unconstitutional that state's statute authorizing one minute of silence at the beginning of the school day for "contemplation, meditation or prayer": "The Board members now say that their purpose in implementing the moment of silence was to enhance discipline and instill in the students the 'intellectual composure' necessary for effective learning. These justifications are clearly the product of afterthought. They are no more than an elaborate effort to inject a secular purpose into a clearly religious activity. . . . It is clear that the educational benefits alleged by the Board members are a mere *pretext*. Their purpose was to institute a devotional exercise in public school classrooms" [italics added]. The court concluded that the school board "must be permanently enjoined from instituting any program similar to the moment of silence. . . . If the defendants are not so enjoined, the moment of silence issue could well be brought before them again. But the defendants would be more careful to *disguise* their purpose the next time. With *a wink and a nod,* they could discuss the secular purposes for the moment of silence and prohibit any discussion of the school prayer issue. Having avoided the factors which lead the Court to rule against them in this case, they could reinstitute the moment of silence" [italics added].

Under the guise of "academic freedom," efforts have been made by some to bring religion into the classroom through the "creation science" door. In 1981, the Louisiana legislature enacted a "Balanced Treatment for Creation-Science and Evolution-Science in Public School Instruction" law which required the teaching of creation science in Louisiana public schools whenever evolution was taught. The Act was declared unconstitutional by a United States District Court and subsequently the United States Court of Appeals, Fifth Circuit, affirmed the district court's judgment; the Court of Appeals declared in *Aguillard* v. *Edwards* (1985): "In truth, notwithstanding the supposed complexities of religion-versus-state issues and the lively debate they generate, this particular case is a simple one, subject to a simple disposal: the Act violates the Establishment Clause of the First Amendment because the purpose of the statute is to promote a religious belief." As to the legislature's claim that the statute had as its purpose to "protect academic freedom," the court responded: "Although we must treat the legislature's statement of purpose with deference, we are not absolutely bound by such statements or legislative disclaimers. . . . Although the record here reflects *self-serving statements* made in the legislative hearings by the Act's sponsor and supporters, this testimonial avowal of secular purpose is not sufficient, in this case, to avoid conflict with the First Amendment" [italics added]. Louisiana officials appealed to the United States Supreme Court, arguing that creation science embodies a scientifically tenable theory that life appeared abruptly in complex form and that such a theory does not depend on religious teaching. Seventy-two Nobel Prize winners and twenty-four scientific organizations urged the Supreme Court to declare the Louisiana statute unconstitutional, telling the Court that the case threatens American science by disparaging scientific facts to promote fundamentalist Christian beliefs. *

The courts have recognized that those who would bring religious teachings and practices into the classroom have attempted to bring in through the back door what the Constitution and the Supreme Court have barred from coming in through the front door. It is too late in the day to blatantly introduce Bible readings, state composed prayers, and postings of the Ten Commandments in public school classrooms; that front door has been closed. The courts have strongly condemned attempts to bring religious exercises through the back door with "self-serving statements" about academic freedom, one minute of silence "for meditation, contemplation or prayer," or some variation thereof, referring to them as "pretexts," "hoaxes," and "disguises." The decisions in this volume clearly demonstrate a general agreement among the courts that the First Amendment prohibits bringing religious exercises and practices into public school classrooms, whether through the front door or the back door.

---

*On June 19, 1987, in a 7–2 vote, the Supreme Court upheld the Court of Appeals' decision. The full text will appear in *Academic Freedom,* Volume 4 of this series.

THE United States Supreme Court declares unconstitutional, in an 8-1 decision, a Champaign, Illinois, school board policy of employing religious teachers of the Catholic, Protestant, and Jewish faiths to give religious instruction in the public schools once a week to those students whose parents signed cards requesting that their children be permitted to attend the religion classes. "Students who did not choose to take the religious instruction were not released from public school duties; they were required to leave their classrooms and go to some other place in the school building for pursuit of their secular studies." Justice Black, delivering the opinion of the Court, argued: " . . . The First Amendment has erected a wall between Church and State which must be kept high and impregnable. Here not only are the State's tax-supported public school buildings used for the dissemination of religious doctrines. The State also affords sectarian groups an invaluable aid in that it helps to provide pupils for their religious classes through use of the state's compulsory public school machinery. This is not separation of Church and State."

McCollum v. *Board of Education*, 333 U.S. 203 (1948)

Mr. Justice Black delivered the opinion of the Court.

This case relates to the power of a state to utilize its tax-supported public school system in aid of religious instruction insofar as that power may be restricted by the First and Fourteenth Amendments to the Federal Constitution.

The appellant, Vashti McCollum, began this action for mandamus against the Champaign Board of Education in the Circuit Court of Champaign County, Illinois. Her asserted interest was that of a resident and taxpayer of Champaign and of a parent whose child was then enrolled in the Champaign public schools. Illinois has a compulsory education law which, with exceptions, requires parents to send their children, aged seven to sixteen, to its tax-supported public schools where the children are to remain in attendance during the hours when the schools are regularly in session. Parents who violate this law commit a misdemeanor punishable by fine unless the children attend private or parochial schools which meet educational standards fixed by the State. District boards of education are given general supervisory powers over the use of the public school buildings within the school districts. Ill. Rev. Stat. ch. 122, § § 123, 301 (1943).

Appellant's petition for mandamus alleged that religious teachers, employed by private religious groups, were permitted to come weekly into the school buildings during the regular hours set apart for secular teaching, and then and there for a period of thirty minutes substitute their religious teaching for the secular education provided under the compulsory education law. The petitioner charged that this joint public-school religious-group program violated the First and Fourteenth Amendments to the United States Constitution. The prayer of her petition was that the Board of Education be ordered to "adopt and enforce rules and regulations prohibiting all instruction in and teaching of religious education in all public schools in Champaign School District Number 71, . . . and in all public school houses and buildings in said district when occupied by public schools."

The board first moved to dismiss the petition on the ground that under Illinois law appellant had no standing to maintain the action. This motion was denied. An answer was then filed, which admitted that regular weekly religious instruction was given during school hours to those pupils whose parents consented and that those pupils were released temporarily from their regular secular classes for the limited purpose of attending the religious classes. The answer denied that this coordinated program of religious instruction violated the State or Federal Constitution. Much evidence was heard, findings of fact were made, after which the petition for mandamus was denied on the ground that the school's religious instruction program violated neither the federal nor state constitutional provisions invoked by the appellant. On appeal the State Supreme Court affirmed. 396 Ill. 14, 71 N. E. 2d 161. Appellant appealed to this Court under 28 U. S. C. § 344 (a), and we noted probable jurisdiction on June 2, 1947.

The appellees press a motion to dismiss the appeal on several grounds, the first of which is that the judgment of the State Supreme Court does not draw in question the "validity of a statute of any State" as required by 28 U. S. C § 344 (a). This contention rests on the admitted fact that the challenged program of religious instruction was not expressly authorized by statute. But the State Supreme Court has sustained the validity of the program on the ground that the Illinois statutes granted the board authority to establish such a program. This holding is sufficient to show that the validity of an Illinois statute was drawn in question within the meaning of 28 U. S. C. § 344 (a). *Hamilton* v. *Regents of U. of Cal.,* 293 U. S. 245, 258. A second ground for the motion to dismiss is that the appellant lacks standing to maintain the action, a ground which is also without merit. *Coleman* v. *Miller,* 307 U. S. 433, 443, 445, 464. A third ground for the motion is that the appellant failed properly to present in the State Supreme Court her challenge that the state program violated the Federal Constitution. But in view of the express rulings of both state courts on this question, the argument cannot be successfully maintained. The motion to dismiss the appeal is denied.

Although there are disputes between the parties as to various inferences that may or may not properly be drawn from the evidence concerning the religious program, the following facts are shown by the record without dispute.[1] In 1940 interested members of the Jewish, Roman Catholic, and a few of the Protestant faiths formed a voluntary association called the Champaign Council on Religious Education. They obtained permission from the Board of Education to offer classes in religious instruction to public school pupils in grades four to nine inclusive. Classes were made up of pupils whose parents signed printed cards requesting that their children be permitted to attend;[2] they were held weekly, thirty minutes for the lower grades, forty-five minutes for the higher. The council employed the religious teachers at no expense to the school authorities, but the instructors were subject to the approval and supervision of the superintendent of schools.[3] The classes were taught in three separate religious groups by Protestant teachers,[4] Catholic priests, and a Jewish rabbi, although for the past several years there have apparently been no classes instructed in the Jewish religion. Classes were conducted in the regular classrooms of the school building. Students who did not choose to take the religious instruction were not released from public school duties; they were required to leave their classrooms and go to some other place in the school building for pursuit of their secular studies. On the other hand, students who were released from secular study for the religious instructions were required to be present at the religious classes. Reports of their presence or absence were to be made to their secular teachers.[5]

The foregoing facts, without reference to others that appear in the record, show the use of tax-supported property for religious instruction and the close cooperation between the school authorities and the religious council in promoting religious education. The operation of the State's compulsory education system thus assists and is integrated with the program of religious instruction carried on by separate religious sects. Pupils compelled by law to go to school for secular education are released in part from their legal duty upon the condition that they attend the religious classes. This is beyond all question a utilization of the tax-established and tax-supported public school system to aid religious groups to spread their faith. And it falls squarely under the ban of the First Amendment (made applicable to the States by the Fourteenth) as we interpreted it in *Everson* v. *Board of Education,* 330 U. S. 1. There we said: "Neither a state nor the Federal Government can set up a church. Neither can pass laws which aid one religion; aid all religions, or prefer one religion over another.[6] Neither can force or influence a person to go to or to remain away from church against his will or force him to profess a belief or disbelief in any religion. No person can be punished for entertaining or professing religious beliefs or disbeliefs, for church attendance or non-attendance. No tax in any amount, large or small, can be levied to support any religious activities or institutions, whatever they may be called, or whatever form they may adopt to teach or practice religion.[7] Neither a state nor the Federal Government can, openly or secretly, participate in the affairs of any religious organizations or groups and *vice versa.* In the words of Jefferson, the clause against establishment of religion by law was intended to erect 'a wall of separation between church and State.'" *Id.* at 15-16. The majority in the *Everson* case, and the minority as shown by quotations from the dissenting views in our notes 6 and 7, agreed that the First Amendment's language, properly interpreted, had erected a wall of separation between Church and State. They disagreed as to the facts shown by the record and as to the proper application of the First Amendment's language to those facts.

Recognizing that the Illinois program is barred by the First and Fourteenth Amendments if we adhere to the views expressed both by the majority and the minority in the *Everson* case, counsel for the respondents challenge those views as dicta and urge that we reconsider and repudiate them. They argue that historically the First Amendment was intended to forbid only government preference of one religion over another, not an impartial governmental assistance of all religions. In addition they ask that we distinguish or overrule our holding in the *Everson* case that the Fourteenth Amendment made the "establishment of religion" clause of the First Amendment applicable as a prohibition against the States. After giving full consideration to the arguments presented we are unable to accept either of these contentions.

To hold that a state cannot consistently with the First and Fourteenth Amendments utilize its public school system to aid any or all religious faiths or sects in the dissemination of their doctrines and ideals does not, as counsel urge, manifest a governmental hostility to religion or religious teachings. A manifestation of such hostility would be at war with our national tradition as embodied in the First Amendment's guaranty of the free exercise of religion. For the First Amendment rests upon the premise that both religion and government can best work to achieve their lofty aims if each is left free from the other within its respective sphere. Or, as we said in the *Everson* case, the First Amendment has erected a wall between Church and State which must be kept high and impregnable.

Here not only are the State's tax-supported public school buildings used for the dissemination of religious doctrines. The State also affords sectarian groups an invaluable aid in that it helps to provide pupils for their religious classes through use of the State's compulsory public school machinery. This is not separation of Church and State.

The cause is reversed and remanded to the State Supreme Court for proceedings not inconsistent with this opinion.

Reversed and remanded.

NOTES

1. Appellant, taking issue with the facts found by the Illinois courts, argues that the religious education program in question is invalid under the Federal Constitution for any one of the following reasons: (1) In actual practice certain Protestant groups have obtained an overshadowing advantage in the propagation of their faiths over other Protestant sects; (2) the religious education program was voluntary in name only because in fact subtle pressures were brought to bear on the students to force them to participate in it; and (3) the power given the school superintendent to reject teachers selected by religious groups and the power given the local Council on Religious Education to determine which religious faiths should participate in the program was a prior censorship of religion.

   In view of our decision we find it unnecessary to consider these arguments or the disputed facts upon which they depend.

2. The Supreme Court described the request card system as follows: " . . . Admission to the classes was to be allowed only upon the express written request of parents, and then only to classes designated by the parents . . . . Cards were distributed to the parents of elementary students by the public-school teachers requesting them to indicate whether they desired their children to receive religious education. After being filled out, the cards were returned to the teachers of religious education classes either by the public-school teachers or the children . . . ." On this subject the trial court found that " . . . those students who have obtained the written consent of their parents therefor are released by the school authorities from their secular work, and in the grade schools for a period of thirty minutes' instruction in each week during said school hours, and forty-five minutes during each week in the junior high school, receive training in religious education . . . . Certain cards are used for obtaining permission of parents for their children to take said religious instruction courses, and they are made available through the offices of the superintendent of schools and through the hands of principals and teachers to the pupils of the school district. Said cards are prepared at the cost of the council of religious education. The handling and distribution of said cards does not interfere with the duties or suspend the regular secular work of the employees of the defendant . . . ."

3. The State Supreme Court said: "The record further discloses that the teachers conducting the religious classes were not teachers in the public schools but were subject to the approval and supervision of the superintendent . . . ." The trial court found: "Before any faith or other group may obtain permission from the defendant for the similar, free and equal use of rooms in the public school buildings said faith or group must make application to the superintendent of schools of said School District Number 71, who in turn will determine whether or not it is practical for said group to teach in said school system." The president of the local school board testified: " . . . The Protestants would have one group and the Catholics, and would be given a room where they would have the class and we would go along with the plan of the religious people. They were all to be treated alike, with the understanding that the teachers they would bring into the school were approved by the superintendent . . . . The superintendent was the last word so far as the individual was concerned . . . ."

4. There were two teachers of the Protestant faith. One was a Presbyterian and had been a foreign missionary for that church. The second testified as follows: "I am affiliated with the Christian church. I also work in the Methodist Church and I taught at the Presbyterian. I am married to a Lutheran."

5. The director of the Champaign Council on Religious Education testified: " . . . If any pupil is absent we turn in a slip just like any teacher would to the superintendent's office. The slip is a piece of paper with a number of hours in the school day and a square, and the teacher of the particular room for the particular hour records the

absentees. It has their names and the grade and the section to which they belong. It is the same sheet that the geography and history teachers and all the other teachers use, and is furnished by the school . . . ."

6. The dissent, agreed to by four judges, said: "The problem then cannot be cast in terms of legal discrimination or its absence. This would be true, even though the state in giving aid should treat all religious instruction alike . . . . Again, it was the furnishing of 'contributions of money for the propagation of opinions which he disbelieves' that the fathers outlawed. That consequence and effect are not removed by multiplying to all-inclusiveness the sects for which support is exacted. The Constitution requires, not comprehensive identification of state with religion, but complete separation." *Everson* v. *Board of Education,* 330 U. S. 1, 59, 60.

7. The dissenting judges said: "In view of this history no further proof is needed that the Amendment forbids any appropriation, large or small, from public funds to aid or support any and all religious exercises . . . . Legislatures are free to make, and courts to sustain, appropriations only when it can be found that in fact they do not aid, promote, encourage or sustain religious teaching or observances, be the amount large or small." *Everson* v. *Board of Education,* 330 U. S. 1, 41, 52–53.

I<small>N</small> a 6-1 vote, the United States Supreme Court decides against the state of New York which had composed the following prayer to be said at the beginning of each school day: "Almighty God, we acknowledge our dependence upon Thee, and we beg Thy blessings upon us, our parents, our teachers and our Country." In holding that the use of this prayer in the public schools was "wholly inconsistent with the Establishment Clause" of the First Amendment, the Court stated: "The First Amendment was added to the Constitution to stand as a guarantee that neither the power nor the prestige of the Federal Government would be used to control, support or influence the kinds of prayer the American people can say—that the people's religions must not be subjected to the pressures of government for change each time a new political administration is elected to office. Under that Amendment's prohibition against governmental establishment of religion, as reinforced by the provisions of the Fourteenth Amendment, government in this country, be it state or federal, is without power to prescribe by law any particular form of prayer which is to be used as an official prayer in carrying on any program of governmentally sponsored religious activity."

Engel v. *Vitale,* 370 U.S. 421 (1962)

Mr. Justice Black delivered the opinion of the Court.

The respondent Board of Education of Union Free School District No. 9, New Hyde Park, New York, acting in its official capacity under state law, directed the School District's principal to cause the following prayer to be said aloud by each class in the presence of a teacher at the beginning of each school day:

"Almighty God, we acknowledge our dependence upon Thee, and we beg Thy blessings upon us, our parents, our teachers and our Country."

This daily procedure was adopted on the recommendation of the State Board of Regents, a governmental agency created by the State Constitution to which the New York Legislature has granted broad supervisory, executive, and legislative powers over the State's public school system.[1] These state officials composed the prayer which they recommended and published as a part of their "Statement on Moral and Spiritual Training in the Schools," saying: "We believe that this Statement will be subscribed to by all men and women of good will, and we call upon all of them to aid in giving life to our program."

Shortly after the practice of reciting the Regents'

prayer was adopted by the School District, the parents of ten pupils brought this action in a New York State Court insisting that use of this official prayer in the public schools was contrary to the beliefs, religions, or religious practices of both themselves and their children. Among other things, these parents challenged the constitutionality of both the state law authorizing the School District to direct the use of prayer in public schools and the School District's regulation ordering the recitation of this particular prayer on the ground that these actions of official governmental agencies violate that part of the First Amendment of the Federal Constitution which commands that "Congress shall make no law respecting an establishment of religion"—a command which was "made applicable to the State of New York by the Fourteenth Amendment of the said Constitution." The New York Court of Appeals, over the dissents of Judges Dye and Fuld, sustained an order of the lower state courts which had upheld the power of New York to use the Regents' prayer as a part of the daily procedures of its public schools so long as the schools did not compel any pupil to join in the prayer over his or his parents' objection.[2] We granted certiorari to review this important decision involving rights protected by the First and Fourteenth Amendments.[3]

We think that by using its public school system to encourage recitation of the Regents' prayer, the State of New York has adopted a practice wholly inconsistent with the Establishment Clause. There can, of course, be no doubt that New York's program of daily classroom invocation of God's blessings as prescribed in the Regents' prayer is a religious activity. It is a solemn avowal of divine faith and supplication for the blessings of the Almighty. The nature of such a prayer has always been religious, none of the respondents has denied this and the trial court expressly so found:

> "The religious nature of prayer was recognized by Jefferson and has been concurred in by theological writers, the United States Supreme Court and State courts and administrative officials, including New York's Commissioner of Education. A committee of the New York Legislature has agreed.
>
> "The Board of Regents as *amicus curiae*, the respondents and intervenors all concede the religious nature of prayer, but seek to distinguish this prayer because it is based on our spiritual heritage . . . ."[4]

The petitioners contend among other things that the state laws requiring or permitting use of the Regents' prayer must be struck down as a violation of the Establishment Clause because that prayer was composed by governmental officials as a part of a governmental program to further religious beliefs. For this reason, petitioners argue, the State's use of the Regents' prayer in its public school system breaches the constitutional wall of separation between Church and State. We agree with that contention since we think that the constitutional prohibition against laws respecting an establishment of religion must at least mean that in this country it is no part of the business of government to compose official prayers for any group of the American people to recite as a part of a religious program carried on by government.

It is a matter of history that this very practice of establishing governmentally composed prayers for religious services was one of the reasons which caused many of our early colonists to leave England and seek religious freedom in America. The Book of Common Prayer, which was created under governmental direction and which was approved by Acts of Parliament in 1548 and 1549,[5] set out in minute detail the accepted form and content of prayer and other religious ceremonies to be used in the established, tax-supported Church of England.[6] The controversies over the Book and what should be its content repeatedly threatened to disrupt the peace of that country as the accepted forms of prayer in the established church changed with the views of the particular ruler that happened to be in control at the time.[7] Powerful groups representing some of the varying religious views of the people struggled among themselves to impress their particular views upon the Government and obtain amendments of the Book more suitable to their respective notions of how religious services should be conducted in order that the official religious establishment would advance their particular religious beliefs.[8] Other groups, lacking the necessary political power to influence the Government on the matter, decided to leave England and its established church and seek freedom in America from England's governmentally ordained and supported religion.

It is an unfortunate fact of history that when some of the very groups which had most strenuously opposed the established Church of England found themselves sufficiently in control of colonial governments in this country to write their own prayers into law, they passed laws making their own religion the official religion of their respective colonies.[9] Indeed, as late as the time of the Revolutionary War, there were established churches in at least eight of the thirteen former colonies and established religions in at least four of the other five.[10] But the successful Revolution against English political domination was shortly followed by intense opposition to the practice of establishing religion by law. This opposition crystallized rapidly into an effective political force in Virginia where the minority religious groups such as Presbyterians, Lutherans, Quakers and Baptists had gained such strength that the adherents to the established Episcopal Church were actually a minority themselves. In 1785–1786, those opposed to the established Church, led by James Madison and Thomas Jefferson, who, though themselves not members of any of these dissenting religious groups, opposed all religious establishments by law on grounds of principle, obtained the enactment of the famous "Virginia Bill for Religious Liberty" by which all religious groups were placed on an equal footing so far as the State was concerned.[11] Similar though less far-reaching legislation was being considered and passed in other States.[12]

By the time of the adoption of the Constitution, our history shows that there was a widespread awareness among many Americans of the dangers of a union of Church and State. These people knew, some of them from bitter personal experience, that one of the greatest dangers to the freedom of the individual to worship in his own way lay in the Government's placing its official stamp of approval upon one particular kind of prayer or one particular form of religious services. They knew the anguish, hardship and bitter strife that could come when zealous religious groups struggled with one another to obtain the Government's stamp of approval from each King, Queen, or Protector that came to temporary power. The Constitution was intended to avert a part of this danger by leaving the government of this country in the hands of the people rather than in the hands of any monarch. But this safeguard was not enough. Our Founders were no more willing to let the content of their prayers and their privilege of praying whenever they pleased be influenced by the ballot box than they were to let these vital matters of personal conscience depend upon the succession of monarchs. The First Amendment was added to the Constitution to stand as a guarantee that neither the power nor the prestige of the Federal Government would be used to control, support or influence the kinds of prayer the American people can say—that the people's religions must not be subjected to the pressures of government for change each time a new political administration is elected to office. Under that Amendment's prohibition against governmental establishment of religion, as reinforced by the provisions of the Fourteenth Amendment, government in this country, be it state or federal, is without power to prescribe by law any particular form of prayer which is to be used as an official prayer in carrying on any program of governmentally sponsored religious activity.

There can be no doubt that New York's state prayer program officially establishes the religious beliefs embodied in the Regents' prayer. The respondents' argument to the contrary, which is largely based upon the contention that the Regents' prayer is "non-denominational" and the fact that the program, as modified and approved by state courts, does not require all pupils to recite the prayer but permits those who wish to do so to remain silent or be excused from the room, ignores the essential nature of the program's constitutional defects. Neither the fact that the prayer may be denominationally neutral nor the fact that its observance on the part of the students is voluntary can serve to free it from the limitations of the Establishment Clause, as it might from the Free Exercise Clause, of the First Amendment, both of which are operative against the States by virtue of the Fourteenth Amendment. Although these two clauses may in certain instances overlap, they forbid two quite different kinds of governmental encroachment upon religious freedom. The Establishment Clause, unlike the Free Exercise Clause, does not depend upon any showing of direct governmental compulsion and is violated by the enactment of laws which establish an official religion whether those laws operate directly to coerce nonobserving individuals or not. This is not to say, of course, that laws officially prescribing a particular form of religious worship do not involve coercion of such individuals. When the power, prestige and financial support of government is placed behind a particular religious belief, the indirect coercive pressure upon religious minorities to conform to the prevailing officially approved religion is plain. But the purposes underlying the Establishment Clause go much further than that. Its first and most immediate purpose rested on the belief that a union of government and religion tends to destroy government and to degrade religion. The history of governmentally established religion, both in England and in this country, showed that whenever government had allied itself with one particular form of religion, the inevitable result had been that it had incurred the hatred, disrespect and even contempt of those who held contrary beliefs.[13] That same history showed that many people had lost their respect for any religion that had relied upon the support of government to spread its faith.[14] The Establishment Clause thus stands as an expression of principle on the part of the Founders of our Constitution that religion is too personal, too sacred, too holy, to permit its "unhallowed perversion" by a civil magistrate.[15] Another purpose of the Establishment Clause rested upon an awareness of the historical fact that governmentally established religions and religious persecutions go hand in hand.[16] The Founders knew that only a few years after the Book of Common Prayer became the only accepted form of religious services in the established Church of England, an Act of Uniformity was passed to compel all Englishmen to attend those services and to make it a criminal offense to conduct or attend religious gatherings of any other kind[17]—a law which was consistently flouted by dissenting religious groups in England and which contributed to widespread persecutions of people like John Bunyan who persisted in holding "unlawful [religious] meetings . . . to the great disturbance and distraction of the good subjects of this kingdom . . . ."[18] And they knew that similar persecutions had received the sanction of law in several of the colonies in this country soon after the establishment of official religions in those colonies.[19] It was in large part to get completely away from this sort of systematic religious persecution that the Founders brought into being our Nation, our Constitution, and our Bill of Rights with its prohibition against any governmental establishment of religion. The New York laws officially prescribing the Regents' prayer are inconsistent both with the purposes of the Establishment Clause and with the Establishment Clause itself.

It has been argued that to apply the Constitution in such a way as to prohibit state laws respecting an establishment of religious services in public schools is to indicate a hostility toward religion or toward prayer. Nothing, of course, could be more wrong. The history of man is inseparable from the history of religion. And perhaps it is not too much to say that since the beginning of that history many people have devoutly believed that "More things are wrought by prayer than this world dreams of." It was doubtless largely due to men who believed this that there grew up a sentiment that caused men to leave the cross-currents of officially established state religions and religious persecution in Europe and come to this country filled with the hope that they could find a place in which they could pray when they pleased to the God of their faith in the language they chose.[20] And there were men of this same faith in the power of prayer who led the fight for adoption of our Constitution and also for our Bill of Rights with the very guarantees of religious freedom that forbid the sort of governmental activity which New York has attempted here. These men knew that the First Amendment, which tried to put an end to governmental control of religion and of prayer, was not written to destroy either. They knew rather that it was written to quiet well-justified fears which nearly all of them felt arising out of an awareness that governments of the past had shackled men's tongues to make them speak only the religious thoughts that government wanted them to speak and to pray only to the God that government wanted them to pray to. It is neither sacrilegious nor antireligious to say that each separate government in this country should stay out of the business of writing or sanctioning official prayers and leave that purely religious function to the people themselves and to those the people choose to look to for religious guidance.[21]

It is true that New York's establishment of its Regents' prayer as an officially approved religious doctrine of that State does not amount to a total establishment of one particular religious sect to the exclusion of all others—that, indeed, the governmental endorsement of that prayer seems relatively insignificant when compared to the governmental encroachments upon religion which were commonplace 200 years ago. To those who may subscribe to the view that because the Regents' official prayer is so brief and general there can be no danger to religious freedom in its governmental establishment, however, it may be appropriate to say in the words of James Madison, the author of the First Amendment:

"[I]t is proper to take alarm at the first experiment on our liberties . . . . Who does not see that the same authority which can establish Christianity, in exclusion of all other Religions, may establish with the same ease any particular sect of Christians, in exclusion of all other Sects? That the same authority which can force a citizen to contribute three pence only of his property for the support of any one establishment, may force him to conform to any other establishment in all cases whatsoever?"[22]

The judgment of the Court of Appeals of New York is reversed and the cause remanded for further proceedings not inconsistent with this opinion.

Reversed and remanded.

Mr. Justice Frankfurter took no part in the decision of this case.

Mr. Justice White took no part in the consideration or decision of this case.

NOTES

1. See New York Constitution, Art. V, § 4; New York Education Law, § § 101, 120 *et seq.*, 202, 214–219, 224, 245 *et seq.*, 704, and 801 *et seq.*

2. 10 N. Y. 2d 174, 176 N. E. 2d 579. The trial court's opinion, which is reported at 18 Misc. 2d 659, 191 N. Y. S. 2d 453, had made it clear that the Board of Education must set up some sort of procedures to protect those who objected to reciting the prayer: "This is not to say that the rights accorded petitioners and their children under the 'free exercise' clause do not mandate safeguards against such embarrassments and pressures. It is enough on this score, however, that regulations, such as were adopted by New York City's Board of Education in connection with its released time program, be adopted, making clear that neither teachers nor any other school authority may comment on participation or nonparticipation in the exercise nor suggest or require that any posture or language be used or dress be worn or be not used or not worn. Nonparticipation may take the form either of remaining silent during the exercise, or if the parent or child so desires, of being excused entirely from the exercise. Such regulations must also make provision for those nonparticipants who are to be excused from the prayer exercise. The exact provision to be made is a matter for decision by the board, rather than the court, within the framework of constitutional requirements. Within that framework would fall a provision that prayer participants proceed to a common assembly while nonparticipants attend other rooms, or that nonparticipants be permitted to arrive at school a few minutes late or to attend separate opening exercises, or any other method which treats with equality both participants and nonparticipants." 18 Misc. 2d, at 696, 191 N. Y. S. 2d, at 492–493. See also the opinion of the Appellate Division affirming that of the trial court, reported at 11 App. Div. 2d 340, 206 N. Y. S. 2d 183.

3. 368 U. S. 924.

4. 18 Misc. 2d, at 671–672, 191 N. Y. S. 2d, at 468–469.

5. 2 & 3 Edward VI, c. 1, entitled "An Act for Uniformity of Service and Administration of the Sacraments throughout the Realm"; 3 & 4 Edward VI, c. 10, entitled "An Act for the abolishing and putting away of divers Books and Images."

6. The provisions of the various versions of the Book of Common Prayer are set out in broad outline in the Encyclopaedia Britannica, Vol. 18 (1957 ed.), pp. 420–423. For a more complete description, see Pullan, The History of the Book of Common Prayer (1900).

7. The first major revision of the Book of Common Prayer was made in 1552 during the reign of Edward VI. 5 & 6 Edward VI, c. 1. In 1553, Edward VI died and was succeeded by Mary who abolished the Book of Common Prayer entirely. 1 Mary, c. 2. But upon the accession of Elizabeth in 1558, the Book was restored with important alterations from the form it had been given by Edward VI. 1 Elizabeth, c. 2. The resentment to this amended form of the Book was kept firmly under control during the reign of Elizabeth but, upon her death in 1603, a petition signed by more than 1,000 Puritan ministers was presented to King James I asking for

further alterations in the Book. Some alterations were made and the Book retained substantially this form until it was completely suppressed again in 1645 as a result of the successful Puritan Revolution. Shortly after the restoration in 1660 of Charles II, the Book was again reintroduced, 13 & 14 Charles II, c. 4, and again with alterations. Rather than accept this form of the Book some 2,000 Puritan ministers vacated their benefices. See generally Pullan, The History of the Book of Common Prayer (1900), pp. vii–xvi; Encyclopaedia Britannica (1957 ed.), Vol. 18, pp. 421–422.

8. For example, the Puritans twice attempted to modify the Book of Common Prayer and once attempted to destroy it. The story of their struggle to modify the Book in the reign of Charles I is vividly summarized in Pullan, History of the Book of Common Prayer, at p. xiii: "The King actively supported those members of the Church of England who were anxious to vindicate its Catholic character and maintain the ceremonial which Elizabeth had approved. Laud, Archbishop of Canterbury, was the leader of this school. Equally resolute in his opposition to the distinctive tenets of Rome and of Geneva, he enjoyed the hatred of both Jesuit and Calvinist. He helped the Scottish bishops, who had made large concessions to the uncouth habits of Presbyterian worship, to draw up a Book of Common Prayer for Scotland. It contained a Communion Office resembling that of the book of 1549. It came into use in 1637, and met with a bitter and barbarous opposition. The vigour of the Scottish Protestants strengthened the hands of their English sympathisers. Laud and Charles were executed, Episcopacy was abolished, the use of the Book of Common Prayer was prohibited."

9. For a description of some of the laws enacted by early theocratic governments in New England, see Parrington, Main Currents in American Thought (1930), Vol. 1, pp. 5–50; Whipple, Our Ancient Liberties (1927), pp. 63–78; Wertenbaker, The Puritan Oligarchy (1947).

10. The Church of England was the established church of at least five colonies: Maryland, Virginia, North Carolina, South Carolina and Georgia. There seems to be some controversy as to whether that church was officially established in New York and New Jersey but there is no doubt that it received substantial support from those States. See Cobb, The Rise of Religious Liberty in America (1902), pp. 338, 408. In Massachusetts, New Hampshire and Connecticut, the Congregationalist Church was officially established. In Pennsylvania and Delaware, all Christian sects were treated equally in most situations but Catholics were discriminated against in some respects. See generally Cobb, The Rise of Religious Liberty in America (1902). In Rhode Island all Protestants enjoyed equal privileges but it is not clear whether Catholics were allowed to vote. Compare Fiske, The Critical Period in American History (1899), p. 76 with Cobb, The Rise of Religious Liberty in America (1902), pp. 437–438.

11. 12 Hening, Statutes of Virginia (1823), 84, entitled "An act for establishing religious freedom." The story of the events surrounding the enactment of this law was reviewed in *Everson* v. *Board of Education,* 330 U. S. 1, both by the Court, at pp. 11–13, and in the dissenting opinion of Mr. Justice Rutledge, at pp. 33–42. See also Fiske, The Critical Period in American History (1899), pp. 78–82; James, The Struggle for Religious Liberty in Virginia (1900); Thom, The Struggle for Religious Freedom in Virginia: The Baptists (1900); Cobb, The

Rise of Religious Liberty in America (1902), pp. 74–115, 482–499.

12. See Cobb, The Rise of Religious Liberty in America (1902), pp. 482–509.

13. "[A]ttempts to enforce by legal sanctions, acts obnoxious to so great a proportion of Citizens, tend to enervate the laws in general, and to slacken the bands of Society. If it be difficult to execute any law which is not generally deemed necessary or salutary, what must be the case where it is deemed invalid and dangerous? and what may be the effect of so striking an example of impotency in the Government, on its general authority." Memorial and Remonstrance against Religious Assessments, II Writings of Madison 183, 190.

14. "It is moreover to weaken in those who profess this Religion a pious confidence in its innate excellence, and the patronage of its Author; and to foster in those who still reject it, a suspicion that its friends are too conscious of its fallacies, to trust it to its own merits .... [E]xperience witnesseth that ecclesiastical establishments, instead of maintaining the purity and efficacy of Religion, have had a contrary operation. During almost fifteen centuries, has the legal establishment of Christianity been on trial. What have been its fruits? More or less in all places, pride and indolence in the Clergy; ignorance and servility in the laity; in both, superstition, bigotry and persecution. Enquire of the Teachers of Christianity for the ages in which it appeared in its greatest lustre; those of every sect, point to the ages prior to its incorporation with Civil policy." *Id.,* at 187.

15. Memorial and Remonstrance against Religious Assessments, II Writings of Madison, at 187.

16. "[T]he proposed establishment is a departure from that generous policy, which, offering an asylum to the persecuted and oppressed of every Nation and Religion, promised a lustre to our country, and an accession to the number of its citizens. What a melancholy mark is the Bill of sudden degeneracy? Instead of holding forth an asylum to the persecuted, it is itself a signal of persecution .... Distant as it may be, in its present form, from the Inquisition it differs from it only in degree. The one is the first step, the other the last in the career of intolerance. The magnanimous sufferer under this cruel scourge in foreign Regions, must view the Bill as a Beacon on our Coast, warning him to seek some other haven, where liberty and philanthropy in their due extent may offer a more certain repose from his troubles." *Id.,* at 188.

17. 5 & 6 Edward VI, c. 1, entitled "An Act for the Uniformity of Service and Administration of Sacraments throughout the Realm." This Act was repealed during the reign of Mary but revived upon the accession of Elizabeth. See note 7, *supra.* The reasons which led to the enactment of this statute were set out in its preamble: "Where there hath been a very godly Order set forth by the Authority of Parliament, for Common Prayer and Administration of the Sacraments to be used in the Mother Tongue within the Church of *England,* agreeable to the Word of God and the Primitive Church, very comfortable to all good People desiring to live in Christian Conversation, and most profitable to the Estate of this Realm, upon the which the Mercy, Favour and Blessing of Almighty God is in no wise so readily and plenteously poured as by Common Prayers, due using of the Sacraments, and often preaching of the Gospel, with the Devotion of the

Hearers: (1) And yet this notwithstanding, a great Number of People in divers Parts of this Realm, following their own Sensuality, and living either without Knowledge or due Fear of God, do wilfully and damnably before Almighty God abstain and refuse to come to their Parish Churches and other Places where Common Prayer, Administration of the Sacraments, and Preaching of the Word of God, is used upon *Sundays* and other Days ordained to be Holydays."

18. Bunyan's own account of his trial is set forth in A Relation of the Imprisonment of Mr. John Bunyan, reprinted in Grace Abounding and The Pilgrim's Progress (Brown ed. 1907), at 103–132.

19. For a vivid account of some of these persecutions, see Wertenbaker, The Puritan Oligarchy (1947).

20. Perhaps the best example of the sort of men who came to this country for precisely that reason is Roger Williams, the founder of Rhode Island, who has been described as "the truest Christian amongst many who sincerely desired to be Christian." Parrington, Main Currents in American Thought (1930), Vol. 1, at p. 74. Williams, who was one of the earliest exponents of the doctrine of separation of church and state, believed that separation was necessary in order to protect the church from the danger of destruction which he thought inevitably flowed from control by even the best-intentioned civil authorities: "The unknowing zeale of *Constantine* and other Emperours, did more hurt to *Christ Jesus* his Crowne and Kingdome, then the raging fury of the most bloody *Neroes*. In the *persecutions* of the later, *Christians* were sweet and fragrant, like spice pounded and beaten in morters: But those *good* Emperours, persecuting some erroneous persons, *Arrius, &c.* and advancing the professours of some Truths of Christ (for there was no small number of *Truths* lost in those times) and maintaining their *Religion* by the materiall Sword, I say by this meanes *Christianity* was *ecclipsed,* and the Professors of it fell asleep . . . ." Williams, The Bloudy Tenent, of Persecution, for cause of Conscience, discussed in A Conference betweene Truth and Peace (London, 1644), reprinted in Narragansett Club Publications, Vol. III, p. 184. To Williams, it was no part of the business or competence of a civil magistrate to interfere in religious matters: "[W]hat imprudence and *indiscretion* is it in the most common affaires of Life, to conceive that *Emperours, Kings* and *Rulers* of the earth must not only be qualified with *politicall* and *state abilities* to *make* and *execute* such *Civill Lawes* which may concerne the common *rights, peace* and *safety* (which is worke and businesse, load and burthen enough for the ablest shoulders in the Commonweal) but also furnished with such *Spirituall* and heavenly *abilities* to governe the *Spirituall* and *Christian Commonweale* . . . ." *Id.,* at 366. See also *id.,* at 136–137.

21. There is of course nothing in the decision reached here that is inconsistent with the fact that school children and others are officially encouraged to express love for our country by reciting historical documents such as the Declaration of Independence which contain references to the Deity or by singing officially espoused anthems which include the composer's professions of faith in a Supreme Being, or with the fact that there are many manifestations in our public life of belief in God. Such patriotic or ceremonial occasions bear no true resemblance to the unquestioned religious exercise that the State of New York has sponsored in this instance.

THE United States Supreme Court, in an 8-1 decision, rules unconstitutional a Pennsylvania statute requiring that "at least ten verses from the Holy Bible shall be read, without comment, at the opening of each public school on each school day" and a Baltimore school board rule providing for opening exercises in the schools of the city, the exercises primarily consisting of the "reading, without comment, of a chapter in the Holy Bible and/or the use of the Lord's Prayer." In declaring the statute and rule unconstitutional, the Court said: "Applying the Establishment Clause principles to the cases at bar we find that the states are requiring the selection and reading at the opening of the school day of verses from the Holy Bible and the recitation of the Lord's Prayer by the students in unison. These exercises are prescribed as part of the curricular activities of students who are required by law to attend school. They are held in the school buildings under the supervision and with participation of teachers employed in those schools . . . . We agree with the trial court's finding [in the Pennsylvania case] as to the religious character of the exercises. Given that finding, the exercises and the law requiring them are in violation of the Establishment Clause. . . . Finally," said the Court, "we cannot accept that the concept of neutrality, which does not permit a State to require a religious exercise even with the consent of the majority of those affected, collides with the majority's right to free exercise of religion. While the free exercise clause clearly prohibits the use of state action to deny the rights of free exercise to *anyone,* it has never meant that a majority could use the machinery of the State to practice its beliefs."

Abington School Dist. v. *Schempp,* 374 U. S. 203 (1963)

Mr. Justice Clark delivered the opinion of the Court.

Once again we are called upon to consider the scope of the provision of the First Amendment to the United States Constitution which declares that "Congress shall make no law respecting an establishment of religion, or prohibiting the free exercise thereof . . . ." These companion cases present the issues in the context of state action requiring that schools begin each day with readings from the Bible. While raising the basic questions under slightly different factual situations, the cases permit of joint treatment. In light of the history of the First Amendment and of our cases interpreting and applying its requirements, we hold that the practices at issue and the laws requiring them are unconstitutional under the Establishment Clause, as applied to the States through the Fourteenth Amendment.

I.

The Facts in Each Case: No. 142. The Commonwealth of Pennsylvania by law, 24 Pa. Stat. § 15–1516, as amended, Pub. Law 1928 (Supp. 1960) Dec. 17, 1959, requires that "At least ten verses from the Holy Bible shall be read, without comment, at the opening of each public school on each school day. Any child shall be excused from such Bible reading, or attending such Bible reading, upon the written request of his parent or guardian." The Schempp family, husband and wife and two of their three children, brought suit to enjoin enforcement of the statute, contending that their rights under the Fourteenth Amendment to the Constitution of the United States are, have been, and will continue to be violated unless this statute be declared unconstitutional as violative of these provisions of the First Amendment. They sought to enjoin the appellant school district, wherein the Schempp children attend school, and its officers and the Superintendent of Public Instruction of the Commonwealth from continuing to conduct such readings and recitation of the Lord's Prayer in the public schools of the district pursuant to the statute. A three-judge statutory District Court for the Eastern District of Pennsylvania held that the statute is violative of the Establishment Clause of the First Amendment as applied to the States by the Due Process Clause of the Fourteenth Amendment and directed that appropriate injunctive relief issue. 201 F. Supp. 815.[1] On appeal by the District, its officials and the Superintendent, under 28 U. S. C. § 1253, we noted probable jurisdiction. 371 U. S. 807.

The appellees Edward Lewis Schempp, his wife Sidney, and their children, Roger and Donna, are of the Unitarian faith and are members of the Unitarian Church in Germantown, Philadelphia, Pennsylvania, where they, as well as another son, Ellory, regularly attend religious services. The latter was originally a party but having graduated from the school system *pendente lite* was voluntarily dismissed from the action. The other children attend the Abington Senior High School, which is a public school operated by appellant district.

On each school day at the Abington Senior High School between 8:15 and 8:30 a.m., while the pupils are attending their home rooms or advisory sections, opening exercises are conducted pursuant to the statute. The exercises are broadcast into each room in the school building through an intercommunications system and are conducted under the supervision of a teacher by students attending the school's radio and television workshop. Selected students from this course gather each morning in the school's workshop studio for the exercises, which include readings by one of the students of 10 verses of the Holy Bible, broadcast to each room in the building. This is followed by the recitation of the Lord's Prayer, likewise over the intercommunications system, but also by the students in the various classrooms, who are asked to stand and join in repeating the prayer in unison. The exercises are closed with the flag salute and such pertinent announcements as are of interest to the students. Participation in the opening exercises, as directed by the statute, is voluntary. The student reading the verses from the Bible may select the passages and read from any version he chooses, although the only copies furnished by the school are the King James version, copies of which were circulated to each teacher by the school district. During the period in which the exercises have been conducted the King James, the Douay and the Revised Standard versions of the Bible have been used, as well as the Jewish Holy Scriptures. There are no prefatory statements, no questions asked or solicited, no comments or explanations made and no interpretations given at or during the exercises. The students and parents are advised that the student may absent himself from the classroom or, should he elect to remain, not participate in the exercises.

It appears from the record that in schools not having an intercommunications system the Bible reading and the recitation of the Lord's Prayer were conducted by the home-room teacher,[2] who chose the text of the verses and read them herself or had students read them in rotation or by volunteers. This was followed by a standing recitation of the Lord's Prayer, together with the Pledge of Allegiance to the Flag by the class in unison and a closing announcement of routine school items of interest.

At the first trial Edward Schempp and the children testified as to specific religious doctrines purveyed by a literal reading of the Bible "which were contrary to the religous beliefs which they held and to their familial teaching." 177 F. Supp. 398, 400. The children testified that all of the doctrines to which they referred were read to them at various times as part of the exercises. Edward Schempp testified at the second trial that he had considered having Roger and Donna excused from attendance at the exercises but decided against it for several reasons, including his belief that the children's relationships with their teachers and classmates would be adversely affected.[3]

Expert testimony was introduced by both appellants and appellees at the first trial, which testimony was summarized by the trial court as follows:

"Dr. Solomon Grayzel testified that there were marked differences between the Jewish Holy Scriptures and the Christian Holy Bible, the most obvious of which was the absence of the New Testament in the Jewish Holy Scriptures. Dr. Grayzel testified that portions of the New Testament were offensive to Jewish tradition and that, from the standpoint of Jewish faith, the concept of Jesus Christ as the Son of God was 'practically blasphemous.' He cited instances in the New Testament which, assertedly, were not only sectarian in nature but tended to bring the Jews into ridicule or scorn. Dr. Grayzel gave as his expert opinion that such material from the New Testament could be explained to Jewish children in such a way as to do no harm to them. But if portions of the New Testament were read without explanation, they could be, and in his specific experience with children Dr. Grayzel observed, had been, psychologically harmful to the child and had caused a divisive force within the social media of the school.

"Dr. Grayzel also testified that there was significant difference in attitude with regard to the respective Books of the Jewish and Christian Religions in that Judaism attaches no special significance to the reading of the Bible *per se* and that the Jewish Holy Scriptures are source materials to be studied. But Dr. Grayzel did state that many portions of the New, as well as of the Old, Testament contained passages of great literary and moral value.

"Dr. Luther A. Weigle, an expert witness for the defense, testified in some detail as to the reasons for and the methods employed in developing the King James and the Revised Standard Versions of the Bible. On direct examination, Dr. Weigle stated that the Bible was non-sectarian. He later stated that the phrase 'non-sectarian' meant to him non-sectarian within the Christian faiths. Dr. Weigle stated that his definition of the Holy Bible would include the Jewish Holy Scriptures, but also stated that the 'Holy Bible' would not be complete without the New Testament. He stated that the New Testament 'conveyed the message of Christians.' In his opinion, reading of the Holy Scriptures to the exclusion of the New Testament would be a sectarian practice. Dr. Weigle stated that the Bible was of great moral, historical and literary value. This is conceded by all the parties and is also the view of the court." 177 F. Supp. 398, 401–402.

The trial court, in striking down the practices and the statute requiring them, made specific findings of fact that the children's attendance at Abington Senior High School is compulsory and that the practice of reading 10 verses from the Bible is also compelled by law. It also found that:

"The reading of the verses, even without comment, possesses a devotional and religious character and constitutes in effect a religious observance. The devotional and religious nature of the morning exercises is made all the more apparent by the fact that the Bible reading is followed immediately by a recital in unison by the pupils of the Lord's Prayer. The fact that some pupils, or theoretically all pupils, might be excused from attendance at the exercises does not mitigate the obligatory nature of the ceremony for . . . Section 1516 . . . unequivocally requires the exercises to be held every school day in every school in the Commonwealth. The exercises are held in the school buildings and perforce are conducted by and under the authority of the local school authorities and during school sessions. Since the statute requires the reading of the 'Holy Bible,' a Christian document, the practice . . . prefers the Christian religion. The record demonstrates that it was the intention of . . . the Commonwealth . . . to introduce a religious ceremony into the public schools of the Commonwealth." 201 F. Supp., at 819.

No. 119. In 1905 the Board of School Commissioners of Baltimore City adopted a rule pursuant to Art. 77, § 202 of the Annotated Code of Maryland.

The rule provided for the holding of opening exercises in the schools of the city, consisting primarily of the "reading, without comment, of a chapter in the Holy Bible and/or the use of the Lord's Prayer." The petitioners, Mrs. Madalyn Murray and her son, William J. Murray III, are both professed atheists. Following unsuccessful attempts to have the respondent school board rescind the rule, this suit was filed for mandamus to compel its rescission and cancellation. It was alleged that William was a student in a public school of the city and Mrs. Murray, his mother, was a taxpayer therein; that it was the practice under the rule to have a reading on each school morning from the King James version of the Bible; that at petitioners' insistence the rule was amended[4] to permit children to be excused from the exercise on request of the parent and that William had been excused pursuant thereto; that nevertheless the rule as amended was in violation of the petitioners' rights "to freedom of religion under the First and Fourteenth Amendments" and in violation of "the principle of separation between church and state, contained therein . . . ." The petition particularized the petitioners' atheistic beliefs and stated that the rule, as practiced, violated their rights

"in that it threatens their religious liberty by placing a premium on belief as against non-belief and subjects their freedom of conscience to the rule of the majority; it pronounces belief in God as the source of all moral and spiritual values, equating these values with religious values, and thereby renders sinister, alien and suspect the beliefs and ideals of your Petitioners, promoting doubt and question of their morality, good citizenship and good faith."

The respondents demurred and the trial court, recognizing that the demurrer admitted all facts well pleaded, sustained it without leave to amend. The Maryland Court of Appeals affirmed, the majority of four justices holding the exercise not in violation of the First and Fourteenth Amendments, with three justices dissenting. 228 Md. 239, 179 A. 2d 698. We granted certiorari. 371 U. S. 809.

II.

It is true that religion has been closely identified with our history and government. As we said in *Engel* v. *Vitale*, 370 U. S. 421, 434 (1962), "The history of man is inseparable from the history of religion. And . . . since the beginning of that history many people have devoutly believed that 'More things are wrought by prayer than this world dreams of.'" In *Zorach* v. *Clauson*, 343 U. S. 306, 313 (1952), we gave specific recognition to the proposition that "[w]e are a religious people whose institutions presuppose a Supreme Being." The fact that the Founding Fathers believed devotedly that there was a God and that the unalienable rights of man were rooted in Him is clearly evidenced in their writings, from the Mayflower Compact to the Constitution itself. This background is evidenced today in our public life through the continuance in our oaths of office from the Presidency to the Alderman of the final supplication, "So help me God." Likewise each House of the Congress provides through its Chaplain an opening prayer, and the sessions of this Court are declared open by the crier in a short ceremony, the final phrase of which invokes the grace of God. Again, there are such manifestations in our military forces, where those of our citizens who are under the restrictions of military service wish to engage in voluntary worship. Indeed, only last year an official survey of the country indicated that 64% of our people have church membership, Bureau of the Census, U. S. Department of Commerce, Statistical Abstract of the United States (83d ed. 1962), 48, while less than 3% profess no religion whatever. *Id.,* at p. 46. It can be truly said, therefore, that today, as in the beginning, our national life reflects a religious people who, in the words of Madison, are "earnestly praying, as . . . in duty bound, that the Supreme Lawgiver of the Universe . . . guide them into every measure which may be worthy of his [blessing . . . .]" Memorial and Remonstrance Against Religious Assessments, quoted in *Everson* v. *Board of Education,* 330 U. S. 1, 71–72 (1947) (Appendix to dissenting opinion of Rutledge, J.).

This is not to say, however, that religion has been so identified with our history and government that religious freedom is not likewise as strongly imbedded in our public and private life. Nothing but the most telling of personal experiences in religious persecution suffered by our forebears, see *Everson* v. *Board of Education, supra,* at 8-11, could have planted our belief in liberty of religious opinion any more deeply in our heritage. It is true that this liberty frequently was not realized by the colonists, but this is readily accountable by their close ties to the Mother Country.[5] However, the views of Madison and Jefferson, preceded by Roger Williams,[6] came to be incorporated not only in the Federal Constitution but likewise in those of most of our States. This freedom to worship was indispensable in a country whose people came from the four quarters of the earth and brought with them a diversity of religious opinion. Today authorities list 83 separate religious bodies, each with membership exceeding 50,000, existing among our people, as well as innumerable smaller groups. Bureau of the Census, *op. cit., supra,* at 46–47.

III.

Almost a hundred years ago in *Minor* v. *Board of Education of Cincinnati,*[7] Judge Alphonso Taft,

father of the revered Chief Justice, in an unpublished opinion stated the ideal of our people as to religious freedom as one of

"absolute equality before the law, of all religious opinions and sects . . . .

"The government is neutral, and, while protecting all, it prefers none, and it *disparages* none."

Before examining this "neutral" position in which the Establishment and Free Exercise Clauses of the First Amendment place our Government it is well that we discuss the reach of the Amendment under the cases of this Court.

First, this Court has decisively settled that the First Amendment's mandate that "Congress shall make no law respecting an establishment of religion, or prohibiting the free exercise thereof" has been made wholly applicable to the States by the Fourteenth Amendment. Twenty-three years ago in *Cantwell* v. *Connecticut,* 310 U. S. 296, 303 (1940), this Court, through Mr. Justice Roberts, said:

"The fundamental concept of liberty embodied in that [Fourteenth] Amendment embraces the liberties guaranteed by the First Amendment. The First Amendment declares that Congress shall make no law respecting an establishment of religion or prohibiting the free exercise thereof. The Fourteenth Amendment has rendered the legislatures of the states as incompetent as Congress to enact such laws . . . ."[8]

In a series of cases since *Cantwell* the Court has repeatedly reaffirmed that doctrine, and we do so now. *Murdock* v. *Pennsylvania,* 319 U. S. 105, 108 (1943); *Everson* v. *Board of Education, supra; Illinois ex rel. McCollum* v. *Board of Education,* 333 U. S. 203, 210–211 (1948); *Zorach* v. *Clauson, supra; McGowan* v. *Maryland,* 366 U. S. 420 (1961); *Torcaso* v. *Watkins,* 367 U. S. 488 (1961); and *Engel* v. *Vitale, supra.*

Second, this Court has rejected unequivocally the contention that the Establishment Clause forbids only governmental preference of one religion over another. Almost 20 years ago in *Everson, supra,* at 15, the Court said that "[n]either a state nor the Federal Government can set up a church. Neither can pass laws which aid one religion, aid all religions, or prefer one religion over another." And Mr. Justice Jackson, dissenting, agreed:

"There is no answer to the proposition . . . that the effect of the religious freedom Amendment to our Constitution was to take every form of propagation of religion out of the realm of things which could directly or indirectly be made public business and thereby be supported in whole or in part at taxpayers' expense . . . . This freedom was first in the Bill of Rights because it was first in the forefathers' minds; it was set forth in absolute terms, and its strength is its rigidity." *Id.,* at 26.

Further, Mr. Justice Rutledge, joined by Justices Frankfurter, Jackson and Burton, declared:

"The [First] Amendment's purpose was not to strike merely at the official establishment of a single sect, creed or religion, outlawing only a formal relation such as had prevailed in England and some of the colonies. Necessarily it was to uproot all such relationships. But the object was broader than separating church and state in this narrow sense. It was to create a complete and permanent separation of the spheres of religious activity and civil authority by comprehensively forbidding every form of public aid or support for religion." *Id.,* at 31-32.

The same conclusion has been firmly maintained ever since that time, see *Illinois ex rel. McCollum, supra,* at pp. 210-211; *McGowan* v. *Maryland, supra,* at 442-443; *Torcaso* v. *Watkins, supra,* at 492-493, 495, and we reaffirm it now.

While none of the parties to either of these cases has questioned these basic conclusions of the Court, both of which have been long established, recognized and consistently reaffirmed, others continue to question their history, logic and efficacy. Such contentions, in the light of the consistent interpretation in cases of this Court, seem entirely untenable and of value only as academic exercises.

IV.

The interrelationship of the Establishment and the Free Exercise Clauses was first touched upon by Mr. Justice Roberts for the Court in *Cantwell* v. *Connecticut, supra,* at 303-304, where it was said that their "inhibition of legislation" had

"a double aspect. On the one hand, it forestalls compulsion by law of the acceptance of any creed or the practice of any form of worship. Freedom of conscience and freedom to adhere to such religious organization or form of worship as the individual may choose cannot be restricted by law. On the other hand, it safeguards the free exercise of the chosen form of religion. Thus the Amendment embraces two concepts,—freedom to believe and freedom to act. The first is absolute but, in the nature of things, the second cannot be."

A half dozen years later in *Everson* v. *Board of Education, supra,* at 14-15, this Court, through MR. JUSTICE BLACK, stated that the "scope of the First Amendment . . . was designed forever to suppress" the establishment of religion or the prohibition of the free exercise thereof. In short, the Court held that the Amendment

"requires the state to be a neutral in its relations with groups of religious believers and non-believers; it does not require the state to be their adversary.

State power is no more to be used so as to handicap religions than it is to favor them." *Id.,* at 18.

And Mr. Justice Jackson, in dissent, declared that public schools are organized

"on the premise that secular education can be isolated from all religious teaching so that the school can inculcate all needed temporal knowledge and also maintain a strict and lofty neutrality as to religion. The assumption is that after the individual has been instructed in worldly wisdom he will be better fitted to choose his religion." *Id.,* at 23-24.

Moreover, all of the four dissenters, speaking through Mr. Justice Rutledge, agreed that

"Our constitutional policy . . . does not deny the value or the necessity for religious training, teaching or observance. Rather it secures their free exercise. But to that end it does deny that the state can undertake or sustain them in any form or degree. For this reason the sphere of religious activity, as distinguished from the secular intellectual liberties, has been given the twofold protection and, as the state cannot forbid, neither can it perform or aid in performing the religious function. The dual prohibition makes that function altogether private." *Id.,* at 52.

Only one year later the Court was asked to reconsider and repudiate the doctrine of these cases in *McCollum* v. *Board of Education.* It was argued that "historically the First Amendment was intended to forbid only government preference of one religion over another. . . . In addition they ask that we distinguish or overrule our holding in the *Everson* case that the Fourteenth Amendment made the 'establishment of religion' clause of the First Amendment applicable as a prohibition against the States." 333 U.S., at 211. The Court, with Mr. Justice Reed alone dissenting, was unable to "accept either of these contentions." *Ibid.* Mr. Justice Frankfurter, joined by Justices Jackson, Rutledge and Burton, wrote a very comprehensive and scholarly concurrence in which he said that "[s]eparation is a requirement to abstain from fusing functions of Government and of religious sects, not merely to treat them all equally." *Id.,* at 227. Continuing, he stated that:

"the Constitution . . . prohibited the Government common to all from becoming embroiled, however innocently, in the destructive religious conflicts of which the history of even this country records some dark pages." *Id.,* at 228.

In 1952 in *Zorach* v. *Clauson, supra,* MR. JUSTICE DOUGLAS for the Court reiterated:

"There cannot be the slightest doubt that the First Amendment reflects the philosophy that Church and State should be separated. And so far as interference with the 'free exercise' of religion and an 'establishment' of religion are concerned, the separation must be complete and unequivocal. The First Amendment within the scope of its coverage permits no exception; the prohibition is absolute. The First Amendment, however, does not say that in every and all respects there shall be a separation of Church and State. Rather, it studiously defines the manner, the specific ways, in which there shall be no concert or union or dependency one on the other. That is the common sense of the matter." 343 U.S., at 312.

And then in 1961 in *McGowan* v. *Maryland* and in *Torcaso* v. *Watkins* each of these cases was discussed and approved. CHIEF JUSTICE WARREN in *McGowan*, for a unanimous Court on this point, said:

"But, the First Amendment, in its final form, did not simply bar a congressional enactment *establishing a church*; it forbade all laws *respecting an establishment of religion*. Thus, this Court has given the Amendment a 'broad interpretation . . . in the light of its history and the evils it was designed forever to suppress. . . .'" 366 U.S., at 441-442.

And MR. JUSTICE BLACK for the Court in *Torcaso*, without dissent but with Justices Frankfurter and HARLAN concurring in the result, used this language:

"We repeat and again reaffirm that neither a State nor the Federal Government can constitutionally force a person 'to profess a belief or disbelief in any religion.' Neither can constitutionally pass laws or impose requirements which aid all religions as against non-believers, and neither can aid those religions based on a belief in the existence of God as against those religions founded on different beliefs." 367 U.S., at 495.

Finally, in *Engel* v. *Vitale*, only last year, these principles were so universally recognized that the Court, without the citation of a single case and over the sole dissent of MR. JUSTICE STEWART, reaffirmed them. The Court found the 22-word prayer used in "New York's program of daily classroom invocation of God's blessings as prescribed in the Regents' prayer . . . [to be] a religious activity." 370 U.S., at 424. It held that "it is no part of the business of government to compose official prayers for any group of the American people to recite as a part of a religious program carried on by government." *Id.*, at 425. In discussing the reach of the Establishment and Free Exercise Clauses of the First Amendment the Court said:

"Although these two clauses may in certain instances overlap, they forbid two quite different kinds of governmental encroachment upon religious freedom. The Establishment Clause, unlike the Free Exercise Clause, does not depend upon any showing of direct governmental compulsion and is violated by the enactment of laws which establish an official religion whether those laws operate directly to coerce non-observing individuals or not. This is not to say, of course, that laws officially prescribing a particular form of religious worship do not involve coercion of such individuals. When the power, prestige and financial support of government is placed behind a particular religious belief, the indirect coercive pressure upon religious minorities to conform to the prevailing officially approved religion is plain." *Id.*, at 430-431.

And in further elaboration the Court found that the "first and most immediate purpose [of the Establishment Clause] rested on the belief that a union of government and religion tends to destroy government and to degrade religion." *Id.*, at 431. When government, the Court said, allies itself with one particular form of religion, the inevitable result is that it incurs "the hatred, disrespect and even contempt of those who held contrary beliefs." *Ibid.*

V.

The wholesome "neutrality" of which this Court's cases speak thus stems from a recognition of the teachings of history that powerful sects or groups might bring about a fusion of governmental and religious functions or a concert or dependency of one upon the other to the end that official support of the State or Federal Government would be placed behind the tenets of one or of all orthodoxies. This the Establishment Clause prohibits. And a further reason for neutrality is found in the Free Exercise Clause, which recognizes the value of religious training, teaching and observance and, more particularly, the right of every person to freely choose his own course with reference thereto, free of any compulsion from the state. This the Free Exercise Clause guarantees. Thus, as we have seen, the two clauses may overlap. As we have indicated, the Establishment Clause has been directly considered by this Court eight times in the past score of years and, with only one Justice dissenting on the point, it has consistently held that the clause withdrew all legislative power respecting religious belief or the expression thereof. The test may be stated as follows: what are the purpose and the primary effect of the enactment? If either is the advancement or inhibition of religion then the enactment exceeds the scope of legislative power as circumscribed by the Constitution. That is to say that to withstand the strictures of the Establishment Clause there must be a secular legislative purpose and a primary effect that neither advances nor inhibits religion. *Everson* v. *Board of Education, supra; McGowan* v. *Maryland, supra*, at 442. The Free Exercise Clause, likewise considered many times here, withdraws from legislative power, state and federal, the exertion of any restraint on the free exercise of religion. Its purpose is to secure religious liberty in the individual by prohibiting any invasions thereof by civil authority. Hence it is necessary in a free exercise case for one to show the coercive effect of the enactment as it operates against him in the practice of his religion. The distinction between the two clauses is apparent—a violation of the Free Exercise Clause is predicated on coercion while the Establishment Clause violation need not be so attended.

Applying the Establishment Clause principles to the cases at bar we find that the States are requiring the selection and reading at the opening of the school day of verses from the Holy Bible and the recitation of the Lord's Prayer by the students in unison. These exercises are prescribed as part of the curricular activities of students who are required by law to attend school. They are held in the school buildings under the supervision and with the participation of teachers employed in those schools. None of these factors, other than compulsory school attendance, was present in the program upheld in *Zorach* v. *Clauson*. The trial court in No. 142 has found that such an opening exercise is a religious ceremony and was intended by the State to be so. We agree with the trial court's finding as to the religious character of the exercises. Given that finding, the exercises and the law requiring them are in violation of the Establishment Clause.

There is no such specific finding as to the religious character of the exercises in No. 119, and the State contends (as does the State in No. 142) that the program is an effort to extend its benefits to all public school children without regard to their religious belief. Included within its secular purposes, it says, are the promotion of moral values, the contradiction to the materialistic trends of our times, the perpetuation of our institutions and the teaching of literature. The case came up on demurrer, of course, to a petition which alleged that the uniform practice under the rule had been to read from the King James version of the Bible and that the exercise was sectarian. The short answer, therefore, is that the religious character of the exercise was admitted by the State. But even if its purpose is not strictly religious, it is sought to be accomplished through readings, without comment, from the Bible. Surely the place of the Bible as an instrument of religion cannot be gainsaid, and the State's recognition of the pervading religious character of the ceremony is evident from the rule's specific permission of the alternative use of the Catholic Douay version as well as the recent amendment permitting nonattendance at the exercises. None of these factors is consistent with the contention that the Bible is here used either as an instrument for nonreligious moral inspiration or as a reference for the teaching of secular subjects.

The conclusion follows that in both cases the laws require religious exercises and such exercises are being conducted in direct violation of the rights of the appellees and petitioners.[9] Nor are these required exercises mitigated by the fact that individual students may absent themselves upon parental request, for that fact furnishes no defense to a claim of unconstitutionality under the Establishment Clause. See *Engel* v. *Vitale, supra*, at 430. Further, it is no defense to urge that the religious practices here may be relatively minor encroachments on the First Amendment. The breach of neutrality that is today a trickling stream may all too soon become a raging torrent and, in the words of Madison, "it is proper to take alarm at the first experiment on our liberties." Memorial and Remonstrance Against Religious Assessments, quoted in *Everson, supra*, at 65.

It is insisted that unless these religious exercises are permitted a "religion of secularism" is established in the schools. We agree of course that the State may not establish a "religion of secularism" in the sense of affirmatively opposing or showing hostility to religion, thus "preferring those who believe in no religion over those who do believe." *Zorach* v. *Clauson, supra*, at 314. We do not agree, however, that this decision in any sense has that effect. In addition, it might well be said that one's education is not complete without a study of comparative religion or the history of religion and its relationship to the advancement of civilization. It certainly may be said that the Bible is worthy of study for its literary and historic qualities. Nothing we have said here indicates that such study of the Bible or of religion, when presented objectively as part of a secular program of education, may not be effected consistently with the First Amendment. But the exercises here do not fall into those categories. They are religious exercises, required by the States in violation of the command of the First Amendment that the Government maintain strict neutrality, neither aiding nor opposing religion.

Finally, we cannot accept that the concept of neutrality, which does not permit a State to require a religious exercise even with the consent of the majority of those affected, collides with the majority's right to free exercise of religion.[10] While the Free Exercise Clause clearly prohibits the use of state action to deny the rights of free exercise to *anyone*, it has never meant that a majority could use the machinery of the State to practice its beliefs. Such a contention was effectively answered by Mr. Justice Jackson for the Court in *West Virginia Board of Education* v. *Barnette*, 319 U.S. 624, 638 (1943):

"The very purpose of a Bill of Rights was to withdraw certain subjects from the vicissitudes of political controversy, to place them beyond the reach of majorities and officials and to establish them as legal principles to be applied by the courts. One's right to . . . freedom of worship . . . and other fundamental rights may not be submitted to vote; they depend on the outcome of no elections.''

The place of religion in our society is an exalted one, achieved through a long tradition of reliance on the home, the church and the inviolable citadel of the individual heart and mind. We have come to recognize through bitter experience that it is not within the power of government to invade that citadel, whether its purpose or effect be to aid or oppose, to advance or retard. In the relationship between man and religion, the State is firmly committed to a position of neutrality. Though the application of that rule requires interpretation of a delicate sort, the rule itself is clearly and concisely stated in the words of the First Amendment. Applying that rule to the facts of these cases, we affirm the judgment in No. 142. In No. 119, the judgment is reversed and the cause remanded to the Maryland Court of Appeals for further proceedings consistent with this opinion.

It is so ordered.

NOTES

1. The action was brought in 1958, prior to the 1959 amendment of § 15-1516 authorizing a child's nonattendance at the exercises upon parental request. The three-judge court held the statute and the practices complained of unconstitutional under both the Establishment Clause and the Free Exercise Clause. 177 F. Supp. 398. Pending appeal to this Court by the school district, the statute was so amended, and we vacated the judgment and remanded for further proceedings. 364 U.S. 298. The same three-judge court granted appellees' motion to amend the pleadings, 195 F. Supp. 518, held a hearing on the amended pleadings and rendered the judgment, 201 F. Supp. 815, from which appeal is now taken.
2. The statute as amended imposes no penalty upon a teacher refusing to obey its mandate. However, it remains to be seen whether one refusing could have his contract of employment terminated for "wilful violation of the school law." 24 Pa. Stat. (Supp. 1960) § 11-1122.
3. The trial court summarized his testimony as follows:
    "Edward Schempp, the children's father, testified that after careful consideration he had decided that he should not have Roger or Donna excused from attendance at these morning ceremonies. Among his reasons were the following. He said that he thought his children would be 'labeled as "odd balls"' before their teachers and classmates every school day; that children, like Roger's and Donna's classmates, were liable 'to lump all particular religious difference[s] or religious objections [together] as "atheism"' and that today the word 'atheism' is often connected with 'atheistic communism,' and has 'very bad' connotations, such as 'un-American' or 'anti-Red,' with overtones of possible immorality. Mr. Schempp pointed out that due to the events of the morning exercises following in rapid succession, the Bible reading, the Lord's Prayer, the Flag Salute, and the announcements, excusing his children

from the Bible reading would mean that probably they would miss hearing the announcements so important to children. He testified also that if Roger and Donna were excused from Bible reading they would have to stand in the hall outside their 'homeroom' and that this carried with it the imputation of punishment for bad conduct.'' 201 F. Supp., at 818.
4. The rule as amended provides as follows:
    "Opening Exercises. Each school, either collectively or in classes, shall be opened by the reading, without comment, of a chapter in the Holy Bible and/or the use of the Lord's Prayer. The Douay version may be used by those pupils who prefer it. Appropriate patriotic exercises should be held as a part of the general opening exercise of the school or class. Any child shall be excused from participating in the opening exercises or from attending the opening exercises upon the written request of his parent or guardian."
5. There were established churches in at least eight of the original colonies, and various degrees of religious support in others as late as the Revolutionary War. See *Engel* v. *Vitale, supra*, at 428, n. 10.
6. "There goes many a ship to sea, with many hundred souls in one ship, whose weal and woe is common, and is a true picture of a commonwealth, or human combination, or society. It hath fallen out sometimes, that both Papists and Protestants, Jews and Turks, may be embarked in one ship; upon which supposal, I affirm that all the liberty of conscience I ever pleaded for, turns upon these two hinges, that none of the Papists, Protestants, Jews, or Turks be forced to come to the ship's prayers or worship, nor compelled from their own particular prayers or worship, if they practice any."
7. Superior Court of Cincinnati, February 1870. The opinion is not reported but is published under the title, The Bible in the Common Schools (Cincinnati: Robert Clarke & Co. 1870). Judge Taft's views, expressed in dissent, prevailed on appeal. See *Board of Education of Cincinnati* v. *Minor*, 23 Ohio St. 211, 253 (1872), in which the Ohio Supreme Court held that:
    "The great bulk of human affairs and human interests is left by any free government to individual enterprise and individual action. Religion is eminently one of these interests, lying outside the true and legitimate province of government."
8. Application to the States of other clauses of the First Amendment obtained even before *Cantwell*. Almost 40 years ago in the opinion of the Court in *Gitlow* v. *New York*, 268 U.S. 652, 666 (1925), Mr. Justice Sanford said: "For present purposes we may and do assume that freedom of speech and of the press—which are protected by the First Amendment from abridgment by Congress—are among the fundamental personal rights and 'liberties' protected by the due process clause of the Fourteenth Amendment from impairment by the States."
9. It goes without saying that the laws and practices involved here can be challenged only by persons having standing to complain. But the requirements for standing to challenge state action under the Establishment Clause, unlike those relating to the Free Exercise Clause, do not include proof that particular religious freedoms are infringed. *McGowan* v. *Maryland, supra*, at 429-430. The parties here are school children and their parents, who are directly affected by the laws and practices against which their complaints are directed. These interests surely suffice to give the parties stand-

ing to complain. See *Engel* v. *Vitale, supra.* Cf. *McCollum* v. *Board of Education, supra; Everson* v. *Board of Education, supra.* Compare *Doremus* v. *Board of Education,* 342 U.S. 429 (1952), which involved the same substantive issues presented here. The appeal was there dismissed upon the graduation of the school child involved and because of the appellants' failure to establish standing as taxpayers.

10. We are not of course presented with and therefore do not pass upon a situation such as military service, where the Government regulates the temporal and geographic environment of individuals to a point that, unless it permits voluntary religious services to be conducted with the use of government facilities, military personnel would be unable to engage in the practice of their faiths.

THE United States Court of Appeals, Second Circuit, decides against parents who had joined in a written demand to New York school officials "that our children be given an opportunity to acknowledge their dependence and love to Almighty God through a prayer each day in their respective classrooms." In deciding that the First Amendment did not require a state to permit "student-initiated" prayers in public schools, the court said: "The authorities acted well within their powers in concluding that plaintiffs must content themselves with having their children say these prayers before nine and after three; their action presented no such inexorable conflict with deeply held religious belief as in *Sherbert* v. *Verner* . . . after all that the states have been told about keeping the 'wall between Church and State . . . high and impregnable . . . ,' it would be rather bitter irony to chastise New York for having built the wall too tall or too strong."

Stein v. *Oshinsky,* 348 F.2d 999 (1965)

FRIENDLY, Circuit Judge.

The decision in Engel v. Vitale, 370 U.S. 421, 82 S.Ct. 1261, 8 L.Ed.2d 601, condemning the "Regents' prayer" as violating the Establishment Clause of the First Amendment, held to be applicable to the states by the Fourteenth, was rendered on June 25, 1962, too late to affect the 1961-62 school year. The case now before us reflects a response to that decision by parents who think their children ought to have some form of religious observance while in public school.

The amended complaint, filed in March, 1963, in the District Court for the Eastern District of New York, made the following allegations: The fifteen plaintiffs, of varying religious faiths, are parents of twenty-one children, ranging from five to eleven years in age. The children attend Public School 184, at Whitestone, N.Y., in grades ranging from kindergarten to the sixth. The defendants are Elihu Oshinsky, principal of the school; the members of the Board of Education of New York City; and the Board of Regents of the University of the State of New York. On October 5, 1962, Mr. Oshinsky "ordered his teachers who were instructing the kindergarten classes to stop the infant children from reciting the simple and ancient prayer:

God is Great, God is Good and We Thank Him for our Food, Amen!

before they ate their cookies and milk in the morning session," and "ordered his teachers who were instruct-

ing the kindergarten classes for the afternoon session to stop the infant children from reciting the simple and ancient prayer:

Thank You for the World so Sweet,
Thank You for the Food We Eat,
Thank You for the Birds that Sing—
Thank You, God, for Everything. . . ."

He also "ordered his teachers to stop the saying of any prayer in any classroom in P. S. 184, Whitestone, New York." The Board of Education and the Board of Regents have instituted a policy banning prayers in the public schools even when the opportunity to pray is sought by the students themselves, and by so doing have "condoned and/or directed" Mr. Oshinsky's actions. The plaintiffs had joined in a written demand to the defendants "that our children be given an opportunity to acknowledge their dependence and love to Almighty God through a prayer each day in their respective classrooms"; defendants had ignored this.

The defendants moved, under F.R.Civ.P. 12(b), to dismiss the complaint for lack of subject-matter jurisdiction and for failure to state a claim on which relief could be granted. Plaintiffs countered with a motion for summary judgment under F.R.Civ.P. 56, supported by an affidavit which added no allegations to those in the complaint and asserted that "the issues presented are purely Constitutional in nature and questions of law. No issues of fact are presented." Defendants filed no affidavits contradicting anything said in the complaint; they urged rather that the motion for summary judgment was premature and that their own motion did not admit the allegations of the complaint save for the purpose of raising the objections there stated. The court denied defendants' motion and granted plaintiffs', 224 F.Supp. 757 (1963). It signed an order prohibiting interference with prayer and requiring that a reasonable opportunity for it be provided each day, but stayed the order pending this appeal.

We see no force in defendants' argument that the posture of the case did not permit the grant of summary judgment to plaintiffs, whatever the merits of their claim and the adequacy of the showing in its support. Although F.R.Civ.P. 56(a) in its initial form would have postponed such a motion until answer had been filed, one of the purposes of the 1946 amendment was to permit a plaintiff to move for summary judgment while a pre-answer rule 12(b) motion was pending. 6 Moore, Federal Practice ¶ 56.07 (2d ed. 1953). We likewise cannot sustain defendants' contention that the complaint did not sufficiently raise a claim of denial of constitutional rights to the free exercise of religion and to freedom of speech "to warrant exercise of federal jurisdiction for purposes of adjudicating it" under 28 U.S.C. § 1343 (3). Bell v. Hood, 327 U.S. 678, 684, 66 S.Ct. 773, 90 L.Ed. 939 (1946). But we think the court erred in its ruling on the merits.

Plaintiffs say that Engel v. Vitale, supra, and the later decisions in Abington Tp. School District v. Schempp and Murray v. Curlett, both at 374 U.S. 203, 83 S.Ct. 1560, 10 L.Ed.2d 844 (1963), held only that under the Establishment Clause of the First Amendment a state may not *direct* the use of public school teachers and facilities for the recitation of a prayer, whether composed by a state official as in Engel or not so composed but having a religious content as in Abington and Curlett; they argue that these decisions did not hold that a state could not *permit* students in public schools to engage in oral prayer on their own initiative. This may be true enough; if the defendants could prevail only by showing that permitting the prayers was prohibited by the Establishment Clause, the question would be whether the use of public property as a situs for the prayers, the consumption of some teacher time in preserving order for their duration, and the possible implication of state approval therefrom would attract the condemnation of People of State of Illinois ex rel. McCollum v. Board of Education, 333 U.S. 203, 68 S.Ct. 461, 92 L.Ed. 649 (1948), or the benediction of Zorach v. Clauson, 343 U.S. 306, 72 S.Ct. 679, 96 L.Ed. 954 (1952), and Sherbert v. Verner, 374 U.S. 398, 409, 83 S.Ct. 1790, 10 L.Ed.2d 965 (1963). Although we note in this connection defendants' serious contention that in the context of closely organized schooling of young children, "student-initiated" prayers are an illusion and any effective routine requires

the active participation of the teachers, we shall assume, *arguendo*, in plaintiffs' favor that the Establishment Clause would not prohibit New York from permitting in its public schools prayers such as those here at issue. Nevertheless New York is not bound to allow them unless the Free Exercise Clause or the guarantee of freedom of speech of the First Amendment compels.

Neither provision requires a state to permit persons to engage in public prayer in state-owned facilities wherever and whenever they desire. Poulos v. State of New Hampshire, 345 U.S. 395, 405, 73 S.Ct. 760, 97 L.Ed. 1105 (1953). It would scarcely be argued that a court had to suffer a trial or an argument to be interrupted any time that spectators—or even witnesses or jurymen—desired to indulge in collective oral prayer. The case of the school children differs from that of spectators—although not from that of witnesses or jurymen—in that, so long as they choose to attend a public school, attendance on their part is compulsory. N.Y. Education Law, Consol.Laws, c. 16, §§ 3201-3229. But "[t]he student's compelled presence in school for five days a week in no way renders the regular religious facilities of the community less accessible to him than they are to others." Abington Tp. School District v. Schempp, supra, 374 U.S. at 299, 83 S.Ct. at 1612 (concurring opinion of Mr. Justice Brennan). We are not here required to consider such cases as that of a Moslem, obliged to prostrate himself five times daily in the direction of Mecca, or of a child whose beliefs forbade his partaking of milk and cookies without saying the blessings of his faith. Cf. Sherbert v. Verner, supra, 374 U.S. at 399 n. 1, 83 S.Ct. 1790. So far as appears, the school authorities might well permit students to withdraw momentarily for such necessary observances—or to forego the milk and cookies, just as they excuse children on holidays important to their religions.

Determination of what is to go on in public schools is primarily for the school authorities. Against the desire of these parents that their children "be given an opportunity to acknowledge their dependence and love to Almighty God through a prayer each day in their respective classrooms," the authorities were entitled to weigh the likely desire of other parents not to have their children present at such prayers, either because the prayers were too religious or not religious enough; and the wisdom of having public educational institutions stick to education and keep out of religion, with all the bickering that intrusion into the latter is likely to produce. The authorities acted well within their powers in concluding that plaintiffs must content themselves with having their children say these prayers before nine or after three; their action presented no such inexorable conflict with deeply held religious belief as in Sherbert v. Verner, supra. After all that the states have been told about keeping the "wall between church and state . . . high and impregnable," Everson v. Board of Education, 330 U.S. 1, 18, 67 S.Ct. 504, 513, 91 L.Ed. 711 (1947), it would be rather bitter irony to chastise New York for having built the wall too tall and too strong.

It was thus error to grant summary judgment to the plaintiffs. We think also that the case calls on us to direct judgment dismissing the complaint. Although denial of the defendants' motions to dismiss would not itself have been appealable, it goes without saying that the grant of summary judgment to the plaintiffs was a proper subject for appeal, 28 U.S.C. § 1291, and 28 U.S.C. § 2106 empowers us to "direct the entry of such appropriate judgment, decree, or order, or require such further proceedings to be had as may be just under the circumstances." Although we have found no authority directly on point, First Nat'l Bank in Yonkers v. Maryland Cas. Co., 290 F.2d 246, 251-252 (2 Cir.), cert. denied, 368 U.S. 939, 82 S.Ct. 381, 7 L.Ed.2d 338 (1961), is very close to being one. A further analogy is furnished by the settled rule, "Where, on an appeal from an order granting or continuing a temporary injunction, or from an order ap-pointing a receiver, the equity of the bill is challenged and the attack upon it appears to be well founded, the power is conferred, and the duty is imposed, upon the appellate court to consider it, and, if it is of the opinion that the relief sought by the bill cannot be granted, to so decide, and thus to save the parties to the suit further expense resulting from the endeavor to secure impossible relief." Guardian Trust Co. v. Kansas City So. Ry. Co., 171 F. 43, 51, 28 L.R.A.,N.S., 620 (8 Cir. 1909) (Sanborn, J.), and cases cited; Metropolitan Water Co. v. Kaw Valley Drainage District, 223 U.S. 519, 523, 32 S.Ct. 246, 56 L.Ed. 533 (1912); Triumph Hosiery Mills, Inc. v. Triumph Int'l Corp., 308 F.2d 196, 200 (2 Cir. 1962); Zentner v. American Fed'n of Musicians, 343 F.2d 758 (2 Cir. 1965). Plaintiffs' attorney has consistently maintained that all the facts are contained in the complaint and are before the court; he did not indicate in argument that any facts warranting a different decision could be alleged or proved. Under these circumstances, we perceive no reason for not bringing this litigation to an end. See 6 Moore, supra, ¶¶ 56.12, 56.13, 56.27[2].

The judgment is reversed, with directions to dismiss the complaint.

THE United States Court of Appeals, Seventh Circuit, concludes that the following verse which a kindergarten teacher required her students to recite prior to their morning snack "is a prayer and that its compulsory recitation by kindergarten students in a public school comes within the proscription by the Supreme Court in the 'school prayer' cases: 'We thank you for the flowers so sweet; We thank you for the food we eat; We thank you for the birds that sing; We thank you for everything.'" The Court declares that "the so-called 'secular purposes' of the verse were merely adjunctive and supplemental to its basic and primary purpose, which was the religious act of praising and thanking the Deity."

DeSpain v. *DeKalb County Community Sch. Dist. 428,* 384 F.2d 836 (1967)

SWYGERT, Circuit Judge.

The plaintiffs, Lyle A. DeSpain and Mary R. DeSpain, are residents of DeKalb, Illinois. They are the parents of Laura I. DeSpain, who at the time the complaint was filed, was five years old and attended kindergarten class at the Ellwood Public School, located in DeKalb County Community School District 428. The plaintiffs brought this action under 28 U.S.C. § 1343 (3) to enjoin the officials of the school district from requiring the plaintiffs' child to recite a prayer during regular school hours. Besides the school district, individually named defendants include the members of the Board of Education and the superintendent of schools, the principal of the Ellwood Public School, and the kindergarten teacher, Esther Watne, who instructed Laura I. DeSpain.

Following a consolidated evidentiary hearing on the request for temporary and permanent injunctive relief, the district court dismissed the plaintiffs' complaint for failure to state a cause of action. DeSpain v. DeKalb County Community School Dist. 428, 255 F.Supp. 655 (N.D.Ill.1966). The court ruled that a verse which Mrs. Watne, the kindergarten teacher, required the children in her class to recite prior to their morning snack is "not a prayer or religious activity within the meaning of the Constitution. . . ." The verse read:

We thank you for the flowers so sweet;
We thank you for the food we eat;
We thank you for the birds that sing;
We thank you for everything.

We are of the view that the verse is a prayer and that its compulsory recitation by kindergarten students in a public school comes within the proscription of the first amendment, as interpreted by the Supreme Court in the "school prayer" cases. School Dist. of Abington Tp., Pa. v. Schempp, 374 U.S. 203, 83 S.Ct. 1560, 10 L.Ed.2d 844 (1963); Engel v. Vitale, 370 U.S. 421, 82 S.Ct. 1261, 8 L.Ed.2d 601 (1962). Accordingly, we reverse.

The evidence showed that for several years prior to the 1965-66 school year Mrs. Watne required the children in her kindergarten class to recite a verse identical to the above-quoted verse except that the last line read, "We thank you, God, for everything." In 1964 Mrs. Watne deleted the word "God," after the plaintiffs complained to Mrs. Watne, the superintendent of schools, the principal, and the Board of Education that the DeSpains' eldest son, then a kindergarten student, was required to recite the verse.

Mrs. DeSpain, who visited the kindergarten class on two occasions, and her daughter testified that immediately before and during the recitation of the verse in question the children folded their hands in their laps and closed their eyes. They also testified that at the conclusion of the verse many children said "Amen." The DeSpains' son testified that during the prior year the conduct of the children during the recitation of the verse was the same. On the other hand, several mothers of other children and Mrs. Watne testified that they did not see the children in a reverential attitude, nor did they hear any of the children say "Amen" after the recitation of the verse.[1]

Dr. A. Donald Davies, an Episcopal priest employed at Seabury Western Theological Seminary, Evanston, Illinois as a professor of Christian Education and Director of the Master of Arts program in Christian Education, testified that a prayer practically identical to the verse recited in Mrs. Watne's class, with the word "God" included in the last line, is found in a manual entitled "God's Love and Care," published by the National Department of Christian Education of the Episcopal church for the training of kindergarten teachers. Dr. Davies further testified that in his opinion the verse at issue is a prayer regardless of the fact that the word "God" was deleted from the last line, that "the intent is to offer thanks to God." In response to a question by the district judge, Dr. Davies stated that if the verse were completely isolated he would not consider it a prayer, but that he would still wonder "what the 'you' was. "

Dr. John Burkhart, a Presbyterian minister and a professor of Systematic Theology at McCormick Theological Seminary in Chicago and Curriculum Consultant for the Presbyterian Board of Christian Education, testified that the verse in question is a prayer in "form and intention." He said that "the 'you' which is the functional word in this prayer would be obviously addressed to someone who is thought to provide everything," and that "this is a common definition of God." He added, "It does not stop being a prayer when the word 'God' is removed, since the children who use it as a prayer, other than where it might have been used in the schools, use it and understand it as a prayer. So, in common context it is a prayer which has simply been modified, but has not lost its prayer connotation or meaning."

Mrs. Watne testified that she used the verse in question as part of her program of good citizenship and her "thankfulness" program. She said its purpose is "for appreciation, gratitude, for the whole world that is in front of them [the children]." She added that the verse was used to teach "social manners," and to thank the "helpers who came to our house . . . [to] help us do things . . . like TV repairmen, the plumber, the milkman. . . . " She admitted, however, that the use, purpose, and effect of the verse in question and the verse which contained the word "God" in the last line, were the same. She also said that in her mind the word "you" referred to God and that the verse was used by her to give thanks to a divine being for the wonders of nature, thanks which she hoped to impart to her pupils. She added, "Why shouldn't I tell them to thank Him?"

The superintendent of schools testified that he had heard the poem in question recited "hundreds of times" and had "never yet felt that it had any religious connotation to it." He added that "when 'God' is used in the public school . . . it is a neutral kind of thing.

There is no kind of theological interpretation of it, except the kind that the individual brings himself to that particular event." He admitted, however, that it would be improper if a plain, ordinary nondenominational prayer is said without comment in the public school by a teacher, and the children are instructed to recite it.

Finally, Edra Lipscomb, a professor in the Education Department at Northern Illinois University, testified that "verses of this kind are commonly used," and that in her opinion "this 'thank you' verse would certainly fit part of this philosophy of helping the children not [only] prepare themselves for life but actually become a part of the living society. . . . " She admitted, however, that according to her information the use of a very similar verse by kindergarten teachers in the Laboratory School at Northern Illinois University was prohibited in 1964.

The district judge decided that "the verse, recited in the setting proved by the testimony in this case, is not a prayer or religious activity within the meaning of the Constitution," because, among other reasons, "[t]he aim of inculcating good manners in the children, the mode of proper serving of a meal, and awaiting eating until all were served, and thanking donors of special treats, were paramount in the teacher's purposes." 255 F.Supp. at 656-657. The judge made the further statement:

[T]his is a case *de minimis*. Despite the theologians' characterization of this verse as a prayer, the court believes that set in the framework of the whole school day, its purpose was not to pray but to instill in the children an appreciation of and gratefulness for the world about them—the birds, the flowers, the food, and everything. They asked no blessing; they sought no divine assistance. Id. at 664.

Both in School Dist. of Abington Tp., Pa. v. Schempp, supra, and in Engel v. Vitale, supra, the Supreme Court admonished the state to observe strict neutrality with respect to religion in public schools. Mr. Justice Clark, speaking for the Court in *Schempp*, referred to the fact that the Supreme Court has consistently held that the establishment clause in the first amendment withdrew all legislative power respecting religious belief or the expression thereof. He then stated the test:

[W]hat are the purpose and the primary effect of the enactment? If either is the advancement or inhibition of religion then the enactment exceeds the scope of legislative power as circumscribed by the Constitution. That is to say that to withstand the strictures of the Establishment Clause there must be a secular legislative purpose and a primary effect that neither advances nor inhibits religion. 374 U.S. at 222, 83 S.Ct. at 1571.

Mr. Justice Black, speaking for the Court in the earlier

Engel case, reviewed the historical purposes underlying the establishment clause. There he wrote:

> When the power, prestige and financial support of government is placed behind a particular religious belief, the indirect coercive pressure upon religious minorities to conform to the prevailing officially approved religion is plain. But the purposes underlying the Establishment Clause go much further than that. Its first and most immediate purpose rested on the belief that a union of government and religion tends to destroy government and to degrade religion. The history of governmentally established religion, both in England and in this country, showed that whenever government had allied itself with one particular form of religion, the inevitable result had been that it had incurred the hatred, disrespect and even contempt of those who held contrary beliefs. 370 U.S. at 431, 82 S.Ct. at 1267.

Neither the *Engel* nor the *Schempp* decision was an attack upon Christianity, religion, or prayer; those cases merely articulated within factual contexts the principles of the first amendment, which was designed to provide a bulwark against those who wish to impose their religious beliefs upon others through governmental action. Thus Mr. Justice Black continued in *Engel*:

> It is neither sacrilegious nor anti-religious to say that each separate government in this country should stay out of the business of writing or sanctioning official prayers and leave that purely religious function to the people themselves and to those the people choose to look to for religious guidance. Id. at 435, 82 S.Ct. at 1269.

With these Supreme Court pronouncements in mind, an application of the test laid down by Mr. Justice Clark in *Schempp* to the facts of this case convinces us that the so-called "secular purposes" of the verse were merely adjunctive and supplemental to its basic and primary purpose, which was the religious act of praising and thanking the Deity.

It is not to be gainsaid that the verse may have commendable virtues in teaching kindergarten children "good manners" and "gratitude," to use Mrs. Watne's words. The fact, however, that children through the use of required schoolroom prayer are likely to become more grateful for the things they receive or that they may become better citizens does not justify the use of compulsory prayer in our public school systems. As the plaintiffs point out, if prayers which tend to teach and inculcate these virtues are not within the ambit of the bar imposed by the first amendment against such religious activity, any religious activity of whatever nature could be justified by public officials on the basis that the activity has beneficial secular purposes; as a result the Supreme Court's admonitions in *Engel* and *Schempp* would

become meaningless.

The Second Circuit in Stein v. Oshinsky, 348 F.2d 999 (2d Cir.), cert. denied, 382 U.S. 957, 86 S.Ct. 435, 15 L.Ed.2d 361 (1965), was presented with a problem similar to the one with which we are faced. In that case a principal of a New York City school ordered the kindergarten teachers, in the language of the complaint, "to stop the infant children from reciting the simple and ancient prayer: 'Thank You for the World so Sweet, Thank You for the Food We Eat, Thank You for the Birds that Sing—Thank You, God, for Everything.'" The plaintiffs, parents of children attending the school, demanded that the school officials give their children an opportunity to recite voluntary prayers in the classroom. When the school officials ignored the demand, suit was instituted in the federal court to force them to grant it. The district court granted the requested relief. The court of appeals reversed the decision, holding that neither the free exercise clause nor the guarantee of freedom of speech of the first amendment requires a state to permit students to engage in public prayer in state-owned facilities "whenever and wherever they desire." In the course of its opinion, the court stated:

> Determination of what is to go on in public schools is primarily for the school authorities. Against the desire of these parents that their children "be given an opportunity to acknowledge their dependence and love to Almighty God through a prayer each day in their respective classrooms," the authorities were entitled to weigh the likely desire of other parents not to have their children present at such prayers, either because the prayers were too religious or not religious enough; and the wisdom of having public educational institutions stick to education and keep out of religion, with all the bickering that intrusion into the latter is likely to produce. The authorities acted well within their powers in concluding that plaintiffs must content themselves with having their children say these prayers before nine or after three. Id. at 1002.

It will be noted that the verse with which the Second Circuit was concerned and the verse at issue here are identical except that in *Oshinsky* the last line contained the word "God." We think this is a distinction without a difference in view of the testimony of Mrs. Watne and the theologians who appeared as witnesses.

The district court characterized this case as *de minimis*. We are tempted to agree. Certainly, this verse was as innocuous as could be insofar as constituting an imposition of religious tenets upon nonbelievers. The plaintiffs have forced the constitutional issue to its outer limits. We are reminded, however, of what the Supreme Court said in *Schempp*:

> [I]t is no defense to urge that the religious practices

here may be relatively minor encroachments on the First Amendment. The breach of neutrality that is today a trickling stream may all too soon become a raging torrent. . . . 374 U.S. at 225, 83 S.Ct. at 1573.

With respect to this facet of the case we also have in mind what the Court said in Everson v. Board of Education, 330 U.S. 1, 18, 67 S.Ct. 504, 91 L.Ed. 711 (1947): "The First Amendment has erected a wall between church and state. That wall must be kept high and impregnable. We could not approve the slightest breach."

The judgment of the district court is reversed.

SCHNACKENBERG, Circuit Judge, (dissenting).

A witness for plaintiffs, Reverend A. Donald Davies, an Episcopalian priest, testified that he was familiar with the curricular content of manuals used in kindergartens, and that in all of them which he had seen there is some verse "like this"[1] in which the child expresses that he has received all of the things mentioned, by saying "thank you" for them. Reverend Davies insisted, however, that the verse in question with "God" removed "is still a prayer". But he admitted that, with the word "God" left out, "They might regard that, then, as an expression of gratitude to the community of animate and inanimate and human things in which they live."

A witness for defendants was Edra Lipscomb,[2] a kindergarten teacher for 19 years, and now a professor at Northern Illinois University, teaching kindergarten courses. According to her testimony, the curriculum followed at the school here involved is typical of kindergarten curriculums now in use, as embodied in a comprehensive compilation thereof introduced in evidence. As to the particular verse under attack in this case, Mrs. Lipscomb testified that verses of this kind are commonly used, and they are not regarded as prayer exercises. She also swore that in a kindergarten workshop in 1964, where she had 40 kindergarten teachers participating, she ascertained that all of those present used such a verse, the purpose of which

"is to help the youngsters become a part of the world around them, and so they do a lot of things in the kindergarten as a part of introduction into society, into the culture, and this 'thank you' verse would certainly fit part of this philosophy of helping the children not prepare themselves for life but actually become a part of the living society, contributing society. Also it is used to establish a quiet atmosphere in preparation for food."

Thus the record of the district court reveals that the daily kindergarten schedule, which was used at the school in question, provides for the children to recite:

Every morning when the sun comes smiling up on everyone

It's lots of fun to say good morning to the sun. Good morning, Sun.

1. We would not be justified in disturbing the findings of fact of the district court; in fact, we are not asked to do so. Certainly we should not rationalize (as do plaintiffs) that the elimination of the word "God" from a verse tends to prove that what remains is a prayer. The verse which remained to be recited by the pupils, after they were served cookies and milk, undoubtedly reflects in their young minds the pleasant prospect of eating. Naturally the recitation of the verse was a vocal expression of their gratitude. Moreover, this court has no right to take on a burden (which plaintiffs have voluntarily assumed) of establishing that a benefactor, to whom each child feels he is speaking, is a deity.

Human lives are replete with incidents where happy or wondrous events evoke voluntary, deep-seated emotions from those who witness them or participate therein. For instance, people may look at a glowing sunset and in admiration exclaim "Thanks for the opportunity of seeing that!" While one who overhears the exclamation might wonder why the remark was made, the fact remains that it is not a prayer. The expression of thanks evinces a sense of gratitude. And gratitude is a virtue, whether evoked by the marvels of nature or by the unidentified suppliers of tasty cookies and milk to kindergarten pupils. The enraptured viewer of the sunset, as well as each eager, usually hungry, child, gives expression to his gratitude.

Despite the elimination of the word "God" from the children's recital of thanks, plaintiffs maintain, in effect, that that word is still there in the minds of the children. Thus we are asked as a court to prohibit, not only what these children are saying, but also what plaintiffs *think* the children are *thinking*. Certainly thought is a matter varying with each child, be he Christian, Jew, atheist or agnostic. One who seeks to convert a child's supposed thought into a violation of the constitution of the United States is placing a meaning on that historic doctrine which would have surprised the founding fathers.

2. There was a conflict in the evidence at the trial in the district court on several issues of fact, (1) as to whether the children took a "devotional attitude" in reciting the verse in question, (2) whether some children said "amen" and "crossed themselves" and (3) whether the children's heads were bowed or they looked either at each other, at the teacher, or at the food. The court found as to these matters that it was "not convinced" that such devotional acts actually occurred. This is a finding of fact which is not clearly contrary to the manifest weight of the evidence and this court has no right, under 28 U.S.C.A. rule 52(a), to make a contrary finding.

3. The district court concluded that this is a case "de minimis". The court supported its conclusion by saying:

"... Despite the theologians' characterization of this verse as a prayer, the court believes that set in the framework of the whole school day, its purpose was not to pray but to instill in the children an appreciation of and gratefulness for the world about them—the birds, the flowers, the food, and everything. They asked no blessing; they sought divine assistance.

"The teacher was exercising her pedagogical function of making the pupils socially acceptable persons, as well-mannered guests, grateful in their appreciation of their provider....

* * * * *

"The court believes that this case presents the situation characterized by Justice Goldberg in the Schempp case, [2] supra, at 308, thus:

'It is of course true that great consequences can grow from small beginnings, but the measure of constitutional adjudication is the ability and willingness to distinguish between real threat and mere shadow.'

[2] School Dist. of Abington Tp., Pa. v. Schempp, 374 U.S. 203, 83 S.Ct. 1560, 10 L.Ed.2d 844 (1963), Justice Goldberg's concurring opinion."

I agree that this is a case *de minimis*. I would affirm.

NOTES

1. The conflicts in the evidence relating to the conduct of the children during the recitation of the verse were resolved in the defendants' favor by the district judge. We believe that the attitude of the children during recitation is immaterial to a determination of the ultimate question which we must decide: Was the required recitation of the verse a proscribed public school activity?

DISSENTING OPINION NOTES

1. We thank you for the flowers so sweet;
We thank you for the food we eat;

We thank you for the birds that sing;
We thank you for everything.

2. She was educated at the University of Illinois, Southern Illinois University, University of Michigan and Indiana University.

THE United States Court of Appeals, Sixth Circuit, decides for a high school student who as a conscientious objector refused to attend the required R.O.T.C. class and as a result was notified by school authorities he would not be awarded his graduation diploma even though he had passed all other requirements. In deciding for the student, the Court concluded its opinion by citing the trial judge: "As the trial judge aptly observed, 'the R.O.T.C. course requirement forced John [the student] to choose between following his religious beliefs and forfeiting his diploma, on the one hand, and abandoning his religious beliefs and receiving his diploma on the other hand.' The State may not put its citizens to such a Hobson's choice consistent with the Constitution without showing a 'compelling state interest . . . within the State's constitutional power to regulate. . . .'"

Spence v. *Bailey,* 465 F.2d 797 (1972)

Mr. Justice Clark:

This is an appeal from a declaratory judgment entered under the provisions of 42 U.S.C. § 1983 and finding that the religious beliefs of John Spence Jr., a conscientious objector attending the Memphis City Schools as a student, had been infringed by a requirement that he participate in the Reserve Officers Training Corps program at the schools. The District Court, 325 F.Supp. 601, found that the compulsory program was contrary to the religious beliefs of Spence Jr. as "a conscientious objector" and that the school authorities had failed to show any compelling state interest in requiring his participation in the program. We affirm.

1. At the time Spence Jr. entered the 11th grade at Central High School in Memphis the state law required that every school student take one year either of physical education or of R.O.T.C. training. No physical education course was offered at Central for male students leaving R.O.T.C. as the only alternative. Nor was any program offered consisting only of those portions of the R.O.T.C. course that were not objectionable to conscientious objectors.

R.O.T.C. was taught by retired U.S. Army officers and the books, manuals and other materials used in the course were prepared by the United States Army. The routine included a study of these materials together with military drills, marksmanship and firearms instruction and military tactics, with the students wearing military uniforms once each week.

There being no physical education course for boys,

Spence Jr. attended R.O.T.C. class for the first three days he was enrolled at Central High. Thereafter he refused to attend the R.O.T.C. class, and his father, the appellee here, petitioned the school authorities to exempt Spence Jr. from attending on account of the latter's conscientious objections.[1] The request was denied and upon Spence Jr. refusing to attend, the school authorities notified him that he would not be awarded his diploma even though he passed all other requirements. Upon his graduation he was not awarded a diploma; however, he was able to enroll in and is now attending college despite this handicap.

2. Appellants do not challenge the sincerity or religious motives of Spence Jr. but contend that the compulsory program is a secular one with, at most, incidental and indirect impact on Spence Jr.'s religious beliefs. They also suggest that he could have avoided R.O.T.C. by attending the Memphis Technical School which does provide courses in physical education. But the record shows that this school is far removed from Spence Jr.'s home; its curriculum does not include the necessary liberal art courses preparatory to college and would not meet Spence Jr.'s requirements. We therefore reject these alternatives.

Appellants cite as support for their position Hamilton v. Regents, 293 U.S. 245, 55 S.Ct. 197, 79 L.Ed. 343 (1934) approving an R.O.T.C. program in a state land grant college and Braunfeld v. Brown, 366 U.S. 599, 81 S.Ct. 1144, 6 L.Ed.2d 563 (1961) upholding a criminal conviction under state blue laws. In *Hamilton* the

34

Court specifically found that the University program served the compelling State interest in military training while Appellants concede here that their military training course had no such compelling State interest.[2] Indeed since Tennessee has made the R.O.T.C. training course optional with physical education, it would be difficult to conclude that the R.O.T.C. program was vital to the State's welfare.

Moreover, other factual differences are present. The enrollment at California's University in *Hamilton* was voluntary while attendance here is required by law. As Mr. Justice Butler noted in *Hamilton*, "California has not drafted or called them to attend the University. They are seeking education offered by the state and at the same time insisting that they be excluded from the prescribed course. . . . " The Court concluded that due process did not confer "the right to be students in the state university free from obligation to take military training as one of the conditions of attendance." At 262, 55 S.Ct. at 204. The distinction here is crucial. See West Virginia State Board of Education v. Barnette, 319 U.S. 624, 631-632, 63 S.Ct. 1178, 87 L.Ed. 1628 (1943); School District of Abington Township, Pa. v. Schempp, 374 U.S. 203, 250-253, 83 S.Ct. 1560, 10 L.Ed.2d 844 (1963) (Brennan, J., concurring). Furthermore the school system here conducts a physical education course for female students at all schools while only Technical High provides it for male students. Indeed, the record shows that physical education for Spence Jr. could have been offered at Central High School since facilities were available less than a hundred yards from the main building. Instead the authorities required Spence Jr. to engage in R.O.T.C. training or go to Technical High. If the appellants had utilized the physical education facilities available, the State would have accomplished its purpose by means which would not have imposed such a heavy burden on Spence Jr.'s free exercise of his religion. As was said in *Braunfeld, supra*, if "the State may accomplish its purpose by means which do not impose such a burden" it must do so. At 607 of 366 U.S., at 1148 of 81 S.Ct.

Braunfeld is one of the Court's recent opinions which have carefully confined the scope of State regulations that may impinge on religious beliefs and practices. We believe that appellants' reliance on it is also misplaced. There the State imposed no penalties upon the religious practitioner, but merely proscribed the purely secular activity of work on Sunday. In Sherbert v. Verner, 374 U.S. 398, 83 S.Ct. 1790, 10 L.Ed.2d 965 (1963), however, the Court struck down an unemployment compensation scheme that tended to penalize those who observed Saturday as a religious holiday. The distinction is clear: the regulation in *Braunfeld* was upheld because it in no way compelled activity that was contrary to religious beliefs and denied no im-

portant State benefits to any religious practitioner. The regulation in *Sherbert* was invalidated because it forced the religious practitioner either to act contrary to his religion (by accepting employment on Saturday) or to be denied important State benefits (unemployment compensation). See Sherbert v. Verner, *supra* at 402-403, 83 S.Ct. 1790. The regulation here involved is clearly similar to that in *Sherbert*, since it compels the conscientious objector either to engage in military training contrary to his religious beliefs, or to give up his public education.

As Mr. Chief Justice Burger said only recently in upholding Amish religious claims in Wisconsin v. Yoder, 406 U.S. 205, 215, 92 S.Ct. 1526, 1533, 32 L.Ed.2d 15 (1972), "only those interests of the highest order and those not otherwise served can overbalance legitimate claims to the free exercise of religion." At 1533. In evaluating rights to the free exercise of religious beliefs, he continued, "we must be careful to determine whether the . . . religious faith" and mode of life of the person are "inseparable and interdependent;" otherwise the faith "may not be interposed as a barrier to reasonable state regulation" if the way of life "is based on purely secular considerations; to have the protection of the Religion Clauses, the claims must be rooted in religious belief." At 215, 92 S.Ct. at 1533.

3. Here the impact on Spence Jr.'s religious beliefs cannot be minimized. As we have indicated the state does not challenge that Spence Jr.'s claims are rooted in deep religious conviction based, as he says, upon "religious training and belief . . . upon a faith to which all else is subordinate and upon which all else is ultimately dependent." As Wisconsin's law requiring compulsory formal education after the 8th grade "would gravely endanger if not destroy the free exercise of . . . religious beliefs," Id. at p. 219, 92 S.Ct. at p. 1535, of *Yoder*, so would Tennessee's law transgress upon Spence Jr.'s.

As the trial judge aptly observed, "the R.O.T.C. course requirement forced John to choose between following his religious beliefs and forfeiting his diploma, on the one hand, and abandoning his religious beliefs and receiving his diploma on the other hand." The State may not put its citizens to such a Hobson's choice consistent with the Constitution without showing a "compelling state interest . . . within the State's constitutional power to regulate . . . " NAACP v. Button, 371 U.S. 415, 438, 83 S.Ct. 328, 341, 9 L.Ed.2d 405 (1963).

Affirmed.

WILLIAM E. MILLER, Circuit Judge (dissenting).

Because of my high regard for the author of the majority opinion in this case, whose illustrious career includes many years service on the highest court in the land, and because of my respect for the opinions of my colleague, Judge McCree, I personally regret that I must note my dissent.

The record clearly indicates that the required R.O.T.C. course at Central High School was prescribed by the duly constituted authorities in lieu of a course in physical education. In addition to the military aspects of the course, it has many other features which the authorities were justified in considering as important training for a student at the high school level, including training in leadership, discipline, hygiene, and other elements. The court in no way committed a student to military service and placed no impediment in his way in the event he should in the future seek to obtain the status of a conscientious objector pursuant to federal statute. Under these circumstances, I find compelling the language of Mr. Justice Cardozo in his concurring opinion in Hamilton v. Regents, 293 U.S. 245, 55 S.Ct. 197, 79 L.Ed. 343 (1934):

There is no occasion at this time to mark the limits of governmental power in the exaction of military service when the nation is at peace. The petitioners have not been required to bear arms for any hostile purpose, offensive or defensive, either now or in the future. They have not even been required in any absolute or peremptory way to join in courses of instruction that will fit them to bear arms. If they elect to resort to an institution for higher education maintained with the state's moneys, then and only then they are commanded to follow courses of instruction believed by the state to be vital to its welfare. This may be condemned by some as unwise or illiberal or unfair when there is violence to conscientious scruples, either religious or merely ethical. More must be shown to set the ordinance at naught. In controversies of this order courts do not concern themselves with matters of legislative policy, unrelated to privileges or liberties secured by the organic law. The First Amendment, if it be read into the Fourteenth, makes invalid any state law "respecting an establishment of religion or prohibiting the free exercise thereof." *Instruction in military science is not instruction in the practice or tenets of a religion. Neither directly nor indirectly is government establishing a state religion when it insists upon such training. Instruction in military science, unaccompanied here by any pledge of military service, is not an interference by the state with the free exercise of religion when the liberties of the constitution are read in the light of a century and a half of history during days of peace and war.* At 265 and 266, 55 S.Ct. at 205 (Emphasis added).

The attempt to distinguish *Hamilton* on the basis that the attendance at the college level in that case was on a voluntary basis, while here attendance was compulsory under Tennessee law, appears to me to be unpersuasive. As I view the record in this case, the R.O.T.C. program did not infringe upon the student's constitutional right of free exercise of religion. As Mr. Justice Cardozo further said in his *Hamilton* concurrence:

Manifestly a different doctrine would carry us to lengths that have never yet been dreamed of. The conscientious objector, if his liberties were to be thus extended, might refuse to contribute taxes in furtherance of a war, whether for attack or for defense, or in furtherance of any other end condemned by his conscience as irreligious or immoral. The right of private judgment has never yet been so exalted above the powers and the compulsion of the agencies of government. One who is a martyr to a principle—which may turn out in the end to be a delusion or an error—does not prove by his martyrdom that he has kept within the law. At 268, 55 S.Ct. at 206.

I see no reason why a conscientious objector, if his liberties are to be so extended, could not with equal plausibility refuse to subject himself to any course which involved the study of military history—for example, a study of the Napoleonic or Punic wars and others of similar character.

I wish to make it clear that my disagreement with the majority in this case is not based upon the notion that there is a compelling state interest. In my opinion there is no objective evidence to support a finding that the required R.O.T.C. program at Central High School in any way impinged upon the student's constitutional right of free exercise of religion. The mere statement in Spence's affidavit that the program did violate his religious faith is based entirely upon a subjective judgment.

As clearly indicated by the decision of the Supreme Court in Wisconsin v. Yoder, et al., 406 U.S. 205, 92 S.Ct. 1526, 1533, 32 L.Ed. 15 (1972), mere subjective evaluation is not enough to establish a religious belief or conviction for First Amendment purposes:

... A way of life, however virtuous and admirable, may not be interposed as a barrier to reasonable state regulation of education if it is based on purely secular considerations; to have the protection of the Religion Clauses, the claims must be rooted in religious belief. Although a determination of what is a "religious" belief or practice entitled to constitutional protection may present a most delicate question, the very concept of ordered liberty precludes allowing every person to make his own standards on matters of conduct in which society as a whole has important interests. Thus, if the Amish asserted their claims because of their subjective evaluation and rejection of the contemporary secular values accepted by the majority, much as Thoreau rejected the social values of his time and isolated himself at Walden Pond, their claim would not rest on a religious basis. Thoreau's choice was philosophical and personal rather than religious, and such belief does not rise to the demands of the Religion Clause. At 92 S.Ct. at 1533.

The Court was able to find in *Yoder* a violation of the Religion Clause in Wisconsin's compulsory school attendance law as applied to members of the Amish faith because, as the Court said, "The record in this case abundantly supports the claim that the traditional way of life of the Amish is not merely a matter of personal preference, but one of deeply religious conviction shared by an organized group, and intimately related to daily living." At 92 S.Ct. at 1533. In the case before us there is no comparable showing.

I would therefore reverse the judgment of the District Court.

NOTES

1. Spence Jr.'s religious beliefs and the resulting conflict were stated by him in these words:

"By reason of religious training and belief, I am conscientiously opposed to participation in war in any form and am opposed to being subjected to combat training for the purpose of being prepared to enter into war. As stated above, my convictions are based upon religious training and belief which is in turn based upon a power or being or upon a faith to which all else is subordinate and upon which all else is ultimately dependent. This sincere and meaningful belief occupies in my life a place parallel to that filled by the Supreme Being, God . . . ."

2. Appellants do say that they have a compelling interest in refusing all applications for exemptions from the R.O.T.C. compulsory rule, otherwise the burden of its administration would be intolerable. Moreover, they argue that a flood of fraudulent conscientious objectors' claims will result if Spence Jr.'s application is allowed. However, similar contentions have been made and rejected heretofore. See Sherbert v. Verner, 374 U.S. 398, 407, 83 S.Ct. 1790, 10 L.Ed.2d 965 (1963).

A United States District Court decides against several students who had challenged the constitutionality of the Massachusetts statute which read: "At the commencement of the first class of each day in all grades in all public schools the teacher in charge of the room in which each such class is held shall announce that a period of silence not to exceed one minute in duration shall be observed for meditation or prayer, and during any such period silence shall be maintained and no activities engaged in." In upholding the constitutionality of the statute, the Court concludes: "We have closely scrutinized the statute and guidelines in our analysis of plaintiffs' claims because First Amendment liberties are at issue. In our view plaintiffs have failed to show the absence of a neutral, secular purpose for the opening moment of silence in the Framingham public schools. The statute and guidelines do not have a primary effect of favoring or sponsoring religion. They do not involve the state in religious exercises or directly in the realm of religion. They do not fall within the proscriptions of the First Amendment."

Gaines v. *Anderson*, 421 F.Supp. 337 (1976)

FRANK J. MURRAY, District Judge.

The plaintiffs bring this action pursuant to 42 U.S.C. § 1983 to challenge the constitutionality of the Massachusetts statute, and the guidelines of the school committee of the town of Framingham adopted to implement it, which requires the observance of a period of silence at the opening of the school day in the public schools. The statute reads:

At the commencement of the first class of each day in all grades in all public schools the teacher in charge of the room in which each such class is held shall announce that a period of silence not to exceed one minute in duration shall be observed for meditation or prayer, and during any such period silence shall be maintained and no activities engaged in.

St.1966, ch. 130, as amended by St.1973, ch. 621; Mass.Gen.Laws ch. 71, § 1A.

On January 12, 1976 the school committee adopted a resolution " . . . that the School Committee comply with the law, Chapter 71, Section 1A of the M.G.L. until such time as the courts rule the Chapter in violation of the Constitution". On January 27, the school committee adopted guidelines to carry out the statutory provisions. The guidelines have been observed since February 2, the day this action was brought. Plaintiffs seek declaratory and injunctive relief to vin-

dicate alleged violations of their rights under the United States Constitution. A three-judge court was convened to hear and determine the claim for injunctive relief. 28 U.S.C. § 2284.

I.

Plaintiffs are twelve students who attend the public schools of the town of Framingham, and the parents of these students.[1] Defendants are the members of the school committee and the superintendent of schools of Framingham. In their complaint plaintiffs allege that the statute as amended and the guidelines violate their rights under the First[2] and Fourteenth[3] Amendments in the following respects: (1) they establish a religious exercise in the public schools in violation of the Establishment Clause of the First Amendment, (2) they mandate a particular format for the religious exercise in violation of the Free Exercise Clause of the First Amendment, and (3) they interfere with the parents' due process rights exclusively to supervise the religious upbringing of their children in violation of the Fourteenth Amendment.

The statute is clear in its requirements. It provides that at the opening of the day in all grades in the public schools a minute of silence shall be maintained during which no overt activities shall take place. The teacher in charge of the schoolroom is required to announce the minute of silence to be observed for meditation or prayer. It is clearly contemplated that this exercise shall be observed in a public building under general supervision of a public school teacher. Under the guidelines teachers are to remind students not observing silence of their obligation to obey the school rules and regulations, and to refer persistent violators to the school principal. If the principal fails to achieve the cooperation of the violator, the principal then is required to follow the established procedures for dealing with breaches of school regulations.[4] Because we conclude that the statute and the guidelines do not advance or inhibit religion, or coerce any student into participating in any activity which infringes his liberty of conscience or interferes with the free exercise of his religion, we do not agree that they violate plaintiffs' rights under the Constitution.

II.

The First Amendment commands in part that "Congress shall make no law respecting an establishment of religion, or prohibiting the free exercise thereof". The Supreme Court has stated the test for measuring the compliance of a challenged statute with the Establishment Clause of the First Amendment in the following language:

> ... what are the purpose and primary effect of the enactment? If either is the advancement or inhibition of religion then the enactment exceeds the scope of legislative power as circumscribed by the Constitution. That is to say that to withstand the strictures of the Establishment Clause there must be a secular legislative purpose and a primary effect that neither advances nor inhibits religion.

Abington School Dist. v. Schempp, 374 U.S. 203, 222, 83 S.Ct. 1560, 1571, 10 L.Ed.2d 844 (1963). In *Committee for Public Education v. Nyquist*, 413 U.S. 756, 93 S.Ct. 2955, 37 L.Ed.2d 948 (1973), the Court referred to a three-part test of any law challenged on establishment grounds: (1) the law must reflect a clearly secular purpose, (2) it must have a primary effect that neither advances nor inhibits religion, and (3) it must avoid excessive government entanglement with religion.

The application of any of these criteria to state action challenged as violative of the Establishment Clause cannot be scientifically precise, *see Tilton v. Richardson*, 403 U.S. 672, 678, 91 S.Ct. 2091, 29 L.Ed.2d 790 (1971), for the line which separates the secular from the sectarian is an elusive one. Application of these criteria requires careful consideration of the values embodied in the First Amendment as revealed by its history and the Supreme Court cases

which have explicated it. It is enough to note here that what is at stake in the First Amendment religion clauses is the policy of separating Church and State to the extent practicable in a nation whose institutions reflect that our heritage is religious and whose people in large measure adhere to a variety of religious beliefs and creeds. The Court's opinions generally have recognized that the underlying policy of the First Amendment's prohibitions is the prevention of such dependence of religion on government and such interference by government with religion "that, as history teaches us, is apt to lead to strife and frequently strain a political system to the breaking point". *Walz v. Tax Commission*, 397 U.S. 664, 694, 90 S.Ct. 1409, 1424, 25 L.Ed.2d 697 (1970) (Harlan, J., concurring); *see Everson v. Board of Education*, 330 U.S. 1, 8-11, 67 S.Ct. 504, 91 L.Ed. 711 (1947); *Engel v. Vitale*, 370 U.S. 421, 425-27, 82 S.Ct. 1261, 8 L.Ed.2d 601 (1962); *Abington School Dist. v. Schempp, supra*, 374 U.S. at 307, 83 S.Ct. 1560 (Goldberg, J., concurring).

In applying the criteria to the statute challenged in this case, we consider and appraise the history of the 1966 enactment, the 1973 amendment,[5] the statutory language employed, and the involvement of the state under the statute in the public school setting.

III.

The plaintiffs infer an unconstitutional purpose from the timing of the 1966 enactment and the meaning of the word "meditation". They argue that the enactment took place in the "aftermath of the invalidation" of Bible reading and prayer in the Massachusetts public schools by the Supreme Judicial Court in *Attorney General v. School Committee of North Brookfield*, 347 Mass. 775, 199 N.E.2d 553 (1964), to fill the void caused by the invalidation. They contend this history leads to the conclusion that it was not the intent of the legislature to further secular ends. We note that the statute was enacted in 1966 after the decisions in *Schempp* in 1963 and *North Brookfield* in 1964, but we think plaintiffs' arguments do not withstand close scrutiny.

The timing of the 1966 enactment does not necessarily support an inference that the Massachusetts Legislature was motivated by an unconstitutional purpose to promote religion. The enactment of this legislation in the aftermath of *Schempp* and *North Brookfield* is completely consistent with a legislative purpose to promote secular purposes in a manner that is constitutionally neutral as to religion. We doubt that timing alone could ever be sufficient to establish an unconstitutional purpose to advance religion. *Compare Epperson v. Arkansas*, 393 U.S. 97, 89 S.Ct. 266, 21 L.Ed.2d 228 (1968). Other materials invariably must be considered. *Cf. McGowan v. Maryland*, 366

U.S. 420, 453, 81 S.Ct. 1101, 6 L.Ed. 2d 393 (1961).

Here, the legislative history, the statutory language, and its likely operation and effect, all suggest that this legislation was designed to serve secular objectives without unconstitutionally advancing religion. Although the legislative history is sparse, the available materials establish that the original bill was entitled "An Act providing for a moment of silent prayer at the beginning of each day in the public schools of the Commonwealth and the recitation of the pledge of allegiance". The pertinent section of the bill provided that "The school day in all the public schools of the [C]ommonwealth shall commence in silence for one moment so that any pupil who so desires may offer a prayer in silence". Upon referral of the bill to the Legislative Committee on Education the word "prayer" was stricken from the title and body of the bill and the word "meditation" was substituted. Subsequently, the Massachusetts Senate changed the bill in certain respects but retained the Committee language of "meditation".

We think that in striking the word "prayer" out of the bill and substituting the word "meditation," the Massachusetts Legislature demonstrated awareness of the distinction between these two words and an intention to further secular purposes without infringing the values protected by the Establishment Clause. A state statute which mandates a moment of silence in a public school setting is not *per se* an invalid exercise of legislative power. All that the statute requires students to do is be silent. Silence during the school day may frequently be necessary if schools are to attain their educative goals, and may serve legitimate secular purposes in aid of the educative function. A quiet moment at the beginning of the day would tend to "'still the tumult of the playground and start a day of study'". *Abington School Dist. v. Schempp, supra,* 374 U.S. at 281, n. 57, 83 S.Ct. at 1602 (quoting the Washington Post, June 28, 1962, § A, at 22, col. 2). The legislature could reasonably believe that students tend to learn greater self-discipline and respect for the authority of the teacher from a required moment of silence. These are legitimate secular ends, and a purpose to advance them is constitutionally permissible.

The word "meditation" did not infuse the statute with the unconstitutional purpose or effect of advancing or inhibiting religion. Meditation—the act of meditating—is not necessarily a religious exercise. Used in its ordinary sense, "meditation" connotes serious reflection or contemplation on a subject which may be religious, irreligious or nonreligious.[6] Thus, the words of the 1966 statute are capable of a reasonable construction by which the constitutional difficulties raised by plaintiffs may be avoided. *See, e. g., Curtis v. Loether,* 415 U.S. 189, 192 n. 6, 94 S.Ct. 1005, 39 L.Ed.2d 260 (1974). We think it is entirely consistent

with the secular goals of public schools for the state to encourage students to turn their minds silently toward serious thoughts and values. As Mr. Justice Brennan wrote:

> It has not been shown that readings from the speeches and messages of great Americans, for example, or from the documents of our heritage of liberty, daily recitation of the Pledge of Allegiance, or *even the observance of a moment of reverent silence at the opening of class,* may not adequately serve the solely secular purposes of the devotional activities without jeopardizing either the religious liberties of any members of the community or the proper degree of separation between the spheres of religion and government. (Emphasis added.)

Abington School Dist. v. Schempp, supra 374 U.S. at 281, 83 S.Ct. at 1602 (Brennan, J., concurring).[7] In our view the prescribed exercise in the 1966 statute was not a state endorsement of religion or interference with liberty of conscience; it did not constitute a religious exercise to achieve secular ends, and, therefore, did not have an unconstitutional effect. We find that the statute met the neutrality requirements of the Establishment Clause.

IV.

We turn next to the question whether the statute continued to withstand the strictures of the Establishment Clause after the words "or prayer" were added to it by the 1973 amendment. Unlike the word "meditation", the word "prayer" in its usual and ordinary sense has a specifically religious meaning.[8] It is settled that the state cannot utilize its power or prestige or influence to advance or encourage religion, *see, e. g., Epperson v. Arkansas, supra* 393 U.S. at 103-04, 89 S.Ct. 266; *Torcaso v. Watkins,* 367 U.S. 488, 495, 81 S.Ct. 1680, 6 L.Ed.2d 982 (1961), and if the amendment here has the purpose or primary effect of encouraging the religious activity of prayer the statute would be rendered unconstitutional. *Abington School Dist. v. Schempp, supra; Engel v. Vitale, supra.* But in appraising the amended statute we are mindful that government's attitude toward religion must be one of "wholesome 'neutrality'", *Abington School Dist. v. Schempp, supra,* 374 U.S. at 222, 83 S.Ct. 1560. The requirements of the First Amendment do not implicate hostility to religion or indifference toward religious groups; they do not import a preference for those who believe in no religion, or demand primary devotion to the secular.

[12] The 1973 amendment is framed in the disjunctive, and the statute as amended permits meditation or prayer without mandating the one or the other. Thus, the effect of the amended statute is to accommodate students who desire to use the minute of

silence for prayer or religious meditation, and also other students who prefer to reflect upon secular matters. This understanding of the operation and effect of the amended statute is reinforced by the legislative history of the amendment and the guidelines adopted by the Framingham school committee.

The bill proposing the amendment originally read: At the commencement of the first class of each day in all grades in all public schools the teacher in charge of the room in which each such class is held shall announce that a period of silence not to exceed one minute in duration shall be observed for meditation *and* prayer, and during any such period silence shall be maintained and no activities engaged in. (Emphasis added.)

House Bill 4890 of 1973. The sponsor of the bill later amended it on the floor by striking out the word "and" and substituting the word "or". This change was a significant one, even if not dispositive, for it indicates a legislative sensitivity to the First Amendment's mandate to take a neutral position that neither encourages nor discourages prayer. Further, the program instituted in the Framingham schools follows the statute precisely. There the only command to the students is the requirement that they be silent for one minute for the purpose of meditation or prayer; there is no command that they meditate or pray.[9] The teachers are directed to dispose of questions raised by students concerning the period of mandated silence with this specific response:

We are doing this in compliance with State Law. Any other questions you have should be discussed with your parents or with someone in your home.

We think that the lack of any mandatory direction to students to meditate or pray clearly indicates a legislative purpose to maintain neutrality, and that the defendants understand this to be the statutory purpose and effect. The fact that the Framingham program provides an opportunity for prayer for those students who desire to pray during the period of silence does not render the program unconstitutional. *See McGowan v. Maryland, supra; Everson v. Board of Education, supra.*

The Supreme Court has held that it is no part of the business of the state to direct the recitation of officially prescribed prayers in the classrooms of public schools, *Engel v. Vitale, supra,* or to require the reading of verses from the Bible and public recitation of the Lord's Prayer at the opening of the school day by pupils in unison. *Abington School Dist. v. Schempp, supra.* In those cases the Court found the prayer exercises to be religious, and violative of the First Amendment even if individual pupils could be excused from attending or participating in the exercises. But the statutory schemes in *Engel* and *Schempp* had features not present in the statute and guidelines before us,

which persuade us that neither *Engel* nor *Schempp* necessarily controls this case. We think that the absence of any mandate by the statute or the teacher to the students to participate in prayer is not an attempt to save an unconstitutional program of school prayer, *see Engel v. Vitale, supra; Abington School Dist. v. Schempp, supra,* but, as we have seen, shows a legislative purpose to maintain neutrality. The Court in *Walz v. Tax Commission, supra,* has pointed out the guidelines that mark the channel limits of constitutional neutrality:

The course of constitutional neutrality in this area cannot be an absolutely straight line; rigidity could well defeat the basic purpose of these provisions, which is to insure that no religion be sponsored or favored, none commanded, and none inhibited. The general principle deducible from the First Amendment and all that has been said by the Court is this: that we will not tolerate either governmentally established religion or governmental interference with religion. Short of those expressly proscribed governmental acts there is room for play in the joints productive of a benevolent neutrality which will permit religious exercise to exist without sponsorship and without interference.

Each value judgment under the Religion Clauses must therefore turn on whether particular acts in question are intended to establish or interfere with religious beliefs and practices or have the effect of doing so. Adherence to the policy of neutrality that derives from an accommodation of the Establishment and Free Exercise Clauses has prevented the kind of involvement that would tip the balance toward government control of churches or governmental restraint on religious practice.

397 U.S. at 669-70, 90 S.Ct. at 1411-12. The line that separates the permissible from the impermissible in this area is elusive. But the statute and guidelines do not create any of the dangers which the First Amendment is designed to prevent. Instead, they serve legitimate secular purposes without departing from the neutrality required by the First Amendment. We are therefore persuaded that the Establishment Clause does not prohibit the practices permitted by the statute and guidelines here.

V.

The plaintiffs have not demonstrated that the statute mandates a religious exercise in violation of the Free Exercise Clause of the First Amendment. The plaintiffs argue that the requirement of a moment of silence infringes "their right to give to their children a religious upbringing consistent with their beliefs, not modified by prayer or meditation required by the State"; that the "sterile" atmosphere of the classroom and the restriction of the period for meditation or prayer to one minute demean their concept of prayer; and that the exposure of the plaintiffs to this atmosphere violates their rights under the Free Exercise Clause. Before addressing this argument we point out what we think is clearly evident: that the free exercise rights of the parents are not at stake since they do not attend school and are not exposed to the minute of silence. *Compare Wisconsin v. Yoder,* 406 U.S. 205, 92 S.Ct. 1526, 32 L.Ed.2d 15 (1972). Although it is not entirely clear whether the plaintiffs' argument concerns the rights of the parents, students, or both, we will assume here that the argument refers to the rights of the students.

The Establishment Clause and the Free Exercise Clause must be read together in light of the underlying purpose they are designed to serve, but the Free Exercise Clause undoubtedly has an independent reach. *Gillette v. United States,* 401 U.S. 437, 461, 91 S.Ct. 828, 28 L.Ed.2d 168 (1971). In *Abington School Dist. v. Schempp, supra,* the distinction between the Free Exercise Clause and the Establishment Clause was stated as follows:

> The Free Exercise Clause . . . withdraws from legislative power, state and federal, the exertion of any restraint on the free exercise of religion. Its purpose is to secure religious liberty in the individual by prohibiting any invasions thereof by civil authority. Hence it is necessary in a free exercise case for one to show the coercive effect of the enactment as it operates against him in the practice of his religion. The distinction between the two clauses is apparent—a violation of the Free Exercise Clause is predicated on coercion while the Establishment Clause violation need not be so attended.

374 U.S. at 222-23, 83 S.Ct. at 1572. There is no showing in this case that any plaintiff was coerced into participating in practices which violate his religious beliefs concerning prayer. *Compare Wisconsin v. Yoder, supra.* Moreover, as we have seen, the statute and guidelines do not compel participation by any student in a religious activity which violates his liberty of conscience. *Compare State Board of Education v. Barnette,* 319 U.S. 624, 63 S.Ct. 1178, 87 L.Ed. 1628 (1943). Unlike the scheme in *Schempp,* the statute and guidelines here do not operate to confront any student with the cruel dilemma of either participating in a repugnant religious exercise or requesting to be excused therefrom. *See Abington School Dist. v. Schempp, supra,* 374 U.S. at 289-293, 83 S.Ct. 1560 (Brennan, J., concurring). If a student's beliefs preclude prayer in the setting of a minute of silence in a schoolroom, he may turn his mind silently toward a secular topic, or simply remain silent, without violating the statute or guidelines or facing the scorn or reproach of his classmates. No rights of plaintiffs under the Free Exercise Clause are violated where the statute and guidelines accommodate those students who desire to pray silently during the minute of silence and whose religious backgrounds permit prayer under those circumstances. *See Gillette v. United States, supra; Braunfield v. Brown,* 366 U.S. 599, 81 S.Ct. 1144, 6 L.Ed.2d 563 (1961). Thus, the neutrality of the statute and guidelines, which we have found to meet the requirements of the Establishment Clause, satisfies the requirements of the Free Exercise Clause.

VI.

Finally, the parent-plaintiffs contend that the statute and guidelines violate their rights under the Due Process Clause of the Fourteenth Amendment exclusively to direct the religious upbringing of their children. We recognize the force of this argument as a general proposition. *See Meyer v. Nebraska,* 262 U.S. 390, 43 S.Ct. 625, 67 L.Ed. 1042 (1923); *Pierce v. Society of Sisters,* 268 U.S. 510, 45 S.Ct. 571, 69 L.Ed. 1070 (1925).[10] As the Court stated in *Wisconsin v. Yoder, supra:*

> The history and culture of Western civilization reflect a strong tradition of parental concern for the nurture and upbringing of their children. This primary role of the parents in the upbringing of their children is now established beyond debate as an enduring American tradition.

406 U.S. at 232, 92 S.Ct. at 1541.

However, the arguments of the parents reflect exactly the free exercise argument advanced on behalf of the students. Compulsion by law of the acceptance of any creed or religious belief or the participation in any form of religious exercise is forbidden by the First Amendment. But the statute and guidelines do not compel the student-plaintiffs to affirm a religious belief repugnant to their parents; they do not compel student assent or even resignation to a religious practice repugnant to their parents. The parents remain free without interference from the statute and guidelines to guide and direct the religious education of their children. They also remain free to instruct their children that, while other students who desire may pray silently, they should not engage in prayer during the moment of silence but merely remain silent as directed by the teacher. Such parental guidance and instructions are not inhibited by the statute and guidelines. Because the statute and the guidelines compel no participation in any religious exercise by the students, the state infringes no parental liberty protected by the Due Process Clause.

We have closely scrutinized the statute and guidelines in our analysis of plaintiffs' claims because First Amendment liberties are at issue. In our view plaintiffs have failed to show the absence of a neutral, secular purpose for the opening moment of silence in the Framingham public schools. The statute and guidelines do not have a primary effect of favoring or sponsoring religion. They do not involve the state in religious exercises or directly in the realm of religion. They do not fall within the proscriptions of the First Amendment.

ORDER

This case came on to be heard before the three-judge court on the merits of the application for injunctive and declaratory relief, and was argued by counsel, and thereupon, upon consideration thereof, and in accordance with the opinion filed herewith, it is hereby

ORDERED: The complaint be and hereby is dismissed.

NOTES

1. There is presently pending the plaintiffs' motion to amend the complaint by adding a paragraph alleging that the parents of the student-plaintiffs are also plaintiffs. The motion is allowed.

2. The strictures of the First Amendment are made applicable to the states by the Fourteenth Amendment. *See Cantwell v. Connecticut*, 310 U.S. 296, 60 S.Ct. 900, 84 L.Ed. 1213 (1940); *Board of Education v. Barnette*, 319 U.S. 624, 63 S.Ct. 1178, 87 L.Ed. 1628 (1943).

3. The provision of the Fourteenth Amendment relied upon by plaintiffs is that "No State shall . . . deprive any person of . . . liberty, . . . without due process of law;

4. The complete guidelines read:
GUIDELINES FOR
IMPLEMENTATION OF
CHAPTER 71, SECTION 1A
OF THE
MASSACHUSETTS GENERAL LAWS
1) The following announcement shall be made each school day morning in each school at the commencement of the first class (it being understood that in the high schools the homeroom period would be considered the first regular period of the day) by the teacher in charge of the room. The announcement shall be made during the period of time when school attendance is taken.
"A one minute period of silence for the purpose of meditation or prayer shall now be observed. During this period silence shall be maintained and no activities engaged in."
At the end of the one minute period, the following shall be announced by the teacher.
"Thank you."
2) If teachers are asked questions concerning this period for meditation or prayer the following should be the response.
"We are doing this in compliance with State Law. Any other questions you have should be discussed with your

parents or with someone in your home."
3) Students not adhering to this regulation shall be reminded by the teacher of their responsibility to obey school rules and regulations. This should be done without detailed explanations or corrective action by the teacher.
4) If a student persists in violating this regulation, the teacher shall refer the student to the principal for corrective action.
5) The principal shall attempt to gain the cooperation of the student in obeying this regulation. If reasonable action on the part of the principal fails to achieve compliance with the regulation, the principal will continue to follow normal established procedures for dealing with breaches of school regulations. These will include a conference or conferences with parents or guardian of the student and, in those situations judged necessary by the principal, suspension of the student from school. The student and his parents or guardian shall be advised of their right to appeal the decision of the principal to the Superintendent of Schools or the School Committee.

5. The 1973 amendment added the words "or prayer" to the statute.

6. *See, e.g.*, the definition of "meditation" in Webster's Third New International Dictionary, p. 1403 (Unabridged 1966):
1: a spoken or written discourse treated in a contemplative manner and intended to express its author's reflection or esp. when religious to guide others in contemplation 2: a private devotion or spiritual exercise consisting in deep continued reflection on a religious theme . . . 3: the act of meditating: steady or close consecutive reflection: continued application of the mind . . . .
Plaintiffs have submitted the affidavits of Rabbi Herman J. Blumberg and Rev. Charles A. Gaines, a Unitarian minister, who state that the terms "prayer" and "meditation" are interchangeable in their faiths. This understanding, however, is not binding on either the state legislature or this court.

7. *See also Opinion of the Justices*, 113 N.H. 297, 307 A.2d 558 (1973); *Opinion of the Justices*, 108 N.H. 97, 228 A.2d 161 (1967); *Reed v. Van Hoven*, 237 F.Supp. 48, 55-56 (W.D.Mich. 1965); Opinion of the Massachusetts Attorney General, Apr. 4, 1966, p. 299; Opinion of the Massachusetts Attorney General, Aug. 20, 1963, p. 84; Choper, Religion in Public Schools: A Proposed Constitutional Standard, 47 Minn.L.Rev. 329, 370-71 (1963); P. Freund, *Religion and the Public Schools, The Legal Issue* (1965).

8. *See, e.g.*, the definition of "prayer" in Webster's Third New International Dictionary, p. 1782 (Unabridged 1966):
. . . 1a: a solemn and humble approach to Divinity in word or thought usu. involving beseeching, petition, confession, praise, or thanksgiving . . . b: an earnest request to someone for something . . . c: prayers *pl*: earnest good wishes . . . 2: the act or practice of praying: the addressing of words or thought to Divinity in petition, confession, praise, or thanksgiving . . . 3: a religious service consisting chiefly of prayers . . . 4: a set form of words used in praying: a formula of supplication, confession, praise, or thanksgiving addressed to God or an object of worship . . . 5: something prayed for: a subject of prayer . . . 6: a slight or

minimal chance (as to succeed or survive). . . .

9.   The plaintiffs appeared to concede this at the oral argument. A member of the panel asked counsel for the plaintiffs whether the statute would be violated in the following circumstances: after the announcement and the minute of silence, a student tells his teacher that he did not meditate or pray during the period. Counsel stated he thought such circumstances would not violate the statute.

10.   The dicta in *Pierce* concerning the rights of the parents to direct the upbringing and education of their children, 268 U.S. at 534-35, 45 S.Ct. 571, apparently have been transformed by time into the holding. *See Wisconsin v. Yoder*, 406 U.S. 205, 233, 92 S.Ct. 1526, 1542, 32 L.Ed.2d 15 (1972): "However read, the Court's holding in *Pierce* stands as a charter of the rights of parents to direct the religious upbringing of their children".

A United States District Court in New Jersey decides that the teaching of the "science of creative intelligence/transcendental meditation" course in the New Jersey public high schools violates the Establishment Clause of the First Amendment. In so deciding, the Court states: "Under the Establishment Clause, a three-part test has evolved to determine whether governmental action in regard to religious activity constitutes a violation of the constitutional prohibition. In order to avoid contravening the Establishment Clause, the law or governmental action in question 'first, must reflect a clearly secular legislative purpose, second, must have a primary effect that neither advances nor inhibits religion, and third, must avoid excessive government entanglement with religion.'" As to the first prong of this test, the Court stated that "the characteristics which are attributed to pure creative intelligence are parallel to characteristics which are attributed to the supreme being or ultimate reality by mankind. In effecting the secular purpose of reducing stress among public school students, however, the governmental entities have not merely introduced the teaching of a simple technique of meditation whereby the meditator contemplates a meaningless sound. . . . owing to the religious nature of the concept of the field of pure creative intelligence and creative intelligence, it is apparent that the governmental agencies have sought to effect a secular goal by the propagation of a religious concept, a belief in an unmanifest field of life which is perfect, pure, and infinite."

"Applying the second prong of the *Nyquist* test," concluded the Court, "the promulgation of a belief in the existence of a pure, perfect, infinite, and unmanifest field of life clearly has a primary effect of advancing religion and religious concepts. . . . Under the final prong of the test, the aid given to the SCI/TM course by both the federal government and the state of New Jersey clearly constitutes an 'excessive government entanglement in religion. . . .' The SCI/TM course fails to pass muster under the three-pronged test enunciated in *Nyquist* and thus violates the Establishment Clause of the First Amendment."

Malnak v. *Yogi*, 440 F.Supp. 1284 (1977)

MEANOR, District Judge.

Plaintiffs move for partial summary judgment to enjoin the teaching of the "Science of Creative Intelligence" in the public schools of New Jersey on the ground that such teaching violates the Establishment Clause of the First Amendment. The material facts are not contested, although the parties vigorously dispute the significance of those facts.

The suit involves 12 named plaintiffs and 20 named defendants. Plaintiffs include eight in-dividuals who pay federal income taxes and are liable to pay state sales taxes and, in some cases, local property taxes. Four of the taxpayers are the parents of two children who attend one of the high schools at which the course was offered; they sue in their own behalfs and as guardians ad litem for their children. The eight taxpayers comprise an unincorporated association known as the Coalition for Religious Integrity, which also is a named plaintiff in this action. The remaining plaintiffs are a clergyman who lives in New

Jersey, Americans United for Separation of Church and State, a nonprofit Maryland corporation, and Spiritual Counterfeit Project, Inc., a nonprofit California corporation.

The first group of defendants are organizations and individuals who are engaged in the dissemination of the Science of Creative Intelligence and in the propagation of the technique of Transcendental Meditation. The organizational defendants are three California corporations and a division of one of the corporations. These defendants seek to disseminate SCI/TM throughout the United States, primarily through the World Plan Executive Council—United States (WPEC-US) and its divisions. At the national level, the organizational structure of a World Plan Executive Council with several divisions apparently occurs in a number of countries throughout the world. *See* Jarvis Deposition at 786. International organizations devoted to the propagation of SCI/TM exist. The structure of the "international level" is changing and the relationship between the international and national organizations is nebulous.

The organizations, primarily under the auspices of the WPECs throughout the world, are implementing a "World Plan" which "is in progress to train one teacher of the Science of Creative Intelligence for every one thousand people in all parts of the globe." Fundamentals of Progress, Exhibit A attached to Jarvis Affidavit, at 2. The "World Plan" has seven stated goals:

(1) To develop the full potential of the individual;

(2) To improve governmental achievements;

(3) To realize the highest ideal of education;

(4) To eliminate the age-old problem of crime and all behavior that brings unhappiness to the family of man;

(5) To maximize the intelligent use of the environment;

(6) To bring fulfillment to the economic aspirations of individuals and society;

(7) To achieve the spiritual goals of mankind in this generation.

Id. The named organizational defendants presumably are entrusted with implementing the "World Plan" within the United States. The individual defendants are officers of these corporations, a person who taught the SCI/TM course in New Jersey high schools, and Maharishi Mahesh Yogi, the principal deviser of the Science of Creative Intelligence and primary exponent of Transcendental Meditation.[1]

The five boards of education which arranged for the teaching of the SCI/TM course at high schools within their jurisdictions also are named as defendants. The New Jersey Department of Education and the New Jersey Board of Education, as well as the Com-

missioner of Education, an individual employee of the Department of Education, and the State of New Jersey itself are sued. In addition, the United States Department of Health, Education and Welfare and the United States are named as defendants.

Plaintiffs base their motion for partial summary judgment on the textbook used in the New Jersey high schools, a ceremony at which attendance by the student is mandatory, the deposition testimony of the president of the WPEC-US, the deposition testimony of two people who taught the SCI/TM course in four of the five high schools at which the course was offered, and a one-page affidavit of a clergyman.

In opposing the motion for partial summary judgment, defendants rely on the same deposition testimony relied upon by plaintiffs and the deposition testimony of three clergymen-practitioners of the TM technique and the deposition testimony of an employee of the United States Office of Education. In addition, defendants rely on affidavits of the president of the WPEC-US, of two teachers of the SCI/TM course in New Jersey high schools, of a linguist, of two professors of religion, and of eleven New Jersey high school students who were enrolled in the SCI/TM course.

Transcendental Meditation, briefly stated, is a technique of meditation in which the meditator contemplates a meaningless sound. Defendants have placed in the record the result of tests which purport to show that a meditator undergoes certain physiological changes during meditation. Other tests purport to show that practitioners of the technique will develop permanent changes in their physiologies, *e.g.*, lowered heart rate and lowered breathing rate.

The "Science of Creative Intelligence" is a theory, devised or promulgated primarily by defendant Yogi, which purports to explain what occurs within a meditator's mind during meditation and to describe an entity or concept which defendants call "creative intelligence." The "Science of Creative Intelligence" posits that during transcendental meditation a meditator reverses the process through which thought develops until the meditator's mind reaches the entity, or "field of life," called "the field of pure creative intelligence," which is at the source of thought, according to the World Plan defendants. The textbook used in the New Jersey high schools states the above, but devotes most of its pages to a description of the nature and qualities of the entity called "creative intelligence."[2]

As stated above, the SCI/TM course was offered as an elective course at five high schools in New Jersey during the 1975-76 academic year. The students at all five high schools used the same textbook and received their mantras,[3] or sound aids, at identical ceremonies. The SCI/TM course was taught four or five days a week by teachers trained by the World Plan defendants. The teachers were paid by the WPEC-US and were not employed by any of the five defendant school boards nor certified by the State Board of Examiners.[4] Aaron Deposition at 621. The SCI/TM course was the only course taught by the SCI/TM teachers.

The undisputed material facts upon which plaintiffs rely and from which plaintiffs assert that the only conclusion possible is that teaching of the SCI/TM course violates the establishment of religion clauses of both the United States and New Jersey constitutions are the textbook and the puja[5] used in the course.

THE TEXTBOOK

The "Science of Creative Intelligence" as a course of study had its genesis in 1972 when "Maharishi, in conjunction with experts in education and science, developed a structure of teaching which was labeled the Science of Creative Intelligence." Jarvis Deposition at 913. As stated above, the "Science of Creative Intelligence" posits that during the practice of Transcendental Meditation the meditator's mind moves from a conscious thought to the source of thought, where the mind comes in contact with the unmanifest and unbounded field of pure creative intelligence, T at 29,[6] which is present, among other places, within every human being. T at 26. Defendants state that attainment of contact with the field of pure creative intelligence places the meditator in a "fourth state of consciousness" known as "restful alertness" or "transcendental consciousness." T at 30. The textbook states that during TM the meditator experiences the field of pure creative intelligence directly. T at 29. Contact with the field of pure creative intelligence infuses the meditator's mind both with creativity, T at 26, and with "all the qualities of creative intelligence," T at 38, clarifies and strengthens the meditator's thoughts, T at 32, expands the meditator's perceptions, T at 30, and "refines" the meditator's nervous system, Jarvis Deposition at 866a. Regular practice of TM will "refine" the meditator's nervous system further so that the expanded perceptions experienced during TM will carry over into the meditator's conscious thoughts and activities. T at 38,86. Regular practice of TM may lead the meditator to the situation in which the meditator's mind is infused with the "expanded awareness" and perceptions that he experiences while meditating during waking, sleeping, and dreaming; this state is called "cosmic consciousness," or "the fifth state of consciousness." T at 86. *See* Jarvis Deposition at 866b.[7]

The textbook states that "[t]he field of pure creative intelligence is the home of all qualities that constitute the universe," T at 292; "all the qualities of which we can conceive are present in the unmanifest field of pure creative intelligence." T at 40. The field of pure creative intelligence also is the source of thought. T at 26, and "a field of unlimited energy, intelligence and happiness." T at 56. The field of pure creative intelligence also is "unbounded." T at 24, and "an inexhaustible reservoir of energy and intelligence, the fountainhead of all currents of creative intelligence." T at 26. The textbook defines "creative intelligence" as "that impelling force which continually gives rise to new expressions of life and order, progressive and evolutionary in nature." T at 20. Thus creative intelligence is a force which springs from the field of pure creative intelligence, *e.g.,* T at 26, which is the source of everything in the universe, *e.g.,* T at 26, 40, 260.

Creative intelligence, like the unbounded field of pure creative intelligence, possesses all the qualities that can be conceived of: "Every quality that is ever expressed in creation is the expression of creative intelligence." T at 40. The textbook specifically lists and discusses fifty "qualities of creative intelligence." "The qualities of creative intelligence can be seen as currents of consciousness arising from the field of pure consciousness, the field of pure creative intelligence." T at 40. The unbounded field of pure creative intelligence is unmanifest and silent. *E. g.,* T at 29, 40. Creative intelligence ranges from the unmanifest field of pure creative intelligence to its manifestations in the universe. T at 22. Manifestations of creative intelligence include everything. "From the individual to the universe, all that we see is the display of creative intelligence." T at 240. The textbook devotes 225 pages to the discussion of fifty specific "qualities of creative intelligence." The textbook states that "[w]hen the conscious mind reaches the field of pure creative intelligence, it becomes saturated with all qualities of creative intelligence. . . ." T at 38. The fifty qualities of creative intelligence which are discussed in the textbook are progress, evolution, purposefulness, intelligence, order, beauty, precision, truth, dynamism, rest, stability, adaptability, gentleness, strength, efficiency, kindness, independence, helpfulness, vigilance, resourcefulness, spontaneity, analysis, synthesis, decisiveness, sweetness, universality, harmony, diversity, joy or happiness, life or liveliness, insight, foresight, thoughtfulness, specificity, expansiveness, courage, generosity, economy, love, justice, cleanliness, purity, freedom, responsibility, creativity, eternity, practicality, success, holism, and fulfillment. The textbook states that during meditation, the meditator's mind

becomes saturated with all qualities of creative intelligence, and then, in whatever area of living these qualities are needed, they express themselves more. That is why when a man meditates, he becomes more efficient in every field of thinking and decision-making, more capable in any undertaking he may choose. Wherever he puts his attention, he begins to display more expressed values of creative intelligence.

* * *

One point that should be emphasized is that the qualities of creative intelligence develop very naturally and spontaneously through regular contact with the field of pure creative intelligence.

We should never try to exhibit qualities of creative intelligence, because their expression must be spontaneous. Every breath of life is spontaneously under the control of creative intelligence, and therefore any trying from our side can only result in stress and strain. Life must be lived very spontaneously, very naturally. We experience in our meditation how very naturally the mind arrives at the goal of all progress, unbounded awareness. We know from our experience how the slightest effort on our part not only stops progress but produces stress. Therefore, we should never try to imitate any quality of creative intelligence. We simply meditate and allow all the qualities of creative intelligence to be displayed spontaneously in our thinking and action.

T at 38. The textbook thus states that a person attains the qualities of creative intelligence, e. g., truthfulness, efficiency, freedom, through regular contact with the field of pure creative intelligence during the practice of Transcendental Meditation. The process is automatic: "We simply meditate and allow all the qualities of creative intelligence to be displayed spontaneously in our thinking and action." Statements of the automatic nature of the process of infusing an individual with all the qualities of creative intelligence through Transcendental Meditation appear throughout the textbook. E. g., T at 49, 260.

The textbook states that Transcendental Meditation is not only the automatic means of attaining all the qualities of creative intelligence, but also is the exclusive manner of obtaining all the qualities of creative intelligence. See T at 94, 132, 217, 262. In this connection, the above-quoted passage states that "[w]e should never try to exhibit qualities of creative intelligence, because their expression must be spontaneous." Since these qualities must be expressed spontaneously and since spontaneous expression of these qualities is developed only through the practice of Transcendental Meditation, it follows that "we should never try to imitate any quality of creative intelligence." The textbook thus appears to indicate that a person should never consciously strive to be kind, truthful, brave, independent, successful, etc. Rather, "[w]e simply meditate and allow all the qualities of creative intelligence to be displayed spontaneously in our thinking and action."[8] T at 38.

The textbook states that the field of pure creative intelligence is the source of everything. For example, the textbook states that the field of pure creative intelligence "is the very source of life-energy, the reservoir of wisdom, the origin of all power in nature, and the fountainhead of all success in the world." T at 98. The textbook states that the field of pure creative intelligence "is the home of all qualities that we can conceive of in the fields of knowledge and action, existence and evolution." T at 260. "The field of pure creative intelligence is the home of all qualities that constitute the universe." T at 292. "[E]verything in creation is nothing other than the expression of unmanifest creative intelligence." T at 260. "[E]very quality that is ever expressed in creation is the expression of creative intelligence." T at 40. "[A]ll aspects of life [are] all manifestations of unmanifest creative intelligence." T at 262. "The entire field of life, from the individual to the cosmos, is nothing but the expression of neverchanging pure creative intelligence in the relative ever-changing expressions of life." T at 92. The field of pure creative intelligence "is at the basis of the 'comprehensive, orderly integrity of the universe.'" T at 174, quoting from a speech given by Maharishi Mahesh Yogi in 1971. The textbook is replete with statements that pure creative intelligence is "the basis of life" or "at the basis of life." E. g., T at 78, 107, 129, 188, 242, 245, 260, 264, 271. For example, the textbook states that the field of pure creative intelligence is "the universal basis of life." T at 188, 129. The textbook also indicates that pure creative intelligence is "the source, course and goal of all existence." T at 171. The citations to the textbook listed above by no means form an exhaustive list of statements attributing the source of everything to the field of pure creative intelligence. Among other qualities specifically mentioned as having their source in the field of pure creative intelligence are thought, e. g., T at 26, 30, 62, 162, 242, activity, T at 32, 102, 192, feelings, T at 102, and "all cultural traditions and values," T at 245. This list also is not exhaustive of the specific qualities which the textbook states have their source in the field of pure creative intelligence.

Defendant Jarvis, president of World Plan Executive Council—United States, agreed in deposition testimony that pure creative intelligence is the source of all creation,[9] but stated that "[i]t is the source in that it is the ultimate constituent." Jarvis Deposition at 1050. Defendant Jarvis thus attributed a passive role to the entity of "level of life," Jarvis Deposition at 1019, called pure creative intelligence.[10] As stated in the textbook and reiterated by defendant Jarvis, the field of pure creative intelligence is the source of creative intelligence, which possesses all the qualities of pure creative intelligence. E. g., T at 40; Jarvis Deposition at 1036. Creative intelligence is the "impelling life force," T at 86, which expresses all the qualities in the universe, which are contained in the field of pure creative intelligence. Creative intelligence ranges from its source in the unmanifest field of creative intelligence to activity in all manifest aspects of life. *See* T at 20. Creative intelligence is coextensive with the field of pure creative intelligence in the sense that both the field of pure creative intelligence and creative intelligence contain "all the qualities of which we can conceive." T at 260. Creative intelligence manifests itself in all aspects of the universe while the field of pure creative intelligence remains always unmanifest, at the core of everything in the universe. T at 292. Creative intelligence thus can be seen as an active extension or projection of the field of pure creative intelligence.

While the field of pure creative intelligence is described as silent, nonchanging, and immovable, the textbook describes creative intelligence as perpetually active in all aspects of the universe. In scores of places, the textbook ascribes activity to creative intelligence, and to qualities of creative intelligence. Identifying creative intelligence as "this impelling life force," T at 86, the textbook later states that creative intelligence "guides and sustains every aspect of the universe." T at 174. The textbook asserts that "the activity of nature is conducted by creative intelligence." T at 114. "Every breath of life is spontaneously under the control of creative intelligence. . . . " T at 38. "Creative intelligence is always giving an evolutionary direction to our thoughts, feelings, and actions." T at 52. "Creative intelligence is always gracefully arranging the parts of our life to form a pleasing whole." T at 62. "We discover that the creative intelligence that structures the blueprint of life in our genes also regulates the movements of the far-distant galaxies and inspires a musician to give expression to the fullness of life." T at 171. The textbook refers to the "activating power of creative intelligence," T at 60, 65, to the "inherent activity" of creative intelligence, T at 82, and to the "endless creative activity of creative intelligence," T at 240, and states that creative intelligence "perpetually creates." T at 242. "Creative intelligence is always acting, ever vigilant to unfold its unbounded resources in every particle of existence." T at 126, *see, e. g.,* T at 110, 128.

"Creative intelligence has structured the body in a manner that allows unbounded awareness to display its full value and enjoy the play of life." T at 224. "It is the love of a mother for her children that inspires her to greatness. Creative intelligence instills unbounded love in her, and this spontaneously generates the limitless creativity and energy needed for all her activities." T at 270. "Creative intelligence is comforting. It provides a family to soothe and nourish us." T at 274. "Creative intelligence is life-supporting. It creates a society that strengthens and upholds the fullness of life in each of its members." T at 282.[11]

In addition to the ascription of activity to creative intelligence, anthropomorphism pervades the textbook's description of creative intelligence. Twenty-five of the textbook's thirty-two lessons begin with the assertion that creative intelligence possesses certain qualities. For example, "[c]reative intelligence is thoughtful and spontaneous," T at 160, "[c]reative intelligence is loving and just," T at 214, "[c]reative intelligence is decisive and sweet," T at 178, "[c]reative intelligence is precise and truthful," T at 72, "[c]reative intelligence is independent and helpful," T at 250. While all the qualities attributed to creative intelligence by the textbook are not exclusively human characteristics, some of them are. For example, neither an animal nor a plant nor an inorganic element nor a law of nature could be said to be thoughtful, just, and truthful. The textbook also anthropomorphizes creative intelligence in many other statements. For example, the textbook states that "[e]ven when we are asleep, creative intelligence is awake, working to refresh us." T at 128.

Among the other characteristics of creative intelligence is omnipotence. In addition to stating repeatedly that "everything in creation is nothing other than the expression of unmanifest creative intelligence," T at 260; *see, e. g.,* T at 92, the textbook states that the field of pure creative intelligence is "the origin of all power in nature." T at 98, and that "the activity of nature is conducted by creative intelligence." T at 114. The textbook speaks of "the unlimited power of creative intelligence." T at 108. On the same page, the textbook states that creative intelligence "accomplishes all great things with no effort." *Id.* A few pages later, the textbook states that "creative intelligence is able to accomplish everything effortlessly by remaining behind the scenes of relative life." T at 118. The textbook states that creative intelligence is self-sufficient and self-illuminating. T at 122, 118. Although self-sufficiency and self-illumination are not necessarily aspects of omnipotence, the context of ultimateness and universality in which the textbook speaks of creative intelligence—"universal existence," T at 292—eliminates all possible conclusions except that the self-sufficiency and self-illumination of creative intelligence is absolute and all-encompassing.

The textbook refers to the field of pure creative intelligence as "the universal basis of all knowledge," T at 189, "the home of all knowledge," T at 149, 189, and "the stable basis of all knowledge." T at 97. The textbook asserts that creative intelligence "uphold[s] all the different fields of knowledge and every expression of life." T at 172. The textbook states that

the activity of nature is conducted by creative intelligence, by that comprehensive, unbounded intelligence, by that enormous computer which takes into account all possible avenues in designing a single channel of action. Because every activity of nature is taken into account and is guided by creative intelligence, nature takes the shortest course." T at 114. It is true, as pointed out by defendants' counsel at oral argument, that a mundane computer is not omniscient because it contains only that data which has been fed into it. A self-activating computer which is "the home of all knowledge," however, is omniscient by definition. The textbook also asserts that the field of pure creative intelligence is *the* reservoir of wisdom." T at 98 (emphasis supplied).

Creative intelligence is omnipresent, according to the textbook. Attestations of the omnipresence of creative intelligence appear scores of times throughout the textbook. For example, in "Lesson 1" the textbook states that "creative intelligence is present everywhere, within us as well as outside us." T at 23. In the central section of the textbook appears the following passage:

Creative intelligence is universal and specific.

* * *

It is present in all forms, words, smells, tastes, and objects of touch. In all objects of experience, in all senses of perception and organs of action, in every phenomenon, in the doer and the work done, in all directions—north, south, east, and west—in all times—past, present, and future—it is uniformly present. In front of man, behind him, to the left and right of him, in him—everywhere, and under all circumstances, creative intelligence is permeating everything."

T at 186. Four pages from the end of the textbook, the book states that "creative intelligence is present everywhere, deep within everything as well as on the surface." T at 292.

Creative intelligence is eternal, according to the textbook. The textbook states that the field of creative intelligence "has existed for all times. It is, always has been, and always will be the nonchanging basis of life, the fountainhead of all currents of creativity." T at 242. The textbook asserts that creative intelligence has existed "in all times—past, present, and future. . . ." T at 186. The textbook asserts:

From the individual to the universe, all that we see is the display of creative intelligence. It is an all-time reality; it goes on and on. And because it is creative, it keeps on creating. In its perpetual play the creation goes on, on the steps of progress. There is no end to it.

T at 240.

The textbook states repeatedly that creative intelligence is both unmanifest or unseen, *e. g.,* T at 30, 41, 107, 132, 252, 295, and unbounded or illimitable or infinite, *e. g.,* T at 24, 44, 74, 100, 126, 157, 180, 208, 244.

The textbook frequently uses synonyms for creative intelligence and for the field of pure creative intelligence. For example, the textbook refers to the field of pure creative intelligence as "pure intelligence." T at 257. In one passage the textbook refers to the field of pure creative intelligence first as "pure intelligence" and in the following line of type as "intelligence." T at 82. Numerous additional references to the field of pure creative intelligence as simply "intelligence" appear throughout the textbook. *E. g.,* T at 56, 60, 62, 89, 114, 157, 172. The textbook also refers to the field of pure creative intelligence as "the unbounded reservoir of intelligence." T at 102.

The field of pure creative intelligence alternatively is called "the field of unlimited happiness," T at 32, 56, and "the unbounded ocean of bliss," T at 152; *see* T at 80, and "that field of unbounded bliss-consciousness," T at 122. The field of pure creative intelligence is "a field of unbounded happiness." T at 162. The textbook gives creative intelligence the synonym "bliss-consciousness." *E. g.,* T at 55, 144. During the practice of Transcendental Meditation, bliss-consciousness, or creative intelligence, is said to "infuse" and "saturate" the meditator's mind. T at 38, 55, 56, 145, 180, 221; *see, e. g.,* T at 95.

The textbook synonymously refers to the field of pure creative intelligence as "universal existence," T at 292, and "perfection of existence," T at 118. The textbook labels the unmanifest field of pure creative intelligence as "the most fundamental field of life." The textbook describes the field of pure creative intelligence as "the unmanifest center of life," T at 36, "the unmanifest field of life," T at 41, "the nonchanging basis of life," *e. g.,* T at 74, 98, "the universal basis of life," T at 188-89, 129, "the wholeness of life," *e. g.,* T at 178, 262, "the holistic field of life," T at 262, "the holistic basis of life," T at 264. The field of pure creative intelligence repeatedly is called the "basis of life," *e. g.,* T at 245, 107, and the textbook uses "the source of life" as a synonym for the field of pure creative intelligence. *See* T at 78. *See also* Jarvis Deposition at 1035.

Another aspect of the field of pure creative intelligence is that it is "full." The textbook uses the word "fullness" as a synonym for the field of pure creative intelligence. For example, the textbook states that "[t]he fullness from which creativity begins is the unmanifest aspect of intelligence. From that fullness the waves of creative intelligence arise and dance into manifestation." T at 22. In other sections of the book, the textbook states that creativity begins in the field of pure creative intelligence and that the waves or currents of creative intelligence also arise from the field of pure creative intelligence. *E. g.,* T at 121, 242. The textbook, especially in the first lesson, states repeatedly that *"fullness is the source, course, and goal of exis-*

tence and progress." E. g., T at 22 (emphasis in original). The textbook later equates "the unbounded wholeness of pure creative intelligence" with "the source, course, and goal of all existence." T at 171. The textbook equates "the goal of all growth and progress" with "the unbounded field of pure creative intelligence." T at 44. The subtitle for Lesson 27 is "Applying Fullness for Success in Life." T at 250. The text of Lesson 27 speaks of applying the field of pure creative intelligence for success in life, thus substituting that phrase for the word "fullness":

When the unmanifest field of pure creative intelligence is incorporated in our awareness through regular practice of Transcendental Meditation, it can be practically applied in all phases of relative life; so we spontaneously succeed in every undertaking.

T at 252. Another instance of synonymous use of "fullness"and "the field of pure creative intelligence" occurs when the textbook refers to both terms as the "nature of life." In Lesson 7, the textbook states that during the practice of Transcendental Meditation "we experience the true nonchanging nature of life." T at 74. In Lesson 27, the textbook states that "the nature of life is fullness, bliss-consciousness. . . ." T at 252.

The textbook states that the field of pure creative intelligence is perfect: "The field of pure creative intelligence is self-sufficient. It is fullness of life, perfection of existence, and therefore unattached to anything in the relative field, free from the influence of action." T at 118. "[N]o sorrow can enter bliss-consciousness, nor can bliss-consciousness know any gain greater than itself." T at 144. The field of pure creative intelligence of course is pure and possesses all qualities in their pure form.

The textbook speaks of certain goals of man and nature. For example, the textbook teaches that "the goal of life [is] perceiving the fullness of life in the waves of practical living." T at 250. The "living of the fullness of life" is the "ultimate success" of an individual. T at 257. The field of pure creative intelligence is the "goal of all existence," as well as its source. T at 171. The textbook instructs that the "true status" of each individual's mind "is unbounded bliss-consciousness." T at 55. If bliss-consciousness "could become permanently established in the mind, the mind would have accomplished its ultimate purpose. . . ." *Id.* Establishing bliss-consciousness in the mind of course occurs only through the practice of Transcendental Meditation. "The purpose of man's life is to gain a state of unlimited energy, intelligence, power, creativity, and bliss." T at 52. If this is the purpose of man's life, how can this purpose be fulfilled? The textbook answers four pages later by stating that this purpose can be fulfilled by contacting the field of pure creative intelligence, T at 56, which is "the inex-haustible fountainhead of energy, creativity, intelligence, and happiness," T at 121, and "the origin of all power in nature." T at 98. It is "the goal of all progress," T at 44, and "[t]he goal of all activity." T at 52.

The textbook frequently states that contact with the field of pure creative intelligence is the exclusive means of obtaining fulfillment. For example, "[t]he experience of the holistic field of pure creative intelligence is an experience of wholeness, fullness, which alone can bring fulfillment to every phase of life." T at 260. Continuing in the same vein, the textbook states:

Our life has so many aspects. All the diverse aspects cannot possibly be attended to individually; fullness of life cannot be gained by amending the parts. What we can do is take care of the holistic value of creation, which lies in the unmanifest field of pure creative intelligence, by opening our awareness to it through Transcendental Meditation.

T at 262.

A fundamental teaching of the textbook is the existence of an unmanifest or uncreated level of life: "LIFE RANGES FROM GROSS TO SUBTLE TO UNMANIFEST." T at 152; *see, e. g.,* T at 41. The textbook explains:

We know from physics that physical existence is composed of many different layers. Beyond the gross surface level of the object are increasingly subtle layers of existence, one within the other—molecular, atomic, subatomic. Beyond the subtlest level, of the object is the unmanifest, unbounded value of the object.

T at 152. The unmanifest level of life is the field of pure creative intelligence: "The ultimate reality of every object is unmanifest creative intelligence." T at 154.

In summary, the textbook teaches that there exists an unmanifest or uncreated field of life which is illimitable or unbounded or infinite. This field of life is present everywhere, both within and without everything and every abstraction in the universe. This field of life is active, has "unlimited power," and encompasses all knowledge. This field of life is pure and perfect. Synonyms for this field of life are "perfection of existence," bliss, and intelligence. This field of life is the field of pure love, *see* T at 218, pure truth, *see* T at 76, and pure justice, *see* T at 220. This field of being has always existed.

Defendants seek to refute the statements in the textbook with conclusional assertions in affidavits and in their briefs the substance of which can be encapsulated thus: no matter what statements appear in the textbook, those statements are "not intended or understood as an [*sic*] religion, religious study or study of God." Jarvis Affidavit ¶ 27. Although defendants' counsel stated at oral argument that he would not call the Science of Creative Intelligence either a philosophy or a science or a religion, defendants' affidavits and brief argue and state that the Science of Creative Intelligence is a "philosophical study," Jarvis Affidavit ¶ 25, or "essays in philosophy," Harned Affidavit ¶ 27; see Db at 24. Based on this assertion, defendants seek to dismiss Creative Intelligence as merely "a philosophical idea," Harned Affidavit ¶ 28, or a "philosophic concept," Jarvis Affidavit ¶ 46[12] and Db at 29. The textbook directly and explicitly contradicts these statements: "Creative intelligence is not just an abstract concept or idea; it is a concrete reality that can be practically applied to bring success and fulfillment to every phase of living." T at 250.

In their papers in opposition to plaintiffs' motion for summary judgment, defendants also select certain descriptions of creative intelligence from the textbook and attempt to refute their obvious meanings. Some of these attempted refutations are supported by imprecise and unpersuasive analogies; others stand as bald assertions of belief by the affiants.

For example, the textbook states that creative intelligence "guides and sustains every aspect of the universe." T at 174. Defendants state:

> Creative intelligence is not understood or taught as sustainer of the universe in a religious sense. It "guides and sustains" in a scientific-philosophic sense, much in the same manner that gravity guides and sustains the path of the planets.

Jarvis Affidavit ¶ 36. The weakness of the analogy requires little comment. Unlike creative intelligence, gravity is not, *inter alia,* the source of life-energy, the home of all knowledge and wisdom, and the origin of all power in nature. *See* T at 98, 149. Unlike creative intelligence, gravity is not kind, or adaptable or practical; nor is gravity an ocean of love. T at 214, 216. Furthermore, gravity does not control everything in the manner in which the textbook states that creative intelligence does. For example, "the activity of nature is conducted by creative intelligence. . . ." T at 114. "Every breath of life is spontaneously under the control of creative intelligence. . . ." T at 38.

The textbook states that

> The activity of nature is conducted by creative intelligence, by that comprehensive, unbounded intelligence, by that enormous computer which takes into account all possible avenues in designing a single channel of action.

T at 114. Plaintiffs contend that this statement and a number of others in the textbook indicate that creative intelligence is "the determining force of the universe." Defendants reply:

> Nor is creative intelligence the determining force in the universe. It may be said to conduct "the activity of nature" in the same way that the DNA molecule conducts growth in the individual and may be likened to an "enormous computer."

Jarvis Affidavit ¶ 37. Some of the problems with this weak analogy are similar to those encountered in the previous analogy. There is no reason to believe that DNA molecules are kind or that DNA molecules are an ocean of love or that DNA molecules are "the ultimate reality" of every object, movement, and activity. *See* T at 154, 192. Moreover, DNA molecules are tangible; they are not the product of someone's imagination or belief, *i. e.,* they are not "philosophic concepts" or "philosophical ideas." In addition, if DNA molecules can be said to contain the code or blueprint for the development of individual organisms, the textbook teaches that creative intelligence places that blueprint there: "the creative intelligence that structures the blueprint of life in our genes also regulates the movements of the far-distant galaxies. . . ." T at 171. Not only does creative intelligence structure "the blueprint of life in our genes," but also "[c]reative intelligence has structured the [human body]. . . ." T at 224.

Defendants state that "bliss-consciousness" is not intended or understood as a religious concept; rather it is merely a term to characterize experiences accompanying a specific level of personal growth." Jarvis Affidavit ¶ 38. The textbook's use of the term "bliss-consciousness" directly contradicts this definition of "bliss-consciousness." At a number of points, the textbook uses "bliss-consciousness" as synonymous with creative intelligence. For example, "[a]s creative intelligence, bliss-consciousness, becomes more infused in the conscious mind, every object becomes more charming, because we are able to perceive more of its full value." T at 55. Again, the textbook states that "[w]e know that the true nature of the self is unbounded pure creative intelligence, bliss-consciousness—that most self-sufficient field of life." T at 121. Still another example is the following quotation:

> In cosmic consciousness a person's whole life is permeated by the light of pure creative intelligence. . . . He is established on that level of existence which is deep within everything—that field of unbounded bliss-consciousness which is self-sufficient and self-illuminating.

T at 122. Of course, "that level of existence which is deep within everything" is referred to elsewhere in the textbook as the field of pure creative intelligence. *See, e. g.,* T at 292.[13]

Defendants state:

> The mere fact that qualities such as beauty, creativity, intelligence and orderliness, are associated with creative intelligence does not make creative intelligence the source of aesthetic values. A Rembrandt painting can be described using similar values, yet it is not the source of aesthetic values in a religious sense.

Jarvis Affidavit ¶ 39. To say that these qualities are

merely "associated with creative intelligence" states a far more modest position than that taken by the textbook. According to the textbook, the field of pure creative intelligence is the "home" of all of these qualities as well as "the home of all qualities that constitute the universe." *E. g.*, T at 292. The field of pure creative intelligence and creative intelligence possess these qualities in their pure and perfect forms. For example, the textbook states that the field of pure creative intelligence is "the field of perfect orderliness." T at 63. The textbook also states the field of pure creative intelligence is "the source of all creativity." T at 242.

The implicit analogy to a Rembrandt painting is not well drawn. Surely no one would suggest that a Rembrandt painting is "the source of all creativity," as the field of pure creative intelligence is said to be. Creativity, beauty, intelligence, and orderliness existed long before Rembrandt put brush to canvas. Neither has any Rembrandt painting "existed for all times," as creative intelligence has; nor has any Rembrandt painting all the other qualities attributed by the textbook to creative intelligence. Finally and most obviously, a Rembrandt painting is a specific and tangible object, not an abstraction produced by belief or imagination.

Defendants admit that creative intelligence is eternal and state that "[p]urely secular ideas and principles, such as freedom and the concepts of truth and justice, are eternal and 'go on and on,' devoid of religious connotations." Jarvis Affidavit ¶ 42. As with defendants' other analogies, one of the weaknesses with this one is that freedom, truth, and justice do not have the other characteristics attributed to creative intelligence by the textbook. For example, neither freedom nor truth nor justice is a "concrete reality," T at 250, which "can be contacted," T at 13, and which "accomplishes all great things with no effort." T at 108. The textbook applies all three of the quotations to creative intelligence. Furthermore, the textbook states that freedom, truth, and justice are merely three of the multitude of qualities contained within the field of pure creative intelligence. *E. g.*, "justice is a quality of creative intelligence." T at 220; *see, e. g.*, T at 72-81, T at 118-125, T at 214-221. Freedom, truth, and justice thus can be seen as eternal as aspects of creative intelligence just as a religious person could see these three concepts as being eternal as aspects of God. Indeed, a person who believes in the existence of both God and creative intelligence theoretically could see creative intelligence as an aspect of God. To an atheist, however, creative intelligence must take on the role of an ultimate essence or supreme being. While an atheist might be able to accept statements that freedom, truth, and justice all were eternal concepts with no relation to God, acceptance of the eternal existence of the field of pure creative intelligence or of creative intelligence, with all its extraordinary characteristics, would require the belief in an essence or being beyond human existence.

Defendants contend that creative intelligence is not all-powerful: "Creative intelligence is understood as 'the origin of all power' in the sense that the stability of mind and body which results from the practice of the TM technique, enables a person to be healthier, to exercise better judgment and thereby be more powerful." This statement differs substantially through understatement and truncation of the relevant textbook quotation from that which is stated in the textbook. The textbook asserts that the field of pure creative intelligence is "the origin of all power in nature." T at 98. Defendants' statement, by truncating the quotation from the textbook, implies that creative intelligence is the origin of all power only in an individual. The textbook, however, speaks of creative intelligence in terms of universality. *E. g.*, T at 126, 188-89. In the entire phrase of which defendants quote only a part, the textbook asserts that the field of pure creative intelligence is "the origin of all power in nature." T at 98. The textbook repeatedly refers to "the unlimited power of creative intelligence," T at 108, and "the unbounded power of creative intelligence," T at 110. The textbook states that creative intelligence conducts the activity of nature, T at 114, including the structuring of the human body, T at 224, and the structuring of the blueprint of each individual's life in his or her genes, T at 171. The textbook states that creative intelligence "can permeate anything," T at 107, "accomplishes all great things with no effort," T at 108, and "is able to accomplish everything effortlessly," T at 118. Creative intelligence is absolutely self-sufficient and self-illuminating, T at 121-22, has "unbounded resources," T at 126, and can know no gain greater than itself, T at 144.

Defendants also contend that

> [w]hile the textbook attempts to describe certain qualities of creative intelligence, it contains nothing intended or understood as inherently religious. Thus, attributes such as loving, just, gentle, strong, efficient, kind, clean, purifying, "a person of full heart," self-sustaining and self-sufficient, are simply human qualities that develop as a result of personal growth.

Jarvis Affidavit ¶ 41. These statements again diverge substantially from what is stated in the textbook. While it may be true that these qualities do develop in an individual as a result of personal growth, the textbook attributes these "simply human qualities," with the exception of "a person of full heart," to a nonhuman, unmanifest, uncreated "concrete reality," T at 250; *e. g.*, T at 214-221, 100-107, 108-117, 222-229. Creative intelligence not only is loving, just, gentle, strong, efficient, kind, clean, purifying, and self-sufficient, but also possesses these qualities, and all other qualities in the universe, *e. g.,* T at 36, 292, in their pure and infinite or "unbounded" states.

Defendants state that

[t]he fact that the textbook mentions that creative intelligence is "the basis of all growth and progress" does not warrant the inference that it is the basis of all growth and progress in a similar sense that physics considers matter and energy to be the basic elements of everything. In addition, concepts such as energy and gravity go "on and on;" however, they are not understood as creators of the universe.

Jarvis Affidavit ¶ 35. Once again, defendants' statements differ substantially from what is stated in the textbook and their analogy is poorly drawn and unpersuasive. While the textbook does state that "[c]reative intelligence is at the basis of all growth and progress," T at 19, this statement must be read in conjunction with the many other assertions in the textbook concerning creative intelligence. The textbook states that creative intelligence is the source of "all existence." T at 171. Creative intelligence is the eternal, "nonchanging basis of life," T at 242, and "the source of all creativity." T at 243. The laws of nature themselves, "which are directly responsible for the creation, maintenance, and evolution of everything in the universe," T at 242, are merely "currents of creative intelligence." T at 110. Creative intelligence uses these laws of nature, or currents of creative intelligence, when creative intelligence creates the manifest universe: "When we investigate more closely the mechanics of manifestation, we find that creative intelligence creates by means of certain traditions, certain specific laws, which themselves are nonchanging. There are innumerable laws of nature functioning at every level of life. . . . " T at 242. "The endless creative activity of creative intelligence takes place within the traditional structure of the laws of nature and is ultimately founded on the most fundamental field of life—the unmanifest field of pure creative intelligence." T at 240. The textbook instructs that "everything in creation is nothing other than the expression of unmanifest creative intelligence. . . . " T at 260. Creative intelligence "structures the blueprint of life in our genes. . . . " T at 171. According to the textbook, "[t]he ultimate reality of every object is unmanifest creative intelligence. Every object, every expressed value in the phenomenal world, is an expression of the nonexpressed, unbounded value of creative intelligence." T at 154.

Creative intelligence thus is not merely "the basis of all growth and progress," but also is the eternal, nonchanging "source of all creativity and the source of 'all existence;'" the textbook continues this theme by stating that "everything in creation is nothing other than the expression of unmanifest creative intelligence. . . . " T at 260.

Defendants' attempt at analogizing creative intelligence to matter and energy, Jarvis Affidavit ¶ 35, is as weak and unpersuasive as defendants' previously discussed analogies and comparisons. Neither matter nor energy has more than the tiniest fraction of the characteristics of creative intelligence. Neither matter nor energy is bliss-consciousness or unbounded awareness or a field of "unlimited power, energy, existence, intelligence, peace, and happiness," as is creative intelligence, according to the textbook. *E. g.,* T at 121, 262, 102. Neither matter nor energy possess the "simply human qualities," Jarvis Affidavit ¶ 41, of creative intelligence. Neither matter nor energy engages in the variegated activities which are conducted by creative intelligence. For example, neither matter nor energy "is always unfolding greater levels of happiness within us," nor are they "always refining our thinking, perception, and action to give clear, truthful expression to the nature of life," as creative intelligence does, to name but a couple of the multitude of activities attributed to creative intelligence by the textbook. T at 144, 74.

Defendants also state that "[e]lectricity, the wheel, the printing press and water can each be considered to be at the basis of all growth and progress within different contexts, yet none can properly be considered the Creator of the Universe." Harned Affidavit ¶ 28. In this statement, defendants passingly mention a crucial consideration, which is the obvious observation that words take their meaning from the context in which they are used. The textbook speaks of creative intelligence only in terms of universality and illimitability. For example, the textbook states that creative intelligence "expresses itself throughout the entire universe. Creative intelligence is always acting, ever vigilant to unfold its unbounded resources in every particle of existence." T at 126. The textbook repeatedly states that creative intelligence is "the universal basis of life," *e. g.,* T at 189, and "the home of all qualities that constitute the universe," *e. g.,* T at 292. Creative intelligence, according to the textbook, has an unlimited supply of resources. T at 126. One of the recurrent promises of the textbook is the experience of universality gained from contact with pure creative intelligence. *E. g.,* T at 188. It is in this context of universality that creative intelligence must be evaluated. Almost needless to say, the implicit comparisons of creative intelligence to electricity, the wheel, the printing press, and water add nothing to defendants' arguments.

As can be seen from the foregoing discussion, one of defendants' methods of refuting the obvious import of textbook statements is to suggest a worldly entity or concept to which the textbook statement arguably might be applied. For example, faced with the textbook statement that creative intelligence "guides and sustains every aspect of the universe," T at 174, defendants claim that creative intelligence is really like gravity guiding the paths of the planets; faced with the textbook statement that creative intelligence conducts the activity of nature, T at 114, defendants argue that creative intelligence is functioning in a fashion similar to that of a DNA molecule; faced with statements in the textbook that creative intelligence is the home of all qualities including beauty, creativity, intelligence, and orderliness, defendants assert that a "Rembrandt painting can be described using similar values. . . ." Jarvis Affidavit ¶ 39. The problem with this approach is that creative intelligence, as described in the textbook, is not truly similar to any of the items to which defendants have compared or analogized it. For defendants' analogies to have any validity, one must, in examining the analogies, exclude from consideration the fact that creative intelligence possesses a plethora of qualities which are not possessed by the items to which it is compared. The weakness of defendants' comparisons perhaps is underscored by juxtaposing and noting the lack of similarity among the items and concepts to which they have compared creative intelligence: gravity, DNA, a Rembrandt painting, energy, the wheel, water, matter, electricity. The dissimilarity of concepts to which creative intelligence has been compared is not surprising in light of the teachings of the textbook. Since "[t]he ultimate reality of every object is creative intelligence," T at 154, creative intelligence presumably is ultimately similar to everything in the universe.

Defendants state that "[c]reative intelligence is not intended to be understood as an all-pervasive 'being' like God." Jarvis Affidavit ¶37. No elaboration on this statement is made in the affidavit. The textbook repeatedly asserts that creative intelligence is all-pervasive. For example, the textbook states that creative intelligence

> is present in all forms, words, smells, tastes, and objects of touch. In all the objects of experience, in all the senses of perception and organs of action, in every phenomenon, in the doer and the work done, in all directions—north, south, east, and west—in all times—past, present, and future—it is uniformly present. In front of man, behind him, to the left and right of him, in him—everywhere, and under all circumstances, creative intelligence is permeating everything.

T at 186. The textbook repeatedly states that "creative intelligence is present everywhere." *E.g.,* T at 23, 36. "The ultimate reality of every object is unmanifest creative intelligence." T at 154. "The universe is a continuous, unified whole, an unbroken field of creative intelligence." T at 137. Creative intelligence, according to the textbook, clearly is all-pervasive. Whether creative intelligence is a "being," essence, principle, intelligence, or entity has no bearing on plaintiff's motion for summary judgment.

In opposition to plaintiffs' motion for summary judgment, defendants also rely upon the depositions of three clergymen. All three clergymen, a Catholic priest, a United Presbyterian minister, and a rabbi, have attended their own pujas, have taken full or partial courses on the Science of Creative Intelligence, which they believe to have been substantially similar in content to that taught in the New Jersey High schools, and practiced Transcendental Meditation. At least one of the clergymen was active in an attempt to introduce the Science of Creative Intelligence into the curriculum of the public high schools in his place of residence and has a daughter who is a teacher of SCI/TM. All three clergymen, based on their understandings of SCI, testified that they did not view their courses in the Science of Creative Intelligence as courses in religion or religious philosophy. Each of the clergymen also testified, based on his understanding of SCI, that he found nothing in the Science of Creative Intelligence course which he took which conflicted with his religion. Two of the clergymen examined the textbook which was used in the New Jersey schools for the first time on the day of their depositions. Prendeville Deposition at 146; Roberts Deposition at 26. The third clergyman testified that he had had a copy of the textbook in his possession for several weeks and had "looked it over kind of carefully." Essrig Deposition at 59. The same clergyman testified that he had attended only a small part of a course on the Science of Creative Intelligence, but also had attended three or four weekend "residence courses" in which he heard several lectures, both live and on video tape, on the subject and had attended "many meetings" at a TM center. *Id* at 19, 54, 56. One of the clergymen testified that in his course on the Science of Creative Intelligence he was provided with a copy of the Bhagavad-Gita and had purchased a copy of Commentaries on the Bhagavad-Gita by Maharishi Mahesh Yogi for use in the course. Roberts Deposition at 71, 57-58. There is no evidence that the Bhagavad-Gita or defendant Yogi's Commentaries thereon were used in connection with the course taught in the New Jersey high schools.

While the court, of course, accepts the statement of each of the clergymen that it is his understanding of the Science of Creative Intelligence course that he took that the course was not a course in religion or religious philosophy, the question whether or not the teaching of the Science of Creative Intelligence, as represented by the textbook and by the deposition testimony of two people who taught the course in New Jersey high schools, constitutes a violation of the establishment clause presents a different question and remains a legal question for resolution by the courts. In addition, it is impossible for this court to determine either what the understanding of each clergyman regarding the Science of Creative Intelligence is or the similarity between the course taken by the clergymen and that offered to New Jersey high school students. There is evidence in the record that the courses taken by the clergymen differed in content both from each other and from the course offered in the New Jersey high schools. One of the clergymen was read three excerpts from the textbook used in New Jersey schools and asked if he had been taught the substance of the quoted excerpts in the course on the Science of Creative Intelligence which he had taken. The clergyman answered "no" to two of the three questions. Prendeville Deposition at 97-101. Later, the same clergyman was asked if he had been taught that "the field of pure creative intelligence is the ocean of life and that all manifest existence and evolutionary processes are waves of that ocean," which is a virtual quotation of a statement appearing on page 20 of the textbook used in New Jersey high schools. The clergyman answered the question with a categorical "No." *Id* at 117. The same clergyman testified that he had been taught in the SCI course which he had taken that the field of pure creative intelligence existed only within each individual. *Id* at 117-18. This teaching clearly contravenes that of the textbook used in New Jersey high schools. *E. g.,* T at 23, 36, 40, 42, 154, 292. The same clergyman's articulated understanding of the meaning of the term creative intelligence differed substantially from the definition which appears in the textbook before the court. *Compare* Prendeville Deposition at 93, 97, 99 *with* T at 20.

As noted earlier, another clergyman testified that he used materials in his course on the Science of Creative Intelligence which were not used in New Jersey or by the other two clergymen. The third clergyman took only a small part of the course, but has attended lectures on the Science of Creative Intelligence from time to time.

None of the three clergymen testified that he had actually read the entire textbook used in the New Jersey high schools. Two of the clergymen saw the book for the first time on the day of their depositions; they could not have spent more than a few minutes in inspecting it. The third clergyman testified that he had had a copy of the textbook in his possession for several weeks and had "looked it over kind of carefully;" he also responded "[y]es, I did," when asked if he had had "a chance to review the book." Essrig Deposition at 59, 22. The same clergyman also testified that he made no notes or other writings during or after his examination of the textbook. *Id.* at 59. Immediately following a conference with defendants' counsel, this clergyman testified that he had "studied" the textbook. *Id.* at 106. The clergyman did not specify the portions of the textbook which he had studied, but did

not remember any reference to the term "bliss-consciousness" in the textbook. *Id.* at 104. The term "bliss-consciousness" appears tens, probably scores, of times throughout the textbook. The term occasionally is used as a synonym for creative intelligence. *E. g.,* T at 55, 144. The same clergyman also stated that he had never heard the term "bliss-consciousness" at any of the lectures on the Science of Creative Intelligence.[14] Essrig Deposition at 102-03.

Aside from the difficulty in determining the basis for the clergymen's understandings of the Science of Creative Intelligence, it is difficult to see the utility of this testimony to the court in light of the fact that the court has a copy of the textbook actually used in the New Jersey high school course and hundreds of pages of deposition testimony of two people who taught that course.

Defendants also submit affidavits from two teachers of the New Jersey SCI/TM courses and eleven identical form affidavits signed by eleven students in New Jersey high schools. Each teacher stated that she does "not understand" the SCI/TM courses which she taught to be courses in religion. Each student's affidavit states the affiant's name, his religious affiliation, the fact that he took an SCI/TM course in a New Jersey high school, and the fact that the student does "not understand" that the SCI/TM course was a study of religion. Since none of these students read more than one-third of the textbook and most read less than one-sixth of the textbook, see Jarvis Affidavit ¶ 32, the students' understandings of the SCI/TM course is impossible to determine. Moreover, the court cannot rely on the unexplained conclusions of third parties when the teachings of the course are in evidence in the form of a textbook, especially if those teachings contradict the unexplained conclusions. In addition, the subjective characterizations by individuals of teachings as religious or not religious in their systems of categorization cannot be determinative of whether or not the teachings are religious within the meaning of the first amendment. *See infra* at 1315-1320.

Defendants also submitted the affidavits of two professors of religion who state that the Science of Creative Intelligence does not constitute a religion under their definitions of religion. These affidavits are discussed *infra* at 1310-1311, 1315-1320.

THE PUJA

The puja is a ceremony at which each student was given his or her mantra, the sound aid essential to practicing Transcendental Meditation. Every student who participated in the SCI/TM course was required to attend a puja as a part of the course; no mantras were given except at pujas. Aaron Deposition at 589. Each student received his or her mantra individually at the conclusion of or during a puja performed in a closed room by the teacher in the presence of one student. The teacher performed a puja in the presence of each individual student prior to imparting a mantra to the student. Aaron Affidavit at 593.

The pujas were conducted on Sundays off the school premises. An appointment was set up for each student so that the teacher could perform the pujas and impart the mantras seriatim without requiring the students to wait while their classmates received their mantras. *Id* at 600. Prior to the appointed Sunday, each student was asked to bring a clean white handkerchief, a few flowers, and three or four pieces of fruit to the puja. Upon each student's arrival, the handkerchief, flowers, and fruit were taken from him or her and placed in a container, and the student was led to a small room. At the request of someone at the site, each student removed his or her shoes before entering the room. The student and teacher entered the room, and the teacher closed the door. Inside the room was a rectangular table which was covered by a white sheet. Metropole Deposition at 344. The table held a brass candleholder and a brass incense holder. The holders contained a candle and incense, both of which were lit by the teacher. *Id.* at 346-47. The table also held three brass dishes which contained, respectively, water, rice, and sandalpaste. *Id.* at 345-46. The table also carried a small brass dish containing camphor. *Id.* at 347-48. In addition, there was a tray on the table and an eight-by-twelve inch color picture of Guru Dev at the back of the table. *Id.* at 348-49; *see* Prendeville Deposition at 73. Guru Dev was a teacher of defendant Yogi and is held by the World Plan defendants to be the latest preserver and disseminator of the Transcendental Meditation technique prior to defendant Yogi. Metropole Deposition at 349. Guru Dev has been dead for over twenty years. *Id.* at 350. As soon as the teacher and student were in the room, the container holding the flowers, fruit, and handkerchief brought by the student was placed on the table. *Id.* at 343. Each student then stood or sat in front of the table while the teacher sang a chant in Sanskrit. The chant lasted three or four minutes. Aaron Deposition at 685. During the singing of the chant, the teacher moved some of the articles from the table onto the tray. *Id.* at 685. *See* Prendeville Deposition at 73-75. At the conclusion of the chant, the teacher imparted the mantra to the student by speaking it aloud. Metropole Deposition at 351. *See* Prendeville Deposition at 23. The teacher then instructed the student in the technique of using the mantra in the practice of Transcendental Meditation for approximately twenty minutes. Aaron Affidavit at 2. Each student then was taken to another room in which he or she meditated alone for the first time for a period of approximately twenty minutes. *Id.* Following the meditation, each student was "asked to

answer in writing several questions concerning the experience." *Id.* Upon completion of the written answers, the teacher and the student met to discuss the student's experience with meditation. *Id.* at 3. Each student spent between one and one-half and two hours engaged in the above-described activities. *Id.* at 2. A week or two prior to the puja, each student was required to sign a document in which the student promised never to reveal his or her mantra. Metropole Deposition at 358. No student received a copy of the document which he or she had signed. *Id.* at 361. The teachers told the students that the puja was not a religious exercise or prayer. Aaron Affidavit at 3; Metropole Affidavit at 2.

As stated above, the chant is sung in Sanskrit. During the several-week teacher training course, the teachers learn the words to the chant by memorizing the Sanskrit words phonetically. Aaron Deposition at 681. Each teacher at the teacher training course is given a sheet of paper on which the Sanskrit words of the chant are written phonetically in English-language characters. Metropole Deposition at 325. The teachers also are given English-language translations of the chant. *Id.* The teachers must memorize the melody to which the chant is sung. Aaron Deposition at 681. In addition, the teachers had to learn certain gestures and hand movements used during the singing of the chant. *Id.* at 681, 685. As a condition precedent to becoming a teacher of SCI/TM, the would-be teachers had to perform the chant in front of and to the satisfaction of defendant Yogi or one of his aides. *Id.* at 682.

The following English translation of the chant which the teachers sing at the puja was supplied by defendants as an exhibit at certain depositions:[15]

"Invocation

Whether pure or impure, where purity or impurity is permeating everywhere, whoever opens himself to the expanded vision of unbounded awareness gains inner and outer purity.

Invocation

To Lord Narayana, to lotus-born Brahma the Creator, to Vashishtha, to Shakti and his son Parashar, To Vyasa, to Shukadeva, to the great Gaudapada, to Govinda, ruler among the yogis, to his disciple, Shri Shankaracharya, to his disciples Padma Pada and Hasta Malaka

And Trotakacharya and Vartika-Kara, to others, to the tradition of our Master, I bow down.

To the abode of the wisdom of the Shrutis, Smritis and Puranas, to the abode of kindness, to the personified glory of the Lord, to Shankara, emancipator of the world, I bow down.

To Shankaracharya the redeemer, hailed as Krishna and Badarayana, to the commentator of the Brahma Sutras, I bow down. To the glory of the Lord

I bow down again and again, at whose door the whole galaxy of gods pray [sic] for perfection day and night.

Adorned with immeasurable glory, preceptor of the whole world, having bowed down to Him we gain fulfillment.

Skilled in dispelling the cloud of ignorance of the people, the gentle emancipator, Brahmananda Sarasvati, the supreme teacher, full of brilliance, Him I bring to my awareness.

Offering the invocation of the lotus feet of Shri Guru Dev, I bow down.

Offering a seat to the lotus feet of Shri Guru Dev, I bow down.

Offering an ablution to the lotus feet of Shri Guru Dev, I bow down.

Offering a cloth to the lotus feet of Shri Guru Dev, I bow down.

Offering sandalpaste to the lotus feet of Shri Guru Dev, I bow down.

Offering full rice to the lotus feet of Shri Guru Dev, I bow down.

Offering a flower to the lotus feet of Shri Guru Dev, I bow down.

Offering incense to the lotus feet of Shri Guru Dev, I bow down.

Offering light to the lotus feet of Shri Guru Dev, I bow down.

Offering water to the lotus feet of Shri Guru Dev, I bow down.

Offering fruit to the lotus feet of Shri Guru Dev, I bow down.

Offering water to the lotus feet of Shri Guru Dev, I bow down.

Offering a betel leaf to the lotus feet of Shri Guru Dev, I bow down.

Offering a coconut to the lotus feet of Shri Guru Dev, I bow down.

Offering camphor light

White as camphor, kindness incarnate, the essence of creation garlanded with Brahman, ever dwelling in the lotus of my heart, the creative impulse of cosmic life, to That, in the form of Guru Dev, I bow down.

Offering light to the lotus feet of Shri Guru Dev, I bow down.

Offering water to the lotus feet of Shri Guru Dev, I bow down.

Offering a handful of flowers.

Guru in the glory of Brahma, Guru in the glory of Vishnu, Guru in the glory of the great Lord Shiva, Guru in the glory of the personified transcendental fulness [sic] of Brahman, to Him, to Shri Guru Dev adorned with glory, I bow down.

The Unbounded, like the endless canopy of the sky, the omnipresent in all creation, by whom the sign of That has been revealed, to Him, to Shri Guru Dev, I bow down.

Guru Dev, Shri Brahmananda, bliss of the Absolute, transcendental joy, the Self-Sufficient, the embodiment of pure knowledge which is beyond and above the universe like the sky, the aim of 'Thou art That' and other such expressions which unfold eternal truth, the One, the Eternal, the Pure, the Immovable, the Witness of all intellects, whose status transcends thought, the Transcendent along with the three gunas, the true preceptor, to Shri Guru Dev, I bow down.

The blinding darkness of ignorance has been removed by applying the balm of knowledge. The eye of knowledge has been opened by Him and therefore, to Him, to Shri Guru Dev, I bow down.

Offering a handful of flowers to the lotus feet of Shri Guru Dev, I bow down."

All spacing, punctuation, and capitalization in the quotation above are identical to the exhibit provided by the defendants.

As can be seen from the English translation, the double invocation of the puja chant takes the form of expressions of reverence for "the Lord," other named entities or individuals, "the tradition of our Master," and Guru Dev, who is portrayed as a personification of a divine being or essence.[16] The translation of the chant reads in part as follows:

To the glory of the Lord I bow down again and again, at whose door the whole galaxy of gods pray [sic] for perfection day and night.

Adorned with immeasurable glory, preceptor of the whole world, having bowed down to Him we gain fulfillment.

This passage makes clear that the chanter is referring to a divine being or essence or entity, "the Lord."[17] No other reasonable interpretation is possible.

The chant continues in the next paragraph to identify Guru Dev as a personification of "Him," or "the Lord:"

Skilled in dispelling the cloud of ignorance of the people, the gentle emancipator, Brahmananda Sarasvati, the supreme teacher, full of brilliance, Him I bring to my awareness.

In this paragraph Brahmananda Sarasvati, who also is known as Guru Dev. see Jarvis Deposition at 995, is referred to as "Him," with a capital aitch. The only prior appearance of the term "Him," with a capital aitch, occurs in the preceding paragraph and the referent of that "Him" is "the Lord." The word "Him" with a capital aitch occurs four additional times in the chant. The referent in each case is "Guru Dev."

The chanter then makes fifteen offerings to Guru Dev and fourteen obeisances to Guru Dev. The chant then describes Guru Dev as a personification of "kindness" and of "the creative impulse of cosmic life," and the personification of "the essence of creation," which, simultaneously with its personification in Guru Dev, lies in the center of the chanter's heart:

> White as camphor, kindness incarnate, the essence of creation garlanded with Brahman, ever dwelling in the lotus of my heart, the creative impulse of cosmic life, to That, in the form of Guru Dev, I bow down.

The chanter then makes three more offerings to Guru Dev and three additional obeisances to Guru Dev. The chant then moves to a passage in which a string of divine epithets are applied to Guru Dev. Guru Dev is called "The Unbounded," "the omnipresent in all creation," "bliss of the Absolute," "transcendental joy," "the Self-Sufficient," "the embodiment of pure knowledge which is beyond and above the universe like the sky," "the One," "the Eternal," "the Pure," "the Immovable," "the Witness of all intellects, whose status transcends thought," "the Transcendent along with the three gunas," and "the true preceptor."[18] Manifestly, no one would apply all these epithets to a human being. The chant ends with another offering and two more obeisances to "Him," to Guru Dev.[19]

The items used in seventeen of the nineteen offerings were explicitly enumerated as being present during the initiation ceremonies of the New Jersey high school students. The items stated as being offered in two of the offerings were not present. *Id.* at 454. Metropole Deposition at 336–48. The materials for five of the nineteen offerings were supplied by each individual student. *See id.* at 338. Defendant Aaron testified that she moved the items that were on the table at the beginning of the puja onto the tray during the singing of the chant. Aaron Deposition at 685. Nothing was on the tray at the beginning of the puja. Metropole Deposition at 348.

A conflict exists between the evidence submitted by defendants as to whether the puja is performed by the initiator for himself or by the initiator for the student. Defendants' experts in religion state that the puja is performed by the teacher for the student. Harned Affidavit ¶ 18; Rao Affidavit ¶ 11. Defendant Jarvis stated that the puja is performed by the teacher for himself. Jarvis Deposition at 896–97. Defendants' counsel also argues that the puja is performed "by the teacher solely for himself." Db at 15. On plaintiffs' motion for summary judgment, defendants' allegation that the puja is performed for the initiator himself, with the students' participation limited to attendance and the contribution of certain offerings, Rao Affidavit ¶ 11, will be accepted as true.

Defendants deny the religiosity of the puja. In refuting the religiosity of the puja, defendants take the same oblique attitude to the question as taken in their discussion of the Science of Creative Intelligence course. Defendants once again eschew direct analysis of the content of the challenged practice, and instead rely upon the subjective interpretations, beliefs, and opinions of defendants and third-parties, who have various degrees of interest in the lawsuit and who have varying degrees of understanding of the facts which form the basis of this lawsuit.

Primary reliance is placed upon the affidavit and deposition testimony of defendant Jarvis. Defendants also rely on the deposition testimony of three clergymen and the affidavits of two professors of religion, the deposition testimony and affidavits of two people who performed several of the initiation ceremonies in relation to the New Jersey high school course, and the affidavits of eleven New Jersey high school students who witnessed performances of the puja in relation to the SCI/TM course.

Defendants seek to characterize the puja as "a ceremony of gratitude," and apparently so represented it to the New Jersey high school students. It is difficult to understand why defendants label the puja "a ceremony of gratitude" because the English translation of the chant fails to reveal one word of gratefulness or thanksgiving. Rather, the puja takes the form of a double invocation of Guru Dev. Putting this difficulty aside for the moment, the question arises as to whom this gratitude is being expressed. Defendants have answered this question by stating that the gratitude is given "to the tradition of teachers who have preserved this teaching," Jarvis Affidavit ¶ 11, "to the knowledge" which each of the "teachers" named in the chant is said to have possessed, Jarvis Deposition at 1006, and to the prior "teachers" themselves, Aaron Deposition at 582. The problem with all of defendants' descriptions of the receiver of the gratitude is that none of the described recipients is capable of receiving it. When one performs a ceremony of gratitude or "thanksgiving," Aaron Deposition at 582, one must have a recipient of that gratitude in mind or the ceremony would be meaningless. In common English usage, ceremonies of gratitude or thanksgiving are performed to divine beings (God, Providence, etc.), animate and sensate beings, and possibly institutions run by human beings. While one may be grateful *for* a body of knowledge or *for* a tradition, that gratitude extends *to* the purveyors or creators of that knowledge or *to* the preservers of the tradition. One would no more perform a ceremony of gratitude to a tradition or to a body of knowledge than one would perform a ceremony of gratitude to a chair or to a useful contrivance or to a machine or to any other inanimate object which would be entirely incapable of perceiving human communication.

The problem with performing the ceremony of gratitude to the teachers themselves is that most of the "teachers" mentioned in the puja chant have been dead for thousands of years, *see* Jarvis Deposition at 1003, and the last "teacher" mentioned in the chant has been dead for nearly a quarter of a century. Dead people are incapable of communication with living human beings unless one believes in the existence of a soul which continues to exist after the death of the body.

As stated earlier, no words of gratitude or thanks appear in the English translation of the puja chant. The chant clearly is labeled "Invocation" twice. An invocation is the invoking or calling upon a spirit, a principle, a person, or a deity for aid. Funk and Wagnells New Standard Dictionary 1290 (1949); The Random House College Dictionary 703 (1973); Webster's New Collegiate Dictionary 444 (1960). The chant clearly invokes the spirit or deity of Guru Dev:

> Skilled in dispelling the cloud of ignorance of the people, the gentle emancipator, *Brahmananda Sarasvati* [*Guru Dev*], the supreme teacher, full of brilliance, *Him I bring to my awareness.*
>
> Offering *the invocation of* the lotus feet of Shri *Guru Dev,* I bow down.

(emphasis supplied).

Defendant Jarvis states in an affidavit that it is his personal understanding that the puja is merely a ceremony of gratitude to the tradition of past teachers and that similar ceremonies are performed in a number of secular contexts in India. While the court of course accepts these statements as accurate reflections of defendant Jarvis' personal understanding, the court also must note that defendant Jarvis made no claim of knowledge in the matter of Indian customs. *See* Jarvis Deposition at 908, 1020. Defendant Jarvis, when asked if he knew what the Sanskrit word "puja" meant, replied, "[n]o, I don't know what the word 'puja' means except to interpret it as a ceremony of gratitude." *Id.* at 935. Directly on the heels of this reply, defendant Jarvis was asked if he were familiar with any puja "other than the one that is performed by the teacher at the time that a mantra is assigned." *Id.* Defendant Jarvis answered: "No." *Id.* In his affidavit, defendant Jarvis also states that he believes that only "3 or 4 ex-teachers" of the more than 7,000 TM teachers in the United States believe that the puja has religious significance. Jarvis Affidavit ¶18.

Defendants also rely on affidavits of two professors of religion. The affidavits are virtually identical and will be treated together. Neither professor practices Transcendental Meditation and presumably has never witnessed a puja; both professors state that they have read the English translation of the puja chant which appears above. Each professor concludes that in his opinion the Puja is not a religious ceremony.

Neither professor offers any textual analysis of the chant. Neither professor offers any analysis of the performance of the ceremony, except to note that each student is present and brings a handkerchief, fruit, and flowers. Rather, the professors offer a broad generalization that "[i]n India, many secular activities begin with a puja ceremony or ceremony of gratitude." Rao Affidavit ¶ 12. The professors then state that secular pujas are part of the cultural life of India. Rao Affidavit ¶ 12. While the court, of course, accepts these generalizations, they shed little or no light on the religiosity or lack thereof of the puja conducted in the presence of New Jersey high school students because there is no indication that the puja performed for the high school students was similar to "secular pujas" performed in India. The only similarity, stated by the professors, between the "secular pujas" of India and the TM puja is that some secular pujas involve the use of flowers, fruit, white handkerchiefs, incense, and rice. Rao Affidavit ¶ 13; Harned Affidavit ¶ 20. Neither professor states that it is common in these "secular pujas" to sing a chant in Sanskrit, a language which has been dead for thousands of years. Neither professor stated that it is common in these secular pujas to sing a chant which includes the words "To the glory of the Lord, I bow down again and again."

The court's statements of what does not appear in the professors' affidavits should not be interpreted as an indication that the court is rejecting any representation of fact contained therein. For the purposes of this motion, the court accepts representations of fact (as distinguished from legal conclusions and arguments) appearing in the professors' affidavits. The court points out the lack of precision in implicitly comparing the TM puja to the "secular pujas" of India merely to demonstrate the lack of utility of these generalizations as an aid in determining the question before the court.

The professors ultimately base their opinions that the puja is not a religious ceremony on their beliefs that religions should be defined subjectively, the keystone being whether or not the participants in the ceremony intend the ceremony to have religious significance. Harned Affidavit ¶ 21; Rao Affidavit ¶ 15, 21. This subjective approach to defining religion and identifying religious ceremonies may account for the failure of the professors to address themselves to the actual performance of the puja and content of the chant. Under the professors' approach, the content of the ceremony would be immaterial if the participants sincerely believed and intended that the puja have no religiosity. As will be developed later, this subjective, or "contextual," approach to defining religion and identifying religious ceremonies is unacceptable as a legal standard under the first amendment. *See* pages 1315–1320 *infra.*

Defendants also rely upon the deposition testimony of three clergymen who practice Transcendental Meditation and who went through a puja in receiving their mantras. Although defendants offered the clergymen as "fact witnesses" and specifically denied that the clergymen were testifying as experts, defendants now seek to rely on the opinions of the clergymen. *See* F.R.Ev. 701. Over the objection of plaintiffs' counsel, each of the three clergymen testified that in his opinion the puja was not a religious ceremony. None of the clergymen implicitly or explicitly held himself out as having extensive knowledge of any religion but their respective denominations. All three clergymen disclaimed knowledge of Indian culture and history and Hindu religion and philosophy. All three clergymen indicated that they accepted representations made to them by their teachers that the puja was a ceremony of gratitude which must be attended by them in order to receive a mantra. All three of the clergymen stated that they did not view the puja as important; one of the clergymen characterized the significance of the puja to him as "trivial," although he also stated that the puja may have had a significance, unknown to him, to other persons. The lack of importance attached to the ritual of the puja may account for the hazy recollections of two of the clergymen. At the time of his puja, none of the clergymen had seen an English translation of the puja chant. A few weeks prior to his deposition, each of the three clergymen was sent the above-quoted translation of the chant by defendants or by defendants' counsel. At his deposition, each of the three clergymen testified that the reading of the translation did not change his opinion that the puja was not a religious ceremony.

In addition to the deposition testimony of the three clergymen, defendants rely on the affidavits of two teachers and eleven high school students of the SCI/TM course who state that they do not understand the puja to be a religious ceremony. Like the clergymen, neither the teachers nor the students claim any qualifications as experts in religion or anything else; they offer statements that they do not understand the puja to be a religious ceremony. Neither the teachers nor the clergymen nor the students offer any reasons for their understandings or lack thereof. While the court accepts the statements, these unexplained statements cannot be determinative of the religiosity of the puja for reasons set out *infra* at 1315–1320, especially in light of the fact that the opinions of the clergymen, teachers, and students are based on facts in the record.

Defendants seek to analogize the puja chant to the Hippocratic Oath. The analogy is not convincing. First, nowhere in the Hippocratic Oath is "the Lord" invoked. The only mention of gods in the Hippocratic Oath occurs in the opening phrase: "I swear by Apollo Physician, by Asclepius, by Health, by Panacea, and by all the gods and goddesses, making them my wit-

nesses. . . ." C. McFadden, Medical Ethics 431–32 (5th ed. 1961). Moreover, the gods mentioned in the Hippocratic Oath are creatures of mythology, inhabitants of a dead religion. Those responsible for administering the oath are neither priests nor trained by priests of these ancient gods, but laymen. In contrast, the puja is sung at the direction of Maharishi Mahesh Yogi, a Hindu monk. The words and offerings of the chant invoke the deified teacher, who also was a Hindu monk, of Maharishi Mahesh Yogi. In the chant, this teacher is linked to names known as Hindu deities. Maharishi Mahesh Yogi places such great emphasis on the singing of this chant prior to the imparting of a mantra to each individual student that no mantras are given except at pujas and no one is allowed to teach the Science of Creative Intelligence/Transcendental Meditation unless he or she performed the puja to the personal satisfaction of Maharishi Mahesh Yogi or one of his aides. Aaron Deposition at 682. *See* Jarvis Deposition at 834. Needless to say, neither Hinduism nor belief in "the Lord" constitute a dead religion. Both of these beliefs are held by hundreds of millions of people.

DISCUSSION

Plaintiffs allege that the teaching of the SCI/TM course in New Jersey high schools violates the establishment clauses of both the United States Constitution and the New Jersey Constitution. The first clause of the first amendment to the United States Constitution states that "Congress shall make no law respecting an establishment of religion, or prohibiting the free exercise thereof." The New Jersey Constitution states that "[t]here shall be no establishment of one religious sect in preference to another." N.J. Const. Art. 1, ¶ 4. The fundamental mandates of the "establishment of religion" clause were enumerated by the Supreme Court thirty years ago:

The "establishment of religion," clause of the First Amendment means at least this: Neither a state nor the Federal Government can set up a church. Neither can pass laws which aid one religion, aid all religions, or prefer one religion over another. Neither can force or influence a person to go to or to remain away from church against his will or force him to profess a belief or disbelief in any religion. No person can be punished for entertaining or professing religious beliefs, for church attendance, or non-attendance. No tax in any amount, large or small, can be levied to support any religious activities or institutions, whatever they may be called, or whatever form they may adopt to teach or practice religion. Neither a state nor the Federal Government can, openly or secretly, participate in the affairs of any religious organizations or groups and *vice versa*. In the words of Jefferson, the clause against establishment of religion by law was intended to erect "a wall of separation between church and State."

Everson v. Board of Education, 330 U.S. 1, 15–16, 67 S.Ct. 504, 511, 91 L.Ed. 711 (1947), quoting *Reynolds v. United States,* 98 U.S. 145, 164, 25 L.Ed. 244 (1878). The Court reaffirmed its commitment to these basic principles in *Torcaso v. Watkins,* 367 U.S. 488, 495, 81 S.Ct. 1680, 1683, 6 L.Ed.2d 982 (1961) (footnotes omitted):

> We repeat and reaffirm that neither a State nor the Federal Government can constitutionally force a person "to profess a belief or disbelief in any religion." Neither can constitutionally pass laws or impose requirements which aid all religions as against non-believers, and neither can aid those religions based on a belief in the existence of God as against those religions founded on different beliefs.

The position of the federal government and the state must be one of neutrality in the area of religious activity. *Abington School District v. Schempp,* 374 U.S. 203, 222, 83 S.Ct. 1560, 10 L.Ed.2d 844 (1963). A three-part test has emerged from the Supreme Court decisions involving the establishment clause. In order to avoid violation of the establishment clause, the federal or state

> law in question, first, must reflect a clearly secular legislative purpose, second, must have a primary effect that neither advances nor inhibits religion, and, third, must avoid excessive government entanglement with religion.

Committee for Public Education v. Nyquist, 413 U.S. 756, 773, 93 S.Ct. 2955, 2965, 37 L.Ed.2d 948 (1973).

Before applying this three-part test, however, the court must determine if the SCI/TM course constitutes a religious activity under the first amendment. Owing to the variety of form and substance which religions may take, the courts have avoided the establishment of explicit criteria, the possession of which indelibly identifies an activity as religious for purposes of the first amendment. This court, therefore, must be guided by the type of activity that has been held to be religious under the first amendment by the courts.

In implementing the establishment clause, the Supreme Court has made clear that an activity may be religious even though it is neither a part of nor derives from a societally recognized religious sect. In *Engel v. Vitale,* 370 U.S. 421, 82 S.Ct. 1261, 8 L.Ed.2d 601 (1962), the New York State Board of Regents, a governmental agency with broad supervisory, executive and legislative powers over the state's public school system, composed a nondenominational prayer and recommended that it be recited by students at the beginning of each school day. Recitation of the prayer

was voluntary; students could remain seated and silent or leave the room during the recitation. The prayer read:

> Almighty God, we acknowledge our dependence upon Thee, and we beg Thy blessings upon us, our parents, our teachers, and our Country.

Id. at 422, 82 S.Ct. at 1262. The Regents put forward the prayer as part of its "Statement on Moral and Spiritual Training in the Schools." Despite the fact that the prayer was not connected to any recognized religious group or groups and had been composed and recommended solely by laymen, the Supreme Court found that "[t]here can, of course, be no doubt that New York's program of daily classroom invocation of God's blessings as prescribed in the Regents' prayer is a religious activity."

Id. at 424, 82 S.Ct. at 1264.

Similarly, in *Torcaso v. Watkins,* 367 U.S. 488, 81 S.Ct. 1680, 6 L.Ed.2d 982 (1961), the Supreme Court held unconstitutional a provision of the Declaration of Rights of the Maryland Constitution which required appointees to state offices to declare a belief in the existence of God as a condition of obtaining their commissions. Although a belief in the existence of God is central to many religions, the Court did not find that this belief in and of itself constituted a religion in the societally accepted meaning of that word nor did the Court find that the belief derived from a particular sect. Rather, the Court found that the Maryland provision violated the establishment of religion clause because it propagated "a particular kind of religious concept." See *id.* at 494, 81 S.Ct. at 1683 (footnote omitted). The Court thus held that governmental aid to the propagation of a "religious concept" would violate the establishment clause. The Court indicated that the Maryland provision violated the establishment clause both in that it prevented nonreligious people from holding public office and in that it aided all "those religions based on a belief in the existence of God as against those religions founded on different beliefs." *Id.* at 495, 81 S.Ct. at 1683–1684 (footnote omitted). The Supreme Court in *Torcaso* and *Engel* interpreted the word "religion" in the first amendment broadly to encompass "religious concept[s]" and religions which do not propound a belief in the existence of God. In a footnote to *Torcaso,* the Court listed certain religions which do not hold a belief in the existence of a Supreme Being: "Among religions in this country which do not teach what would generally be considered a belief in the existence of God are Buddhism, Taoism, Ethical Culture, Secular Humanism and others." *Id.* at 495 n.11, 81 S.Ct. at 1684 (citations omitted).

In a statutory context, the Supreme Court has given a broad meaning to the phrase "religious training and belief" in construing section 6(j) of the Universal Military Service and Training Act. *Welsh v. United States,* 398 U.S. 333, 90 S.Ct. 1792, 26 L.Ed.2d 308 (1970); *United States v. Seeger,* 380 U.S. 163, 85 S.Ct. 850, 13 L.Ed.2d 733 (1965). Section 6(j) provided in part:

> Nothing contained in this title shall be construed to require any person to be subject to combatant training and service in the armed forces of the United States who, by reason of religious training and belief, is conscientiously opposed to participation in war in any form. Religious training and belief in this connection means an individual's belief in a relation to a Supreme Being involving duties superior to those arising from any human relation, but does not include essentially political, sociological, or philosophical views or a merely personal moral code.

Despite the fact that the Court was called upon to construe a statute, which contained an explanation of the phrase "religious training and belief," the Court held:

> If an individual deeply and sincerely holds beliefs that are purely ethical or moral in source and content but that nevertheless impose upon him a duty of conscience to refrain from participating in any war at any time, those beliefs certainly occupy in the life of that individual "a place parallel to that filled by . . . God" in traditionally religious persons. Because his beliefs function as a religion in his life, such an individual is as much entitled to a "religious" conscientious objector exemption under § 6(j) as is someone who derives his conscientious opposition to war from traditional religious convictions.

Welsh v. United States, supra, 398 U.S. at 340, 90 S.Ct. at 1796, *quoting United States v. Seeger, supra,* at 176, 85 S.Ct. 850.

The majority opinion in neither *Seeger* nor *Welsh* grappled with the problem of defining religion as it is used in the first amendment. The significance of these cases for purposes of this court's analysis derives not from the definitions of "religious training and belief" at which the Supreme Court arrived, but rather from the fact that the Court defined the phrase broadly in an exercise of statutory construction, an area in which the Court is far more circumscribed in defining terms than it is in the area of constitutional interpretation. *See Welsh, supra,* 398 U.S. at 346, 90 S.Ct. 1792 (Harlan, J., concurring).

In light of *Engel, supra,* and *Abington School District v. Schempp, supra,* a panel of the Seventh Circuit held that the first amendment's establishment clause was violated by a teacher who had her kindergarten students recite the following poem or prayer prior to their morning snack:

We thank you for the flowers so sweet;
We thank you for the food we eat;
We thank you for the birds that sing;

We thank you for everything.
DeSpain v. DeKalb County Community School District 428, 384 F.2d 836, 837 (7th Cir. 1967), *cert. denied,* 390 U.S. 906, 88 S.Ct. 815, 19 L.Ed.2d 873 (1968). The Seventh Circuit held that recitation of this simple poem or prayer by five-year-olds constituted an establishment of religion because the word "you" referred to "the Deity." *Id.* at 839.

In *Founding Church of Scientology v. United States,* 133 U.S.App.D.C. 299, 409 F.2d 1146 (1969), the court confronted the question whether or not a philosophy or system of beliefs called Scientology was a religion under the first amendment. Although Scientology postulated the existence of no supreme essence or being and disavowed mysticism and supernaturalism, the court held that the Founding Church's claim that its theories and philosophy constituted a religion for purposes of the first amendment revealed a prima facie case for such status. *Id.* at 1160. The Court noted that the theories of Scientology included a belief

> that man is essentially a free and immortal spirit (a "thetan" in Scientological terminology) which merely inhabits the "mest body" ("mest" is an acronym of the words matter, energy, space, time). Man is said to be characterized by the qualities of "beingness," "havingness," and "doingness." The philosophical theory was developed that the world is constructed on the relationships of "Affinity," "Reality," "Communication," which taken together are denominated "the ARC Triangle."

Id. at 1152. In *Founding Church,* the Scientologists claimed that Scientology was a religion entitled to protection under the first amendment whereas the proponents of the Science of Creative Intelligence state that their teachings and activities are not religious in nature. The case is noteworthy, however, as another example of a court giving a broad definition to the term religion under the first amendment. The court also noted that whether or not Scientology was a religion for purposes of the first amendment did not depend on the representations of its proponents, but was a proper subject for legal contest. *Id.* at 1160.

Defendants point out that none of the above-discussed decisions explicitly defined religion within the meaning of the first amendment. The lack of a precise definition is not surprising in light of the fact that a constitutional provision is involved. This court knows of no decision defining press or speech within the meaning of the first amendment. The meaning of these terms, and many other constitutional terms, have expanded with the passage of time and the development of the nation. The drafters of the Constitution certainly attributed a meaning to the term "the press" which would not encompass means of communication now deemed to be part of "the press."

See, e. g., Rosenbloom v. Metromedia, Inc., 415 F.2d 892, 895 (3d Cir. 1969). Similarly, philosophies and theories recognized as religions or religious practices were unheard of by the drafters of the Constitution and the Bill of Rights. New religions appear in this country frequently and they cannot stand outside the first amendment merely because they did not exist when the Bill of Rights was drafted. As stated by Mr. Justice Frankfurter in *McGowan v. Maryland,* 366 U.S. 420, 465–66, 81 S.Ct. 1101, 1156, 6. L.Ed.2d 393 (1961) (Frankfurter, J., concurring),

Of course, the immediate object of the First Amendment's prohibition was the established church as it had been known in England and in most of the Colonies. But with foresight those who drafted and adopted the words, "Congress shall make no law respecting an establishment of religion," did not limit the constitutional proscription to any particular, dated form of state-supported theological venture. The Establishment Clause withdrew from the sphere of legitimate legislative concern and competence a specific, but comprehensive, area of human conduct; man's belief or disbelief in the verity of some transcendental idea and man's expression in action of that belief or disbelief.

When courts are faced with forms of "the press" or forms of "religion" unknown in prior decisional law, they must look to the prior interpretations of the constitutional provisions for guidance as to the substantive characteristics of theories or practices which have been found to constitute "religion" under the first amendment. The Supreme Court has interpreted the religion clauses of the first amendment several times in its recent history. *E. g., Committee for Public Education v. Nyquist,* 413 U.S. 756, 93 S.Ct. 2955, 37 L.Ed.2d 948 (1973); *Epperson v. Arkansas,* 393 U.S. 97, 89 S.Ct. 266, 21 L.Ed.2d 228 (1968); *Abington School District v. Schempp,* 374 U.S. 203, 83 S.Ct. 1560, 10 L.Ed.2d 844 (1963); *Engel v. Vitale,* 370 U.S. 421, 82 S.Ct. 1261, 8 L.Ed.2d 601 (1963); *Torcaso v. Watkins,* 367 U.S. 488, 81 S.Ct. 1680, 6 L.Ed.2d 982 (1961); *Everson v. Board of Education,* 330 U.S. 1, 67 S.Ct. 504, 91 L.Ed. 711 (1947); *Cantwell v. Connecticut,* 310 U.S. 296, 60 S.Ct. 900, 84 L.Ed. 1213 (1940). The historical development and purpose of the religion clauses have been elaborated in a number of these cases, especially in *Engel* and in *Everson.* Religion, as comprehended by the first amendment now includes mere affirmation of belief in a supreme being, *Torcaso, supra,* invocation of a supreme being in a public school, *Engel, supra,* and reading verses from the Bible without comment, *Schempp, supra.*

Defendants argue that all of the above-discussed decisions are inapposite to the issues in this suit because the activity in question in each of the prior cases was represented or conceded to be religious in nature whereas defendants in the instant action assert that the activities are not religious in nature. The court notes the distinction but cannot accept defendants' conclusion that the decisions are not relevant. The cases, at the very least, reveal the types of activity and belief that have been considered religious under the first amendment.

Finding no guidance in the decisional law, defendants urge the court to adopt a "definitional approach" which is "substantive and contextual."[20] Harned Affidavit ¶12. Under the cases discussed *supra,* it is the usual practice of courts to examine the substance, or content, of a challenged activity and the context in which it occurs. This court is following this usual practice in the instant case.

Defendants illustrate their concept of a "substantive and contextual" approach by means of an analogy:

Imagine I watch an athlete, who bows his head, folds his hands and closes his eyes for a moment during athletic competition. Although this occurs in a secular context, I assume he is praying. When I mention this to him, he denies that he is praying and asserts that he is merely trying to empty his mind of every distraction so he can concentrate entirely upon the athletic event. I refuse to believe him because whenever I have seen persons act in this manner, they have been engaged in prayer. But the athlete responds that if his actions did have religious significance, he would act similarly after his victories in order to express his gratitude to God. Yet he does not do so. Furthermore, he says, if he were devout, he would certainly not maintain the extravagant life style, that has gained him notoriety in the newspapers. In the end, I am persuaded that his actions have no religious significance. He has provided me with the complete context in which it is possible to accurately assess whether or not his actions have any religious significance. In the context of this athlete's life and ideas, these actions have no religious significance.

Harned Affidavit ¶ 13. Although defendants label this approach "substantive and contextual," the analogy is devoid of substantive analysis and places determinative emphasis on the athlete's subjective characterization of his activity. To inject some substantive analysis into the analogy, the narrator might ask the athlete how he emptied his mind of distraction. If the athlete replied that when he closes his eyes he pictures in his mind's eye a black dot which expands until it blots out all distracting thoughts and noises, then the narrator again would conclude that the action carried no religious significance. If, however, the athlete states that after he closes his eyes he invokes and contacts That, the narrator no doubt would ask a definition of "That." If the athlete answered that "That" is the eternal, omnipresent source of everything in the universe, the narrator might respond, "oh, then you were praying." The athlete would answer: "Oh, no. Prayers are directed to God, which is a projection of the human imagination of an ideal and around which the theologies and religions of the world have grown. There's nothing religious about That. That is an objective reality. I know because I contact it frequently and it helps me." Although the athlete steadfastly and sincerely denies the religiosity of his action, it is doubtful that the narrator would have any hesitation in concluding that the athlete had engaged in what society would recognize as a religious activity. The difference in interpretation does not depend on the sincerity or cognition of the athlete. Rather, the difference is semantical. The athlete is cognizant of his action and sincerely believes that he has contacted "That." He fails to characterize the activity as religious because he believes religions to consist of moral precepts and rituals and an abstraction known as God. The narrator thus would be faced with a situation in which the questioned action had no religious significance in the eyes of the athlete, but clearly would be viewed as religious by society. The difference derives from the different definitions of religion held by the athlete and by society.

As noted by defendants' expert, "religion is notoriously difficult to define." Harned Affidavit ¶ 7. Judge (now Chief Justice) Burger has noted that resort to dictionary definitions reveals that "the terms 'religion' and 'religious' in ordinary usage are not rigid concepts." *Washington Ethical Society v. District of Columbia*, 101 U.S.App.D.C. 371, 249 F.2d 127, 129 (1957). Subjective characterizations of actions and beliefs as religious or scientific or philosophical will vary among individuals because of their varying concepts of religion or science or philosophy. To allot "critical," Harned Affidavit ¶ 21; Rao Affidavit ¶ 21, or determinative weight on the question whether or not an activity or belief is "religious" under the first amendment to the proponents' subjective characterizations of their activities and beliefs would be to inject a variable into the first amendment test which would preclude a fair and uniform standard. Under this approach, courts would be bound to accept the proponents' representations of its activities and beliefs as religious or secular unless the court determined by evaluating the proponents' demeanors in the witness box that the proponents were insincere in their characterizations of their activities and beliefs. The courts thus would be forced to examine and to accept the intellectual classification system of each proponent of certain activities or beliefs. The only inquiry left to the courts would be into the sincerity with which the proponents hold their systems of classification. "Religion" under the first amendment would take on a different meaning in each case, and similar or virtually identical practices would be religious or not religious under the first amendment depending on the classification system of a particular proponent. For example, one of the clergymen meditators deposed as a fact witness on behalf of defendants testified that "[r]eligion to me, is my personal relationship to God. The concepts about Gods in other religions are philosophy." Roberts Deposition at 85. If this clergyman were to offer a course in the philosophical and moral teachings of a religion other than his own in a public high school, some taxpayers no doubt would sue under the establishment clause to enjoin the teaching of the course. In deciding whether or not the teachings were religious, if the court were required to place determinative weight on the characterization of the teachings by the clergyman and his students, then the court would be bound to rule that a system of teachings considered by society to be religious are not religious under the first amendment. In the context of the life and ideas of the clergyman and his students, to whom the teachings were presented as philosophical, the teachings carry no religious significance; they are merely philosophical discourses. A substantive analysis of the teachings, of course, would tend to show their religious nature and a court certainly would be justified in finding the course "religious" under the first amendment despite the sincere characterization by the clergyman of the teachings as secular philosophy.

In a vein similar to defendants' clergyman-fact witness, defendant Jarvis testified to an intensely personal and subjective definition of God: "To me, God is a personal appreciation, something that is developed in my heart and mind with respect to my relationship and communication with my creator, and it falls into my religious development because I include God within my own religious life."[21] Jarvis Deposition at 1049. In contradistinction to God, "a personal appreciation" of his creator, defendant Jarvis defined creative intelligence as an objectively demonstrable phenomenon. *Id.* at 878. If Mr. Jarvis believes that his religion derives from "a personal appreciation" of his creator, then it is not surprising that he would fail to view what he believes to be an objectively demonstrable phenomenon and the teachings thereon to be religious in nature.

The problem of placing heavy emphasis on subjective characterizations of certain beliefs and activities by the proponents of those beliefs and activities is illustrated by *Welsh v. United States*, 398 U.S. 333, 90 S.Ct. 1792, 26 L.Ed.2d 308 (1970). Welsh sought classification as a conscientious objector under section 6(j) of the Universal Military Training and Service Art. Section 6(j) allowed classification of a registrant as a conscientious objector only if his objection to war sprang from religious beliefs. Although Welsh disavowed that his conscientious objection to war derived from religious beliefs, the Supreme Court held that Welsh's beliefs were religious within the meaning of the Act. The Court of Appeals had relied on Welsh's disavowal of a religious basis for his objection in upholding the Appeal Board's denial of conscientious objector status to Welsh. In reversing the Court of Appeals, the Supreme Court stated that the lower court had placed:

undue emphasis on the registrant's interpretation of his own beliefs. The Court's statement in [*United States v.*] *Seeger* that a registrant's characterization of his own belief as "religious" should carry great weight does not imply that his declaration that his views are nonreligious should be treated similarly. When a registrant states that his objections to war are "religious," that information is highly relevant to the question of the function his beliefs have in his life. But very few registrants are fully aware of the broad scope of the word "religious" as used in § 6(j), and accordingly a registrant's statement that his beliefs are nonreligious is a highly unreliable guide for those charged with administering the exemption.

Id. at 341, 90 S.Ct. at 1797. The Court also noted that Welsh had amended his original disavowal through a letter to his Appeal Board which stated that his beliefs "were certainly religious in the ethical sense of the word." *Id.*

The unreliability of proponents' characterizations of their actions and beliefs is illustrated by the instant case. The first organization in the country to offer instruction in the technique of Transcendental Meditation was incorporated in California in 1959 by Maharishi Mahesh Yogi and others under the name of the Spiritual Regeneration Movement Foundation. Jarvis Deposition at 858, 861. Until 1965, the Spiritual Regeneration Movement Foundation was the only organization in the United States which offered instruction in Maharishi Mahesh Yogi's teachings. *Id.* at 852. Defendant Jarvis served as secretary of this corporation from 1963 to 1965. *Id.* at 854. One of the articles of the certificate of incorporation, as amended, of the Spiritual Regeneration Movement Foundation stated that "this corporation is a religious one, the educational purpose shall be to give instruction in a simple system of meditation." *Id.* at 861. The proponents of SCI/TM before the court today characterize their activities as secular in nature.

To the extent that the standard recommended by defendants places critical or determinative weight on the subjective characterization of the proponents of their activities and beliefs, it must be rejected. The inappropriateness of a standard which places such importance on the proponents' characterization of their beliefs and activities is particularly apparent in the context of an establishment clause case in which the proponents have enlisted the aid of governmental entities in the propagation of their beliefs, teachings, theories, and activities. While the characterization of proponents is properly admissible evidence, proponents cannot propagate concepts which society recognizes as religious in nature merely because the proponents view the concepts as secular.

The court finds it unnecessary to improvise an unprecedented definition of religion under the first amendment because it appears that this case is governed by the teachings of prior Supreme Court decisions. Careful inspection of the facts in this suit reveal that the novel aspects of the case are more apparent than real.

The textbook clearly teaches[22] and assumes that there exists and has existed eternally an unmanifested or uncreated field of life which is unbounded or infinite. This field of life is present everywhere, both within and without everything in the universe; it permeates everything and every being and is the ultimate reality of everything in the universe. This field of life is active in the form of "creative intelligence," is the source of all power in the universe, has "unlimited power," and encompasses all knowledge. This field of life is pure and perfect and contains all qualities of the universe in their pure, perfect, and infinite form. This field of life is alternately termed perfection of existence, bliss, and intelligence. This field of being contains love, justice, and truth in their pure and infinite forms. Contact with this field of being bestows upon individuals the ability to choose between right and wrong spontaneously, without regard to moral codes and laws. T at 180. Manifestly, the textbook describes some sort of ultimate reality which in its various forms is given the name "god" in common usage. Over a dozen years ago, a unanimous Supreme Court took judicial cognizance of "the ever-broadening understanding of the modern religious community" concerning the concept of God. *United States v. Seeger*, 380 U.S. 163, 180, 85 S.Ct. 850, 861, 13 L.Ed.2d 733 (1965). The Court noted that "[t]he eminent Protestant theologian, Dr. Paul Tillich ... identified God not as a projection 'out there' or beyond the skies but as the ground of our very being." *Id.* The Court then quoted Dr. Tillich as follows:

I have written of the God above the God of theism .... In such a state [of self-affirmation] the God of both religious and theological language disappears. But something remains, namely, the seriousness of that doubt in which meaning within meaningless is affirmed. The source of this affirmation of meaning within meaningless, of certitude within doubt, is not the God of traditional theism but the "God above God," the power of being, which works through those who have no name for it, not even the name God.

Id., quoting P. Tillich, II Systematic Theology 12

(1957).

The Court followed this excerpt with a quotation from a contemporaneous pronouncement of the Ecumenical Council of the Catholic Church:

Ever since primordial days, numerous peoples have had a certain perception of that hidden power which hovers over the course of things and over the events that make up the lives of men; some have even come to know of a Supreme Being and Father.

*   *   *

The Church regards with sincere reverence those ways of action and of life, precepts and teachings which, although they differ from the ones she sets forth, reflect nonetheless a ray of that Truth which enlightens all men.

Id. at 182, 85 S.Ct. at 862, *quoting* Council Daybook, Vatican II, 3d Sess. 282 (1965).

Finally the Court quoted the views of a leader in the Ethical Culture Movement on that Movement's conception of the term "God:"

What ultimate reality is we do not know; but we have the faith that it expresses itself in the human world as the power which inspires in men moral purpose.

*   *   *

Thus the "God" that we love is not the figure on the great white throne, but the perfect pattern, envisioned by faith, of humanity as it should be, purged of the evil elements which retard its progress toward "the knowledge, love and practice of the right."

Id. at 183, 85 S.Ct. at 863, *quoting* D. Muzzey, Ethics As a Religion (1951).

In his concurring opinion, Mr. Justice Douglas outlined concepts of "god" as expounded in Hinduism and Buddhism. Concerning Hindu conceptions of "god," Mr. Justice Douglas notes:

Though Hindu religion encompasses the worship of many Deities, it believes in only one single God, the eternally existent One Being with his manifold attributes and manifestations.

*   *   *

Philosophically, the Supreme Being is the transcendental Reality which is Truth, Knowledge, and Bliss. It is the source of the entire universe.

Id. at 189–90, 85 S.Ct. 866 (Douglas, J., concurring).
Mr. Justice Douglas continued:

Buddhism—whose advent marked the reform of Hinduism—continued somewhat the same concept [of God or Brahman]. As stated by Nancy Wilson Ross, "God—if I may borrow that word for a moment—the universe, and man are one indissolu-

ble existence, one total whole. Only THIS—capital THIS—is. Anything and everything that appears to us as an individual entity or phenomenon, whether it be a planet or an atom, a mouse or a man, is but a temporary manifestation of THIS in form; every activity that takes place, whether it be birth or death, loving or eating breakfast, is but a temporary manifestation of THIS in activity. When we look at things this way, naturally we cannot believe that each individual person has been endowed with a special and individual soul or self. Each one of us is but a cell, as it were, in the body of the Great Self, a cell that comes into being, performs its functions, and passes away, transformed into another manifestation. Though we have temporary individuality, that temporary, limited individuality is not either a true self or our true self. Our true self is the Great Self; our true body is the Body of Reality, or the Dharmakaya, to give it its technical Buddhist name.

*   *   *

. . . if "God" is taken to mean a personal Creator of the universe, then the Buddhist has no interest in the concept. *Id.*, p. 39. But if "God" means something like the state of oneness with God as described by some Christian mystics, then the Buddhist surely believes in "God," since this state is almost indistinguishable from the Buddhist conception of Nirvana, "the supreme Reality; . . . the eternal, hidden and incomprehensible Peace."

Id., pp. 39–40.

Id. at 190–91, 85 S.Ct. at 866, *citing* Conze, Buddhism (1959) (Douglas, J., concurring).

The foregoing quotations, of course, are not relied upon by this court for their technical accuracy. Rather, the quotations demonstrate the substantive content attributed to the term "God" by contemporary society. It cannot be doubted that the concepts encompassed by this substantive content are recognized as "religious" concepts. The similarity, indeed, virtual identity, between some of the concepts used in the quotations to describe "God" and the terms used in the textbook to describe creative intelligence is unmistakable. For example, compare the Buddhist concept that "[o]ur true self is the Great Self," with the textbook statement that "[w]e know that the true nature of the self is unbounded pure creative intelligence, bliss-consciousness—that most self-sufficient field of life." T at 121. Compare the Buddhist concept that "God—if I may borrow that term for a moment—the universe, and man are one indissoluble existence," with the textbook statement that "[t]he universe is a continuous, unified whole, an unbroken field of creative intelligence." T at 137. Compare the Buddhist concept that "[a]nything and everything that appears to us as an individual entity or phenomenon, is but a temporary manifestation of THIS. . . . " with the textbook statements that "everything in creation is nothing other than the expression of unmanifest creative intelligence," T at 260, and that "all aspects of life [are] manifestations of unmanifest creative intelligence." T at 262. Compare the Buddhist concept of Nirvana as "the eternal, hidden and incomprehensible Peace," with the textbook's description of the field of pure creative intelligence as the eternal, T at 242, unmanifest, T at 30, unbounded, T at 24, silent, T at 82, nonchanging, T at 94, immovable, T at 40, field of unbounded harmony, T at 138.

Compare the Hindu concept of the Supreme Being as Truth, Knowledge, and Bliss with the textbook statements asserting that the field of pure creative intelligence is "an ocean of bliss," T at 152, "a field of unlimited happiness," T at 32, the basis of all knowledge, T at 97, "the home of all knowledge," T at 149, and truth, T at 76, 81. Compare the Hindu concept that the Supreme Being is the source of the entire universe with the textbook statement that creative intelligence lies at the basis of every individual life and of everything, T at 189, and is the source of all existence. T at 171.

Compare the Catholic concept of God as Truth with the textbook's indication that the field of pure creative intelligence is truth. T at 76, 81. Compare the Protestant theologian's concept of God as "the very ground of our being" with the textbook's description of the field of pure creative intelligence as "the very source of life-energy," T at 98, and the "universal basis of life," T at 188–89, and "the stable foundation of our life [sic]," T at 271.

These concepts concerning God or a supreme being of some sort are manifestly religious when they appear as tenets of Christianity or Buddhism or Hinduism. These concepts do not shed that religiosity merely because they are presented as a philosophy or as a science.[23] Similarly, whether an unmanifest and eternal field of life with all the characteristics attributed to it as the textbook attributes to creative intelligence is called a supreme being, god, the ultimate reality, Brahman, Tao, Allah, Nirvana, THIS, creative intelligence and the field of creative intelligence, the Father, Son, and Holy Spirit, it, or the One is immaterial to determining the religious nature of the concept; although the precise conceptions or definitions of the ultimate reality or supreme being will differ from religion to religion, the religious nature of the concept is incontrovertible. Whether "God" is considered an ultimate universal principle or being or essence or entity or field of life on which the universe is based, has no bearing on the religious nature of the concept. It cannot be doubted that concepts of "God" or an ultimate level of life or ultimate reality are religious concepts.[24] E. g., Engel v. Vitale, supra; Tor-

caso v. Watkins, supra; Seeger v. United States, supra; DeSpain v. DeKalb County Community School District, supra.

The puja chant is an invocation of a deified human being who has been dead for almost a quarter of a century. An icon of this deified human being rests on the back of a table on which is placed a tray and offerings. During the singing of the chant, which identifies the items on the table and in the room as offerings to this deity, some of these offerings are lifted from the table by the chanter and placed onto the tray. It cannot be doubted that the invocation of a deity or divine being is a prayer. Engel v. Vitale, supra, 370 U.S. at 424, 82 S.Ct. 1261. The religious nature of prayer has been recognized by many courts, e. g., Engel v. Vitale, supra;[25] DeSpain v. DeKalb County Community School District, supra, and the proposition needs no further demonstration here.

A recognition of the religious nature of the teachings and activities questioned is largely determinative of this suit since the entanglement of both the federal and state governmental entities is apparent. Under the establishment clause, a three-part test has evolved to determine whether governmental action in regard to religious activity constitutes a violation of the constitutional prohibition. In order to avoid contravening the establishment clause, the law or governmental action in question

> first, must reflect a clearly secular legislative purpose, second, must have a primary effect that neither advances nor inhibits religion, and third, must avoid excessive government entanglement with religion.

Committee for Public Education v. Nyquist, supra, 413 U.S. at 773, 93 S.Ct. at 2965. (citations omitted).

The secular purpose of the governmental associations with the SCI/TM course apparently is to make available to public school students the alleged benefits of the technique of Transcendental Meditation. Practice of the technique is alleged by its proponents to reduce stress in individuals; the reduction in stress allegedly would result in an increase in educability and sociability among the students taking the course. This purpose appears to be secular. In effecting this secular purpose, however, the governmental agencies did not merely offer a course in the technique of Transcendental Meditation. In fact, the teaching and practice of the technique occupies a minor fraction of the class time of the SCI/TM course. Instruction in the technique takes less than twenty minutes. Aaron Affidavit at 2. Ten or fifteen minutes of each class are spent in practicing the technique, Metropole Deposition at 416. Approximately 70 percent of the class time is devoted to the teaching of the theory of the Science of Creative Intelligence, the focal point of which is the textbook. As stated earlier, the textbook posits that during the practice of Transcendental Meditation the meditator comes into contact with the field of pure creative intelligence, "the ultimate reality of every object," T at 154. As outlined above, most of the book is devoted to attributing various characteristics to the field of pure creative intelligence and creative intelligence. As demonstrated above, the characteristics which are attributed to pure creative intelligence are parallel to characteristics which are attributed to the supreme being or ultimate reality by mankind. In effecting the secular purpose of reducing stress among public school students, however, the governmental entities have not merely introduced the teaching of a simple technique of meditation whereby the meditator contemplates a meaningless sound. Rather, the SCI/TM course teaches that the meaningless sound is merely a vehicle used by the meditator to contact directly the "perfection of existence," a level of life or being beyond and unmanifest to the mundane universe and observable or knowable solely through direct "contact" as outlined by the textbook,[26] or possibly through its manifestations, i. e., the universe. Owing to the religious nature of the concept of the field of pure creative intelligence and creative intelligence, it is apparent that the governmental agencies have sought to effect a secular goal by the propagation of a religious concept, a belief in an unmanifest field of life which is perfect, pure, and infinite. In addition, students wishing to learn the technique of Transcendental Meditation are compelled to attend a religious ceremony, the puja. These means of effecting ostensibly secular ends are prohibited by the establishment clause. *Abington School District v. Schempp, supra; Engel v. Vitale, supra.*

Applying the second prong of the *Nyquist* test, the promulgation of a belief in the existence of a pure, perfect, infinite, and unmanifest field of life clearly has a primary effect of advancing religion and religious concepts. *Abington School District v. Schempp, supra; Engel v. Vitale, supra.* Under the final prong of the test, the aid given to the SCI/TM course by both the federal government and the state of New Jersey clearly constitutes an "excessive government entanglement in religion." *Lemon v. Kurtzman,* 403 U.S. 602, 91 S.Ct. 2105, 29 L.Ed.2d 745 (1971). The course is offered as part of the curriculum at five New Jersey public high schools and the federal government has provided funds to aid in the establishment of the SCI/TM course in the public schools.

The SCI/TM course fails to pass muster under the three-pronged test enunciated in *Nyquist* and thus violates the establishment clause of the first amendment.[27]

SUMMARY JUDGMENT

Plaintiffs move for partial summary judgment under Rule 56(a) to enjoin the teaching of SCI/TM in the New Jersey public schools. Rule 56(c) provides in part:

> The judgment sought shall be rendered forthwith if the pleadings, depositions, answers to interrogatories, and admissions on file, together with the affidavits, if any, show that there is no genuine issue as to any material fact and that the moving party is entitled to a judgment as a matter of law.

The record before the court on this motion for summary judgment is unusually complete. The court has in evidence the 296-page textbook used in the course, a detailed description of the puja and defendants' translation of the chant sung therein, hundreds of pages of deposition testimony by two people who taught four of the five SCI/TM courses in New Jersey high schools, and other depositions and affidavits. This large quantity of evidence fails to reveal any dispute between the parties as to the operative facts. Defendants, however, argue that the court cannot and should not grant plaintiffs' motion for summary judgment. Defendants advance essentially three arguments in support of their position.

First, defendants argue that a trial must be held to determine the sincerity with which defendants categorize their teachings as being "not religious." For purposes of this summary judgment motion, the court, of course, accepts the sincerity of defendants' categorization of their teaching as not religious and their statement that only a tiny fraction of the more than seven thousand trained TM teachers in the United States view the SCI/TM course as religious, Jarvis Affidavit ¶¶ 16, 23. The reasons why defendants' characterization of their teachings cannot be determinative of the religious nature of those teachings were stated *supra* at 1315–1320.

In connection with their first argument, defendants state that "[i]n *Theriault v. Silber,* 391 F.Supp. 578 (W.D.Tex.1975) and *United States v. Kuch,* 288 F.Supp. 439 (D.D.C.1968) it was determined that certain organizations were not religious because they did not sincerely hold the beliefs they professed." Db at 34. This statement raises a different issue of sincerity, the sincerity with which the alleged adherents of certain activities or beliefs profess those beliefs. Plaintiffs, of course, do not contest the sincerity with which defendants adhere to their teachings, such as the teaching that the practice of Transcendental Meditation brings the practitioner into direct contact with an unmanifest, eternal, pure, and perfect field of life.

Second, defendants argue that the court should not grant plaintiffs' motion for summary judgment because the court is faced with a novel issue of law in that no court previously has set forth explicit criteria, the possession of which unmistakably denominate beliefs, teachings, or activities as religious within the meaning of the first amendment. The courts have recognized certain teachings and beliefs as religious in nature.

While defendants' teachings wear novel labels, the underlying teachings fall well within the concepts which courts previously have found to be religious.

In this posture, it is difficult to see the need for a bench trial. Counsel for defendants indicated at oral argument that the factual record is unlikely to be supplemented by a bench trial. The principal deviser of the Science of Creative Intelligence and the primary teacher of the technique of Transcendental Meditation, Maharishi Mahesh Yogi, is unlikely to testify at trial.[28] Defendants' counsel stated at oral argument that their only anticipated addition to the record now before the court was the testimony of two or three experts on religion. The experts would be called upon to give their opinions as to definitions of the term "religion" and their interpretations of the SCI/TM course. Defendants' counsel acknowledged at oral argument that the expert opinions could be reduced to writing, and defendants have submitted the affidavits of two experts in religion in opposing plaintiffs' motions for summary judgment.

In these affidavits, defendants' experts point out a longstanding debate among academicians as to "the virtues of a functionalist/inclusive as opposed to a substantive/exclusive definition of religion." Harned Affidavit ¶ 7. Defendants' experts urge the court to construct a definition of religion which would exclude theories or practices which (1) did not contain certain attributes, such as, priests, houses of worship, symbols, dogmas concerning after-life and salvation, and (2) were not characterized by its adherents as religious. Defendants' experts state no rationale for this court's construction of an "exclusive" definition of religion except that "functionalist" definitions of religion tend to be overinclusive. Defendants' experts also admit that their narrow "exclusive" approach to defining religion is inappropriate under the free exercise clause, but maintain its validity for purposes of the establishment clause. *Id.* ¶ 11. *See* pages 1315–1320 *supra*.

The approach to defining religion offered by defendants' experts is directly contrary to holdings of both the Supreme Court and lower federal courts. *E. g., Engel v. Vitale, supra; Torcaso v. Watkins, supra; DeSpain v. DeKalb County Community School District 428, supra.* The courts never have excluded certain beliefs or practices from the application of the religion clauses on the ground that the beliefs or practices lacked this or that type of teaching or practice which is connected to conventionally recognized religions. In addition, the courts have deemed activities and teachings religious even though the activities did not derive from a particular religious sect. *E. g., Engel v. Vitale, supra; Torcaso v. Watkins, supra.* An expert's definition of religion never can be determinative and can be of only tangential relevance to the meaning of constitutional terms. The court is interested in the term religion as it is used in the Constitution and has

no interest in attempting to decide an academic dispute among theologians as to the best approach to defining religion for their professional purposes. For example, defendants' experts assert that "[e]lements commonly associated with religion," such as, clergy, places of worship, explicit moral codes, are not part of SCI/TM. *See* Harned Affidavit ¶ 24; Rao Affidavit ¶ 23. None of these elements need be present, however, for a court to determine that a practice or belief is religious within the meaning of the first amendment.[29] *See, e.g., Torcaso v. Watkins, supra.*

While expert opinion is invaluable in certain cases, a court, in dealing with a constitutional term, must be governed more by prior judicial findings than by the opinions of experts.[30] Since the concepts being taught by defendants repeatedly have been recognized as religious by the courts, *see supra* at 1320–23, the conclusions of experts that SCI/TM does not constitute "religion as I know it," Harned Affidavit ¶ 30; Rao Affidavit ¶ 27, fails to raise a material issue of fact which would necessitate a bench trial. In addition, the prior judicial recognition of teachings such as those of defendants as religious dispels the novelty of the legal question, and, thus, the necessity of a bench trial.

Finally, defendants argue that plaintiffs' motion for summary judgment cannot be granted unless the court infers that the teachings of the SCI/TM course are religious within the meaning of the first amendment. Defendants point out that all inferences to be drawn from the underlying facts on a motion for summary judgment "must be viewed in the light most favorable to the party opposing the motion." *Adickes v. S. H. Kress & Co.,* 398 U.S. 144, 158–59, 90 S.Ct. 1598, 1609, 26 L.Ed.2d 142 (1970), *quoting United States v. Diebold, Inc.,* 369 U.S. 654, 655, 82 S.Ct. 993, 8 L.Ed.2d 176 (1962); *Goodman v. Mead Johnson & Co.,* 534 F.2d 566, 573 (3d Cir. 1976). The courts in all three cases reversed summary judgments on the ground that "[a] study of the record in this light leads us to believe that inferences contrary to those drawn by the trial court might be permissible." *United States v. Diebold, Inc., supra,* at 655, 82 S.Ct. at 994. In light of the prior judicial recognition of teachings such as those of defendants as religious, no inference is possible except that the teaching of SCI/TM and the puja are religious in nature; no other inference is "permissible" or reasonable, especially because the court is dealing with the meaning of a constitutional term and not with a factual dispute such as was involved in *Adickes, supra, Diebold, supra,* and *Goodman, supra.*

Although defendants have submitted well over 1500 pages of briefs, affidavits, and deposition testimony in opposing plaintiffs' motion for summary judgment, defendants have failed to raise the slightest doubt as to the facts or as to the religious nature of the teachings of the Science of Creative Intelligence and the puja. The teaching of the SCI/TM course in New

Jersey public high schools violates the establishment clause of the first amendment, and its teaching must be enjoined.

Plaintiffs will submit an order in conformity with this opinion with consent as to form within 10 days.

NOTES

1. Plaintiffs have been unable to effect service of process on Maharishi Mahesh Yogi, apparently a citizen of India, on account of his prolonged absence from this country.
2. Creative intelligence arises out of the field of pure creative intelligence. The court notes the distinction, but for purposes of discussion the two entities will be considered as complimentary portions of a single entity. *See* discussion at 1290–1291, 1292–1293 *infra*.
3. "Mantra" has been defined as a meaningless sound which is essential to the practice of Transcendental Meditation and which is "known" to have a positive effect on the nervous system. Metropole Deposition at 352; Aaron Deposition at 664; Jarvis Deposition at 886. Defendants attach great importance to the selection of mantras for individuals and deny that use of a randomly selected sound in meditation will produce the beneficial effects alleged to result from the practice of their method of meditation. *See* Jarvis Deposition at 887–90.
4. *See* N.J.S.A. 18A:6–34 *et seq.*
5. The puja is a ceremony at which each student was given his or her mantra, the sound aid essential to practicing the TM technique.
6. The letter "T" in the citations represents the textbook used in the New Jersey high schools, "Science of Creative Intelligence for Secondary Education: First-Year Course."
7. The practice of TM by a person who has attained cosmic consciousness may lead to further refinement of his nervous system and increased faculties of perception until a state called unity consciousness is reached. If a person, through the practice of TM, develops his faculties of perception to their full potential and attains the highest level of refinement of his nervous system, the person is said to have attained the highest form of consciousness, which is called interchangeably either God consciousness or Brahman consciousness. Jarvis Deposition at 866b & 866e–f; Aaron Deposition at 650–57. Defendant Aaron, a SCI/TM teacher at two of the New Jersey high schools, stated at deposition that she did not mention unity consciousness or Brahman or God consciousness to her classes. Aaron Deposition at 660.
8. The practice of Transcendental Meditation automatically bestows upon a practitioner the ability to tell what is right from what is wrong:

   > A more and more exact sense of judgment between right and wrong comes naturally as one's consciousness grows, but when consciousness is highest and creative intelligence is infused into the nature of one's mind to the fullest extent, the mind knows without doubt what is right and wrong. By natural inclination and natural taste, wrong actions and wrong thoughts are not even considered. So the real art of performing right action is in having a mind that is right at all times. To be right, the mind has to be in that state of lasting contentment and purity which alone belongs to the state of cosmic consciousness.

   T at 180. The textbook states that the laws and traditions of one's culture and religion provide guidelines "to proper modes of thinking and behavior" prior to the attainment of cosmic consciousness. T at 180–81. Once a practitioner of Transcendental Meditation achieves cosmic consciousness, however, mundane moral codes apparently are superfluous. *See id.*
9. Defendant Jarvis also acknowledged that pure creative intelligence is the source of religion, philosophy, and knowledge. Jarvis Deposition at 1019.
10. Defendant Jarvis apparently was referring to only the field of pure creative intelligence in the quoted sentence. While the field of pure creative intelligence remains unmanifest and silent, according to the textbook, no such passivity is attributed to creative intelligence by the textbook. As noted in footnote 2, *supra*, the court is regarding the field of pure creative intelligence and creative intelligence as complementary aspects of the same entity.
11. In addition to the ascription of activity to creative intelligence as an entity, the textbook ascribes activity to certain qualities of creative intelligence. The specific qualities of creative intelligence are the means through which creative intelligence "expresses itself." T at 258, 13. For example, the textbook states that "[t]he functioning of creative intelligence is such that under similar circumstances, similar results occur. . . . There is something definite; nothing is random, and it is this specific value of creative intelligence that automatically carries out evolution everywhere." T at 64. "The progressive and evolutionary qualities of creative intelligence are at the basis of all growth everywhere; they continually propel life on increasing steps of progress towards the fullness of life." T at 42. "[T]he functioning of the orderly quality of [creative intelligence] reveals the intelligence governing individual and cosmic life." T at 60. "Creative intelligence is precise and truthful. . . . It is this precise quality of creative intelligence that structures the finer levels of existence and unfolds the truth of life to our awareness." T at 72. "The precise and truthful qualities of creative intelligence direct the growth of everything in nature with precision and exactness." T at 80. "[T]he precise quality of creative intelligence structures with minute detail all the manifest expressions of life, while the truthful quality of creative intelligence provides the nonchanging platform from which these changing expressions arise." T at 82. "It is this efficient quality of creative intelligence that kindly and effortlessly guides everything to its goal in the fullness of life." T at 108. "The harmonizing and diversifying qualities of creative intelligence enable every thing in nature to fulfill its own specific role while contributing to the harmonious functioning of the whole." T at 140. "The integrative quality of creative intelligence promotes the progress, and evolution of all values of life—physical and nonphysical, abstract and concrete." T at 170.

    > Throughout creation there is the expression of life, and underneath there is stability. The wide range of variety in creation is based on the nonvariable unity of existence, intelligence. To be able to put the changing and nonchanging aspects of life together—this is the integrative quality of creative intelligence.

    T at 172. "The generous and economical qualities of creative intelligence endlessly and precisely give and give and give until every aspect of life is full to overflowing." T at 206. "The generous and economical qualities of creative intelligence provide abundance of wealth with precision in every bit of life." T at 213. Through Transcendental Meditation, "[t]he clean and purifying qualities of creative intelligence cleanse the body, senses, mind, and heart simultaneously." T at 224. "The liberating and responsible qualities of creative intelligence make such diverse expression of life grow freely within the dignity of its own individual structure." T at 238. "The creative and traditional qualities of creative intelligence provide patterns of change through which everything quickly progresses to the fullness of life." T at 240. "The holistic and fulfilling qualities of creative intelligence bring fulfillment to life by enabling us to perceive the fullness of life in every individual expression of life." T at 258.

12. In apparent contradiction to the statement in his affidavit, Mr. Jarvis, president of WPEC-US, testified at deposition that creative intelligence is an objectively demonstrable phenomenon, "demonstrable in its expression. For instance, I move my hand." Jarvis Deposition at 878. Mr. Jarvis also testified at deposition that SCI/TM was not a philosophy. *Id.* at 1016.

13. At other points, the textbook refers to "bliss-consciousness" as a state of mind which can be achieved through Transcendental Meditation. *E. g.,* T at 95. Presumably, this use of "bliss-consciousness" differs from its use as a synonym for creative intelligence. This situation illustrates a recurrent technique of the textbook, which is the attribution of different meanings to identical, seemingly technical terms, such as "bliss-consciousness" and "fullness," in different sections of the textbook. No doubt, this technique contributed to the fact that no high school class in New Jersey managed to complete more than nine of the 32 lessons contained in the textbook. Jarvis Affidavit at ¶ 32. The vagueness engendered by this technique is compounded by the fact that the textbook, although labelled a "Science" and now called "essays in philosophy," is virtually devoid of reliable definitions. The 296-page textbook defines one term: creative intelligence. All other definitions apparently are left to classroom discussion as all other terms are undefined or are defined capriciously, varying from sentence to sentence. An example of whimsical definition occurs on page 23 of the textbook. The first sentence on page 23 reads: "Perceiving the fullness of life means perceiving creative intelligence functioning in every expression of life." Thus it appears that fullness of life means perceiving creative intelligence functioning in every aspect of life. A few paragraphs later on the same page, however, the textbook states that "[t]he fullness of life is already within us—it only needs to be enlivened." If fullness of life means creative intelligence functioning in every aspect of life, however, how can the fullness of life be within us waiting to be enlivened? The next page of the textbook states that it is the field of pure creative intelligence that is within us and it is creative intelligence which "only needs to be enlivened." T at 24. It thus appears that fullness of life is a synonym for creative intelligence instead of a synonym for creative intelligence functioning in every expression of life. The paragraph which begins by informing the reader that the fullness of life is within us waiting to be enlivened, however, continues as follows:

> Fullness of life means making use of the fullness of creative intelligence—living a life that is always creative and interesting, ever lively with new discoveries

and insights, life that is always intelligent, orderly and purposeful, our creative energies being productively channeled into ever greater achievements. Fullness of life means enjoying the full range of our potentialities—inner strength and stability, outer adaptability, ease of expression, and enjoyment. T at 23. Appropriately, the text of lesson one ends three sentences later with the question "[w]hat does fullness of life mean to you?" T at 23. The textbook does not state whether the student is to pick one of the definitions appearing on page 23 or use his imagination to create a definition for himself. In either case, clarity and precision of communication suffer.

As stated earlier, "fullness of life" is the main theme of the three-year curriculum of "The Science of Creative Intelligence," the three sub-themes adopted for each year being "perceiving the fullness of life," "developing the fullness of life," and "living the fullness of life." T at 11. Despite the obvious importance of the term "fullness of life" to an intellectual understanding of the course, the textbook never offers an explicit, reliable definition. In numerous places, the textbook uses "fullness of life" synonymously with creative intelligence or the field of pure creative intelligence. *E. g.,* T at 126. *But see* T at 216, where the textbook states "[l]ove is the fullness of life." The purpose of this nebulous approach to technical terms is never stated, but the lack of precise definition of terms and the use of identical terms for different referents seems an unusual and unnecessarily confusing approach to be taken by an introductory textbook in a science or philosophy course. Other instances of imprecise and poor usage of words occur throughout the textbook. For example, 25 of the 32 lessons in the textbook begin with the words "two qualities of creative intelligence." These words are followed immediately, not by the names of two qualities, but by two adjectives.

14. The same clergyman testified that there was no connection between the teachings embodied in the Science of Creative Intelligence and the technique of Transcendental Meditation. *See id.* at 71, 99. The clergyman apparently was oblivious to the fact that defendants teach that the Science of Creative Intelligence explains the mechanics of the practice of Transcendental Meditation, including the teaching that the alleged benefits of the practice of Transcendental Meditation derive not from the contemplation of a meaningless sound but from contact with an unmanifest field of life known as the field of pure creative intelligence. *E. g.,* T at 23, 24, 26, 38.

15. This translation was attached to the Prendeville Deposition and was marked as defendants' exhibit AA. This translation is based upon the Sanskrit chant and the translation thereof appearing in a book called "The Holy Tradition," which was written by Maharishi Mahesh Yogi. *See* Jarvis Deposition at 764, 986–88.

16. Maharishi Mahesh Yogi has referred to the divinity of Guru Dev in other contexts. *See* Jarvis Deposition at 811–12.

17. The court is aware that defendant Jarvis, although not an expert in the culture, history, or religions of India, *see* Jarvis Deposition at 908, 1020, testified that it is his personal understanding that the use of the word "Lord" in the term "Lord Narayana" denotes merely "the highest possible human appreciation and esteem [for human beings], like we would say Lord Mountbatten or something like that." Jarvis Deposition at 996. Ignoring for the moment the inaccuracies in this weak analogy and

accepting the statement *arguendo,* Mr. Jarvis' understanding of the word "Lord" when the word is attached to a proper noun can have no application to the term "the Lord" standing alone. In addition, it is impossible to imagine that "the whole galaxy of gods pray [*sic*] for perfection" at the door of "Lord Mountbatten" or at the door of any other titled person.

18. The similarity between the epithets applied to Guru Dev in this chant and the description of the field of pure creative intelligence in the textbook is unmistakable.

19. In addition to the obeisance to "the Lord" and the identification of Guru Dev with this divinity, Guru Dev is depicted in the chant as a Guru in the glory of the three major gods of Hinduism and is said to be a personification of the Supreme Being of Hindu philosophy:

> Guru in the glory of Brahma, Guru in the glory of Vishnu, Guru in the glory of the great Lord Shiva, Guru in the glory of the personified transcendental fulness [*sic*] of Brahman, to Him, to Shri Guru Dev adorned with glory, I bow down.

As stated by Mr. Justice Douglas in *United States v. Seeger,* 380 U.S. 163, 189–90, 83 S.Ct. 850, 865, 13 L.Ed.2d 733, 750 (1965) (Douglas, J., concurring) (emphasis in original):

> In the Hindu *religion* the Supreme Being is conceived in the forms of several cult Deities. The chief of these, which stand for the Hindu Triad, are Brahma, Vishnu and Siva.

* * *

Indian *philosophy,* which comprises several schools of thought, has advanced different theories of the nature of the Supreme Being. According to the Upanishads, Hindu sacred texts, the Supreme Being is described as the power which creates and sustains everything, and to which the created things return upon dissolution. The word which is commonly used in the Upanishads to indicate the Supreme Being is Brahman.

20. Defendants preface this "definitional approach" with the assertion that "the free exercise clause may require a broad definition of religion in order to protect individual liberty; however, the establishment clause has a more narrow scope." Harned Affidavit ¶ 11. This statement by one of defendants' experts in religion is clearly improper and inadmissible under Rule 56(e) because the professor presents no credentials as an expert in constitutional law. Defendants argue that "[u]nlike the free-exercise clause of the First Amendment, the establishment clause does not encompass multifarious heterodox beliefs." Defendants' Second Supplemental Brief at 2. Defendants cite no authority for this assertion and the proposition appears dubious. As stated by Mr. Justice Rutledge:

> "Religion" appears only once in the Amendment. But the word governs two prohibitions and governs them alike. It does not have two meanings, one narrow to forbid "an establishment" and another, much broader, for securing "the free exercise thereof." "Thereof" brings down "religion" with its entire and exact content, no more and no less, from the first into the second guaranty, so that Congress and now the states are as broadly restricted concerning the one as they are regarding the other.
>
> No one would claim today that the Amendment is constricted, in "prohibiting the free exercise" of religion, to securing the free exercise of some formal or creedal observance, of one sect or of many. It secures all forms of religious expression, creedal, sectarian or nonsectarian, wherever and however taking place, except conduct which trenches upon the like freedoms of others or clearly and presently endangers the community's good order and security. . . . The word connotes the broadest content, determined not by the form or formality of the teaching or where it occurs, but by its essential nature regardless of those details.
>
> "Religion" has the same broad significance in the twin prohibition concerning "an establishment." The Amendment was not duplicitous. "Religion" and "establishment" were not used in any formal or technical sense. The prohibition broadly forbids state support, financial or other, of religion in any guise, form or degree.

Everson v. Board of Education, supra, 330 U.S. at 32–33, 67 S.Ct. at 519–520 (Rutledge, J., dissenting). While Mr. Justice Rutledge was speaking for four members of the court in dissent in *Everson,* the majority and dissent agreed that the establishment clause must have a broad interpretation and application. *See Abington School District v. Schempp, supra,* 374 U.S. at 216–17, 83 S.Ct. 1560.

To the extent that the religion clauses differ in the protections afforded, the application of the two clauses of course will differ. For example, the establishment clause has a broader application than does the free exercise clause in the sense that a plaintiff may bring suit under the establishment clause even though he has suffered no injury to or impairment of his religious beliefs while a plaintiff cannot bring suit under the free exercise clause unless he can allege a direct governmental infringement upon his religious beliefs or practices. *See, e. g., Engel v. Vitale, supra,* 370 U.S. at 430–31, 82 S.Ct. 1261; *McGowan v. Maryland, supra,* 366 U.S. at 466–67, 81 S.Ct. 1101 (Frankfurter, J., concurring). The establishment clause protects every individual's right to freedom of belief while the free exercise clause protects the individual's freedom to practice his religion. *See, e. g., Abington School District v. Schempp, supra,* 374 U.S. at 217–18, 83 S.Ct. 1560; *Cantwell v. Connecticut,* 310 U.S. 296, 303–04, 60 S.Ct. 900, 84 L.Ed.2d 1213 (1940).

The case at bar is illustrative of the different functions of the religion clauses. While defendants deny the religious nature of their teachings and activities, the adherents to certain teachings and activities who sought the protection of the free exercise clause never could deny the religious nature of their teachings and activities.

The fact that the religion clauses offer different protections gives no reason to infer that the word "religion," which appears only once in the religion clauses, has a meaning under the establishment clause different from its meaning under the free exercise clause. While it is possible for a group of individuals to attach religious significance to activities which society regards as nonreligious and seek protection for the practice of those activities under the free exercise clause, a court cannot afford that protection unless the activities embody religious teachings. *E. g., People v. Woody,* 61 Cal.2d 716, 40 Cal.Rptr. 69, 394 P.2d 813 (1964) (In Bank). *See* note 26 *infra.* In *Woody,* a group of individuals believed that the eating of peyote put them into direct contact with God. The California Supreme Court held that a state criminal statute proscribing the use of peyote could not be applied to the adherents to this belief because application of the law to them would violate the free exercise clause. If subsequent medical research which revealed that peyote had beneficial properties lead the state to repeal the criminal statute, a public school would be able to teach that peyote has beneficial effects but the school could not teach that use of peyote puts the user in touch with God without violating the establishment clause. The activity is not religious per se, but is religious in light of the beliefs or teachings attached to it.

Similarly, principles which society at large finds beneficial and useful are not religious in nature merely because similar principles are common to the dogmas of many religious sects. For example, a public school could teach its students that it is wrong to steal or murder without violating the establishment clause. The public school could not teach its students to refrain from stealing because God has proscribed it. The principle is not necessarily religious, but becomes religious if taught as a divine law.

21. In this connection, defendant Jarvis also testified that it is his belief that God created the physical universe and human beings. Jarvis Deposition at 1059. When asked if he believed that God created pure creative intelligence, defendant Jarvis expressed uncertainty: "That is a question I have not as yet answered for myself." *Id.* at 1051. Later defendant Jarvis stated: "I can accept the statement that God created pure creative intelligence, but I don't understand it enough to develop that statement." *Id.* at 1060. Defendant Jarvis also attributed a passive role to creative intelligence as the ultimate source of everything in the universe: "It is the source in that it is the ultimate constituent," which God would use to create. *Id.* at 1050. While the field of pure creative intelligence may be inactive, any description of creative intelligence as passive is contradicted directly by the textbook. *See* pages 1292–1293 *supra.*

Defendants call attention to defendant Jarvis' religious views as demonstrative of the lack of religiosity in SCI/TM, Db at 26, and these views illustrate one of the problems with the teachings of the SCI/TM course. While defendant Jarvis is able to accept as a matter of religious faith that God created creative intelligence, he was unable to explain in terms of reason how something that has existed "always," was created by God who also has existed always. The same metaphysical conundrum no doubt would confront some high school students of SCI/TM. In addition, those students who doubt or deny the existence of God or any other unmanifest field of life will be subjected to inculcation of a belief in an unmanifest field of life which is pure, perfect, and unbounded.

22. The court, of course, does not concern itself with the truth or falsity of defendants' teachings. *See United States v. Ballard,* 322 U.S. 78, 85–88, 64 S.Ct. 882, 88 L.Ed. 1148 (1944).

23. A philosophy may well posit the existence of a supreme being without functioning as a religion in the sense of having clergy and houses of worship. For purposes of the first amendment, these philosophies are the functional equivalent of religions. Surely the prohibition of the establishment clause could not be avoided by governmental aid to the inculcation of a belief in a supreme being through philosophical instruction instead of through conventionally recognized religious instruction.

24. Plaintiffs have placed in the record an affidavit of a professor of theology which states that certain attributes, which plaintiffs contend are ascribed to creative intelligence by the World Plan defendants, are possessed exclusively by God in the tradition of both Hebrew and Christian theology. Although defendants ridicule this affidavit as "meaningless," Db at 28, they do not refute it; defendants' only response to the affidavit is a paragraph in the affidavit of a professor of religious studies which entirely misinterprets plaintiffs' affidavit. *See* Harned Affidavit ¶ 29. In light of the discussion *supra* at 1320–1322, however, the court finds no need to rely, and does not rely, on the affidavit in ruling on plaintiffs' motion for partial summary judgment.

25. In *Engel v. Vitale, supra,* the New York State Board of Regents composed and recommended the use of a prayer. Only the teacher of each class was required to recite the prayer. *Id.* at 438, 82 S.Ct. 1261 (Douglas, J., concurring). Attendance by the students was not mandatory. *Id.* at 423 n.2, 82 S.Ct. 1261. In the instant case, attendance by all students taking the elective SCI/TM course is mandatory. The students also are asked to participate in the ceremony to the extent of bringing flowers, fruit, and a handkerchief which are used as offerings to the deified Guru Dev during the puja chant. The compulsion placed on students in the SCI/TM course to attend a religious ceremony thus is greater than that placed on the students in *Engel.* While the prayer in *Engel* was recited daily and the puja is performed only once for each student, the prayer in *Engel* was recited without any of the trappings which are part of the puja. The fact that the puja chant is sung in Sanskrit, of course, has no bearing on the religious nature of the ceremony.

26. The distinction between teaching that the practice of Transcendental Meditation will bring about certain physiological and psychological changes in the meditator and teaching that the practice of Transcendental Meditation brings the meditator into direct contact with a pure, perfect, and infinite field of life, the field of pure creative intelligence, is illustrated by *People v. Woody,* 61 Cal.2d 716, 40 Cal.Rptr. 69, 394 P.2d 813 (1964) (In Bank). Defendants in *Woody* were convicted of violation of California laws prohibiting the use of certain narcotic drugs and hallucinogens. Defendants appealed the conviction on the ground that application of the statute to them impinged on their first amendment right to the free exercise of religion because the eating of peyote, a hallucinogen, was part of their religious practices. In addition to, or concurrent with, the psychological changes undergone by a peyote eater, defendants believed that "those who partake of peyote enter into direct contact with God." 40 Cal.Rptr. at 73, 394 P.2d at 817. Although the California Supreme Court recognized the right of the state, pursuant to its police power, to proscribe the use of peyote when taken merely to produce hallucinations and other psychological changes in the user, the court held that the law could not be applied to defendants because defendants believed that partaking of peyote not only produced hallucinations but also brought them into direct contact with God.

Similarly, defendants here do not teach that use of a mantra merely will bring about certain beneficial physiological and psychological changes; rather, defendants teach that a mantra is a vehicle which will bring a practitioner of Transcendental Meditation into direct contact with an unmanifest, pure, perfect, eternal, and infinite field of life, the field of pure creative intelligence. The fact that a practitioner of Transcendental Meditation may undergo certain physiological and psychological changes without believing that he is contacting with the field of pure creative intelligence, *see, e. g.,* Essrig Deposition at 70, 71, 99, just as an eater of peyote can experience hallucinations without believing that he is contacting God, does not make defendants' teachings any less religious.

27. In light of the court's holding under the Federal Constitution, plaintiffs' claims of violation of the New Jersey Constitution need not be addressed.

28. Plaintiffs' various attempts to effect service of process on Maharishi Mahesh Yogi have been unsuccessful. Maharishi Mahesh Yogi has not been present in the United States for approximately two years. Pursuant to Rule 4(i)(d) of the Federal Rules of Civil Procedure and to Rule 4:4-4(e) of the New Jersey Court Rules, plaintiffs eventually sought to effect service on Maharishi Mahesh Yogi by delivering a copy of the summons and complaint to the Clerk of this court to be mailed by registered mail, return receipt requested, to Maharishi Mahesh Yogi at the World Plan Administrative Center in Switzerland. The summons and complaint were returned to the Clerk, the envelope stamped "Nicht abgeholt/Non reclame/Non ritirato." A crossed out signature appears in a box marked "Signature of the employee of the office of destination" on the return receipt, which is taped to the envelope.

29. Atheism may be a religion under the establishment clause in that the government cannot aid the propagation of a belief in the nonexistence of a supreme being. *See Abington School District v. Schempp, supra,* 374 U.S. at 225, 83 S.Ct. 1560; *Zorach v. Clauson,* 343 U.S. 306, 314, 72 S.Ct. 679, 96 L.Ed. 954 (1952).

30. Courts frequently decide on the basis of the operative facts whether or not certain activities stand within the meaning of terms used in the Constitution. For example, in *Rosenbloom v. Metromedia, Inc.,* 415 F.2d 892, 895 (3d Cir. 1969), *aff'd,* 403 U.S. 29, 90 S.Ct. 917, 25 L.Ed.2d 85 (1971), the Third Circuit held that radio and television were within the meaning of the word press as used in the first amendment. In *Heflin v. Sanford,* 142 F.2d 798 (5th Cir. 1944), the Fifth Circuit held that compelled national service was not involuntary servitude within the meaning of the thirteenth amendment.

Under the doctrine of "constitutional fact," the Supreme Court has held that the courts must decide whether an activity falls within the meaning of con-

stitutional terms. For example, in *Pennekamp v. Florida,* 328 U.S. 331, 66 S.Ct. 1029, 90 L.Ed. 1295 (1946), the Supreme Court held that it was not bound by lower court findings that newspaper editorials "were unlawfully critical of the administration of justice in certain cases then pending," *id.* at 333, 66 S.Ct. at 1030, because

> [t]he Constitution has imposed upon this Court final authority to determine the meaning and application of those words of that instrument which require interpretation to resolve judicial issues. With that responsibility, we are compelled to examine for ourselves the statements in issue and the circumstances under which they were made to see whether or not they do carry a threat of clear and present danger to the impartiality and good order of the courts or whether they are of a character which the principles of the First Amendment, as adopted by the Due Process Clause of the Fourteenth Amendment, protect.

Id. at 335, 66 S.Ct. at 1031 (footnote omitted).

Similarly, in *Edwards v. South Carolina,* 372 U.S. 229, 83 S.Ct. 680, 9 L.Ed. 697 (1963), the Supreme Court, held that it was required to examine the underlying facts from which it would determine whether or not petitioner's actions came within the meaning of the "constitutionally protected rights of free speech, free assembly, and freedom to petition for redress of their grievances." *Id.* at 235, 83 S.Ct. at 638. In *Blackburn v. Alabama,* 361 U.S. 199, 80 S.Ct. 274, 4 L.Ed.2d 242 (1960), the Court rejected the findings of a lower court that petitioner's confession was voluntary within the meaning of the due process clause of the fourteenth amendment and held that the Court had a duty to scrutinize the underlying facts and detemine whether or not the confession was voluntary under the fourteenth amendment. *Id.* at 205, 80 S.Ct. 274.

In addition, the Supreme Court has held that "the meaning of an armband for the purpose of expressing certain views is the type of symbolic act that is within the Free Speech Clause of the First Amendment." *Tinker v. Des Moines Independent Community School District,* 393 U.S. 503, 505, 89 S.Ct. 733, 736, 21 L.Ed.2d 731 (1969), citing *West Virginia Board of Education v. Barnette,* 319 U.S. 624, 63 S.Ct. 1178, 87 L.Ed. 1628 (1943); *Stromberg v. California,* 283 U.S. 359, 51 S.Ct. 532, 75 L.Ed. 1117 (1931).

The Supreme Court also has held that certain "associational" rights are within the meaning of speech, peaceable assembly, and petition for redress of grievances as used in the first amendment. *E. g., United Mine Workers, District 12 v. Illinois State Bar Association,* 389 U.S. 217, 88 S.Ct. 353, 19 L.Ed.2d 426 (1967); *NAACP v. Button,* 371 U.S. 415, 83 S.Ct. 328, 9 L.Ed.2d 405 (1963).

THE New York Supreme Court, Appellate Division, decides against an art teacher who had been dismissed for using classroom facilities and school time to preach and encourage student acceptance of the beliefs of a religious organization known as The Anointed Music & Publishing Company led by Brother Julius. The Court declares: "Such conduct on petitioner's part was clearly a violation of the Establishment of Religion Clause of the First Amendment of the Federal Constitution and section 3 of article XI of our State Constitution, which prohibits the use of State property in aid or maintenance of any school in which any denominational tenet is taught."

La Rocca v. *Board of Ed. of Rye City School Dist.*, 406 N.Y.S.2d 348 (1978)

MEMORANDUM BY THE COURT

Proceeding pursuant to CPLR article 78 *inter alia* to review a determination of the respondent Board of Education of the Rye City School District, which, after a hearing, dismissed the petitioner from her position as a teacher.

Determination confirmed and proceeding dismissed on the merits, without costs or disbursements.

Petitioner, a tenured teacher of art in the Rye Senior High School, was charged by her principal and the Superintendent of the Rye City School District with insubordination, neglect of duty and inefficiency. The Board of Education determined that there was probable cause to credit the charges and thereafter petitioner was served with a notice of charges pursuant to section 3020-a of the Education Law. There were four charges, the first three of which charged, in essence, that petitioner, from September, 1972 to the date of the notice, had engaged in proselytization at the Rye Senior High School for a religious organization known as The Anointed Music & Publishing Company (Tampco) led by Brother Julius. The fourth charge was that petitioner had disobeyed the direction of her principal, given her at the end of the 1973-1974 academic year, to cease engaging in the proselytizing activities specified in the first three charges. The hearing held between May 22, 1975 and June 23, 1976, resulted in a transcript totalling more than 3,300 pages, in addition to more than 60 exhibits. The hearing panel ruled that petitioner had committed the acts of proselytization listed in charges 1, 2 and 3 during the

period from September, 1972 through January 30, 1975. As to the fourth charge, insubordination, the panel found that the school district had not sustained its burden of proof. Two of the panel members recommended that petitioner be suspended without pay for the balance of the 1976-1977 school year and for the entire 1977-1978 school year. The third panel member recommended that the petitioner's employment with the school district be terminated.

The board reviewed the entire record and, in its determination, set forth at some length the basis in the evidence for its acceptance of the hearing panel's findings of guilt on the charges of proselytization and concluded, again with a full explanation of its reasons therefor, that the petitioner's services should be terminated.

Petitioner initiated the instant CPLR article 78 proceeding to review the board's determination. We confirm the determination based upon our review of the record, which shows that there is substantial evidence to sustain the findings that petitioner, during the period from September, 1972 to January 30, 1975, proselytized students to attend meetings of Tampco in Meriden, Connecticut, and Rye, New York, offered students transportation to those meetings, encouraged students to recruit for Tampco, used classroom facilities during school time to preach and encourage student acceptance of the religious beliefs of Tampco and Brother Julius and, during school hours and on school property, encouraged students to study the Bible and to adopt therefrom the beliefs of Tampco and Brother Julius. There is also substantial evidence to sustain the further findings of the board that petitioner improperly used her influence and authority as a teacher to recruit students for Tampco and as followers of Brother Julius and to preach their precepts and beliefs under the guise of offering students guidance and assistance in dealing with their school, family and personal problems. The evidence shows that in so doing, petitioner encouraged students interested in her religion to disregard their parents' wishes and to lie to them about their involvement in her religious group. Finally, there is undisputed evidence to sustain the third charge that petitioner placed herself in situations which suggested that the public high school in which she taught was being used for proselytization of religious beliefs in violation of the constitutional mandate of separation of church and State by using her office for a prayer session during school hours and, also during school hours, repeatedly trying to induce students to become members of Tampco and to adopt its religious beliefs.

Such conduct on petitioner's part was clearly in violation of the establishment of religion clause of the First Amendment of the Federal Constitution and section 3 of article XI of our State Constitution, which prohibits the use of State property in aid or maintenance of any school in which any denominational tenet is taught (see *Illinois ex rel. McCollum v. Board of Educ.*, 333 U.S. 203, 216–217, 68 S.Ct. 461, 92 L.Ed. 649; *Judd v. Board of Educ.*, 278 N.Y. 200, 15 N.E.2d 576). Nor is the penalty of dismissal imposed by the respondent so disproportionate to the offense as to be shocking to one's sense of fairness, especially in the light of the fact that the petitioner, in her testimony before the hearing panel, stated that if she were to return to teaching she would not feel required to abide by the directive she had been given by her school superiors to cease her proselytizing activities in school and that if, based on her religion, she believed something to be true, she would feel free to express that belief regardless of where she would be or to whom she was speaking (see *Matter of Pell v. Board of Educ.*, 34 N.Y.2d 222, 233, 356 N.Y.S.2d 833, 841, 313 N.E.2d 321, 326; *Matter of Harris v. Mechanicville Cent. School Dist.*, 57 A.D.2d 231, 233–234, 394 N.Y.S.2d 302, 304; *Matter of Hatta v. Board of Educ.*, 57 A.D.2d 1005, 394 N.Y.S.2d 301).

THE United States Court of Appeals, Eighth Circuit, decides that the Sioux Falls School Board's policy and rules regarding observance of religious holidays, religion in the curriculum, etc., do not violate the Establishment and Free Exercise Clauses of the First Amendment. The Court states: "Rather than entangling the schools in religion, the rules provide the means to ensure that the district steers clear of religious exercises." In conclusion, the court said: "We recognize that this opinion affirming the district court will not resolve for all times, places or circumstances the question of when Christmas carols, or other music or drama having religious themes, can be sung or performed by students in elementary and secondary schools without offending the First Amendment. The constitutionality of any particular school activity conducted pursuant to the rules, in association with any particular holiday, cannot be determined unless and until there is a specific challenge, supported by evidence, to the school district's implementation of the rules."

In his dissenting opinion, Judge McMillian declares: "There is nothing unconstitutional about the use of religious subjects or materials in public schools *as long as it is presented as part of a secular program of education.* However, to the extent the policy and rules adopted by the Sioux Falls School District authorizes the observance of religious holidays, particularly Christmas assemblies, in a manner other than as part of a secular program of education, I would hold the policy and rules violate the Establishment Clause."

Florey v. *Sioux Falls School Dist.,* 619 F.2d 1311 (1980)

HEANEY, Circuit Judge.

I.

In response to complaints that public school Christmas assemblies in 1977 and prior years constituted religious exercises, the School Board of Sioux Falls, South Dakota, set up a citizens' committee to study the relationship between church and state as applied to school functions.[1] The committee's deliberations, which lasted for several months, culminated in the formulation of a policy statement and set of rules outlining the bounds of permissible school activity. After a public hearing, the School Board adopted the policy statement and rules recommended by the committee.[2]

The appellants brought suit for declaratory and injunctive relief, alleging that the policy statement and the rules adopted by the School Board violate the Es-

tablishment and Free Exercise Clauses of the First Amendment to the United States Constitution. The district court reviewed the practices of the Sioux Falls School District and found that the 1977 Christmas program that was the subject of the initial complaints "exceeded the boundaries of what is constitutionally permissible under the Establishment Clause." The court also found, however, that programs similar to the 1977 Christmas program would not be permitted under the new School Board guidelines and concluded that the new rules, if properly administered and narrowly construed, would not run afoul of the First Amendment. *Florey v. Sioux Falls Sch. Dist. 49-5,* 464 F.Supp. 911 (D.S.D.1979).

The appellants' claim is that the School Board policy and rules are unconstitutional both on their face and as applied. At the time of the district court proceeding, however, no holiday season had passed with the rules in effect. Consequently, little evidence was presented on the actual implementation of the rules, and the district court made no findings in that regard. The record does contain some evidence of the interpretation given the rules by school administrators with respect to the Christmas holiday. We may consider that evidence, as well as the district court's observations on the 1977 Christmas program, in discerning the meaning of the rules, but because of the absence of district court findings on their application, we limit our review to the constitutionality of the rules on their face.

II.

The close relationship between religion and American history and culture has frequently been recognized by the Supreme Court of the United States.[3] Nevertheless, the First Amendment to the Constitution explicitly prescribes the relationship between religion and government: "Congress shall make no law respecting an establishment of religion, or prohibiting the free exercise thereof . . . ."[4] This apparently straightforward prohibition can rarely be applied to a given situation with ease, however. As the Supreme Court has noted, "total separation [between church and state] is not possible in an absolute sense." *Lemon v. Kurtzman*, 403 U.S. 602, 614, 91 S.Ct. 2105, 2112, 29 L.Ed.2d 745 (1971). As a result, the Court has developed a three-part test for determining when certain governmental activity falls within the constitutional boundaries:

First, the [activity] must have a secular . . . purpose; second, its principal or primary effect must be one that neither advances nor inhibits religion, . . . finally, the [activity] must not foster "an excessive governmental entanglement with religion."

Id. at 612-613, 91 S.Ct. at 2111 (quoting *Walz v. Tax Commission*, 397 U.S. 664, 674, 90 S.Ct. 1409, 1414, 25 L.Ed.2d 697 (1970)).

A. *Purpose.*

The appellants' contention that the School Board's adoption of the policy and rules was motivated by religious considerations is unsupportable. The record shows that the citizens' committee was formed and the rules drawn up in response to complaints that Christmas observances in some of the schools in the district contained religious exercises. The motivation behind the rules, therefore, was simply to ensure that no religious exercise was a part of officially sanctioned school activities. This conclusion is supported by the opening words of the policy statement: "It is accepted that no religious belief or non-belief should be promoted by the school district or its employees, and none should be disparaged." The statement goes on to affirmatively declare the purpose behind the rules:

The Sioux Falls School District recognizes that one of its educational goals is to advance the students' knowledge and appreciation of the role that our religious heritage has played in the social, cultural and historical development of civilization.

The express language of the rules also leads to the conclusion that they were not promulgated with the intent to serve a religious purpose. Rule 1 limits observation of holidays to those that have both a religious *and* a secular basis. Solely religious holidays may not be observed. Rule 3 provides that music, art, literature and drama having a religious theme or basis may be included in the school curriculum only if "presented in a prudent and objective manner and as a traditional part of the cultural and religious heritage of the particular holiday." Similarly, Rule 4 permits the use of religious symbols only as "a teaching aid or resource" and only if "such symbols are displayed as an example of the cultural and religious heritage of the holiday and are temporary in nature." We view the thrust of these rules to be the advancement of the students' knowledge of society's cultural and religious heritage, as well as the provision of an opportunity for students to perform a full range of music, poetry and drama that is likely to be of interest to the students and their audience.

This purpose is quite different from the express and implied intent of the states of New York, Pennsylvania and Maryland in the Supreme Court "School Prayer Cases." First, we emphasize the different character of the activities involved in those cases. The challenged law in *Engel v. Vitale*, 370 U.S. 421, 82 S.Ct. 1261, 8 L.Ed.2d 601 (1962), provided for the recitation of a state-authored prayer at the start of each school day. The Supreme Court had no difficulty characterizing this practice as a religious activity:

There can, of course, be no doubt that New York's program of daily classroom invocation of God's blessings as prescribed in the Regents' prayer is a religious activity. It is a solemn avowal of divine faith and supplication for the blessings of the Almighty. The nature of such a prayer has always been religious . . . .

Id. at 424-425, 82 S.Ct. at 1264.

Since prayer, by its very nature, is undeniably a religious exercise, the conclusion is inescapable that the advancement of religious goals was the purpose sought by the school officials in *Engel*. Indeed, the state officials published the prayer in a document entitled "Statement on Moral and Spiritual Training in the Schools." There can be little doubt that their intent was to promote "spiritual" ends.

Similarly, in *Abington School Dist. v. Schempp*, 374 U.S. 203, 83 S.Ct. 1560, 10 L.Ed.2d 844 (1963), the Supreme Court emphasized the "pervading religious character of the ceremony" involving daily Bible reading in the schools. *Id.* at 224, 83 S.Ct. at 1572. Again, when a state intentionally sets up a system that by its essential nature serves a religious function, one can only conclude that the advancement of religion is the desired goal. As explained more fully in the next section of this opinion, however, the programs permitted under the Sioux Falls rules are not unquestionably religious in nature. Thus, we are not required to infer that the Sioux Falls School Board intended to advance religion.

Moreover, in the Supreme Court prayer cases, compulsory religious exercises were imposed on all schools by state law. The Sioux Falls rules, by contrast, do not require the individual schools to have holiday activities; they merely permit the inclusion of certain programs in the curriculum in the event that classroom teachers feel that such programs would enhance their overall instructional plan. The rules are an attempt to delineate the scope of permissible activity within the district, not to mandate a statewide program of religious inculcation.

The appellants argue that the "legislative" history of Rule 1 compels the conclusion that the rule was designed to advance religion. The basis for this argument is a proposed amendment to Rule 1 introduced before both the citizens' committee and the School Board. The proposed amendment would have added to Rule 1 the following words: "Such observances shall be limited to secular aspects of these holidays." The amendment was defeated by both the citizens' committee and the School Board. The School Board rejected the proposal, appellants assert in their brief, "because it wanted to allow schools to observe the religious basis of holidays." This, they maintain, is an unconstitutional purpose.

We do not agree that the rejection of the proposed amendment renders the School Board rules constitutionally infirm. First, the record is devoid of evidence indicating the reasons the proposal was rejected. A number of possibilities suggest themselves, including the ambiguity of the proposed addition. The appellants' assertion that the rejection was due to the School Board's desire "to observe the religious basis of holidays" is thus unsupported. Furthermore, even if the appellants' contention were correct, the Constitution does not necessarily forbid the use of materials that have a "religious basis." Government involvement in an activity of unquestionably religious origin does not contravene the Establishment Clause if its "present purpose and effect" is secular. *McGowan v. Maryland,* 366 U.S. 420, 445, 81 S.Ct. 1101, 1115, 6 L.Ed.2d 393 (1961). Thus, although the rules permit the schools to observe holidays that have both a secular and a religious basis, we need not conclude that the School Board acted with unconstitutional motives. To the contrary, we agree with the district court's findings that the School Board did not adopt the policy statement and rules for the purpose of advancing or inhibiting religion.

B. *Effect.*

The appellants contend that, notwithstanding the actual intent of the School Board, the "principal or primary effect" of the rules is to either advance or inhibit religion. See *Lemon v. Kurtzman, supra,* 403 U.S. at 612, 91 S.Ct. at 2111. We cannot agree. The First Amendment does not forbid all mention of religion in public schools; it is the *advancement* or *inhibition* of religion that is prohibited. *Committee for Public Education v. Nyquist,* 413 U.S. 756, 788, 93 S.Ct. 2955, 2973, 37 L.Ed.2d 948 (1973). Hence, the *study* of religion is not forbidden "when presented objectively as part of a secular program of education." *Abington School Dist. v. Schempp, supra,* 374 U.S. at 225, 83 S.Ct. at 1573. We view the term "study" to include more than mere classroom instruction; public performance may be a legitimate part of secular study. This does not mean, of course, that religious ceremonies can be performed in the public schools under the guise of "study." It does mean, however, that when the primary purpose served by a given school activity is secular, that activity is not made unconstitutional by the inclusion of some religious content. As the district court noted in its discussion of Rule 3, "[t]o allow students *only* to study and *not* to perform [religious art, literature and music when] such works . . . have developed an independent secular and artistic significance would give students a truncated view of our culture." 464 F.Supp. at 916 (emphasis in original).

The appellants assert, however, that something more than secular study is authorized by the Sioux Falls rules. They point to Rule 1, which states that holidays that have a religious and secular basis may be "observed" in the public schools. "Observation," they maintain, necessarily connotes religious ceremony or exercise and the rule thus has the impermissible effect of advancing religion.

A review of the policy statement and rules as a whole leads us to conclude that the appellants' emphasis of the word "observe" is misplaced and their interpretation of it incorrect. First, as noted in section II.A. of this opinion, the rules must be read together with the policy statement of the School Board. That statement makes it clear that religion is to be neither promoted nor disparaged in the Sioux Falls schools. Consequently, any ambiguity in the meaning of the word "observed" must be resolved in favor of promoting that policy. Moreover, the only evidence presented on the definition of the word "observed" was the testimony of the School Superintendent, Dr. John Harris. Dr. Harris explained that "observed" means "that programs with content relating to both the secular and religious basis of [the holiday] could be performed, could be presented in the school." (Transcript at 65.) As noted earlier, we view performance or presentation to be a legitimate and important part of "study" in the public schools. Thus, the use of the word "observe" does not mean that the rules have the effect of advancing religion so long as the religious content of the programs is "presented objectively as part of a secular program of education." *Abington School Dist. v. Schempp, supra,* 374 U.S. at 225, 83 S.Ct. at 1573.

To determine whether religion is advanced or inhibited by the rules, then, we must look to see if a genuine "secular program of education" is furthered by the rules. It is unquestioned that public school students may be taught about the customs and cultural heritage of the United States and other countries. This is the principal effect of the rules. They allow the presentation of material that, although of religious origin, has taken on an independent meaning.

The district court expressly found that much of the art, literature and music associated with traditional holidays, particularly Christmas, has "acquired a significance which is no longer confined to the religious sphere of life. It has become integrated into our national culture and heritage."[5] Furthermore, the rules guarantee that all material used has secular or cultural significance: Only holidays with both religious and secular bases may be observed; music, art, literature and drama may be included in the curriculum only if presented in a prudent and objective manner and only as a part of the cultural and religious heritage of the holiday; and religious symbols may be used only as a teaching aid or resource and only if they are displayed as a part of the cultural and religious heritage of the holiday and are temporary in nature. Since all programs and materials authorized by the rules must deal with the secular or cultural basis or heritage of the holidays and since the materials must be presented in a prudent and objective manner and symbols used as a teaching aid, the advancement of a "secular program of education," and not of religion, is the primary effect of the rules.

The appellants argue that, despite the secular benefits, inclusion of material with a religious theme, basis or heritage invalidates the rules. In support of this assertion, the appellants point out that several of appellants' witnesses, all of them ordained clergymen, testified that the singing of Christmas carols would have some religious effect on them. But the appellants misread the test laid down by the Supreme Court. As noted, *Lemon v. Kurtzman, supra,* permits a given activity if "its *principal* or *primary* effect [is] one that neither advances nor inhibits religion." 403 U.S. at 612, 91 S.Ct. at 2111 (emphasis added). It would be literally impossible to develop a public school curriculum that did not in some way affect the religious or

nonreligious sensibilities of some of the students or their parents. School administrators should, of course, be sensitive to the religious beliefs or disbeliefs of their constituents and should attempt to avoid conflict,[6] but they need not and should not sacrifice the quality of the students' education. They need only ensure that the primary effect of the school's policy is secular. The district court's finding that they have done this by the challenged rules is not clearly erroneous.

The distinction between an activity that primarily advances religion and one that falls within permissible constitutional limits may be illustrated by comparing the 1977 kindergarten Christmas program found by the district court to be an impermissible religious activity and the programs authorized by the new School Board guidelines. The 1977 program at one of the elementary schools contained a segment that, in the words of the district court, "was replete with religious content including a responsive discourse between the teacher and the class entitled, 'The Beginners Christmas Quiz.'" The "Quiz" read as follows:

> Teacher: Of whom did heav'nly angels sing,
> And news about His birthday bring?
> Class: Jesus.
> Teacher: Now, can you name the little town
> Where they the Baby Jesus found?
> Class: Bethlehem.
> Teacher: Where had they made a little bed
> For Christ, the blessed Saviour's head?
> Class: In a manger in a cattle stall.
> Teacher: What is the day we celebrate
> As birthday of this One so great?
> Class: Christmas.

This "Quiz" and other similar activities constituted, the district court found, "a predominately religious activity" which exceeded constitutional bounds. We agree with this characterization and with the district court's observation that similar programs would be prohibited by the new rules. The administration of religious training is properly in the domain of the family and church. The First Amendment prohibits public schools from serving that function.

C. *Entanglement.*

The appellants contend that the new guidelines in Sioux Falls unconstitutionally "foster 'an excessive government entanglement with religion.'" *See Lemon v. Kurtzman, supra,* 403 U.S. at 613, 91 S.Ct. at 2111. All the Supreme Court cases cited by the appellants in support of the "entanglement" test deal with governmental aid to sectarian institutions, not with the permissible scope of activity in the public schools. In a "parochaid" case, the court is presented with a situation in which the state is involving itself with a concededly religious activity or institution. The real danger is the potential for state repression of such institutions. In the present case, by contrast, the school district is called upon to determine whether a given activity is religious. This type of decision inheres in every curriculum choice and would be faced by school administrators and teachers even if the rules did not exist. Indeed, the rules are guidelines designed to aid in the decisionmaking process. Rather than entangling the schools in religion, the rules provide the means to ensure that the district steers clear of religious exercises. We think the district court was correct in finding that the new rules do not unconstitutionally entangle the Sioux Falls school district in religion or religious institutions.

III.

The appellants also contend that implementation of the policy and rules of the Sioux Falls School Board should be enjoined because the rules violate the Free Exercise Clause of the First Amendment. This contention does not withstand scrutiny.[7]

The public schools are not required to delete from the curriculum all materials that may offend any religious sensibility. As Mr. Justice Jackson noted in *McCollum v. Board of Education,* 333 U.S. 203, 235, 68 S.Ct. 461, 477, 92 L.Ed. 649 (1948),

> Authorities list 256 separate and substantial religious bodies to exist in the continental United States. Each of them . . . has as good a right as this plaintiff to demand that the courts compel the schools to sift out of their teaching everything inconsistent with its doctrines. If we are to eliminate everything that is objectionable to any of these warring sects or inconsistent with any of their doctrines, we will leave public education in shreds.

These inevitable conflicts with the individual beliefs of some students or their parents, in the absence of an Establishment Clause violation, do not necessarily require the prohibition of a school activity. On the other hand, forcing any person to participate in an activity that offends his religious or nonreligious beliefs will generally contravene the Free Exercise Clause, even without an Establishment Clause violation. *See Wisconsin v. Yoder,* 406 U.S. 205, 92 S.Ct. 1526, 32 L.Ed.2d 15 (1972). In this case, however, the Sioux Falls School Board recognized that problem and expressly provided that students may be excused from activities authorized by the rules if they so choose.[8]

IV.

We recognize that this opinion affirming the district court will not resolve for all times, places or circumstances the question of when Christmas carols, or other music or drama having religious themes, can be

sung or performed by students in elementary and secondary public schools without offending the First Amendment. The constitutionality of any particular school activity conducted pursuant to the rules, in association with any particular holiday, cannot be determined unless and until there is a specific challenge, supported by evidence, to the school district's implementation of the rules. We simply hold, on the basis of the record before us, that the policy and rules adopted by the Sioux Falls Board of Education, when read in the light of the district court's holding that segments of the 1977 Christmas program at one of the elementary schools were impermissible, are not violative of the First Amendment.[9]

For the foregoing reasons, the judgment of the district court is affirmed.

APPENDIX

I. POLICY

Recognition of Religious Beliefs and Customs

It is accepted that no religious belief or non-belief should be promoted by the school district or its employees, and none should be disparaged. Instead, the school district should encourage all students and staff members to appreciate and be tolerant of each other's religious views. The school district should utilize its opportunity to foster understanding and mutual respect among students and parents, whether it involves race, culture, economic background or religious beliefs. In that spirit of tolerance, students and staff members should be excused from participating in practices which are contrary to their religious beliefs unless there are clear issues of overriding concern that would prevent it.

The Sioux Falls School District recognizes that one of its educational goals is to advance the students' knowledge and appreciation of the role that our religious heritage has played in the social, cultural and historical development of civilization.

II. RULES

Observance of Religious Holidays

The practice of the Sioux Falls School District shall be as follows:

1. The several holidays throughout the year which have a religious and a secular basis may be observed in the public schools.
2. The historical and contemporary values and the origin of religious holidays may be explained in an unbiased and objective manner without sectarian indoctrination.
3. Music, art, literature and drama having religious themes or basis are permitted as part of the

curriculum for school-sponsored activities and programs if presented in a prudent and objective manner and as a traditional part of the cultural and religious heritage of the particular holiday.

4. The use of religious symbols such as a cross, menorah, crescent, Star of David, creche, symbols of Native American religions or other symbols that are a part of a religious holiday is permitted as a teaching aid or resource provided such symbols are displayed as an example of the cultural and religious heritage of the holiday and are temporary in nature. Among these holidays are included Christmas, Easter, Passover, Hannukah, St. Valentine's Day, St. Patrick's Day, Thanksgiving and Halloween.

5. The school district's calendar should be prepared so as to minimize conflicts with religious holidays of all faiths.

Religion in the Curriculum

Religious institutions and orientations are central to human experience, past and present. An education excluding such a significant aspect would be incomplete. It is essential that the teaching *about*—and not *of*—religion be conducted in a factual objective and respective manner.

Therefore, the practice of the Sioux Falls School District shall be as follows:

1. The District supports the inclusion of religious literature, music, drama and the arts in the curriculum and in school activities provided it is intrinsic to the learning experience in the various fields of study and is presented objectively.

2. The emphasis on religious themes in the arts, literature and history should be only as extensive as necessary for a balanced and comprehensive study of these areas. Such studies should never foster any particular religious tenets or demean any religious beliefs.

3. Student-initiated expressions to questions or assignments which reflect their beliefs or non-beliefs about a religious theme shall be accommodated. For example, students are free to express religious belief or non-belief in compositions, art forms, music, speech and debate.

Dedications and Commencement

Traditions are a cherished part of the community life and the Sioux Falls School District expresses an interest in maintaining those traditions which have had a significance to the community. Such ceremonies should recognize the religious pluralism of the community.

Therefore, the practice of the Sioux Falls School District shall be as follows:

1. A dedication ceremony should recognize the religious pluralism of the community and be appropriate to those who use the facility. An open invitation should be extended to all citizens to participate in the ceremony.

2. Traditions, i.e., invocation and benediction, inherent in commencement ceremonies, should be honored in the spirit of accommodation and good taste.

3. Because the baccalaureate service is traditionally religious in nature, it should be sponsored by agencies separate from the Sioux Falls School District.

McMILLIAN, Circuit Judge, dissenting.

I dissent. Before discussing the three-part Establishment Clause test and applying its analysis to this case, I would note that this case involves a close question in one of the most sensitive areas of constitutional law, the relationship between religion and public education.[1] The Supreme Court's Establishment Clause cases have developed "controlling constitutional standards [which] have become firmly rooted and the broad contours . . . are now well defined," *Committee for Public Education & Religious Liberty v. Nyquist,* 413 U.S. 756, 761, 93 S.Ct. 2955, 2959, 37 L.Ed.2d 948 (1973) (*Nyquist*), but those standards are not easily applied and the precedents do not squarely address this case. This is not a financial aid case; rather, this is a variation of the school prayer (*Engel v. Vitale,* 370 U.S. 421, 82 S.Ct. 1261, 8 L.Ed.2d 601 (1962)) and Bible reading (*School District v. Schempp,* 374 U.S. 203, 83 S.Ct. 1560, 10 L.Ed.2d 844 (1963)(*Schempp*)) cases. Preparing and presenting Christmas assemblies is not a religious activity in the obvious sense that reciting a nondenominational prayer or reading from the Bible are religious activities. Prayer is "a solemn avowal of divine faith and supplication for the blessings of the Almighty." *Engel v. Vitale, supra,* 370 U.S. at 424, 82 S.Ct. at 1264. Similarly, reading from the Bible is a religious exercise.[2] *Schempp, supra,* 374 U.S. at 224, 83 S.Ct. at 1572. When compared with school prayers or Bible reading, Christmas assemblies, and in particular the singing of Christmas carols, appear ambiguous in character. Nonetheless, I am of the opinion that the preparation and presentation of Christmas assemblies in the public schools violates the Establishment Clause.

"The problem, like many problems in constitutional law, is one of degree." *Zorach v. Clauson,* 343 U.S. 306, 314, 72 S.Ct. 679, 684, 96 L.Ed. 954 (1952). I quite agree with the majority that singing Christmas carols in the public schools is not necessarily a violation of the Establishment Clause. At 1315—1316. "[N]ot every involvement of religion in public life is unconstitutional. . . . " *Schempp, supra,* 374 U.S. at 232, 83 S.Ct. at 1576 (Brennan, J., concurring). As noted by the majority, the Christmas carol is a music form which is undoubtedly worthy of study. At 1316—1317 n.5. Nothing in my analysis should be taken to mean that the study of Christmas carols and other Christmas traditions, "when presented objectively as part of a secular program of education, may not be effected consistently with the First Amendment." *Schempp, supra,* 374 U.S. at 225, 83 S.Ct. at 1573. "Music without sacred music, architecture minus the cathedral, or painting without the scriptural themes would be eccentric and incomplete, even from a secular point of view." *Illinois ex rel. McCollum v. Board of Education,* 333 U.S. 203, 236, 68 S.Ct. 461, 477, 92 L.Ed. 649 (1948) (Jackson, J., concurring) (*McCollum*). Similarly, western European history would be incomplete without the Crusades, the Inquisition or the Reformation, as would early American history (and the history of the Establishment Clause itself, *see Nyquist, supra,* 413 U.S. at 770 n. 28, 93 S.Ct. at 2964) without the Puritans, the Quakers or the Transcendentalists. To return to the metaphor of music, nothing in my analysis would limit a music curriculum to fugues and minuets, *see Lemon v. Kurtzman,* 403 U.S. 602, 614, 91 S.Ct. 2105, 2112, 29 L.Ed.2d 745 (1971)(*Lemon*), and exclude oratorios.

I. *The Three-part Test*

The Establishment Clause provides that "Congress shall make no law respecting an establishment of religion. . . . " U.S. Const. amend I. Although phrased in absolute terms, the Establishment Clause has never been held to require "total separation" of church and state in an absolute sense. *Lemon, supra,* 403 U.S. at 614, 91 S.Ct. at 2112; *cf. McDaniel v. Paty,* 435 U.S. 618, 98 S.Ct. 1322, 55 L.Ed.2d 593 (1978) (state statute barring the clergy from public office held unconstitutional). However, the Establishment Clause definitely has "a secular reach far more penetrating in the conduct of Government than merely to forbid an 'established church.'" *McCollum, supra,* 333 U.S. at 213, 68 S.Ct. at 466 (Frankfurter, J., concurring).[3] The line of separation is certainly neither straight nor easily determined. *See Committee for Public Education & Religious Liberty v. Regan,* __ U.S.__ __, 100 S.Ct. 840, 851, 63 L.Ed.2d 94 (1980) (Blackmun, J., dissenting) (*Regan*) ("the wavering line" separating church and state). As described in *Lemon, supra,* 403 U.S. at 614, 91 S.Ct. at 2112, "the line of separation, far from being a [high and impregnable] 'wall,' is a blurred, indistinct, and variable barrier depending on all the circumstances of a particular relationship." Although in my view the line of separation has become unnecessarily blurred,

[t]he fact is that the line which separates the secular from the sectarian in American life is elusive. The difficulty of defining the boundary with precision inheres in a paradox central to our scheme of liberty. While our institutions reflect a firm conviction that we are a religious people, those institutions by solemn constitutional injunction may not officially involve religion in such a way as to prefer, discriminate against, or oppress, a particular sect or religion.

Schempp, supra, 374 U.S. at 231, 83 S.Ct. at 1576 (Brennan, J., concurring). Further, "[n]either [a state nor the federal government] can constitutionally pass laws or impose requirements which aid all religions as against non-believers, and neither can aid those religions based on a belief in the existence of God as against those religions founded on different beliefs." *Torcaso v. Watkins,* 367 U.S. 488, 495, 81 S.Ct. 1680, 1683-1684, 6 L.Ed.2d 982 (1961) (citations and footnotes omitted). "By reason of the First Amendment government is commanded 'to have no interest in theology or ritual,' for on those matters 'government must be neutral.'" *Engel v. Vitale, supra,* 370 U.S. at 443, 82 S.Ct. at 1273 (Douglas, J., concurring), *citing McGowan v. Maryland,* 366 U.S. 420, 453, 81 S.Ct. 1101, 1119, 6 L.Ed.2d 393 (1961) (Douglas, J., dissenting).

The focus of an Establishment Clause analysis is whether the challenged action involves "the three main concerns against which the Establishment Clause sought to protect: 'sponsorship, financial support, and active involvement of the sovereign in religious activity.'" *Tilton v. Richardson,* 403 U.S. 672, 677, 91 S.Ct. 2091, 2095, 29 L.Ed.2d 790 (1971) *citing Walz v. Tax Commissioner,* 397 U.S. 664, 668, 90 S.Ct. 1409, 1411, 25 L.Ed.2d 697 (1970).

The mode of analysis for Establishment Clause questions is defined by the three-part test that has emerged from [the Supreme] Court's decisions. In order to pass muster, a statute must have a secular legislative purpose, must have a principal or primary effect that neither advances nor inhibits religion, and must not foster an excessive government entanglement with religion.

Wolman v. Walter, 433 U.S. 229, 235-36, 97 S.Ct. 2593, 2599, 53 L.Ed.2d 714 (1977), *citing Roemer v. Maryland Public Works Board,* 426 U.S. 736, 748, 96 S.Ct. 2337, 2345, 49 L.Ed.2d 179 (1976); *Nyquist, supra,* 413 U.S. at 772-73, 93 S.Ct. at 2965-2966; *Lemon, supra,* 403 U.S. at 612-13, 91 S.Ct. at 2111. The three-part test "has been clearly stated, if not easily applied." *Meek v. Pittenger,* 421 U.S. 349, 358, 95 S.Ct. 1753, 1759, 44 L.Ed.2d 217 (1975). In recent Supreme Court cases it has been applied to "those [cases] involving public aid in varying forms to sectarian educational institutions," the second of the two general categories of religion and education cases raising Establishment Clause questions identified by Mr.

Justice Powell in *Nyquist, supra,* 413 U.S. at 772, 93 S.Ct. at 2965 (footnote omitted). At issue here is the first category: "those [cases] dealing with religious activities within the public schools." *Id.* (footnote omitted); *cf. Lanner v. Wimmer,* 463 F.Supp. 867, 881 (D. Utah 1978) (accreditation of Bible history classes by public school held to violate Establishment Clause). The action challenged here is necessarily less substantive than the kind of action at issue in the financial aid cases, but the tests of secular legislative purpose, impermissible effect, and excessive entanglement are equally applicable. "[T]hese tests or criteria should be 'viewed as guidelines' within which to consider 'the cumulative criteria developed over many years and applying to a wide range of governmental action challenged as violative of the Establishment Clause.'" *Id.* 413 U.S. at 773 n.31, 93 S.Ct. at 2965 n.31, *citing Tilton v. Richardson, supra,* 403 U.S. at 677-78, 91 S.Ct. at 2095-2096; *see also Meek v. Pittenger, supra,* 421 U.S. at 358-59, 95 S.Ct. at 1759-1760.

As noted by the majority, there was little evidence presented below about the actual implementation of the school district's policy and rules for the observance of religious holidays. At 1313. At the center of the controversy in the present case is the Christmas assembly. At oral argument counsel for the school district and for appellants supplied a few additional details about the Christmas assemblies. The other holiday observances were not discussed. The contents of the Christmas holiday observances varies from teacher to teacher; the complexity of the material depends upon the grade level; the lower grades tend to have class parties while the upper grades tend to have school assemblies; the assemblies are typically concerts which feature traditional Christmas music and songs, including Christmas carols such as "Silent Night" and "O Come All Ye Faithful"; the assemblies are usually held during the evening at the particular school; assembly attendance is not compulsory and students could excuse themselves; assembly activity is not graded but assembly preparation is part of the general classroom work and may involve as much as two months of the school year (this time is, of course, not devoted entirely to assembly preparation). This kind of Christmas assembly is a traditional feature in many public schools and in many communities across the country. However, widespread observances or "mere longevity of custom does not in itself insulate a practice from constitutional scrutiny." *Fox v. City of Los Angeles,* 22 Cal. App.3d 792, 587 P.2d 663, 671, 150 Cal.Rptr. 867, 875 (1978) (banc) (Bird, C. J., concurring) (cross displayed in city hall windows at Easter enjoined as violation of Establishment Clause in state constitution), *citing* 70 Cal.App.3d 885, 139 Cal.Rptr. 180, 184 (App. 1977). "[H]istorical acceptance without more [does] not alone [suffice], as 'no one acquires a vested or pro-

tected right in violation of the Constitution by long use.'" *Nyquist, supra,* 413 U.S. at 792, 93 S.Ct. at 2975, *citing Walz v. Tax Commissioner, supra,* 397 U.S. at 678, 90 S.Ct. at 1416.

II. *The Secular Legislative Purpose Test*

First, I am not totally persuaded that the policy and rules reflect a clearly secular legislative purpose. It cannot be overlooked that complaints about the religious content of several Christmas assemblies prompted the formation of the citizens' advisory committee and the adoption of the policy and rules by the school board. Against this background I am inclined to view the school board's rejection of the proposed "secular aspects only" amendment as indicative of a purpose to permit more than the study (including performance when appropriate) of religion, subjects with religious content or significance and religious traditions. *Cf. Meltzer v. Board of Education,* 577 F.2d 311, 317 (5th Cir. 1978)(banc) (Brown, C. J., dissenting in part) (majority upheld guidelines for distribution of religious literature in public schools against Establishment Clause attack), *cert. denied,* 439 U.S. 1089, 99 S.Ct. 872, 59 L.Ed.2d 56 (1979). In addition, the rules refer exclusively to "religious holidays." No doubt this singular orientation reflects the non-existence of agnostic or atheistic occasions. The rules do not address the observance of *non-religious* holidays, such as Veterans Day, Arbor Day, Memorial Day, Labor Day, the birthdays of various presidents or civic leaders (i.e. the controversy over whether Martin Luther King's birthday should be a holiday). To the extent the policy and rules focus only on religious holidays, I would find the policy and rules unconstitutionally operate as a preference of religion.

Like the majority, I too accept "the thrust of these rules to be the advancement of the students' knowledge of society's cultural and religious heritage." At 1314. The opening words of the policy statement takes the commendable position that "no religious belief or non-belief should be promoted by the school district or its employees, and none should be disparaged." At 1319 (Appendix). I do not deny that knowledge of society's cultural and religious heritage and the encouragement of tolerance (religious and other kinds) and mutual understanding are admirable secular goals. However, I find several problems in the relationship between the rules and these secular goals. First, I do not understand how the *observance* of religious holidays promotes these secular goals. Moreover, I do not understand how the observance of particular religious holidays (*i.e.* Christian and Jewish holidays; *but see* note 4 *infra*), but not others (*i.e.,* Ramadan, North American Indian holidays, Hindu holidays) encourages student knowledge and appreciation of religious and cultural diversity. For example, the observance of the holidays of religions less familiar to most American public school children than either Christian or Jewish holidays would seem more likely to increase student knowledge and promote religious tolerance.

Second, even assuming the observance of religious holidays does advance these secular goals, those secular goals can be achieved in public education without the "observance" of religious holidays. As Mr. Justice Brennan observed in *Schempp*,

> *Torcaso* and the *Sunday Law Cases* forbid the use of religious means to achieve secular ends where non-religious means will suffice. . . . While I do not question the judgment of experienced educators that the challenged practices [Bible reading] may well achieve valuable secular ends [fostering harmony and tolerance among the pupils, enhancing the authority of the teacher, and inspiring better discipline], it seems to me that the State acts unconstitutionally if it either sets about to attain even indirectly religious ends by religious means, or if it uses religious means to serve secular ends where secular means would suffice.

374 U.S. at 281, 83 S.Ct. at 1603. Here the school district seeks to accomplish secular goals by religious means, the observance of religious holidays. Surely the school district can advance student knowledge and tolerance of religious diversity as effectively by *non* religious means, that is, through the study of comparative religions or as part of the history or social studies curriculum. In any case, the observance of religious holidays as a means of accomplishing the secular goals of knowledge and tolerance clearly discriminates against non-belief.

Third, even if the secular goals of student knowledge and religious tolerance are promoted by religious means and nonreligious means are inadequate, why should the rules limit such observance only to those holidays which have "a religious and a secular basis"? Why require these holidays to have a secular basis at all? Ostensibly it is the religious basis of these particular holidays (and the different religions thus represented) which is critical to the promotion of student knowledge and tolerance of religious diversity. In this context, a particular holiday's *secular* basis is irrelevant. Nonetheless, the inclusion of a secular basis requirement does balance and diffuse the religious basis requirement and thereby appears, at first glance, to shield the rules from constitutional attack.

Finally, the rules state that several holidays have "a religious and a secular basis" but fail to explain what is meant by those terms. The rules identify such holidays as Christmas, Easter, Passover, Chanukah, Valentine's Day, St. Patrick's Day, Thanksgiving, and Halloween. On the one hand, I find it very difficult to articulate exactly what is meant by "secular basis"

and to discern the secular basis of some of the holidays (i.e. Easter). Secular basis presumably refers to something other than religiously neutral symbols (i.e. snowmen and jingle bells instead of Nativity scenes and the Star of Bethlehem), association with majoritarian (Christian) cultural traditions, commercialization, or observance contemporaneous with Christian religious holidays.[4]

On the other hand, I find it equally difficult to ascertain what is meant by "religious basis," particularly as applied to holidays like Valentine's Day. Valentine's Day does have a certain degree of secular (and commercial) significance as an occasion for the exchange of expressions of love and affection. However, the religious origin of Valentine's Day can only be characterized as remote (it is the name day of a Roman Christian martyr of the second century AD) and its contemporary religious significance minimal. The same observation is more or less true of St. Patrick's Day and Halloween, particularly insofar as those holidays are "celebrated" today. Furthermore, the "religious basis" of the holidays listed in the rules varies rather markedly, for example, from Valentine's Day to Easter. In fact, Thanksgiving arguably seems to me the one holiday listed in the rules which has both a discernible secular and religious basis; Thanksgiving commemorates an event of some significance (perhaps apocryphal) in early American colonial history and is a national holiday set aside for giving thanks to God. Thanksgiving is a federal legal public holiday. *See* 5 U.S.C. § 6103(a).

Christmas is especially difficult. Despite its many and diverse secular manifestations, Christmas remains an event of immense and undiminished significance to Christians: the celebration of the birth of Christ. *Cf. McGowan v. Maryland, supra*, 366 U.S. at 431–53, 81 S.Ct. at 1108–1119 (Sunday closing laws upheld as establishing uniform day-of-rest and recreation with only remote or incidental religious benefit). Unlike Thanksgiving, Christmas has no *inherent* secular basis as the anniversary of an American historical event. Christmas has nevertheless acquired an undeniable secular importance and general acceptance as a holiday season over the years. As noted in *Allen v. Morton*, 161 U.S.App.D.C. 239, 495 F.2d 65 (1973), which involved an Establishment Clause challenge to the annual "Christmas Pageant of Peace" celebrated on federal parkland adjacent to the White House that included the display of a life-size Nativity scene or "creche," Christmas holiday observances are often associated with the laudable secular theme of expressing a national desire for "Peace on Earth, Goodwill Toward Men." *Id.* at 69. Christmas is also a federal legal public holiday, 5 U.S.C. § 6103(a), and is observed directly and indirectly in many government activities: for example, the President lights a national

Christmas tree, the post office issues commemorative stamps for the Christmas season which feature artwork with Christian themes, local governments display Christmas trees and Christmas decorations on public buildings, city streets and city squares.

Nonetheless, what is constitutionally unobjectionable for adults or in a non-public school context, *but see Fox v. City of Los Angeles, supra,* 587 P.2d at 666, 150 Cal.Rptr. at 870, may be prohibited for public school children. *See, e.g., Tilton v. Richardson, supra,* 403 U.S. at 685, 91 S.Ct. at 2099 (Burger, C.J.) (distinction between elementary and secondary education and university education); *Schempp, supra,* 374 U.S. at 294–300, 83 S.Ct. at 1612 (Brennan, J., concurring) ("Of special significance to this distinction is the fact that we are here usually dealing with adults, not with impressionable children as in the public schools."). To the extent the school district seeks to justify the *observance* of the Christmas holiday as an occasion to advance the students' knowledge of cultural and religious knowledge, diversity, and tolerance or to promote peace among mankind,[5] these objectives could be accomplished by the *observance* of a more neutral "holiday," for example United Nations Day. "Such substitutes would, I think, be unsatisfactory or inadequate only to the extent that the present activities do in fact serve religious goals." *Schempp, supra,* 374 U.S at 281, 83 S.Ct. at 1602–1603 (Brennan, J., concurring).

Even assuming the school board acted with a secular legislative purpose, "the propriety of a legislature's purposes may not immunize from further scrutiny a law which either has a primary effect that advances religion, or which fosters excessive entanglements between Church and State." *Nyquist, supra,* 413 U.S. at 774, 93 S.Ct. at 2966.

III. *The Primary Effect Test*

Second, do the rules, particularly to the extent they permit the preparation and presentation of Christmas assemblies, have a principal or primary effect which either advances or inhibits religion? Unlike the majority, I think they do. Christmas assemblies have a substantial impact, both in favor of one religion and against other religions and nonbelief, on the school district employees, the students, the parents and relatives of the students and community.

> When a [school district] so openly promotes the religious meaning of one religion's holidays, the benefit reaped by that religion and the disadvantage suffered by other religions is obvious. Those persons who do not share those holidays are relegated to the status of outsiders by their own government; those persons who do observe those holidays can take pleasure in seeing . . . their belief given official sanction and special status.

Fox v. City of Los Angeles, supra, 587 P. 2d at 670, 150

Cal.Rptr. at 874 (Bird, C. J., concurring). By sponsoring Christmas assemblies which feature programs of traditional Christmas music, including Christmas carols, only during the Christmas season, the school district has in effect endorsed the beliefs of one religion. The school district has placed "the power, prestige and financial support of government" behind the Christmas holiday. *See Engel v. Vitale, supra,* 370 U.S. at 430–31, 82 S.Ct. at 1267. The school district devotes considerable faculty time to the preparation and presentation of these assemblies; students expend considerable classroom time to the same end.

"The unconstitutionality of this practice crystallizes when we consider *what* is being displayed *where* and *when.*" *Fox v. City of Los Angeles, supra,* 587 P.2d at 670, 150 Cal.Rptr. at 874 (Bird, C.J., concurring) (emphasis in original). Viewed in context, I do not think Christmas assemblies can accurately be described as merely arts festivals or choral concerts. These assemblies contain material that is unmistakably Christmas-oriented and are held only during the Christmas season, not in October or April. The programs of Christmas assemblies may include songs, poems, or dramatic presentations, all of which may have artistic merit, but the subject and particularly the timing of these assemblies are no less revealing than the term "Christmas assembly." In contrast, Christmas carols presented *as a musical form* could be performed at any time during the school year, not just at Christmas. Even though generally performed during the evening (when the school buildings are not being used educationally), assembly preparations are conducted in public school buildings, during the school day, by public school teachers.

It is not enough that the challenged activity has a principal or primary effect that neither advances nor inhibits religion. *Compare Lemon, supra,* 403 U.S. at 612, 91 S.Ct. at 2111, *with Nyquist, supra,* 413 U.S. at 783–84 & n.39, 93 S.Ct. at 2971. The majority identifies the principal effect of the rules to be education about the customs and cultural heritage of the United States and other countries. Even accepting this characterization (I would emphasize instead the musical or dramatic impact of the Christmas assemblies) of the principal secular effect, this principal secular effect is not separable from the religious effect. Moreover, the religious effect is not "remote, indirect or incidental" to the secular effect. *See generally* L. Tribe, American Constitutional Law 840 (1978). In *Nyquist,* the Supreme Court cautioned against using the principal or primary effect test to make "metaphysical" distinctions between primary and secondary effects. 413 U.S. at 783–84 n.39, 93 S.Ct. at 2970–2971. The Supreme Court stated that "[o]ur cases simply do not support the notion that a law found to have a 'primary' effect to promote some legitimate end under the

State's police power is immune from further examination to ascertain whether it also has the direct and immediate effect of advancing religion." *Id.* In other words, the primary effect test forbids any government action that has a substantial religious impact. *See Meltzer v. Board of Education, supra,* 577 F.2d at 318 (Brown, C.J., dissenting in part) (outlines a nondiscriminatory impact principle), *citing Gillette v. United States,* 401 U.S. 437, 450, 91 S.Ct. 828, 836, 28 L.Ed.2d 168 (1971); *Allen v. Morton, supra,* 495 F.2d at 87 (Leventhal, J., concurring); *Fox v. City of Los Angeles, supra,* 587 P.2d at 673 & n.11, 150 Cal.Rptr. at 877 (Bird, C.J., concurring). As discussed above, I would find that Christmas assemblies do have a substantial religious (or non-secular) effect, an effect which cannot be "offset" by a primary secular effect under the formulation of the primary effect test set forth in *Nyquist.* I do not dispute that Christmas assemblies have secular effects (cultural education, promotion of religious diversity, musical and dramatic value); however, "[s]uch secular objectives, no matter how desirable and irrespective of whether judges might possess sufficiently sensitive calipers to ascertain whether the secular effects outweigh the sectarian benefits, cannot serve today any more than they could 200 years ago to justify such a direct and substantial advancement of religion." 413 U.S. at 785 n.39, 93 S.Ct. at 2971.

IV. *The Excessive Entanglement Test*

Third, I think the rules necessarily foster an excessive entanglement of the school district with religion. As noted by the majority, the rules call upon the school district to determine whether a given activity is religious. At 1318.

The [school board] may also find itself effectively defining religion or censoring the content of religious materials. . . . [T]he secular public school system could become the focal point for the competition of all religious beliefs [and nonbelief]. The courts and other state officials would be under a continuing duty to make certain that one faith was not in effect being endorsed and promoted by [the observance of religious holidays]. Indeed, it is ironic that the more fairly and objectively the guidelines are enforced, the more the school board will become immersed in serious religious judgments.

Meltzer v. Board of Education, supra, 577 F.2d at 319 (Brown, C.J., dissenting in part). "A comprehensive, discriminating, and continuing state surveillance will inevitably be required to ensure that [the rules] are obeyed and the First Amendment otherwise respected." *Lemon, supra,* 403 U.S. at 619, 91 S.Ct. at 2114. Of course, it is precisely this type of "excessive and enduring entanglement between state and church," *id.,* which is proscribed by the Establishment Clause.

[T]he Establishment Clause embodied the Framers' conclusion that government and religion have discrete interests which are mutually best served when each avoids too close a proximity to the other. It is not only the nonbeliever who fears the injection of sectarian doctrines and controversies into the civil polity, but in as high degree it is the devout believer who fears the secularization of a creed which becomes too deeply involved with and dependent upon the government. It has rightly been said of the history of the Establishment Clause that "our tradition of civil liberty rests not only on the secularism of a Thomas Jefferson but also on the fervent sectarianism . . . of a Roger Williams."

Schempp, supra, 374 U.S. at 259–60, 83 S.Ct. at 1591 (Brennan, J., concurring) (footnotes omitted), *citing* P. Freund, The Supreme Court of the United States 84 (1964).

In addition to administrative entanglement, the rules also enmesh the school district in another type of entanglement first articulated in *Lemon, supra,* 403 U.S. at 623, 91 S.Ct. at 2116, that is, "the potential for political divisiveness related to religious belief and practice." *See also Meek v. Pittenger, supra,* 421 U.S. at 372, 95 S.Ct. at 1766; *Nyquist, supra,* 413 U.S. at 797–98, 93 S.Ct. at 2978; *see generally* L. Tribe, American Constitutional Law 866 (1978). As in the case of financial aid to parochial schools, proponents in favor of religious holiday observances, opponents against religious holiday observances and advocates for specific religious (or non-religious) holidays will engage in considerable political activity either to elect school board members whose views are compatible with their own views or to influence the school board.

It would be unrealistic to ignore the fact that many people confronted with issues of this kind will find their votes aligned with their faith.

Ordinarily political debate and division, however vigorous or even partisan, are normal and healthy manifestations of our democratic system of government, but political division along religious lines was one of the principal evils against which the First Amendment was intended to protect. The potential divisiveness of such conflict is a threat to the normal political process.

Lemon, supra, 403 U.S. at 622, 91 S.Ct. at 2116 (citations omitted).

V. *The Free Exercise Challenge*

Appellants also argue that the rules on the observance of religious holidays violate the Free Exercise Clause. In view of my Establishment Clause analysis, I do not reach this issue. However, I do not agree with the majority that the availability of excusal from participation in activities authorized under the rules refutes the Free Exercise challenge. At 1318–1319.

[T]he excusal procedure itself necessarily operates in such a way as to infringe the rights of free exercise of those children who wish to be excused. [The Supreme Court] held in *Barnette* and *Torcaso*, respectively, that a State may require neither public school students nor candidates for an office of public trust to profess beliefs offensive to religious principles. By the same token the State could not constitutionally require a student to profess publicly his disbelief as the prerequisite to the exercise of his constitutional right of abstention. . . . [B]y requiring what is tantamount in the eyes of teachers and schoolmates to a profession of disbelief, or at least of nonconformity, the procedure may well deter those children who do not wish to participate for any reason based upon the dictates of conscience from exercising an indisputably constitutional right to be excused. Thus the excusal provision in its operation subjects them to a cruel dilemma. In consequence, even devout children may well avoid claiming their right and simply continue to participate in exercises distasteful to them because of an understandable reluctance to be stigmatized as atheists or nonconformists simply on the basis of their request.

Schempp, supra, 374 U.S. at 288–90, 83 S.Ct. at 1606–1607 (Brennan, J., concurring) (citations and footnotes omitted).

VI. *Conclusion*

Of course, "every vestige, however slight, of co-operation or accommodation between religion and government" is *not* unconstitutional.[6] *Id.* at 294, 83 S.Ct. at 1609; *cf. Sherbert v. Verner,* 374 U.S. 398, 83 S.Ct. 1790, 10 L.Ed.2d 965 (1963) (free exercise clause required accommodation of state unemployment compensation benefits program for member of Seventh Day Adventist Church); *Zorach v. Clauson, supra,* 343 U.S. at 312, 72 S.Ct. at 683 (released time for religious instruction off school premises). There is nothing unconstitutional about the use of religious subjects or materials in public schools *as long as it is presented as part of a secular program of education.* However, to the extent the policy and rules adopted by the Sioux Falls School District authorizes the observance of religious holidays, particularly Christmas assemblies, in a manner other than as part of a secular program of education, I would hold the policy and rules violate the Establishment Clause.

The above analysis may be regarded by some as hypersensitive or even antireligious. It is not. Judicial scrutiny of the relationship between religion and government must be particularly scrupulous in the context of the public school.

The secular public school did not imply indifference to the basic role of religion in the life of the people, nor rejection of religious education as a means of fos-

tering it. The claims of religion were not minimized by refusing to make the public schools agencies for their assertion. The nonsectarian or secular public school was the means of reconciling freedom in general with religious freedom. The sharp confinement of the public schools to secular education was a recognition of the need of a democratic society to educate its children, insofar as the State undertook to do so, in an atmosphere free from pressures in a realm in which pressures are most resisted and where conflicts are most easily and most bitterly engendered. Designed to serve as perhaps the most powerful agency for promoting cohesion among a heterogeneous democratic people, the public school must keep scrupulously free from entanglement in the strife of sects. The preservation of the community from divisive conflicts, of Government from irreconcilable pressures by religious groups, of religion from censorship and coercion however subtly exercised, requires strict confinement of the State to instruction other than religious, leaving to the individual's church and home, indoctrination in the faith of his choice.

McCollum, supra, 333 U.S. at 216–17, 68 S.Ct. at 468 (Frankfurter, J., concurring).

It is implicit in the history and character of American public education that the public schools serve a uniquely *public* function: the training of American citizens in an atmosphere free of parochial, divisive, or separatist influences of any sort—an atmosphere in which children may assimilate a heritage common to all American groups and religions. This is a heritage neither theistic nor atheistic, but simply civic and patriotic.

Schempp, supra, 374 U.S. at 241–42, 83 S.Ct. at 1582 (Brennan, J., concurring) (citations omitted) (emphasis in original) (speaking in terms of division along *religious* lines).

I would reverse the judgment of the district court.

NOTES

1. The committee consisted of the school district's director of music, Jewish, Catholic and Protestant clergy, an attorney, a member of the American Civil Liberties Union, and parents and teachers of students in the district.

2. The policy statement and rules are set out in the appendix to this opinion. The rules challenged in this case are those contained under the heading "Observance of Religious Holidays."

3. *See, e.g., Abington School Dist. v. Schempp,* 374 U.S. 203, 212, 83 S.Ct. 1560, 1566, 10 L.Ed.2d 844 (1963) ("It is true that religion has been closely identified with our history and government."); *Engel v. Vitale,* 370 U.S. 421, 434, 82 S.Ct. 1261, 1268, 8 L.Ed.2d 601 (1962) ("The history of man is inseparable from the history of religion."); *Zorach v. Clauson,* 343 U.S. 306, 313, 72 S.Ct. 679, 684, 96 L.Ed. 954 (1952) ("We are a religious people

whose institutions presuppose a Supreme Being.").

4. The First Amendment has been made applicable to the states by the Fourteenth Amendment. *Engel v. Vitale, supra,* 370 U.S. at 422, 82 S.Ct. at 1262; *Zorach v. Clauson, supra,* 343 U.S. at 309, 72 S.Ct. at 681; *Cantwell v. Connecticut,* 310 U.S. 296, 303, 60 S.Ct. 900, 903, 84 L.Ed. 1213 (1940).

5. The singing of "Christmas carols" appears to be a primary focal point of appellants' objections to the rules. These carols had their origin in England, France, Germany, and other European countries. The first carols written in the United States appeared in the Nineteenth Century, but European carols were sung far earlier. The earliest printed collection of carols was published in 1521. Many of the popular carols of today, including *Adeste Fideles, Hark the Herald Angels Sing* and *Joy to the World,* were written in the early part of the Eighteenth Century. The most popular of all, *Silent Night, Holy Night,* was probably composed in Austria in 1818 and first published in 1840. Carols were banned for a period in the New England Colonies by the Puritans, but they have been sung in homes, schools, churches and public and private gathering places during the Christmas season in every section of the United States since that time. Today, carols are sung with regularity on public and commercial television and are played on public address systems in offices, manufacturing plants and retail stores in every city and village. *See* T. Coffin, The Book of Christmas Folklore (1973); R. Myers, Celebrations, The Complete Book of American Holidays; 5 Encyclopedia Americana 693 (International ed. 1968).

  Many carols have a religious theme; some do not. As in the centuries gone by, some persons object to the singing of carols with a religious basis in any place but the church or home because they feel that to do so debases religion; others have the same objection but because they feel it enhances religion. We take no part in this argument, it being entirely clear to us that carols have achieved a cultural significance that justifies their being sung in the public schools of Sioux Falls, South Dakota, if done in accordance with the policy and rules adopted by that school district.

6. In keeping with the goal of avoiding conflict with students' religious beliefs, the Sioux Falls policy statement includes the following:

  The school district should utilize its opportunity to foster understanding and mutual respect among students and parents, whether it involves race, culture, economic background or religious beliefs. In that spirit of tolerance, students and staff members should be excused from participating in practices which are contrary to their religious beliefs unless there are clear issues of overriding concern that would prevent it.

  The school district may, of course, excuse students from participating in this or any other school activity. But excusing students from participation does not solve Establishment Clause problems, *Abington School Dist. v. Schempp, supra,* 374 U.S. at 224–225, 83 S.Ct. at 1572–1573, and we find this aspect of the school district rules to be irrelevant to our Establishment Clause analysis.

7. The free exercise issue is stressed by amicus curiae, but it seems to have been added to the appellants' appeal brief as an afterthought. Neither the complaint, the trial briefs, nor the district court opinion mention the Free Exercise Clause; all are concerned only with the Establishment Clause.

8. *See* note 6 *supra.*

9. For a contrary view, see Note, *Religious—Holiday Observances in the Public Schools,* 48 N.Y.U.L.Rev. 1116 (1973). The authors of that Note would permit programs relating to religious holidays but would prohibit the display of any religious art or symbols as a part of the program and would further prohibit the singing of carols or songs that express reverence to God, Jesus, Buddha, Mohammed, or any other religious prophet or leader.

Dissenting Opinion Notes

1. The Court's historic duty to expound the meaning of the constitution has encountered few issues more intricate or more demanding than that of the relationship between religion and the public schools. Since undoubtedly we are "a religious people whose institutions presuppose a Supreme Being," *Zorach v. Clauson,* 343 U.S. 306, 313, 72 S.Ct. 679, 684, 96 L.Ed. 954, deep feelings are aroused when aspects of that relationship are claimed to violate the injunction of the First Amendment that government may make "no law respecting an establishment of religion, or prohibiting the free exercise thereof. . . . " Americans regard the public schools as a most vital civic institution for the preservation of a democratic system of government. It is therefore understandable that the constitutional prohibitions encounter their severest test when they are sought to be applied in the school classroom.

  School District v. Schempp, 374 U.S. 203, 230, 83 S.Ct. 1560, 1576, 10 L.Ed.2d 844 (1963) (Brennan, J., concurring) (*Schempp*).

2. Surely the place of the Bible as an instrument of religion cannot be gainsaid, and the State's recognition of the pervading religious character of the ceremony is evident from the rule's specific permission of the alternative use of the Catholic Douay version as well as the recent amendment permitting nonattendance at the exercises. None of these factors is consistent with the contention that the Bible is here used either as an instrument for nonreligious moral inspiration or as a reference for the teaching of secular subjects.

  Schempp, supra, 374 U.S. at 224, 83 S.Ct. at 1572.

3. Its authors did not simply prohibit the establishment of a state church or a state religion, an area history shows they regarded as very important and fraught with great dangers. Instead they commanded that there should be "no law *respecting* an establishment of religion." A law may be one "respecting" the forbidden objective while falling short of its total realization. A law "respecting" the proscribed result, that is, the establishment of religion, is not always easily identifiable as one violative of the Clause. A given law might not *establish* a state religion but nevertheless be one "respecting" that end in the sense of being a step that could lead to such establishment and hence offend the First Amendment.

  Lemon, supra, 403 U.S. at 612, 91 S.Ct. at 2111 (emphasis in original).

4. For example, Passover is often paired with Easter as is Chanukah with Christmas; however, Chanukah is not a major Jewish holiday and the rules, to the extent they suggest Chanukah has a religious significance to Jews comparable to that of Christmas to Christians, distort Judaism. Brief of American Jewish Congress as amicus curiae at 2 n.2. The rules do not include Rosh Hashanah or Yom Kippur.

5. Likewise, in *Schempp* the school authorities argued that Bible-reading and other religious recitations in public

schools served, primarily, secular purposes, including "the promotion of moral values, the contradiction to the materialistic trends of our times, the perpetuation of our institutions and the teaching of literature." 374 U.S. at 223; [83 S.Ct. at 1572]. . . .

It may assist in providing a historical perspective to recall that the argument here is not a new one. The Preamble to Patrick Henry's Bill Establishing a Provision for Teachers of the Christian Religion, which would have required Virginians to pay taxes to support religious teachers and which became the focal point of Madison's Memorial and Remonstrance . . . , contained the following listing of secular purposes: "The general diffusion of Christian knowledge hath a natural tendency to correct the morals of men, restrain their vices, and preserve the peace of society. . . . "

Nyquist, supra, 413 U.S. at 784–85 n.39, 93 S.Ct. at 2971 n.39 *citing Everson v. Board of Education,* 330 U.S.

1, 72–74, 67 S.Ct. 504, 538–539, 91 L.Ed. 711 (1947) (Appendix to dissent of Rutledge, J., reprinting the Bill in full).

6. For example, chaplains are provided in the armed forces and in prisons; public meetings (*see Bogen v. Doty,* 598 F.2d 1110 (8th Cir. 1979)) and legislative sessions are frequently opened by prayers; legislatures are served by chaplains; judicial sessions are opened with references to God; the currency of the Unites [sic] States carries the motto "In God We Trust;" businesses are closed by Sunday closing laws.

See Schempp, supra, 374 U.S. at 296–304, 83 S.Ct. at 1610–1614 (Brennan, J., concurring); *Engel v. Vitale, supra,* 370 U.S. at 435 n. 21, 82 S.Ct. at 1269; *but cf. id.* at 437–41 &nn.1–6, 82 S.Ct. at 1270–1272 (Douglas, J., concurring) ("Our system at the federal and state levels is presently honeycombed with [government financing of religious exercise].").

T HE United States Supreme Court decides that the Kentucky statute requiring the posting of a copy of the Ten Commandments on the wall of each public school classroom in the state is unconstitutional as violating the Establishment Clause of the First Amendment. The court concludes "that Kentucky's statute requiring the posting of the Ten Commandments in public school rooms has no secular legislative purpose, and is therefore unconstitutional."

Stone v. *Graham*, 449 U.S. 39 (1980)

PER CURIAM.

A Kentucky statute requires the posting of a copy of the Ten Commandments, purchased with private contributions, on the wall of each public classroom in the State.[1] Petitioners, claiming that this statute violates the Establishment and Free Exercise Clauses of the First Amendment,[2] sought an injunction against its enforcement. The state trial court upheld the statute, finding that its "avowed purpose" was "secular and not religious," and that the statute would "neither advance nor inhibit any religion or religious group" nor involve the State excessively in religious matters. App. to Pet. for Cert. 38–39. The Supreme Court of the Commonwealth of Kentucky affirmed by an equally divided court. 599 S.W.2d 157 (1980). We reverse.

This Court has announced a three-part test for determining whether a challenged state statute is permissible under the Establishment Clause of the United States Constitution:

"First, the statute must have a secular legislative purpose; second, its principal or primary effect must be one that neither advances nor inhibits religion . . . ; finally the statute must not foster 'an excessive government entanglement with religion.'" *Lemon* v. *Kurtzman,* 403 U.S. 602, 612–613 (1971) (citations omitted).

If a statute violates any of these three principles, it must be struck down under the Establishment Clause. We conclude that Kentucky's statute requiring the posting of the Ten Commandments in public school rooms has no secular legislative purpose, and is therefore unconstitutional.

The Commonwealth insists that the statute in question serves a secular legislative purpose, observing that the legislature required the following notation in small print at the bottom of each display of the Ten

Commandments: "The secular application of the Ten Commandments is clearly seen in its adoption as the fundamental legal code of Western Civilization and the Common Law of the United States." 1978 Ky. Acts, ch. 436, § 1 (effective June 17, 1978), Ky. Rev. Stat. § 158.178 (1980).

The trial court found the "avowed" purpose of the statute to be secular, even as it labeled the statutory declaration "self-serving." App. to Pet. for Cert. 37. Under this Court's rulings, however, such an "avowed" secular purpose is not sufficient to avoid conflict with the First Amendment. In *Abington School District* v. *Schempp,* 374 U.S. 203 (1963), this Court held unconstitutional the daily reading of Bible verses and the Lord's Prayer in the public schools, despite the school district's assertion of such secular purposes as "the promotion of moral values, the contradiction to the materialistic trends of our times, the perpetuation of our institutions and the teaching of literature." *Id.,* at 223.

The pre-eminent purpose for posting the Ten Commandments on schoolroom walls is plainly religious in nature. The Ten Commandments are undeniably a sacred text in the Jewish and Christian faiths,[3] and no legislative recitation of a supposed secular purpose can blind us to that fact. The Commandments do not confine themselves to arguably secular matters, such as honoring one's parents, killing or murder, adultery, stealing, false witness, and covetousness. See Exodus 20:12–17; Deuteronomy 5:16–21. Rather, the first part of the Commandments concerns the religious duties of believers: worshipping the Lord God alone, avoiding idolatry, not using the Lord's name in vain, and observing the Sabbath Day. See Exodus 20:1–11; Deuteronomy 5:6–15.

This is not a case in which the Ten Commandments are integrated into the school curriculum, where the Bible may constitutionally be used in an appropriate study of history, civilization, ethics, comparative religion, or the like. *Abington School District* v. *Schempp, supra,* at 225. Posting of religious texts on the wall serves no such educational function. If the posted copies of the Ten Commandments are to have any effect at all, it will be to induce the schoolchildren to read, meditate upon, perhaps to venerate and obey, the Commandments. However desirable this might be as a matter of private devotion, it is not a permissible state objective under the Establishment Clause.

It does not matter that the posted copies of the Ten Commandments are financed by voluntary private contributions, for the mere posting of the copies under the auspices of the legislature provides the "official support of the State ... Government" that the Establishment Clause prohibits. 374 U.S., at 222; see *Engel* v. *Vitale,* 370 U.S. 421, 431 (1962).[4] Nor is it significant that the Bible verses involved in this case are merely posted on the wall, rather than read aloud as in *Schempp* and *Engel,* for "it is no defense to urge that the religious practices here may be relatively minor encroachments on the First Amendment." *Abington School District* v. *Schempp, supra,* at 225. We conclude that Ky. Rev. Stat. § 158.178 (1980) violates the first part of the *Lemon* v. *Kurtzman* test, and thus the Establishment Clause of the Constitution.[5]

The petition for a writ of certiorari is granted, and the judgment below is reversed.

It is so ordered.

NOTES

1. The statute provides in its entirety:
   "(1) It shall be the duty of the superintendent of public instruction, provided sufficient funds are available as provided in subsection (3) of this Section, to ensure that a durable, permanent copy of the Ten Commandments shall be displayed on a wall in each public elementary and secondary school classroom in the Commonwealth. The copy shall be sixteen (16) inches wide by twenty (20) inches high.
   "(2) In small print below the last commandment shall appear a notation concerning the purpose of the display, as follows: 'The secular application of the Ten Commandments is clearly seen in its adoption as the fundamental legal code of Western Civilization and the Common Law of the United States.'
   "(3) The copies required by this Act shall be purchased with funds made available through voluntary contributions made to the state treasurer for the purposes of this Act." 1978 Ky. Acts, ch. 436, § 1 (effective June 17, 1978), Ky. Rev. Stat. § 158.178 (1980).
2. The First Amendment provides in relevant part: "Congress shall make no law respecting an establishment of religion, or prohibiting the free exercise thereof. . . ." This prohibition is applicable to the States through the Fourteenth Amendment. *Abington School District* v. *Schempp,* 374 U.S. 203, 215–216 (1963).
3. As this Court commented in *Abington School District* v. *Schempp, supra,* at 224: "Surely the place of the Bible as an instrument of religion cannot be gainsaid. . . ."
4. Moreover, while the actual copies of the Ten Commandments were purchased through private contributions, the State nevertheless expended public money in administering the statute. For example, the statute requires that the state treasurer serve as a collecting agent for the contributions. Ky. Rev. Stat. § 158.178 (3) (1980).

I<small>N</small> 1982, the House of Representatives of the Commonwealth of Massachusetts was considering a bill requiring a period of voluntary prayer or meditation in public schools. The Massachusetts legislature asked the justices of the Supreme Judicial Court of Massachusetts to answer the question: "Would the enactment of said bill which allows voluntary permissible prayer and meditation in the public schools of the Commonwealth be constitutional under the First and Fourteenth Amendments of the United States Constitution?" The justices, in answering that the bill "if enacted, would violate the First and Fourteenth Amendments to the Constitution," stated: "Neither the fact that the opening period may sometimes result in silent meditation, nor that its observance is by a student volunteer, can serve to free it from the limitations of the Establishment Clause."

Opinions of the Justices to the House of Representatives, Mass., 440 N.E.2d 1159 (1982)

On September 30, 1982, the Justices submitted the following answer to questions propounded to them by the House of Representatives.

To the Honorable the House of Representatives of the Commonwealth of Massachusetts:

The undersigned Justices of the Supreme Judicial Court respectfully submit their response to the questions set forth in an order adopted by the House of Representatives on August 3, 1982, and transmitted to us on August 5, 1982.

The order recites that House No. 1454, a bill pending before the General Court, provides for a period of voluntary prayer or meditation in public schools, and that grave doubt exists as to its constitutionality if enacted into law. A copy of the bill was transmitted with the order. The bill entitled, "An Act requiring a period for voluntary prayer or meditation in public schools," would amend G.L. c. 71, § 1A, by striking out the present § 1A and inserting in its place the following sections:

"*Section 1A.* At the commencement of the first class of each day in all grades in all public schools the teacher in charge of the room in which each class is held shall announce that a period of voluntary prayer or meditation may be offered by a student volunteer, not to exceed one minute in duration.

Section B. Such prayer shall not establish a religion in Public Schools, just as the prayer by the

Chaplains of the Senate and House of Representatives, and the Crier of the Supreme Court, does not establish [a] religion in our government."

The order presents two questions to us:

"1. Would the enactment of said bill which allows voluntary permissible prayer and meditation in the public schools of the commonwealth be constitutional under Article II of Part I of the Constitution of the Commonwealth?

"2. Would the enactment of said bill which allows voluntary permissible prayer and meditation in the public schools of the commonwealth be constitutional under the First and Fourteenth Amendment of the United States Constitution?"[1]

We treat the questions presented by the House of Representatives in reverse order because if the proposed statute would violate the First Amendment of the United States Constitution, as applicable to the States through the Fourteenth Amendment, *Cantwell v. Connecticut,* 310 U.S. 296, 303, 60 S.Ct. 900, 903, 84 L.Ed. 1213 (1940), its constitutionality under the Massachusetts Constitution is irrelevant. See, e.g., *Moe v. Secretary of Admin. & Fin.,* 382 Mass. 629, ___, Mass.Adv.Sh. (1981) 464, 479, 417 N.E.2d 387. We note also that "the criteria which have been established by the United States Supreme Court for judging claims arising under the First Amendment . . . are equally appropriate to claims brought under cognate provisions of the Massachusetts Constitution." *Colo. v. Treasurer & Receiver Gen.*, 378 Mass. 550, 558, 392 N.E.2d 1195 (1979).

Section 1A of House No. 1454 is almost indistinguishable in substance from the statute this court held unconstitutional in *Kent v, Commissioner of Educ.*, 380 Mass. 235, 402 N.E.2d 1340 (1980). In *Kent,* this court was called upon to review the constitutionality of a version of G.L. c. 71, § 1A, as appearing in St.1979, c. 692. That version read as follows: "At the commencement of the first class of each day in all grades in all public schools the teacher in charge of the room in which each such class is held shall announce that a period of prayer may be offered by a student volunteer, and during any such period an excusal provision will be allowed for those students who do not wish to participate." The plaintiffs in *Kent,* public school children and their parents, challenged the statute as violative of the First Amendment to the United States Constitution which states in pertinent part that "Congress shall make no law respecting an establishment of religion, or prohibiting the free exercise thereof. . . ." The court held the law to be unconstitutional because the statute was religious in character and had a sectarian purpose and effect. *Kent, supra,* at ___ __ ___, Mass.Adv.Sh. at 810–813 (1980) 402 N.E.2d 1340. We concluded that enforcement by the Commonwealth of the legislation in regard to school prayer would violate the principle of separation of church and State as embodied in the First Amendment.[2]

The only discernible distinction between the statute in *Kent* (St.1979, c. 692) and House No. 1454 is that House No. 1454 does not exclusively contemplate that the student volunteer will offer a prayer. The student may offer a period of meditation. We think that the addition of the words "or meditation" is of no constitutional significance in this context.[3] House No. 1454 contemplates that, at least in some instances, viz., at the student volunteer's discretion, prayers will be orally recited. The proposed statute, on its face, demonstrates an intent to return prayer to the public schools. The United States Supreme Court, however, has consistently held that the Establishment Clause withdraws all legislative power respecting religious belief or the expression thereof. *School Dist. of Abington Township v. Schempp,* 374 U.S. 203, 222, 83 S.Ct. 1560, 1571, 10 L.Ed.2d 844 (1963). "Under the authorities the Establishment Clause is interpreted to prohibit religious observances on public school property even when these are nondenominational and participation in them on the part of pupils is voluntary." *Kent, supra* at _____, Mass.Adv.Sh. at 808, 402 N.E.2d 1340.

Neither the fact that the opening period may sometimes result in silent meditation, nor that its observance is by a student volunteer, can serve to free it from the limitations of the Establishment Clause. See *Engel v. Vitale,* 370 U.S. 421, 430, 82 S.Ct. 1261, 1266, 8 L.Ed.2d 601 (1962); *Kent, supra* at 811–812. "The Court's opinion in the *Schempp* case articulated and applied two tests or guidelines for the decision of Establishment Clause cases of that order. The Court said (374 U.S. at 222, 83 S.Ct. at 1571): ' . . . The test may be stated as follows: what are the purpose and the primary effect of the enactment? If either is the advancement or inhibition of religion then the enactment exceeds the scope of legislative power as circumscribed by the Constitution. That is to say that to withstand the strictures of the Establishment Clause *there must be a secular legislative purpose and a primary effect that neither advances nor inhibits religion.*' (Emphasis added.)" *Kent, supra* at _____, Mass.Adv.Sh. at 809, 402 N.E.2d 1340.

The purpose of House No. 1454 is clear—the bill seeks to encourage the recitation of prayer in public schools. The opening exercise, if the student volunteer chooses to offer a prayer, is a religious ceremony and is intended by the bill to be so. The effect of the statute would be to return prayer to the public schools. Such a bill would, if enacted, come into clear conflict with the prohibitions of the Establishment Clause of the First Amendment. We advert once more to the opinion of the court in *Kent:* "When prayers [are to be] daily heard in most classrooms of many public schools in the Commonwealth, and this occur[s] as a result of legislative enactment, it [is] more than a strain to attempt to argue that religion [is] not being advanced in the sense of the Constitution." *Kent, supra,* ___ __ ___, Mass.Adv.Sh. at 811–812, 402 N.E.2d 1340.

Section B of House No. 1454, by asserting that the school prayer bill "shall not establish a religion in Public Schools, just as the prayer by the Chaplains of the Senate and House of Representatives . . . does not establish [a] religion in our government," attempts to invade the rightful province of the judiciary to adjudicate whether a law conflicts with the requirements of the Constitution. "'This,' in the words of Mr. Chief Justice Marshall, 'is of the very essence of judicial duty.'" *Colo. v. Treasurer & Receiver Gen., supra* 378 Mass. at 553, 392 N.E.2d 1195, quoting from *Marbury v. Madison,* 5 U.S. (1 Cranch) 137, 178, 2 L.Ed. 60 (1803). In any event, the drafters of this bill appear mistakenly to analogize school prayer to ceremonial practices similar to the one this court held constitutional in *Colo. v. Treasurer & Receiver Gen., supra* 378 Mass. at 561, 392 N.E.2d 1195.

Any suggestion that the court's decision in *Colo. v. Treasurer & Receiver Gen., supra,* provides an answer to the question presented here is in error. The *Colo* court emphatically distinguished the opening prayer of the Legislature from the practice of prayer in public schools by stating that "such invocations are easily distinguishable from the practice of daily prayer . . . in the [public] schools. There the State, by incorporating religious exercises into the context of a compulsory school day, lends at least implicit support to the notion that children should be indoctrinated to accept religion. The purpose of a school is to teach impressionable children, many of whom, because of their ages, cannot be expected to comprehend that school-sponsored prayers are not necessarily 'lessons' to be learned like other aspects of the school program. . . . By contrast, mature legislators may reasonably be assumed to have fully formed their own religious beliefs or nonbeliefs." (Citations omitted.) *Colo, supra* at 559, 392 N.E.2d 1195.[4] Thus we conclude that the ritual practice of a short prayer before a mature audience is distinguishable from government–sponsored prayer from children whose attendance in school is compulsory.[5]

We conclude that House No. 1454, if enacted, would violate the First and Fourteenth Amendments to the United States Constitution. Our answer to question 2 is, "No." Our answer to question 2 makes it unnecessary for us to respond to question 1. Accordingly, we beg to be excused from responding thereto.

The foregoing opinion and answer is submitted by the Chief Justice and the Associate Justices subscribing hereto on the thirtieth day of September, 1982.

EDWARD F. HENNESSEY
HERBERT P. WILKINS
PAUL J. LIACOS
RUTH I. ABRAMS
FRANCIS P. O'CONNOR

We cannot join in this response of the Justices because we find that this case is utterly indistinguishable from *Colo v. Treasurer & Receiver Gen.*, 378 Mass. 550, 392 N.E.2d 1195 (1979), on the substantive issues (there will always be accidental differences). In *Colo,* the court found nothing constitutionally offensive in expending public monies to pay the salaries of chaplains of the Massachusetts House of Representatives and Senate who open each day's activities with a prayer. The following language in *Colo* fits school prayer as proposed in the questions like a glove: "There is no evidence that a great degree of government entanglement with religion is occasioned by the employment of legislative chaplains [substitute "student volunteers"]. The prayers offered are brief, the content unsupervised by the State, and attendance completely voluntary. There is no evidence that the State has become embroiled in any difficult decisions about which religions are to be represented or what sorts of invocations are to be offered." *Colo, supra* at 559, 392 N.E.2d 1195.

The Justices strain at distinguishing *Colo* by quoting its dictum to the effect that a short prayer may "indoctrinate" (the word belongs to *Colo*) children into the habit of saying a prayer, whereas mature legislators have already been either indoctrinated or not in the habit of prayer, and the prayer in opening the legislative session is really a meaningless liturgy anyway, or to use the Justices' language, a "ritual practice." To state this is to refute it.

We just cannot see any real difference between *Colo* and the suggested format for school prayer. Indeed, *Colo* presents a stronger case for prayer banning under the majority's secularistic interpretation of the First Amendment to the United States Constitution because of the salaries paid to the chaplains from public funds.

JOSEPH R. NOLAN
NEIL L. LYNCH

NOTES

1. Responding to our invitation for briefs from interested persons, the Massachusetts Board of Education has argued that the questions should be answered in the negative; the Committee to Restore Voluntary Prayer in School has argued that the questions should be answered in the affirmative.

2. We are not persuaded by the argument of amicus curiae, the Committee to Restore Voluntary Prayer in School, that the recent decision of *Widmar v. Vincent*, _____ U.S. _____, 102 S.Ct. 269, 70 L.Ed.2d 440 (1981), limited the holding in *School Dist. of Abington Township v. Schempp*, 374 U.S. 203, 83 S.Ct. 1560, 10 L.Ed.2d 844 (1963), on which we relied in *Kent v. Commissioner of Educ.*, (1980) 380 Mass. 235, 402 N.E.2d 1340. The facts in *Widmar* are wholly dissimilar. In *Widmar*, university students who were members of a registered religious group challenged a regulation adopted by the University of Missouri that prohibited the use of University grounds or buildings for purposes of religious worship or teaching. *Widmar, supra* at 272. The University routinely provided its facilities for meetings of registered organizations. *Id.* The *Widmar* Court framed the issue before it as follows: "In order to justify discriminatory exclusion from a public forum based on the religious content of a group's intended speech, the University must therefore satisfy the standard of review appropriate to content-based exclusions. It must show that its regulation is necessary to serve a compelling state interest and that it is narrowly drawn to achieve that end." *Id.* at 274. The Court went on to note that "it is on the bases of speech and association rights that we decide the case" and that the Court need not reach "the questions that would arise if State accommodation of Free Exercise and Free Speech rights should, in a particular case, conflict with the prohibitions of the Establishment Clause." *Id.* at 276 n. 13.

   Thus, the Court never cited its decision in *Schempp*, as there was no need to distinguish *Schempp* from *Wid-*

mar. The Court concluded that the basis for its decision was "narrow": "Having created a forum generally open to student groups, the University seeks to enforce a content-based exclusion of religious speech. Its exclusionary policy violates the fundamental principle that a state regulation of speech should be content-neutral, and the University is unable to justify this violation under applicable constitutional standards." *Id.* at 278.

In the *Schempp* case, by contrast, the Court relied only on the Establishment Clause claim in striking down statutes that provided for prayers and other religious exercises in public schools. *Schempp, supra* 374 U.S. at 205, 83 S.Ct. at 1562. The *Schempp* case is also readily distinguishable, on its facts, from *Widmar.* Compare *Schempp, supra* at 223, 83 S.Ct. at 1572, with *Widmar, supra* at 276 n. 14.

3. In *Gaines v. Anderson,* 421 F.Supp. 337 (D.Mass.1976), a three-judge panel in the Federal District Court ruled on the constitutionality of an earlier version of § 1A of G.L. c. 71, as amended by St.1973, c. 621, which provided for a period of silence or meditation at the commencement of the school day. The *Gaines* court noted that although the word "prayer" has a sectarian meaning, the word "meditation" does not. *Gaines, supra* at 342–343 & n. 8. As such, the choice given to the student to pray or to meditate on purely secular matters did not violate the Establishment Clause of the First Amendment. Rather, the secular and pedagogical practice of preparing the students to engage in a day of study by requiring them to turn their thoughts silently to serious matters, was constitutionally permissible. *Gaines, supra* at 346.

4. We note that the Justices comprising the quorum in *Colo v. Treasurer and Receiver Gen.,* 378 Mass. 550, 392 N.E.2d 1195 (1979), were all included in the unanimous full court decision in *Kent v. Commissioner of Educ.,* 380 Mass. 235, 402 N.E.2d 1340 (1980).

5. Courts and commentators have noted that school children who are particularly susceptible to the influence of their teachers and who are intellectually undeveloped have little real and meaningful choice in deciding to decline participation in a religious exercise. See *Schempp, supra* 374 U.S. at 290 n. 69, 83 S.Ct. at 1607 (Brennan, J., concurring); *Reed v. Van Hoven,* 237 F.Supp. 48, 52 (W.D.Mich. 1965); Choper, Religion in the Public Schools: A Proposed Constitutional Standard, 47 Minn.L.Rev. 329, 343 (1963); Comment, Religious Garb in the Public Schools—A Study in Conflicting Liberties, 22 U.Chi.L.Rev. 888, 893 (1955).

A United States District Court in Tennessee declares unconstitutional a Tennessee statute which provided that in the "first class of each day in all grades in all public schools, the teacher in charge of the room in which such class is held shall announce that a period of silence not to exceed one minute of duration shall be observed for meditation or prayer or personal beliefs and during any such period, silence shall be maintained." In deciding that the statute violated the Establishment Clause, the court stated: "The founders of our nation knew personally the dangers and the persecution that are set afoot when governments take a position either for or against religious beliefs, and they recognized very well that 'freedom to worship was indispensable in a country whose people came from the four quarters of the earth and brought with them a diversity of religious opinion.' Bringing their convictions to bear, the framers of our Constitution were determined that every *individual* must be free to practice or not to practice religious beliefs in accordance with the dictates of his own conscience, and that *government* must stay out of religious affairs entirely. The issue here, then, concerns power—the power of the legislature—and it is clear that on both sides of the spectrum, the state lacks power either to handicap or to favor religions. . . . "

Beck v. *McElrath,* 548 F.Supp. 1161 (1982)

MORTON, Chief Judge.

In this civil action plaintiffs seek declaratory relief pursuant to 42 U.S.C. § 1983, the First and Fourteenth Amendments to the United States Constitution, and Article I, Section 3 of the Tennessee Constitution. It is alleged that an enactment by the General Assembly of Tennessee must be declared unconstitutional.

I.

The challenged provision states:

At the commencement of the first class of each day in all grades in all public schools, the teacher in charge of the room in which such class is held shall announce that a period of silence not to exceed one minute of duration shall be observed for meditation or prayer or personal beliefs and during any such period, silence shall be maintained.

1982 Tenn.Pub.Acts ch. 899, § 1 (amending Tenn. Code Ann. § 49-1922). The basic question presented in this lawsuit concerns whether the General Assembly could enact this amendment in light of the Establish-

ment Clause.

As a preliminary matter, defendants point out that prayer has never been prohibited in public schools, and that those who generally state that prayer is prohibited do so incorrectly. This statement is obviously correct, for "the Free Exercise Clause . . . recognizes the value of religious training, teaching and observance and, more particularly, the right of every person to freely choose his own course with reference thereto, free of any compulsion from the state." *School District v. Schempp,* 374 U.S. 203, 222, 83 S.Ct. 1560, 1571, 10 L.Ed.2d 844 (1963). Defendants also point out that the Constitution does not require an anti-religious government. This statement is also clearly supported by the above-quoted authority. Moreover, the Supreme Court has expressly noted elsewhere that the First Amendment "requires the state to be a neutral in its relations with groups of religious believers and non-believers; it does not require the state to be their adversary. State power is no more to be used so as to handicap religions, than it is to favor them." *Everson v. Board of Education,* 330 U.S. 1, 18, 67 S.Ct. 504, 513, 91 L.Ed. 711 (1947). Identifying these concepts as constitutional realities, defendants set out to fashion an argument in support of the challenged statute. Such realities under the Free Exercise Clause are not determinative of the issues in this case, however. Defendants recognize, as does the court, that no issue in this case touches upon alleged infringement of rights secured under that clause. To the contrary, it is claimed that the state has attempted to promote, rather than inhibit, religious exercises in the public schools. The Establishment Clause, as an interrelated and complementary provision, prohibits action by the state which transcends the bounds of neutrality on the opposite side of the issue to which the identified realities address themselves. A decision cannot be reached in this case without also looking at the other side of the coin, so to speak, for "[w]hile the Free Exercise Clause clearly prohibits the use of state action to deny the rights of free exercise to *anyone*, it has never meant that a majority could use the machinery of the State to practice its beliefs." *Schempp, supra,* 374 U.S. at 226, 83 S.Ct. at 1573.

II.

The history of the First Amendment as it relates to religious freedom has been detailed on numerous occasions. Most commonly recognized is the principle that the framers of the Constitution sought to prevent the establishment of any single denomination as a state church, because it is well known that "[a] large proportion of the early settlers of this country came here from Europe to escape the bondage of laws which compelled them to support and attend government favored churches." *Everson, supra,* 330 U.S. at 8, 67 S.Ct. at 508. The story behind the religion clauses goes further, however. With Thomas Jefferson and James Madison as leading proponents of complete individual freedom in matters concerning religion,

> [t]he people [in Virginia], as elsewhere, reached the conviction that individual religious liberty could be achieved best under a government which was stripped of all power to tax, to support, or otherwise to assist any or all religions, or to interfere with the beliefs of any religious individual or group.

Id. at 11, 67 S.Ct. at 509. Thus governments in this country are not only powerless to establish an official church; governments in this country are powerless to support, assist, suppress, or hinder religious beliefs in any respect whatsoever. The meaning of the Establishment Clause, in particular, can therefore be stated as follows:

> Neither a state nor the Federal Government can set up a church. Neither can pass laws which aid one religion, aid all religions, or prefer one religion over another. Neither can force nor influence a person to go to or to remain away from church against his will

or force him to profess a belief or disbelief in any religion. No person can be punished for entertaining or professing religious beliefs or disbeliefs, for church attendance or nonattendance. No tax in any amount, large or small, can be levied to support any religious activities or institutions, whatever they may be called, or whatever form they may adopt to teach or practice religion. Neither a state nor the Federal Government can, openly or secretly, participate in the affairs of any religious organizations or groups and vice versa. In the words of Jefferson, the clause against establishment of religion by law was intended to erect "a wall of separation between Church and State."

Id. at 115–116, 67 S.Ct. at 511–12 (citations omitted). Upon this foundation, the test which generally confronts legislation alleged to contravene the Establishment Clause has been stated as follows:

> [T]o pass muster under the Establishment Clause the law in question first must reflect a clearly secular legislative purpose, second, must have a primary effect that neither advances nor inhibits religion, and, third, must avoid excessive government entanglement with religion.

Committee for Public Education and Religious Liberty v. Nyquist, 413 U.S. 756, 774, 93 S.Ct. 2955, 2965, 37 L.Ed.2d 948 (1973).

A.

Defendants suggest that the statute merely provides for enforcement of a moment of silence in public schools. This approach begs the preeminent question, however. Plaintiffs do not challenge simply a moment of silence here; they challenge a moment of silence which, by legislative mandate in Tennessee, "shall be observed for meditation or prayer or personal beliefs." It may well be, as defendants contend, that a moment of silence in and of itself is nondiscriminatory and may serve a secular purpose in aid of the educative function. Certainly a statutory enactment is unnecessary to provide for a moment of silence. The court is unable to agree, however, that the statute reflects such a clearly secular purpose. In the abstract it is true that "meditation" and "reflection upon personal beliefs" can be viewed as carrying meanings that do not touch upon religion. Individual terms within a statute are not to be construed in a purely abstract sense or in a vacuum, however. As all terms in the statute are viewed together and accorded reasonable meaning, it is difficult to escape the conclusion that the legislative purpose was advancement of religious exercises in the classroom. Ordinary principles of statutory construction do not comprehend the straining that defendants would urge upon the court.

At the very best, it might be said that the statute

on its face is ambiguous, and that the court should consider underlying legislative history. If that is the case, the record of debate upon this statute is devastating to defendants' position. The overwhelming intent among legislators supporting the bill, including the sponsors, was to establish prayer as a daily fixture in the public schoolrooms of Tennessee. Even if much that was said can be passed off as political rhetoric, it is rhetoric clearly inconsistent with standards set in place by the Constitution, and therefore reflects upon an inappropriate purpose. There were indications that certain legislators have concluded that prayer should be a routine part of a school day because a majority of their constituents support such a practice. But such reliance, even upon the sentiments of a public majority whose existence might be subject to judicial notice, takes no account of the principle that:

> The very purpose of a Bill of Rights was to withdraw certain subjects from the vicissitudes of political controversy, to place them beyond the reach of majorities and officials and to establish them as legal principles to be applied by the courts. One's right to ... freedom of worship ... and other fundamental rights may not be submitted to vote; they depend on the outcome of no elections.

West Virginia Board of Education v. Barnette, 319 U.S. 624, 638, 63 S.Ct. 1178, 1185, 87 L.Ed. 1628 (1943). If this is not correct, by leaving political favor and majority sentiment to carry the day on all issues we have no need for a Constitution at all, and we might determine our most basic rights by consulting the latest Gallup Poll.

In support of their contention that the legislative purpose was secular in nature, defendants partially quote the comments of Senator Henry. It is instructive to note, however, that Senator Henry was speaking in support of an amendment which would have deleted from the bill any reference to prayer. Senator Henry argued to no avail his conviction that "the prayer proposition I really don't think we ought to legislate." Immediately following his comments another senator rose in opposition to the same amendment and opened his remarks by stating:

> If there is one thing the people of this state want, they want prayer in public schools. The fact of the matter is this is a vote on prayer in public schools. Now Senator Henry ... just has a different point of view. But if you want to get recorded as being against prayer in public school, you vote for his amendment.

The amendment was defeated by a vote of 24 to 7, and thus it is quite as likely as not that the Senate intentionally turned away from the secular objective supported by Senator Henry. In any event, his remarks were hardly endorsed by the Senate and certainly do not support a finding of a secular purpose.

Defendants also refer to statements by Senator Dunavant and Senator Davis, each of whom spoke in opposition to Senator Henry's amendment. But Senator Dunavant's remarks consisted for the most part of a defense for the bill based upon the absence of coercion. Senator Davis agreed with Senator Dunavant and echoed his sentiments, indicating that "[t]he kids can pray, which we hope that most of them will, but they don't have to." The real import of their remarks, in other words, appears to be that although the subject legislation would indeed serve to promote prayer in schools, it would be constitutionally acceptable so long as children were not forced to pray. Such reasoning, whether defendants consciously adopt it or not, overlooks the distinction that "a violation of the Free Exercise Clause is predicated on coercion while the Establishment Clause violation need not be so attended." *Schempp, supra,* 374 U.S. at 223, 83 S.Ct. at 1572. *See also Engel v. Vitale,* 370 U.S. 421, 82 S.Ct. 1261, 8 L.Ed.2d 601 (1962). Moreover, it does nothing to dispel the appearance of a legislative purpose directed almost solely toward the promotion of religion, because:

> That a child is offered an alternative may reduce the constraint; it does not eliminate the operation of influence by the school in matters sacred to conscience and outside the school's domain. The law of imitation operates, and nonconformity is not an outstanding characteristic of children.

McCollum v. Board of Education, 333 U.S. 203, 227, 68 S.Ct. 461, 473, 92 L.Ed. 649 (1948) (Frankfurter, J., concurring).

Certain modifications in the statutory language were approved, ostensibly in an effort to bring that language into line with constitutional requirements. But a mere cursory reading of the legislative history discloses that the purpose for which the statute was enacted remained constant—the legislature sought to set aside a time for daily religious exercises in public schools. Certainly no other purpose is apparent which substantially influenced the legislature as a body, or which can be viewed as more than a "merely adjunctive and supplemental" secular purpose. *DeSpain v. DeKalb County Community School District,* 384 F.2d 836, 839 (7th Cir. 1967), *cert. denied,* 390 U.S. 906, 88 S.Ct. 815, 19 L.Ed.2d 873 (1968).

B.

The second factor to be considered under *Nyquist* concerns the primary effect of legislation. Schools were not in session when the hearing in this case was conducted, and no evidence was produced. Nevertheless, the effect of this statute should be examined. *See, e.g., Nyquist, supra* (case resolved on basis of pleadings, without evidentiary hearing). The natural effect must be determined from the face of the statute, if for no other reason because the legislature did not provide any guidelines for implementing its requirements.

The court is convinced that the primary effect of this statute must be the promotion of religious exercises. Stated otherwise, it is presumed that the effect will be that which was intended by the legislature. As a practical matter, the statute's effect may well differ from one classroom to another in the absence of implementing guidelines. For example, some teachers might simply call for a moment of silence; some might call for a moment of silence and instruct students that they are to meditate, pray, or reflect upon their personal beliefs; and some, in straightforward execution of the legislative intent, might instruct students that a time is being provided for them to pray. If, for that matter, teachers merely recite the statute to students and announce that its terms will be followed, the primary effect would appear to be obvious. Unavoidably, students will understand that they are being encouraged not only to be silent, but also to engage in religious exercises. It cannot be seriously argued, and certainly cannot be assured, that nice distinctions concerning the potential meanings of "meditation" and "personal beliefs" will naturally arise in the minds of public school students.

C.

In light of conclusions discussed above, a detailed examination of potential administrative entanglements under the third prong of the *Nyquist* test is not necessary here. Suffice it to say that the bill not only leaves school officials and teachers in the position of administering the law, but also leaves them to interpret its requirements. As they perform these tasks, "public funds, though small in amount, are being used to promote a religious exercise. Through the mechanism of the State, all of the people are being required to finance a religious exercise that only some of the people want and that violates the sensibilities of others." *Schempp, supra,* 374 U.S. at 229, 83 S.Ct. at 1575 (Douglas, J., concurring). Varying degress of potential entanglement are as difficult to enumerate as are the potential effects, and appear to be no less problematical.

III.

It cannot be denied, as the Supreme Court has explicitly recognized, "that religion has been closely identified with our history and government," *Schempp, supra,* 374 U.S. at 213, 83 S.Ct. at 1566, that indeed "[t]he history of man is inseparable from the history of religion," *Engel, supra,* 370 U.S. at 434, 82 S.Ct. at 1268, that the founders of our country "believed devotedly that there was a God and that the unalienable rights of man were rooted in Him," *Schempp, supra,* 374 U.S. at 213, 83 S.Ct. at 1566, and that an exceedingly large majority of people in this nation identify themselves as holding religious beliefs, *see id.,* 374 U.S. at 213, 83 S.Ct. at 1566. Religion has occupied, and continues to occupy, a prominent role in this society. As a corollary, and as no less an abiding principle, total religious freedom has held an exalted position in this country. The founders of our nation knew personally the dangers and the persecution that are set afoot when governments take a position either for or against religious beliefs, and they recognized very well that "freedom to worship was indispensable in a country whose people came from the four quarters of the earth and brought with them a diversity of religious opinion." *Schempp, supra,* 374 U.S. at 214, 83 S.Ct. at 1567. Bringing their convictions to bear, the framers of our Constitution were determined that every *individual* must be free to practice or not to practice religious beliefs in accordance with the dictates of his own conscience, and that *government* must stay out of religious affairs entirely. The issue here, then, concerns power—the power of the legislature— and it is clear that on both sides of the spectrum, the state lacks power either to handicap or to favor religions, *Everson, supra,* 330 U.S. at 18, 67 S.Ct. at 513. The absence of power under our Constitution to enact legislation respecting religion is complete, however popular a measure might be and whether it would *favor* or *oppose* a particular religion or all religions. Justice Rutledge, dissenting in the *Everson* case, forcefully stated this principle, as follows:

Our constitutional policy ... does not deny the value or the necessity for religious training, teaching or observance. Rather it secures their free exercise. But to that end it does deny that the state can undertake or sustain them in any form or degree. For this reason the sphere of religious activity, as distinguished from the secular intellectual liberties, has been given the twofold protection and, as the state cannot forbid, neither can it perform or aid in performing the religious function. The dual prohibition makes that function altogether private.

Everson, supra, 330 U.S. at 52, 67 S.Ct. at 529.

Even if all of the tests and what might be viewed as technical requirements are to be set aside, the ultimate question in a case such as this nevertheless concerns whether the legislation at issue is neutral; whether it favors religion, or whether it opposes religion. It if is not neutral it must be struck down:

The wholesome "neutrality" of which [Supreme Court] cases speak ... stems from a recognition of the teachings of history that powerful sects or groups might bring about a fusion of governmental and religious functions or a concert of dependency of one upon the other to the end that official support of the

State or Federal Government would be placed behind the tenets of one or of all orthodoxies. This the Establishment Clause prohibits. And a further reason for neutrality is found in the Free Exercise Clause, which recognizes the value of religious training, teaching and observance, and, more particularly, the right of every person to freely choose his own course with reference thereto, free of any compulsion from the state. This the Free Exercise Clause guarantees.

Schempp, supra, 374 U.S at 222, 83 S.Ct. at 1571.

Under our Constitution, individuals can exercise their religious beliefs or individuals can refuse to exercise religious beliefs, and they may do so as groups, but Congress and state legislatures must leave them alone. Individuals can promote their religious beliefs or individuals can oppose religious beliefs, and they may do so as groups, but Congress and state legislatures cannot. The statute before the court was not intended to be a neutral measure, and it cannot be viewed as such. It is therefore violative of the Establishment Clause.

A United States District Court in Texas "holds that the pratice of initiating, leading, or encouraging the recitation or singing of the 'Aldine school prayer' is in violation of the First Amendment." The prayer had been posted on the wall over the entrance to the gymnasium at Aldine Senior High School and had been "recited or sung by students to music played by the Aldine School band at athletic contests, pep rallies, and at graduation ceremonies. . . . These activities take place before or after regular school hours, but are sponsored by Aldine Senior High School and form a part of the school's regular extracurricular program. The recitation or singing is frequently initiated by the high school principal or other school employees." The Court argued, in part: "Since these extracurricular events were school sponsored and so closely identified with the school program, the fact that the religious activity took place in a non-religious setting might create in a student's mind the impression that the state's attitude toward religion lacks neutrality. . . . This court has found that defendants' practice carries with it the implied recognition and approval of religious activity. Not only are the words in question recited or sung on school property at school events but also, most significantly, this frequently takes place at the initiation of the principal of Aldine High School or another employee of the District. . . . The court believes that when the nature and circumstances of defendants' actions are viewed in their entirety, the natural consequences of these actions would be the advancement of religion by indicating to students that the state advocates religious belief."

Doe v. *Aldine Independent School Dist.*, 563 F.Supp. 883 (1982)

SINGLETON, Chief Judge.

In this action, an anonymous plaintiff brought suit against the Aldine Independent School District (the District) for violation of plaintiff's constitutional rights. Specifically, plaintiff contended that the recitation and singing of a school prayer on Aldine Independent School District property constituted a violation of the first amendment prohibition against the establishment of religion. Plaintiff requested a preliminary injunction, a declaratory judgment, damages, and attorneys fees.[1] Presently before the court is plaintiff's motion for summary judgment on the issue of the constitutionality of the activity which is the source of plaintiff's complaint.

I. Statement of Stipulated Facts

The words of the prayer which are the source of the controversy are the following: "Dear God, please bless our school and all it stands for. Help keep us free from sin, honest and true, courage and faith to make our school the victor. In Jesus' name we pray, Amen." These words are posted in raised block letters on the wall over the entrance to the gymnasium at Aldine Senior High School and are recited or sung by students to music played by the Aldine School band at athletic contests, pep rallies, and at graduation ceremonies. These events take place in the gymnasium and at the football stadium, which are the property of the District. These activities take place before or after regular school hours, but are sponsored by Aldine Senior High School and form a part of the school's regular extracurricular program. The recitation or singing is frequently initiated by the high school principal or other school employees. Although students are required to assemble in the gymnasium for certain school programs, attendance at any event during which the prayer is recited or sung is voluntary. In addition, no one is required to sing or recite the words, nor is anyone obliged to stand when the words are recited or sung.

II. The Establishment Violation

The first amendment to the United State Constitution provides that "Congress shall make no law respecting an establishment of religion, or prohibiting the free exercise thereof. . . . " This amendment was made applicable to the states by the Supreme Court in *Everson v. Board of Education,* 330 U.S. 1, 67 S.Ct. 504, 91 L.Ed. 711 (1947). In this same case, the Court, quoting the words of Thomas Jefferson, clearly articulated the purpose behind the first amendment's prohibition "to erect a wall of separation between church and state." Id. at 16, 67 S.Ct. at 512. The Court also set forth its view of the effect the constitutional prohibition has on the operation of government:

> The "establishment of religion" clause of the first amendment means at least this: Neither a state nor the Federal Government can set up a church. Neither can pass laws which aid one religion over another. Neither can force nor influence a person to go to or to remain away from church against his will or force him to profess a belief or disbelief in any religion. No person can be punished for entertaining or professing religious beliefs or disbeliefs, for church attendance or non-attendance. No tax in any amount, large or small, can be levied to support any religious activities or institutions, whatever they may be called, or whatever form they may adopt to teach or practice religion. Neither a state nor the Federal Government can, openly or secretly, participate in the affairs of any religious organizations or groups and vice versa.

Id. at 15, 67 S.Ct. at 511.

In the instant case, the court has before it two interrelated questions: (1) whether the activities[2] of the defendants violated the establishment clause or (2) whether, as defendants contend, the restriction of those activities would mean an impermissible encroachment on the individual student's constitutional right to freely exercise his or her religion.

There is no doubt that the words of the Aldine school song constitute a prayer since they call on God for His blessing and contain an avowal of divine faith. *Engel v. Vitale,* 370 U.S. 421, 424–25, 82 S.Ct. 1261, 1263–64, 8 L.Ed.2d 601 (1962); *Hall v. Bradshaw,* 630 F.2d 1018, 1020 (4th Cir.1980).

A. The Test for an Establishment Clause Violation

The Supreme Court has confronted this issue before in the public school setting and, as a result of its appreciation for the delicacy of the situation and concern that constitutional rights be protected, has formulated a test for ascertaining if a school has imper-

missibly participated in an establishment of religion. *Lemon v. Kurtzman,* 403 U.S. 602, 612–613, 91 S.Ct. 2105, 2111, 29 L.Ed.2d 745 (1971). This test comprises three questions: (1) Does the policy or practice have a nonreligious purpose? (2) Is the primary effect of the policy or practice one which neither advances nor inhibits religion? and (3) Does the policy or practice avoid an excessive entanglement with religion? If the answers to all three questions are yes, the school's activity is not an unconstitutional participation in the establishment of religion. *Id.* at 612–13, 91 S.Ct at 2111. *Lubbock Civil Liberties Union v. Lubbock Independent School District,* 669 F.2d 1038 (5th Cir.1982).

B. The Secular Purpose Question

In answer to the first question of the *Kurtzman* test, defendants (speaking through amicus curiae)[3] assert that the school prayer has the clear secular purpose of instilling "in the students a sense of school spirit or pride . . . [which] has a beneficial effect on the student body and contributes to an increase in morale, and concomitantly lessens disciplinary problems." Brief of Amicus Curiae at 9. This argument misconstrues the law on this point. A school district or other governmental body cannot seek to advance nonreligious goals and values, no matter how laudatory, through religious means. *Abington School District v. Schempp,* 374 U.S. 203, 83 S.Ct. 1560, 10 L.Ed.2d 844 (1963). In *Hall v. Bradshaw,* 630 F.2d 1018 (4th Cir.1980), the court stated, "If a state could avoid the application of the first amendment in this manner [by using religious means to further nonreligious goals], any religious activity of whatever nature could be justified by public officials on the basis that it has beneficial secular purposes" (at 1020–21). Additionally, when a nonreligious purpose may be promoted through nonreligious means, a state may not employ religious ones. *Abington School District v. Schempp,* 374 U.S. at 278, 83 S.Ct. at 1601 (Brennan, J., concurring); *Lubbock Civil Liberties Union v. Lubbock Independent School District,* 669 F.2d at 1045.

In the instant case it is apparent that the goals and values Aldine School District seeks to instill in its students may be encouraged through nonreligious means. Therefore, as a matter of law, defendants' practice of posting the disputed words over the gymnasium and of encouraging its recitation fails to satisfy the secular purpose requirement of the first question of the Supreme Court's test.

C. The Primary Effect Question

Defendants contend that the primary effect of the singing or reciting the prayer neither advances nor inhibits religion because the students are under no obligation to participate, state employees have only a limited involvement,[4] and the contested activities do not take place in a religious setting. These assertions are based on a misunderstanding of the applicable law. The degree of state employee involvement has no bearing on this issue. That a state employee may be minimally involved in an activity may bear on the question of whether there is state action, but not on the question of whether the primary effect of a practice is to advance or inhibit religion. Also, despite defendants' insistence to the contrary, the fact that participation in a religious activity is not obligatory will not prevent a constitutional conflict. The limits of the first amendment are not avoided by simply making the singing of the prayer voluntary. As has been emphasized repeatedly by the courts, voluntariness is not relevant to a first amendment inquiry. *Engel v. Vitale,* 370 U.S. 421, 430, 82 S.Ct. 1261, 1266, 8 L.Ed.2d 601; *Lubbock Civil Liberties Union v. Lubbock Independent School District,* 669 F.2d at 1046; *See Abington School District v. Schempp,* 374 U.S. at 223, 83 S.Ct. at 1572.

In this case, Aldine Senior High School sponsored the events where the prayer was sung. Pep rallies, football games, and graduation ceremonies are considered to be an integral part of the school's extracurricular program and as such provide a powerful incentive for students to attend. As said in *Lubbock,* "it is the Texas compulsory education machinery that draws the students to the school event and provides any audience at all for the religious activities . . ." (at 1026). Since these extracurricular events were school sponsored and so closely identified with the school program, the fact that the religious activity took place in a nonreligious setting might create in a student's mind the impression that the state's attitude toward religion lacks neutrality. The Supreme Court has noted that "to an impressionable student even the mere appearance of secular involvement in religious activities might indicate that the state had placed its imprimature on a particular religious creed. This symbolic inference is too dangerous to permit." *Roemer v. Board of Public Works,* 426 U.S. 736, 750, 754, 96 S.Ct. 2337, 2346, 2348, 49 L.Ed.2d 179 (1976).

This court has found that defendants' practice carries with it the implied recognition and approval of religious activity. Not only are the words in question recited or sung on school property at school events but also, most significantly, this frequently takes place at the initiation of the principal of Aldine High School or another employee of the District. *See Hall v. Bradshaw,* 630 F.2d at 1021. The court believes that when the nature and circumstances of defendants' actions are viewed in their entirety, the natural consequences of these actions would be the advancement of religion by indicating to students that the state advocates religious belief. In view of this probable effect on Aldine students, the defendants cannot satisfactorily respond to the question of the activities' primary effect.

D. The Entanglement Question

Defendants contend that they have avoided an excessive entanglement with religion because (1) the prayer is recited only at times which do not impinge on the educational function of the school, and (2) both attendance at events where the prayer is sung or recited and participation in the actual singing are voluntary.

This memorandum has already dealt with defendants' position concerning voluntary participation and so turns to defendants' first assertion.

The entanglement analysis is concerned with procedural matters. Here the relevant inquiry is whether the state must engage in continuing administrative supervision of the religious activity. *Brandon v. Board of Education of Guilderland Central School District,* 635 F.2d 971, 979 (2d Cir. 1980). If the state must so supervise, then church and state are excessively intertwined. *Lubbock Civil Liberties Union v. Lubbock Independent School District,* 669 F.2d at 1047.

In this case, it is apparent that Aldine High School personnel are active in the supervision of the events where the religious activity occurs. The facts here are similar to those of *Lubbock* where the court found that in compliance with Texas state law, the Lubbock Independent School District had exercised supervision over students who were meeting voluntarily before and after school hours for religious purposes on school grounds. *Id.* at 1047. In that case, the continuing supervision plus the use of the District's facilities resulted in a finding of excessive entanglement with religion. *Id.*

The finding in *Lubbock* controls on the entanglement question. Aldine School District facilities were used as the site of the religious activity and District employees were involved in supervising both the school property and the events which took place there. Therefore, as a matter of law, the court concludes that the defendant did not avoid an excessive entanglement with religion and has not met the third prong of the *Kurtzman* test.

III. *Free Exercise of Religion*

Finally, defendants have taken the position that restriction on the activity at issue would be an improper interference on the students' right to the free exercise of religion. Amicus Brief at 8. However, the activity which the court addresses is not an independent, unofficial invocation of God's help by the students, but rather a state initiated, encouraged, and supervised regular practice which occurs on school property during extracurricular events which are an important part of the school's program. The distinction is significant and controlling. The former is an inviolable right; the latter, according to the purpose, effect, and entanglement analysis of the Supreme Court, is an impermissible establishment of religion.

Accordingly, this court holds that the practice of initiating, leading, or encouraging the recitation or singing of the "Aldine School Prayer" and the posting of the words to the prayer is in violation of the first amendment, and plaintiff's motion for summary judgment is hereby GRANTED.

NOTES

1. The request for a preliminary injunction was withdrawn when at the hearing it was revealed that plaintiff was no longer a student at Aldine Senior High School.

2. The prayer is at times recited and at times sung. The singing of the prayer involves no constitutional distinction. Each of these practices, under the circumstances of this case, is proscribed by the first amendment. Though the act of posting the prayer on the gymnasium wall is distinct from the initiation of its singing and recitation, the court proceeds with the analysis as though both acts are part of the same religious practice. It would seem, however, that the posting of the words alone is unconstitutional in light of *Stone v. Graham,* 449 U.S. 39, 101 S.Ct. 192, 66 L.Ed.2d 199 (1980).

3. The court combines three sources of information in determining the defendants' position on the various legal issues in this case; the memorandum in opposition to plaintiff's motion for summary judgment, the amicus curiae brief filed by Congressman Jack Fields, and the arguments proffered at the hearing on the motion for summary judgment by attorney for defendants, Mr. James Wunderlich. The amicus brief does not speak for the defendants, but in this case the amicus seems to offer the most elaborate statement of defendants' basic arguments.

4. In the amicus curiae brief it was asserted that only the band and choir director was involved in the singing of the song. Amicus Brief at 9. This assertion is in apparent conflict with the stipulated fact that the principal frequently initiated the singing of the prayer.

   The court does not resolve issues of fact in determining that the principal initiates the recitations which resolution would, of course, be improper in ruling on a motion under Rule 56 of the Federal Rules of Civil Procedure. Rather, the court considers the fact established because the Aldine High School Principal, Vernon L. Lewis, so testified at the hearing and defendants in no manner contested the principal's construction of the Aldine High School practice with regard to this religious activity.

   Nevertheless, it is undisputed that at least the band and choir director did initiate recitation or singing of the school prayer. This degree of state involvement is sufficient to raise a first amendment question.

A United States District Court in New Mexico declares unconstitutional a New Mexico statute which read: "Each local school board may authorize a period of silence not to exceed one minute at the beginning of the school day. This period may be used for contemplation, meditation, or prayer, provided that silence is maintained and no activities are undertaken." In its opinion, the Court stated: "In this case, the moment of silence clearly has the potential for impermissibly fostering religion, and it has caused precisely the sort of political divisiveness along sectarian lines which the Establishment Clause was designed to avoid. . . . The Court therefore concludes that § 22-5-4.1 [the statute authorizing local school boards to implement a daily moment of silence] as implemented by the defendants causes excessive entanglement between church and state. The statute is therefore unconstitutional and its implementation by the defendants illegal."

Duffy v. *Las Cruces Public Schools,* 557 F.Supp. 1013 (1983)

BURCIAGA, District Judge.

THIS MATTER comes before the Court for resolution of the merits of the plaintiff's complaint. At issue is the constitutionality of § 22-5-4.1, NMSA 1978, a statute authorizing local school boards in New Mexico to implement a daily moment of silence in public schools within the local school districts. Having considered the evidence adduced at trial, the arguments of counsel and the relevant authorities, the Court concludes that § 22-5-4.1 represents an unconstitutional infringement on the Establishment Clause of the First Amendment. This memorandum opinion shall constitute the Court's findings of fact and conclusions of law.

FINDINGS OF FACT

Plaintiff Jerry Duffy is a taxpayer and a citizen of New Mexico. He brought this action on his own behalf, and on behalf of his son, John P. Duffy, a minor. John Duffy is also a citizen of New Mexico, and currently attends public school in the Las Cruces Public School District [hereinafter, the District].

The District, a defendant herein, is responsible for administering that part of the New Mexico public school system which operates in and near Las Cruces. The District's governing body is the Board of Education of the Las Cruces Public Schools [hereinafter, the Board]. The Board adopts and oversees enforcement of the policies governing the operations of the District.

Defendants Joan M. Pucelik, Walter L. Rubens, Vincent Boudreau, Mrs. Tom Salopek, and Everett Crawford are the current members of the Board. Each was duly elected by the qualified voters residing in the District. At all pertinent times prior to June 30, 1982, Defendant John E. Stablein was the Superintendent of Schools for the District. Stablein was selected by the Board to serve as Superintendent. Since July 1, 1982, Harold W. Floyd has served as Superintendent. The Superintendent of Schools is responsible for administering policies enacted by the Board in the schools of the District.

The challenged statute, § 22-5-4.1, NMSA 1978, provides that:

Each local school board may authorize a period of silence not to exceed one minute at the beginning of the school day. This period may be used for contemplation, meditation or prayer, provided that silence is maintained and no activities are undertaken.

The law was introduced during the 1981 Session of the New Mexico Legislature as House Bill 205. The legislation was sponsored by Representatives Randall Sabine and William O'Donnell, both of whom reside in Dona Ana County, in or near Las Cruces. H.B. 205 was passed by the Legislature during the 1981 session, and signed into law by Governor Bruce King.

In late 1980 or early 1981, Representative O'Donnell asked Mr. William McEuen, General Counsel to the State Department of Education, to draft a bill which would permit students to pray in school. O'Donnell acted at the urging of a Mrs. Jean Walsh. O'Donnell instructed McEuen to confer with Walsh for advice on the matter. O'Donnell also instructed McEuen to provide recommended language for a bill which would authorize some form of prayer in New Mexico public schools.

Mrs. Walsh directed McEuen's attention to the case of *Gaines v. Anderson,* 421 F.Supp. 337 (D.Mass. 1976). In that case, the court upheld the constitutionality of a statute very similar to that being challenged in this case. In drafting H.B. 205, McEuen relied heavily on the statute which was at issue in *Gaines v. Anderson.* H.B. 205 adopts verbatim the material language of the Massachusetts statute. The word "contemplation" was not in the Massachusetts law, but was inserted into H.B. 205, purportedly to demonstrate the neutrality of the statute.

Although there is no formal written legislative history of H.B. 205, it is clear that the pre-eminent purpose of § 22-5-4.1, NMSA 1978, was to establish a devotional exercise in the classrooms of New Mexico public schools. The motive of Representative O'Donnell was to establish prayer in the public schools, as can be seen in his instructions to McEuen. And McEuen perceived the intent of O'Donnell to be to establish prayer in the public schools. In the memorandum to O'Donnell which contained the proposed bill which became H.B. 205, McEuen said that his purpose was to recommend wording for "a bill which would authorize some form of prayer in our public schools."

The plain language of the statute also supports the conclusion that the legislative purpose was to establish prayer in the public schools. Obviously, inclusion of the word "prayer" is a clear indication of the legislative purpose. Indeed, it could hardly be more clear. The defendants urge that the inclusion of the words "contemplation" and "meditation" indicates the "neutral" intent of the legislature. The Court is not persuaded by this argument. It is clear that McEuen inserted these words solely for the purpose of attempting to disguise the religious nature of the bill.

H.B. 205 authorized local school boards to implement the moment of silence. The defendants affiliated with the District and the Board chose to implement the exercise in the public schools of Las Cruces. Therefore, consideration of the purpose behind the implementation is clearly appropriate to this inquiry.

It is clear that the purpose of the Board was to provide a program of prayer in District schools. In the summer of 1981, the Board began discussing the possible implementation of the moment of silence. These discussions were also undertaken at the urging of Jean Walsh. The matter was discussed at various Board meetings throughout the summer of 1981. During these meetings, only the religious aspect of the statute was discussed. At no time did any Board member avow any secular purpose for the moment of silence. It is clear that the defendant Board members and the other persons who attended the Board meetings in the summer of 1981, perceived the sole purpose of § 22-5-4.1, NMSA 1978, to be to permit prayer in the public schools.

Superintendent Stablein was initially opposed to the implementation of § 22-5-4.1. Stablein believed the law to be improper in that it authorized prayer in public schools. He was also concerned about the dispute in which the Board was likely to become embroiled. A school bond election was about to be held, and Stablein was concerned that the school prayer issue would sublimate the bond issue; he did not want to "miff" the voters on the eve of the bond election.

The testimony of the Board members themselves makes clear that they had no secular purpose in implementing the moment of silence. The Board members who voted to implement the exercise did so only because of the pressure being exerted on them by constituents who favored prayer in public schools. While it perhaps cannot be said that the Board members favored prayer in public schools as an abstract proposition, it is clear that they intended to implement a program of prayer in the schools in order to avoid the political wrath of their constituents.

The Board members now say that their purpose in implementing the moment of silence was to enhance discipline and instill in the students the "intellectual composure" necessary for effective learning. These justifications are clearly the product of afterthought. They are no more than an elaborate effort to inject a secular purpose into a clearly religious activity. There is no credible evidence before the Court to support the defendants' contention.

These justifications were never uttered publicly at the Board meetings at which the moment of silence was discussed. It is unlikely that the moment of silence carries any significant benefits to the educational process, and it is clear that the benefits the Board claims to have been seeking could have been better accomplished by means other than the moment of silence. Add to this the fact that no moment of silence was ever considered by the Board prior to the enactment of H.B. 205, despite the educational benefits the defendants now claim arise from the moment of silence. It is clear that the educational benefits alleged by the Board members are a mere pretext. Their purpose was to institute a devotional exercise in public school classrooms.

The Court finds that the primary effect of § 22-5-4.1 and its implementation by the Las Cruces Board of

Education is to advance religion. It is clear that the Legislature intended the moment of silence to be a devotional exercise. It was regarded as such by both the Board members and the members of the community who spoke at the meetings where it was discussed. The memorandum advising parents of the implementation of the program could also be understood as stating that a voluntary, silent devotional exercise was to be instituted in the public schools.

It does not matter whether the moment of silence would be regarded as a proper devotional exercise by a cleric or another person knowledgeable in such affairs. The ill lies in the public's *perception* of the moment of silence as a devotional exercise. If the public perceives the State to have approved a daily devotional exercise in public school classrooms, the effect of the State's action is the advancement of religion.

The dangers inherent in the sovereign placing its imprimatur on a religious exercise are particularly acute where children are involved. As established by Gordon Cawelti, an expert in the fields of curriculum and discipline, children are extremely impressionable and easily influenced. They exhibit a tendency to conform with each other in dress and behavior, and it is psychologically disturbing for a child to be different from his peers. There is a clear and present danger that the children will perceive the moment of silence as government approval of religion.

The fact that § 22-5-4.1 allows not only prayer, but also meditation and contemplation is of no moment. It cannot be seriously argued and certainly cannot be assumed that schoolchildren can discern the nice distinctions concerning the meanings of "meditation," "contemplation," and "prayer."

As discussed above, the Board discussions which preceded implementation, as well as the communications announcing implementation of the moment of silence, left the clear impression that school prayer was the issue. The manner of conducting the moment lends further support to this impression. Under the regulations approved by the Board, the moment of silence is required to occur as soon as possible after the tardy bell. No leeway is allowed which would permit its observance at any other time. If the moment of silence were meant to instill discipline and intellectual composure, such regulations would be inappropriate. Instead, teachers would have the option of invoking the moment of silence before each class, after each recess, or after the students return from lunch. The fact that the moment of silence is rigidly held at the same time every day suggests to the public that it has no disciplinary or educational significance.

The defendants' expert witnesses concede that there has been no meaningful research on the practical effects of the moment of silence on the educational process. The Court finds that there are no significant educational benefits from the moment of silence as implemented by the defendants. The evidence to the contrary is entitled to no weight in the view of the Court. The marginal benefits that may be realized are clearly outweighed by the danger in the public's perception of the moment of silence as a State-approved religious activity.

The moment of silence as implemented by the defendants requires a good deal of governmental involvement in the act of prayer which would not exist had § 22-5-4.1 not been instituted. The exercise is undertaken on school grounds during school hours. Teachers have the duty to maintain silence by all of the students, and to insure that no other activities are undertaken. The Superintendent of Schools and, ultimately, the Board are responsible for seeing that Board policies, including the moment of silence, are carried out in the classrooms of the District.

It is clear that the moment of silence has caused a good deal of political divisiveness, much of which is along sectarian lines in the community, and has the potential to cause a good deal more. During the time immediately preceding the adoption of the moment of silence, a concerted effort in favor of adoption was conducted by local religious groups. The effort included petition drives by local churches and an impressive letter-writing campaign. It is, of course, significant that the proponents of adoption regarded § 22-5-4.1 as a method of instituting prayer in the public schools. The opponents were less organized, but they did exist. Their uncoordinated efforts were to little avail, and their protests were overwhelmed by the religious groups' campaign to adopt the moment of silence.

The matter was certainly divisive within the school system itself. A poll was conducted among the student councils and the teachers to determine their views on the matter. Although the members of student councils cannot be considered a truly representative sample for determining student attitudes, the Court finds it significant that 27% of the students polled were against implementation of the moment of silence. Even more unsettling is the fact that the teachers polled disapproved of the moment of silence by a margin of 47.26% to 42.36%. Indeed, at least four teachers have refused to conduct the moment of silence in their classrooms.

The Superintendent is aware that there are teachers in the District who refuse to conduct the moment of silence. Their refusal is punishable as a failure to follow Board policy. Defendant Stablein decided that, for the time being, there would be no disciplinary action against these teachers. However, it is clear that future action against these teachers is not foreclosed.

The most compelling evidence of political divisiveness, however, came from the Board members themselves. It is clear that their concern about the upcoming bond election was a major factor in their decision to implement § 22-5-4.1. They worried that the voters would not consider the substantive merits of the bond proposal, but would instead cast their votes along sectarian lines depending on the Board's decision on the moment of silence. Thus, they were concerned that school prayer would be the dominant issue in the bond election. In order to avoid that possibility, they instituted the moment of silence. By so doing, they refused to independently judge the secular merits of the moment of silence proposal and willingly submitted to the religious arguments.

The moment of silence was observed in District schools beginning on October 12, 1981. Each of the 16,000 students in District schools is affected. Although the program was allegedly adopted on a "trial basis," there is no indication that the program will be voluntarily discontinued.

CONCUSIONS OF LAW

The plaintiff brings this action under 42 U.S.C. § 1983 to redress the violation, under color of state law, of rights guaranteed to him by the Constitution of the United States and the Constitution of the State of New Mexico. He seeks injunctive relief under § 1983 and declaratory relief under 28 U.S.C. § 2201. The Court has jurisdiction over the subject matter under 28 U.S.C. § 1343(3).

The most commonly recognized purpose of the First Amendment is to prevent any single denomination from being established as a state church. *Everson v. Board of Education,* 330 U.S. 1, 8, 67 S.Ct.504, 507, 91 L.Ed. 711 (1947); *Beck v. McElrath,* 548 F.Supp. 1161 at 1162 (M.D.Tenn., 1982). However, the protection of the First Amendment does not stop there. Not only is the State prohibited from adopting a state religion, but also from passing any law relating to the establishment of religion. The Supreme Court has made clear the scope of the prohibition.

Neither a state nor the Federal Government can set up a church. Neither can pass laws which aid one religion, aid all religions, or prefer one religion over another. Neither can force nor influence a person to go to or to remain away from a church against his will or force him to profess a belief or disbelief in any religion. No person can be punished for entertaining, or professing religious beliefs or disbeliefs, for church attendance or nonattendance. No tax in any amount, large or small, can be levied to support any religious activities or institutions, whatever they may be called, or whatever form they may adopt to teach or practice religion. Neither a state nor the Federal Government can, openly or secretly, participate in the affairs of religious organizations or groups and vice versa. In the words of Jefferson, the clause against establishment of religion by law was

intended to erect "a wall of separation between Church and State."
Everson, supra 330 U.S. at 11, 67 S.Ct. at 509.

In the recent past, the Supreme Court has considered a number of cases touching upon issues similar to those in this case. These cases have resulted in a three-prong analysis which may be stated as follows:

[T]o pass muster under the Establishment Clause the law in question first must reflect a clearly secular legislative purpose, second, must have a primary effect that neither advances nor inhibits religion, and, third, must avoid excessive government entanglement with religion.
Committee for Public Education v. Nyquist, 413 U.S. 756, 774, 93 S.Ct. 2955, 2966, 37 L.Ed.2d 948 (1973). *See also Lemon v. Kurtzman,* 403 U.S. 602, 612–613, 91 S.Ct. 2105, 2111, 29 L.Ed.2d 745 (1971).

In this case, the plaintiff challenges § 22-5-4.1, NMSA 1978, under the Establishment Clause. The Court finds that § 22-5-4.1 does in fact violate the Establishment Clause of the First Amendment.

Establishment Clause

Secular Legislative Purpose

The first inquiry into the Establishment Clause analysis goes to the purpose of the legislature in adopting § 22-5-4.1. Based on the Court's findings of fact, it must be concluded that the legislature had no clearly secular purpose in adopting the law. Having failed to pass the first test of the *Lemon v. Kurtzman* analysis, the law must be deemed unconstitutional irrespective of the two remaining tests, which also will be addressed below. *Stone v. Graham,* 449 U.S. 39, 101 S.Ct. 192, 66 L.Ed.2d 199 (1980).

Of course, both the defendants and the legislative sponsors of the statute deny that they acted with a religious purpose. The evidence indicates otherwise.

At the core of the Establishment Clause is the requirement that a government justify in secular terms its purpose for engaging in activities which may appear to endorse the beliefs of a particular religion. Although courts have rarely looked behind the stated legislative purposes, it is clear that an avowed secular purpose, if found to be self-serving, may "not be sufficient to avoid conflict with First Amendment." *Stone v. Graham,* 449 U.S. 39, 41, 101 S.Ct. 192, 193, 66 L.Ed.2d 199 (1980).
American Civil Liberties Union v. Rabun County Chamber of Commerce, 678 F.2d 1379, 1390 (11th Cir.1982).

In this case, the legislative avowals of secular purpose are clearly self-serving and the Court is not bound by them. *Karen B. v. Treen,* 653 F.2d 897 (5th Cir.1981); *Hall v. Bradshaw,* 630 F.2d 1018 (4th Cir.1980); *McLean v. Arkansas Board of Education,*

529 F.Supp. 1255 (E.D.Ark.1982). In determining the true purpose of the legislature, the most appropriate starting place is the statute itself.

The presence of the word "prayer" in § 22-5-4.1 is compelling evidence that there was no secular purpose sought to be achieved. As the court observed in *Karen B. v. Treen,*

> the plain language of [the challenged statutes] makes apparent their predominantly religious purpose. Prayer is perhaps the quintessential religious practice for many of the world's faiths, and it plays a significant role in the devotional lives of most religious people. Indeed, since prayer is a primary religious practice in itself, its observance in public school classrooms has, if anything, a more obviously religious purpose than merely displaying a copy of a religious text in a classroom.

653 F.2d at 901.

The defendants, of course, argue that the words "contemplation" and "meditation" indicate a neutral purpose, and even legislative sensitivity to the people's right to freedom of religion. See *Gaines v. Anderson, supra.* The Court cannot accept this characterization. As discussed in the findings of fact, the Court views the inclusion of these words as a transparent ruse meant to divert attention from the statute's true purpose. Viewed in this light, it can hardly be said that the statute reflects sensitivity to the right to religious freedom. Indeed, it reflects the opposite. The inclusion of the words "contemplation" and "meditation" indicates that the legislature knowingly set out to denigrate the right to freedom of religion, and then sought to conceal the result by including these so-called alternatives to prayer. *See, e.g., Lubbock Civil Liberties Union v. Lubbock Independent School District,* 669 F.2d 1038 (5th Cir.1982) (school gatherings for "educational, moral, religious or ethical" purposes found unconstitutional); *Beck v. McElrath, supra.* The plain language of the statute indicates a religious purpose.

In addition to the statutory language, the courts may consider other factors in determining legislative purpose. Matters such as the historical context of the statute, the events leading up to passage of the act, and the contemporaneous statements of the legislative sponsors may be considered. *McLean, supra* at 1263–1264. In this case, these factors completely undercut the defendants' arguments. As indicated in the Court's findings of fact, the events preceding adoption of the moment of silence and the statements of the legislative sponsors clearly indicate that the purpose of the statute was to return prayer to the schools.

The defendants next argue that as long as some identifiable secular purpose is served by the statute, it does not run afoul of the Establishment Clause even if there is also a religious purpose. The authority for this proposition is mysterious at best.

The Court has found that no secular purpose is served by the statute. But even if there were such a secular purpose, it is clear that the defendants misapprehend the law. "[T]he state cannot escape the proscriptions of the Establishment Clause merely by identifying a beneficial secular purpose. The inquiry goes beyond this." *Hall v. Bradshaw,* 630 F.2d at 1020. If the State could avoid the application of the First Amendment in this manner, "any religious activity of whatever nature could be justified by public officials on the basis that it has beneficial secular purposes." *DeSpain v. DeKalb County Community School District,* 384 F.2d 836, 839 (7th Cir. 1967). *See also American Civil Liberties Union v. Gallatin Area School District,* 307 F.Supp. 637, 641 (W.D.Pa.1969). The defendants' argument is without merit.

Finally, the defendants argue that their purpose was merely to accommodate the exercise of the children's right to freedom of religon. *See Lanner v. Wimmer,* 662 F.2d 1349, 1357 (10th Cir.1981). *Lanner* is inapposite. *Lanner* involved a released time program which allowed students to attend religious classes offered by private entities off school grounds. Such programs are considered an accommodation of religion. *See Zorach v. Clauson,* 343 U.S. 306, 72 S.Ct. 679, 96 L.Ed. 954 (1952). The defendants apparently argue that a religious activity undertaken on campus, during school hours and under the supervision of teachers paid by the State is the equivalent of the program at issue in *Lanner.* That is clearly not the case. Here, the moment of silence goes far beyond a mere accommodation of the public's right to worship as it pleases. It establishes a devotional exercise on school grounds during school hours with teacher supervision. Far from being an accommodation of religion, it is an establishment of religion with the added element of being compulsory.

The Court concludes that § 22-5-4.1 was enacted and implemented for a religious purpose by the Legislature and the Board. The statute is therefore unconstitutional and its implementation illegal.

Primary Effect of Statute

In order to survive the Establishment Clause, a statute must have a primary effect which neither inhibits nor advances religion.

> [R]eligious activity under the aegis of the government is strongly discouraged, and in some circumstances—for example, the classroom—is barred. The sacred practice of religious instruction and prayer, the Framers foresaw, are best left to private institutions—the family and houses of worship.

Brandon v. Board of Education, 635 F.2d 971, 973 (2d Cir.1980). The Court concludes that the primary effect of the enactment and implementation of § 22-5-4.1 is advancement of religion.

In analyzing this matter, it must always be remembered that we are dealing with children attending public schools. As the Second Circuit Court of Appeals has observed:

Our nation's elementary and secondary schools play a unique role in transmitting basic and fundamental values to our youth. To an impressionable student, even the mere appearance of secular involvement in religious activities might indicate that the state has placed its imprimatur on a particular religious creed. This symbolic inference is too dangerous to permit.

Id. at 978.

In this case, the danger is clear. The debates leading to the adoption of the moment of silence left the clear impression that the issue was prayer in the public schools in the minds of both its supporters and opponents. Once the moment of silence was adopted, the policy of allowing prayer at the beginning of each school day "implies recognition of religious activities ... as an integral part of the District's ... program...." *Lubbock Civil Liberties Union, supra,* 669 F.2d at 1045.

This, in combination with the impressionability of secondary and primary age schoolchildren and the possibility that they would misapprehend the involvement of the District in these [matters], renders the primary effect of the policy impermissible advancement of religion.

Id. To like effect, *see Brandon, supra,* 635 F.2d at 973.

The Establishment Clause protects against "sponsorship, financial support, and active involvement of the sovereign in religious activity." *Walz v. Tax Commission,* 397 U.S. 664, 668, 90 S.Ct. 1409, 1411, 25 L.Ed.2d 697 (1970). Here, the State has chosen to sponsor and actively involve itself in the matter of prayer. "A prayer, however, is undeniably religious and has, by its nature, both a religious purpose and effect." *Hall, supra,* 630 F.2d at 1020. By authorizing a time for prayer in the classrooms, the defendants have placed the imprimatur of the State on that religious activity. In so doing, they have impermissibly advanced religion. No other significant secular effects are present, the Court having rejected the testimony of Dr. Thomas Thompson. It is clear, therefore, that the primary effect of § 22-5-4.1 and its implementation is the advancement of religion. The statute is unconstitutional and its implementation is illegal.

Excessive Entanglement

The third inquiry in the three-prong Establishment Clause analysis is whether the challenged activity fosters an excessive entanglement of church and state. In this case, it is clear that there is such excessive entanglement.

The moment of silence is intended to provide a time, place and atmosphere for prayer. The time chosen is during school hours, and the place is the school grounds. The atmosphere of silence is instilled and maintained by the teachers. These facts alone have been found sufficient to constitute excessive entanglement. *Brandon, supra* at 979; *Karen B., supra* at 903; *Lubbock Civil Liberties Union, supra.* Here, there is an even greater entanglement. The Superintendent is obligated to enforce the policies of the Board, including the moment of silence. He is responsible for ensuring that District teachers observe the moment of silence. The Superintendent, in turn, answers to the Board. The Board is ultimately responsible for enforcement of the moment of silence policy.

As the Supreme Court observed in *Lemon v. Kurtzman, supra,* "the very restrictions and surveillance necessary to ensure that teachers play a strictly nonideological role give rise to entanglements between church and state." 403 U.S. at 620–621, 91 S.Ct. at 2114–2115.

The Court's conclusion is further supported by the evidence of political divisiveness. Both students and teachers are sharply divided over the moment of silence. Feelings ran high in the community, particularly among the proponents of adoption. Board members feared that refusal to adopt the moment of silence would result in the defeat of their bond proposal, a matter which should have been completely unrelated to the moment of silence.

A broader base of entanglement of yet a different character is presented by the divisive potential of these state programs. ... It would be unrealistic to ignore the fact that many people confronted with issues of this kind will find their votes aligned with their faith. Ordinarily, political debate and division, however vigorous or even partisan, are normal and healthy manifestations of our democratic system of government, but political division along religious lines was one of the principal evils against which the First Amendment was intended to protect.

Lemon, supra, 403 U.S. at 622, 91 S.Ct. at 2115.

Any government activity with "the potential for impermissible fostering of religion" can cause the sort of divisiveness the Establishment Clause was meant to guard against. *Id.* at 619, 91 S.Ct. at 2114.

By placing its imprimatur on the particular kind of belief embodied in prayer, the state necessarily offends the sensibilities not only of nonbelievers but of devout believers among the citizenry who regard prayer "as a necessarily private experience." (Citation omitted.)

Hall v. Bradshaw, supra, 630 F.2d at 1021. In this case, the moment of silence clearly has the potential for impermissibly fostering religion, and it has caused precisely the sort of political divisiveness along sectarian lines which the Establishment Clause was designed to avoid. *See Lemon, supra* 403 U.S. at 622, 91 S.Ct. at 2115; *Committee for Public Education v. Nyquist,* 413 U.S. at 794–798, 93 S.Ct. at 2976–2978.

The Court therefore concludes that § 22-5-4.1 as implemented by the defendants causes excessive entanglement between church and state. The statute is therefore unconstitutional and its implementation by the defendants illegal.

The defendants seem to argue at several points that the encroachment on the plaintiff's rights is minor because the decision of whether to pray during the moment of silence is left with the students. It is well-settled that voluntary exercises are not beyond the reach of the Establishment Clause. *See School District of Abington Township v. Schempp,* 374 U.S. 203, 83 S.Ct. 1560, 10 L.Ed.2d 844 (1963); *Engel v. Vitale,* 370 U.S. 421, 82 S.Ct. 1261, 8 L.Ed.2d 601 (1962); *Lubbock, supra; Karen B., supra; Collins v. Chandler Unified School District,* 644 F.2d 759 (9th Cir.1981). And, the fact that some might regard the encroachment on religious freedom in this case to be minor is no defense. *Stone v. Graham,* 449 U.S. 39, 101 S.Ct. 192, 66 L.Ed.2d 199 (1980).

The Supreme Court has rejected the argument that relatively minor encroachments may escape scrutiny under the Establishment Clause, for "[t]he breach of neutrality that is today a trickling stream may all too soon become a raging torrent." *Abington School District v. Schempp,* 374 U.S. 203, 225, 83 S.Ct. 1560, 1573, 10 L.Ed.2d 844 (1963). *Hall v. Bradshaw, supra* at 1021. Although the encroachment may seem minor to some, it violates the Establishment Clause nonetheless.

Free Exercise of Religion Clause

The plaintiff also claims an encroachment on his right to freely exercise his own religion. While the coercive effect of the moment of silence is clearly present, plaintiff has failed to prove that he or his minor son have been denied the right to freely exercise their religion. On the record, therefore, it cannot be said conclusively that the moment of silence violates the Free Exercise Clause of the First Amendment.

Defendant's Request for Declaratory Judgment

The defendants have counterclaimed for declaratory relief. The defendants seek a judgment declaring that they have an inherent right, apart from § 22-5-4.1, to institute a program of daily periods of silence as a means of encouraging discipline and intellectual composure, and that such a program does not offend either the federal or state constitutions. In addition, the defendants ask the Court to declare that they may continue the moment of silence regardless of the constitutionality of § 22-5-4.1 so long as prayer is neither suggested nor encouraged. In light of the foregoing conclusions of the Court, this relief must be denied.

What the defendants seek, in essence, is an abstract declaration that the defendants could institute a moment of silence in the absence of § 22-5-4.1, assuming there was a secular purpose, a neutral effect, and no excessive entanglement. However, this abstract proposition cannot be divorced from the realities reflected in the Court's findings. The defendants basically ask the Court to declare that if the facts were different, the moment of silence would be lawful. This the Court cannot do.

It may be that a school board has the power to implement a moment of silence without § 22-5-4.1. But that is not the question before the Court. The defendants did not ground their authority in the Board's inherent powers. They relied on § 22-5-4.1. They did not adopt the program for purposes of intellectual composure or discipline. Instead, they acted with a religious purpose. Further, while one can conceive of facts indicating that a period of silence neither advances nor inhibits religion, in this case the public perceives the moment of silence as a means of instituting prayer in the public schools. The facts found by the Court are not the facts which are assumed in the defendants' request for declaratory relief.

The Court sees similar difficulties with a declaratory judgment which would allow the moment of silence to be continued even if § 22-5-4.1 is found unconstitutional. Indeed, the Court concludes that the defendants must be permanently enjoined from instituting any program similar to the moment of silence. The reasons therefor are clear.

If the defendants are not so enjoined, the moment of silence issue could well be brought before them again. But the defendants would be more careful to disguise their purpose the next time. With a wink and a nod, they could discuss the secular purposes for the moment of silence, and prohibit any mention of the school prayer issue. Having avoided the factors which lead the Court to rule against them in this case, they could reinstitute the moment of silence.

It would be inimical to allow such a situation to develop. The Court believes that the defendants wish to follow the law. But being human, they might well again accede to constituent pressure and adopt a reworked moment of silence. This reworked moment of silence, free from the patent defects which render it unconstitutional in this case, could not, in the view of the Court, be separated in the mind of the public from the exercise which the Court today finds unconstitutional.

The Court must, therefore, prohibit any future implementation of the moment of silence. This will guarantee that the defendants will not again be pressured into adopting such a program, and insures the integrity of the holding of the Court. It would be a total and inescapable contradiction for the Court to say that § 22-5-4.1 is unconstitutional on the one hand, and on the other to say that an identical program instituted in the wake of the finding of unconstitutionality is valid.

The Court must therefore deny the defendants the relief they have requested, and the counterclaim will be dismissed.

Wherefore,

IT IS ORDERED, ADJUDGED AND DECREED that:

1.   The enactment of § 22-5-4.1, NMSA 1978, by the Legislature of the State of New Mexico exceeds the scope of legislative power as circumscribed by the First and Fourteenth Amendments of the United States Constitution;

2.   Section 22-5-4.1, NMSA 1978, and its implementation in the Las Cruces Public Schools violates the First Amendment of the United States Constitution;

3.   Section 22-5-4.1, NMSA 1978, and its implementation in the Las Cruces Public Schools violates Article II, Section 11 of the Constitution of the State of New Mexico in that it gives a preference by law to a particular mode of worship;

4.   The defendants shall be enjoined from conducting the minute of silence described in § 22-5-4.1, NMSA 1978, both now and in the future; and

5.   The defendants shall take nothing on their counterclaim, and that counterclaim should be dismissed.

A Permanent Injunction, Declaratory Judgment and Final Judgment shall be entered concurrently herewith.

A United States District Court in New Jersey declares unconstitutional a New Jersey statute requiring that public school principals and teachers "shall permit students to observe one minute of silence to be used solely at the discretion of the individual student, before the opening exercises of each school day for quiet and private contemplation or introspection." In declaring the statute unconstitutional the court stated: "All the evidence points to the religious intent of this enactment—the period of more than a decade during which the New Jersey legislature sought to evade *Engel* and *Abington Township* in order to reintroduce a mandatory time for prayer in the public schools; the debate upon the bill which was in terms of public prayer and state involvement in religion; the time and manner in which the minute of silence was mandated, following the form and posture of school prayer which was outlawed in the early 1960's. . . . I conclude that Bill 1064 does not have a bona fide secular purpose and, in fact, has a religious purpose."

May v. *Cooperman*, 572 F.Supp. 1561 (1983)

DEBEVOISE, District Judge.

This is an action for declaratory and injunctive relief brought pursuant to 42 U.S.C. § 1983 and 28 U.S.C. § § 2201 and 2202. Plaintiffs seek to have declared unconstitutional a State statute, namely, New Jersey P.L. 1982, Ch. 205 which provides that:

1. Principals and teachers in each public elementary and secondary school of each school district in this State shall permit students to observe a 1 minute period of silence to be used solely at the discretion of the individual student, before the opening exercises of each school day for quiet and private contemplation or introspection.

2. This act shall take effect immediately.

Plaintiffs are public school children and parents of such children who either are not religious and view the minute of silence as an enforced religious observance or else are religious and oppose required participation in this particular observance. One plaintiff, Jeffrey May, is a teacher in the Edison Township school who declined to conduct a minute of silence in his classroom on the ground that it is a religious observance and who was threatened with discipline for this failure.

Defendants are Saul Cooperman, Commissioner of New Jersey's Department of Education which is responsible for implementing the minute of silence bill, the Edison Township Board of Education and the Old Bridge Township Board of Education.

The statute became effective on December 16, 1982, when the New Jersey State Senate overrode the Governor's veto, the Assembly having overriden the veto on December 13. By reason of the approaching Christmas recess the full effect of the statute was not felt until January 1983, when the public schools reopened.

This action was filed on January 10, at which time I issued an order temporarily restraining implementation of the statute. Subsequently the parties and the New Jersey Assembly and New Jersey Senate, which intervened as defendants, agreed to an extension of the temporary restraint until the trial of the case, thus in effect converting the temporary restraining order into a preliminary injunction.

The original defendants did not take an active role in the defense of the case. This inactivity flowed, no doubt, from the fact that the State's Governor and Attorney General had concluded that the statute violated the United States Constitution and that they could not in good faith defend it. However, the intervening defendants vigorously contested the action both during pretrial discovery proceedings and at the trial itself.

The trial commenced on September 13, 1983. Both sides produced extraordinarily useful witnesses. Each witness was articulate and effectively testified as to a

115

significant aspect of the case. The witnesses viewed the statute, its purpose and effect from very different perspectives. Each witness held strong views concerning the educational and/or religious implications of the statute. All of their views were essential for an understanding of the issues and contributed significantly to the resolution of these issues.

The Facts

In the early 1960's the United States Supreme Court held that school-sponsored prayer and Bible reading in the public schools are unconstitutional. *School District of Abington Township v. Schempp,* 374 U.S. 203, 83 S.Ct. 1560, 10 L.Ed.2d 844 (1963); *Engel v. Vitale,* 370 U.S. 421, 82 S.Ct. 1261, 8 L.Ed.2d 601 (1962). These decisions required modification of the exercises which traditionally had been conducted in New Jersey's public schools at the start of each day. These exercises typically included reading from the Old Testament and recital of the Lord's Prayer.

There was very substantial opposition to the Supreme Court's decisions, and in many parts of the United States various measures were proposed to change the ruling or evade it. In New Jersey legislation was proposed from time to time with the rather obvious purpose of reintroducing opening prayer in some form in the public schools.

At first such proposed legislation specifically mentioned prayer. For example, A. 146 (1969), which authorized "a brief period of silent prayer or meditation", was vetoed by Governor Hughes who had doubts as to its constitutionality. In 1971 a similar bill (A. 597 (1970)) was vetoed by Governor Cahill on similar grounds.

In 1978 the legislature adopted A. 648 which mandated "a brief period of silent meditation" at the beginning of each day and explicitly disavowed any intent to create a religious exercise. Governor Byrne declined to approve the bill and it failed to become law. He based his decision in part on the bill's possible violation of the Establishment Clause or the Free Exercise Clause of the First Amendment and in part on the lack of any useful purpose of the bill.

In 1980 Assemblyman Zangari introduced A. 2197 which called for a one minute period of silence in each public school during each school day. On May 4, 1981 Governor Byrne returned this bill unsigned on the grounds that it was either unconstitutional or unnecessary.[1]

The statute which is the subject of this case was introduced as Assembly Bill No. 1064 on March 8, 1982. Its principal sponsor was Assemblyman Zangari, who was joined by 54 other members of the Assembly. Assemblyman Zangari had previously introduced three other bills on related subjects: one calling for an amendment to the United States Constitution to permit prayer in public places, including public schools (A. 162 (1980)), another providing for a period of prayer or scripture reading in each school before the beginning of the school day (A. 2196 (1980)), and still another providing for a one minute period of silence after the beginning of each school day (A. 2197 (1980), referred to above).

The New Jersey legislature does not preserve an official record of its hearings and debates, and consequently this source of information concerning the purpose of legislation is not available.[2] However, several witnesses described some of the legislative committee meetings which they attended by reason of their interest in the Bill.

Joseph Chuman, leader of the Society for Ethical Culture for Bergen County testified in opposition to the Bill before Senator Feldman's Education Committee on June 21, 1982. The hearing on the Bill lasted 1½ to 2 hours. Three committee members, including Senator Feldman, were present. Two representatives of education organizations and a representative of the American Civil Liberties Union spoke against the Bill. Assemblyman Zangari spoke in favor. He argued that it would serve a useful psychological purpose. He pointed out that although he was a Catholic he went to Protestant schools and was encouraged to participate, which never did him any harm. When Chuman spoke to him afterwards Assemblyman Zangari asserted that he would be happy to see verbal prayer and Bible reading in the schools. Asked about the effect on atheists, he stated that they were so few in number their views could be discounted. Mr. Chuman could recall no discussion before the Committee of the educational purposes of the Bill.

Marianne Rhodes, Associate Director of Government Relations of the New Jersey School Board Association, attended a May 17, 1982 hearing of an Assembly Committee and a September 23, 1982 hearing of the Senate Education Committee. She made memoranda of the discussions concerning Bill A. 1064. At the Assembly Committee hearing Assemblyman Zangari stated that the Bill had been reduced to 54 words and that it was important that society get back to deeply embedded religious values. He quoted President Reagan as advocating adoption of a constitutional amendment allowing school prayer.

Ms. Rhodes recorded that at the September 23 Senate hearing Senator Ewing and Assemblyman Zangari spoke for the Bill. In response to Senator Feldman's question why the Bill was necessary since students could pray whenever they wished, Assemblyman Zangari stated that "They [students] publicly won't do it [pray] unless they are directed."

The Rev. Dudley E. Sarfaty is Associate General Secretary of the New Jersey Council of Churches, a group composed of representatives of 15 Protestant denominations. He attended the sessions of the Assembly at which the question of overriding the Governor's veto was debated. He made notes of these sessions. Assemblyman Michael F. Adubato urged that it would be a good thing if the State subsidized parochial education, and the Bill was a step in the right direction. Senator Dumont stated that the kind of ceremony required by the minute of silence Bill would cut down crime and disruption and that the legislature should not be rigid on matters of church and state. Senator Cardinale asserted that "We know what the people want" and asked rhetorically whether the members of the State Senate were the servants of the people or the courts. The only argument which Rev. Sarfaty heard touching on possible educational benefits of the Bill was Senator Dumont's assertion that the minute of silence would cut down crime and disruption.

It is significant what those who opposed the Bill conceived its purposes and effect to be, because in many instances they were among those most directly affected by it.

The Ethical Cultural Society of Bergen County styles itself as a liberal religious organization, the purpose of which is to further respect for the individual. It viewed the Bill as an attempt to return prayer to the public schools in another guise and opposed the Bill in the legislature.

The New Jersey School Board Association is a body created by statute comprised of representatives of 611 school districts in the State. Its purpose is to promote public education in New Jersey and to assist local school boards. In the past, at the direction of a very substantial majority of the delegates from the constituent school boards, it opposed legislative efforts to mandate prayer or silent meditation in the public schools on the ground that the practice had no educational value. A small minority of the Association's delegates opposed the Association's position on the ground that prayer should be returned to the schools. By virtue of the strong stand which the delegates had taken on previous prayer and meditation bills, the Association's directors urged the legislature to defeat Bill No. 1064. The rationale offered for its adoption, the calming effect which a moment of silence would have upon students, was viewed as a pretext for a religious purpose.

The American Baptist Churches of New Jersey, the coordinating body of 235 American Baptist Churches in the State, has consistently opposed the prayer and meditation bills introduced into the New Jersey legislature. It has done this on religious grounds. The mandated silence was viewed as an attempt by the State to impose something having the appearance and nature of a religious observance. At the very heart of the American Baptist faith is the tradition of religious liberty and opposition to any move by the state to in-

trude into religious affairs. Legislation mandating prayer, meditation and silence is conceived to be state intrusion into religious matters, the effect of which will be to cheapen and "trivialize" true religion. Significantly some American Baptist pastors and members did not agree with the position taken by their denomination's coordinating body. They did not agree because they viewed the minute of silence Bill as a useful way to bring religion into the schools.

The New Jersey Education Association is a labor organization having 117,000 members working in New Jersey's public schools. Of this number 84,000 are teachers. The organization opposed Assembly Bill 1064, perceiving it to be a back door approach to bringing prayer into the public schools.

Despite the opposition, both the Senate and the Assembly voted to override the Governor's veto of the minute of silence Bill and it became law on December 16, 1982. It was in effect only briefly before the temporary restraining order was issued in this case, but it is instructive to examine the impact which the Bill had in several school districts during the short period when it was being implemented.

The intervenors produced evidence of experiences in the Sayreville school system through the testimony of an elementary school teacher, Evelyn A. Swenson, the testimony of an elementary school principal, John D. Singer, and the tape of a CBS television news broadcast showing interviews of students, a school board member and teachers after implementation of Assembly Bill 1064.

Sayreville is a community having a large number of middle income, blue collar inhabitants and a large number of first and second generation citizens of Central European and Scandinavian ancestry. It also has Black, Asian and Hispanic inhabitants.

For many years the Sayreville public schools had commenced each day with a psalm, the Lord's Prayer, the salute to the flag and a patriotic song. In 1969, following the Supreme Court's school prayer decision, the Sayreville Board of Education adopted a resolution which was designed to give people an opportunity to pray. The resolution, which was moved by Board member DiPoalo provided:

Approval was granted for a 2 minute meditation period to be instituted in our school system after the salute to the flag in the morning for any child who wants to pray, with the provision that no student be forced to pray if he is unwilling, nor deny any student the right to pray.

From that time on all the Sayreville public schools have commenced the day with opening exercises which culminated in a moment of silence. Soon after adoption of the 1969 resolution it became apparent that two minutes of silence was not feasible and by tacit agreement the period of silence was reduced in practice to 30–45 seconds.

Mrs. Swenson testified that at the outset she explained to students the meaning of meditation as silent, private, serious contemplation or thinking. She instructed her students to close their eyes in order that they would not distract each other. It was an opportunity to pray, but no one was required to do so. Some children sat with their hands clasped. Once or twice she noticed a child crossing himself. No parents or children ever expressed concern about the practice, and Mrs. Swenson viewed the ceremony as a helpful way to start the school day. On other occasions during the day she uses periods of silence for specific purposes. For example in science class she may ask the students to maintain silence and determine how many different sounds they can hear. Or in reading class she may ask the students to imagine a particular person or event.

In 1978 the 1969 resolution was modified by the adoption of Policy 808 specifying procedures for opening exercises. It provided for the salute to the flag as a part of each day's opening exercises and stated that, "Opening exercises may also include the singing of patriotic songs and a moment of silent meditation."

Although the language of Policy 808 differed from the 1969 resolution in that there was no reference to prayer and in that the mandated two minutes of silence was changed to a moment of silence, there was in fact no change in the Sayreville opening exercises after 1978. The effect of the 1978 enactment was simply to ratify the existing practice of reducing the length of the period of silence to 30 to 45 seconds.

The adoption of Assembly Bill 1064 required no change in Sayreville's opening exercises, except that perhaps, literally construed, the Bill would require that the moment of silence come first in the sequence of opening events and that it last for 60 seconds.

The intervenors placed in evidence a tape of a two minute CBS interview of various persons in Sayreville concerning Sayreville's experience with its moment of silence. The interview was conducted on December 17, 1982, the day after the override of the Governor's veto. Children were shown practicing contemplation; a high school student described his experiences going back to fourth grade; a principal stated that the moment of silence created no disciplinary problems and had a salutary effect; School Board member DiPoalo, who had introduced Sayreville's 1969 meditation and prayer resolution, referred to nuclear and other crises facing today's world and opined that "people better do a little praying."

The reaction in Princeton was quite different from that in Sayreville. The school system has 2400-2500 students. Religiously the community is heterogeneous. A majority of the residents are of Catholic or Protestant backgrounds. Fifteen to twenty percent of the population is Jewish. Students from forty countries are in the school system and most of the major religions of the world find adherents among the student body.

The minute of silence Bill was the subject of considerable discussion among at least the high school students. It was generally considered a form of prayer which some students opposed and some approved. One high school student, Denice Fishburne, collected 200 signatures on a petition in opposition to the Bill. Another student collected 100 signatures.

Princeton's Superintendent of Schools, Dr. Paul D. Houston, testified at the trial. He stated that immediately after the override of the Governor's veto he began receiving telephone calls from parents who did not wish their children to be in class when the minute of silence was observed, as they viewed the exercise as a form of enforced prayer. Principals telephoned him expressing fear that enforcing the statute would cause student disruption and stating that many students and some teachers would not observe the new law. Dr. Houston refrained from implementing the statute until he met with the school board. The board was uniformly opposed to the law, believing it to be unconstitutional as a compulsory religious observance in the public schools. By consensus it was agreed that the statute would not be implemented in the Princeton public schools pending a court determination of its validity. In Dr. Houston's opinion there is no educational justification for requiring that all students be silent at the same time. Moreover, were it to be implemented, arrangements would have to be made to excuse large numbers of students who did not wish to participate. He observed that teachers can and do provide for silent contemplation when it fits in with an educational purpose.

Mark Tulloss, an eighth grade student in Roosevelt, New Jersey, had discussed the Bill in his history class. He and most of his classmates opposed a minute of silence on the ground that it constituted prayer, but after the veto override the principal of his school gave instructions that at the start of each day every student was to observe the minute of silence by standing up, bowing his head and closing his eyes. Tulloss remained silent during those periods, but refused to bow his head or close his eyes. He continued reading. The reaction of his classmates to the exercise was that it was "boring", "stupid".

Paramus is a community of 30,000 people, the Jewish, Protestant and Catholic faiths each being equally represented among the population. Dr. Paul Shelly, Superintendent of the Paramus school system, testified that students and teachers generally perceived the minute of silence Bill as an effort to circumvent the Supreme Court decision and to reintroduce prayer into the schools. The State Board of Education sent no guidelines to the various school districts after the Bill became effective; it simply distributed a copy of the Bill. There were objections to implementing the Bill in Paramus, and Dr. Shelly simply informed teachers that the law had been passed, without elaborating upon how it should be implemented.

Plaintiff Cary Butler, a 17 year old student in the Hillsborough Township High School did not wish to participate in the moment of silence when the entire school was directed by the principal to sit for the minute of silence and be perfectly quiet and still. It was a matter Cary had discussed at home and he and his family concluded that the enforced minute of silence violated their beliefs. He asked his teacher to leave, and the teacher sent him to the school office for a determination. In the hall another teacher directed him to stand still and be quiet, which he refused to do on the ground that it would be enforced prayer. Cary was charged with insubordination and suspended, but shortly he was permitted to return to classes and leave his homeroom during the minute of silence. This dispensation was not granted to other students, the principal preferring to handle requests on a case-by-case basis.

Plaintiff Gary Drew and his wife are Roman Catholics who have six year old and nine year old daughters in the Old Bridge Township public schools. They object to use of the minute of silence in the schools because they believe religious training and observance should be taught in the home and the church. They do not wish to have their young and impressionable children subjected to whatever practice teachers may employ in implementing what they view as an essentially religious observance. They did not instruct their children to leave their classrooms when the minute of silence was observed, because they were concerned that it would unduly embarrass them.

The pain that such a move would cause a young child is illustrated by the circumstances in which Rita Rothenberg and her family found themselves. Mr. and Mrs. Rothenberg asked their young son Joshua to decline to participate in the minute of silence on religious grounds. The thought of being separated from the other children so upset Joshua that his parents did not persist in their request that he leave the room during the minute of silence.

Plaintiff Jeffrey May is a high school teacher in the Edison school system. He is an agnostic and views the minute of silence as a form of prayer in which he cannot in good conscience participate.

On December 22, 1982 he and all other faculty members received a memorandum from the principal of his high school. The memorandum directed all faculty members and students to participate in a minute of silence as directed by the State Legislature. Mr. May informed his principal that he could not and would not participate because he views the law to be unconstitutional and because it violated his conscience and personal philosophical beliefs. He was nevertheless directed to take part. He refused to do so and was threatened with disciplinary action.

The foregoing represent types of reactions in the public schools in New Jersey after Bill 1064 became effective.

Dr. Calvin Thompson, a psychologist, testified for the intervenors. He had conducted a study in the Las Cruces, New Mexico Public School District of the public perception of the moment of silence law in effect in that District. The District had 14,000 school children. Its population is largely middle class with approximately 50% of the population being of Hispanic origin and approximately 50% being "Anglo". There is a small number of Black and Indian inhabitants. The population is predominantly Christian —Catholic and Protestant—with a lesser number of Jewish inhabitants.

Las Cruces' moment of silence law is described in *Duffy v. Las Cruces Pub. Schools*, 557 F.Supp. 1013 (D.N.M.1983). Dr. Thompson studied the effect of the practice by televising a number of classrooms before, during, and after the moment of silence, by watching the period of silence and by conducting structured interviews with students. On the basis of his study Dr. Thompson concluded that most persons viewed the moment of silence as simply silence and not as prayer. He concluded that it served as a transitional tool separating outside activities from school work and that it was a moment which could be used for meditation or prayer. Some of the students who were interviewed stated that they used the moment for prayer. In any given observation he made, from 0 to 20% of the students assumed positions which could be interpreted as having the probability of being a religious act.[3] Dr. Thompson was of the opinion that the public perception of the moment of silence in New Jersey would be similar to the perception in New Mexico. Dr. Thompson provided interesting data, but I think care must be exercised in generalizing on the basis of it. There are major differences between New Jersey and New Mexico. More important, there are major differences between the many communities in New Jersey. As the other evidence in the case clearly demonstrates, attitudes toward the minute of silence differ greatly from one New Jersey community to another. Las Cruces may reflect attitudes in some of them but certainly not in all or perhaps even in very many of them.

Having described the genesis of Bill 1064 and the reaction to its becoming effective, it is necessary to examine briefly its religious and educational implications.

Plaintiffs offered the testimony of Dr. Langdon

Gilkey, professor of theology at the University of Chicago Divinity School and a Baptist minister. Dr. Gilkey teaches historical theology and the relationship of theological views to contemporary culture. He offered a definition of religion which is serviceable for the purpose of this case and can be used to analyze the facts established here. It is a definition which, I believe, is in accord with the developing concept of religion reflected in more recent Supreme Court decisions, *see* Judge Adams' discussion of the definition of religion for constitutional purposes in his concurring opinion in *Malnak v. Yogi,* 592 F.2d 197, 200–215 (3d Cir.1979).

All religions, according to Dr. Gilkey, have three components: (i) each embodies a view of ultimate reality—especially as it concerns the human predicament and the resolution of the difficulties human beings confront as they proceed through life; (ii) each religion prescribes a way of life, which constitutes a response to the ultimate reality perceived by that religion; and (iii) each religion with its view of ultimate reality and its way of life is embodied in an historical community of faith which links the past, the present and the future.

The second element of religion—the way of life which responds to the perception of the ultimate reality—includes such practices as participation in the sacraments and prayer. This is the point at which Assembly Bill 1064 is charged with impinging upon or furthering religion.

In the Christian, Jewish and Islamic religions God is viewed as the ultimate reality and prayer is usually central to the way of life which responds to that ultimate reality. In other religions, such as Buddhism, God may not be the ultimate reality and the response may be meditation or other observances rather than prayer.

Even where a principal component of a religion's way of life is prayer, the forms of prayer may differ widely, being conditioned by historical and cultural traditions, by time and by place. In the traditional American culture silence, bowing one's head and clasping one's hands is associated with prayer. This reflects the development of Protestantism, Reform Judaism, and Catholicism. Historically, however, Catholics kneeled and Jews raised their hands. Members of the Islamic faith may kneel on prayer rugs, face east and call out loud upon Allah. For Quakers silence itself is prayer. For others prayer must be vocal. With the increasing cultural and religious diversity in the United States, with traditional western religions being supplemented by adherents of and converts to eastern religions, diversity in the forms of prayer has proliferated.

What the minute of silence Bill has done is to mandate that all students assume the posture of one traditional form of prayer. While this may provide the opportunity for many persons to engage in their kind of prayer, the enforcement of silence either in a seated or standing position prevents others from engaging in their kinds of prayer.

Like the Rev. George D. Younger, who testified as to the views of the American Baptist Churches of New Jersey, Dr. Gilkey was of the opinion that legislative acts such as Bill 1064 which may lead to objective prayer will have the effect of causing a rejection of genuine religion in all of its three components. That is to say, the intervention of the state is counter-productive—enforcement of religious observances will induce cynicism and resistance on the part of any healthy person and the rejection of that which the state is seeking to instill.

Intervenors maintain that Bill 1064 has a secular purpose, namely, providing a period of transition from the many concerns of the students outside of school to the work of the school. In support of this thesis the intervenors offered the testimony of Dr. Adam Scrupski, an associate professor at Rutgers Graduate School of Education. He was of the opinion that the minute of silence can serve a useful pedagogical function as a supplement to or as an opening exercise forming the boundary between school and not-school. Silence connotes seriousness and solemnity, as in a courtroom, library or place of worship, and having a teacher administer the period of silence serves to accentuate his or her role in the educational process. There is a need for a boundary, according to Dr. Scrupski, and a ritual such as a moment of silence serves to provide the boundary. He viewed the salute to the flag as a less effective boundary than it once was, although it can still serve that purpose.

The experience in Sayreville's schools certainly suggests that in combination with the flag salute and a song a brief period of silence serves a transition purpose.

The circumstances of Dr. Scrupski's retention as the intervenor's expert casts some doubt on the proposition that the State legislators enacted Bill 1064 in a search for the best method of effecting a transition from non-school to school activities. In the spring of 1983, long after the temporary restraining order was entered, Dr. Scrupski happened to discuss the Bill with a friend who worked on the staff of one of the Legislature's Committees on Education. The staff member asked him if there might be a secular purpose for the law. In the words of Dr. Scrupski, "He was interested in knowing if I thought there was a secular consequence, a good reason, so to speak". (Tr. at 546). Dr. Scrupski found a secular consequence and was retained to testify concerning it.

I will not summarize the testimony of plaintiffs' experts, Dr. Peter J. Kuriloff, associate professor of education at the University of Pennsylvania and Dr. Stanley L. Rosner, a professor at the College of Education at Temple University. Their testimony and that of the other witnesses of both parties convinces me beyond any doubt whatsoever that one minute of silence as a transitional device for all grade levels in all schools for all kinds and conditions of students has little educational justification. Frequently the bustle of the playground cannot be transformed into serious school work by a requirement to sit still; rather some alternative action must be engaged in to transfer the students' attention to the work of the school. For young children a minute of silence may be an eternity, while many older students could handle it with ease. For hyperactive or handicapped children a minute of silence may be an impossibility. There is no evidence that any school in New Jersey was having any difficulty effecting a transition from non-school to school. Even in Sayreville which incorporated a period of silence at the end of its active opening exercises, the authorities found that they could not handle more than 30 to 40 seconds of mandated silence and simply disregarded the Board of Education resolution which mandated a longer period.

It is unclear whether Bill 1064 requires that every student remain present during the minute of silence or whether it simply requires that every student be given an opportunity to observe a minute of silence with the right of those who do not wish to participate to absent themselves. If the former interpretation is adopted, it is quite clear from the Princeton experience that significant numbers of students and teachers will refuse to observe silence on religious or other grounds based on conscience. If the latter interpretation is adopted, varying numbers of students and teachers will elect to stay away from the observance. In either situation the exercise will have only marginal utility as a transitional device for all students.

Having set forth the evidence in some detail, it is possible to draw from it certain generalized factual findings[4]:

1. From a religious perspective New Jersey's population is diverse. It includes persons holding deep religious convictions; it includes persons who are indifferent to religion; it includes persons who, as a matter of conviction, belong to no organized religious body and engage in no religious observances.

2. The very substantial portion of New Jersey's population which considers itself religious exhibits great diversity as to all three aspects of religion, that is to say, as to views of the nature of ultimate reality, as to the outward practices observed to express views of ultimate reality, and as to the particular religious bodies to which adherence is given.

3. Prayer, which is a common practice of many different religious bodies, takes many forms. Each form of prayer can be associated with particular views of ultimate reality and with particular religious bodies.

4. A short period of group silence at the commencement of the day or at the commencement of an undertaking constitutes one of the traditional forms of prayer of major religious bodies in New Jersey.[5]

5. The purpose of Bill 1064 was to mandate a period at the start of each school day when all students would have an opportunity to engage in prayer. This conclusion is drawn from the facts that:

   a. Until the early 1960's when the United States Supreme Court held that school-sponsored prayer and Bible reading in public schools are unconstitutional, the New Jersey public schools traditionally included prayer and Bible reading as part of their opening exercises.

   b. There was and is substantial public sentiment that prayer should be a part of opening exercises.

   c. In response to this public sentiment and, in some cases, by reason of personal conviction, many New Jersey legislators introduced one bill after another in an attempt to reintroduce prayer in the public schools notwithstanding the Supreme Court's ruling.

   d. Assembly Bill 1064 prescribing a minute of silence is but the most recent of such bills motivated by these sentiments.

   e. The driving force behind the Bill came from those who deeply and sincerely believed that an opportunity for prayer in the public schools at the beginning of each day should be mandated.

   f. Similarly one driving force in opposition to the Bill came from religious persons who perceived the minute of silence as a State prescribed religious observance violating their deeply and sincerely held belief that the State cannot involve itself in religious matters.

   g. Other opposition to the Bill came from nonreligious persons who perceived the minute of silence as an enforced religious observance.

6. The purpose of the Bill, urged at the trial, to provide a transition from non-school life to school work is an after-the-fact rationalization and not the real purpose of the Bill. This conclusion is drawn from the facts that:

   a. There is no evidence that any school lacked an effective means of making the transition from non-school to school through such devices as the salute to the flag, a song, a period of announcements and taking attendance and the like.

   b. The agencies having the most knowledge and experience with educational matters, namely the school boards and teacher organizations throughout the State, overwhelmingly opposed the Bill on the ground that it had no educational value.

   c. While the minute of silence might serve as a

transition device for some students of more mature years, it could not serve as such a device for younger students, certain handicapped students, and others.

d. The attempt to develop rational support for the thesis that a minute of silence served a transitional purpose commenced after this law suit was underway rather than before the Bill was adopted.

7. As implemented the Bill requires all students to assume a posture identified as the posture of prayer of certain religious groups.

8. Although the Bill is designed to give persons an opportunity to pray, in fact it only gives an opportunity to pray to those whose prayers can be performed in the prescribed posture. Others whose prayers require action and/or sound are precluded from engaging in prayer during the minute of silence.

9. The experiences of various schools during the weeks when the minute of silence was enforced suggests that some students will use the minute of silence to pray; some will use it to engage in thoughtful meditation; some will tolerate it though considering it boring and stupid; some who believe it violates their religious convictions will nevertheless submit to it, not wishing to risk public ridicule; some who believe it violates their religious convictions will either refuse to observe it or will absent themselves from the place where others are observing it.

The Law

The First Amendment of the United States Constitution provides that "Congress shall make no law respecting an establishment of religion, or prohibiting the free exercise thereof. . . ." The Fourteenth Amendment makes the First Amendment binding on the states. *Everson v. Board of Education,* 330 U.S. 1, 67 S.Ct. 504, 91 L.Ed. 711 (1947).

Bill 1064 requires that public school principals and teachers "shall permit students to observe 1 minute of silence to be used solely at the discretion of the individual student, before the opening exercises of each school day for quiet and private contemplation or introspection." "Contemplation" has been defined in Webster's as "meditation on spiritual things" and "introspection" has been defined as "looking into or within, as one's own mind" or "inspecting, as one's own thoughts or feelings." Very simply, the issue posed in this case is whether, Bill 1064 constitutes a law respecting an establishment of religion or prohibiting the free exercise thereof. I conclude that Bill 1064 does constitute such a law.[6]

The test, stated negatively, is that "[A] legislative enactment does not contravene the Establishment Clause if it has a secular legislative purpose, if its principal or primary effect neither advances nor inhibits religion, and if it does not foster an excessive government entanglement with religion." *Committee for*

Public Education v. Regan, 444 U.S. 646, 100 S.Ct. 840, 63 L.Ed.2d 94 (1980); *Committee for Public Education v. Nyquist,* 413 U.S. 756, 93 S.Ct. 2955, 37 L.Ed.2d 948 (1973); *Lemon v. Kurtzman,* 403 U.S. 602, 91 S.Ct. 2105, 29 L.Ed.2d 745 (1971); *Gilfillan v. City of Philadelphia,* 637 F.2d 924 (3d Cir.1980); *Malnak v. Yogi, supra.* The statute under review does not pass muster under any of these criteria.

As found above, the purpose of Bill 1064 is religious not secular. Intervenors urge that "the unambiguous language of New Jersey's moment of silence law evidences a legislative interest to promote a secular purpose in a manner that is constitutionally neutral to religion." (Intervenors' Brief at 11, 12). Unless one examines the statute in a total vacuum, this conclusion is without rational basis. All the evidence points to the religious intent of this enactment—the period of more than a decade during which the New Jersey legislature sought to evade *Engel* and *Abington Township* in order to reintroduce a mandatory time for prayer in the public schools; the debate upon the Bill which was in terms of public prayer and State involvement in religion; the time and manner in which the minute of silence was mandated, following the form and posture of school prayer which was outlawed in the early 1960's.

This obvious attempt to cross the forbidden line becomes all the more apparent in light of the pretextual nature of the secular purpose advanced in this case. True, intervenors' witnesses testified that the Bill can serve as a useful boundary between non-school activities and school work. However, only the utterly naive would conclude that the Bill's advocates were fighting passionately for establishment of such a boundary. It is abundantly clear that once the Governor's veto had been overridden and litigation commenced, Bill 1064 became a statute in search of a secular purpose.

The intervenors urge, quite correctly, that "constitutional analysis of legislative purpose does not involve a judicial inquiry into supposed illicit legislative motive." (Intervenors' Brief at 26). There is a distinction, I believe, between the motives and purposes of individual legislators and an institutional legislative purpose. Legislators may have the purest of personal motives and produce unconstitutional legislation, and contrariwise individual legislators with wrongful motives may vote for a bill and produce legislation which is both beneficent and constitutional. This is illustrated by *United States v. O'Brien,* 391 U.S. 367, 88 S.Ct. 1673, 20 L.Ed.2d 672 (1968), which upheld the provision of the Universal Military Training and Service Act of 1948 making it an offense to willfully and knowingly mutilate, destroy and change by burning a registration certificate. In light of the overwhelmingly obvious and important secular purpose of the Act, the

Supreme Court upheld the constitutionality of this provision even though an incidental effect may have been to circumscribe a person's ability to express his views about the Act by burning his draft registration card. The Court noted that "this Court will not strike down *an otherwise constitutional statute* on the basis of an alleged illicit legislative motive". 391 U.S. at 383, 88 S.Ct. at 1682 (emphasis added). It declined, therefore, to give significance to the statements of one Senator and two House members as probative of the claim that the purpose of the provision at issue was to stifle free speech rather than to advance a secular purpose.

The present case is a far cry from *O'Brien.* Here there is no overwhelming secular purpose. Both the history of this kind of legislation and the circumstances of the adoption of this particular Bill point inescapably to an essentially religious purpose. The statements of the legislators in committee, on the floor and to the public as disclosed by the evidence in this case are consistent with and confirmatory of an institutional purpose to accomplish something the Constitution forbids.

Intervenors point to the language of Justice Brennan's concurring opinion in *Abington School District v. Schempp, supra,* as support for the proposition that a moment of silence is a secular device:

The second justification [of prayer and Bible reading] assumes that religious exercises at the start of the school day may directly serve solely secular ends—for example, by fostering harmony and tolerance among the pupils, enhancing the authority of the teacher, and inspiring better discipline.

*   *   *

I have previously suggested that Torcaso and the Sunday Law Cases forbid the use of religious means to achieve secular ends where nonreligious means will suffice. That principle is readily applied to these cases. It has not been shown that readings from speeches and messages of great Americans, for example, or from the documents of our heritage of liberty, daily recitation of the Pledge of Allegiance, *or even the observance of a moment of reverent silence at the opening of class,* may not adequately serve the secular purposes of the devotional activities without jeopardizing either the religious liberties of any members of the community or the proper degree of separation between the spheres of religion and government.

374 U.S. at 280, 281, 83 S.Ct. at 1602–1603 (emphasis added).

The question of the purpose and effect of a minute or moment of silence was not at issue in *Abington.* That question is at issue in the present case, and I think a showing has been made that New Jersey's minute of silence does jeopardize the religious liberties of members of the community and breaches the proper degree of separation between the spheres of religion and government.

The conclusion I have reached is consistent with the most recent federal district court cases passing on the constitutionality of moment of silence laws. *Duffy v. Las Cruces Public Schools, supra; Beck v. McElrath,* 548 F.Supp. 1161 (M.D.Tenn.1982); *see also Opinions of the Justices to the House, etc.,* 387 Mass. 1201, 440 N.E.2d 1159 (Sup.Jud.Ct.1982); *contra, Gaines v. Anderson,* 421 F.Supp. 337 (D.Mass.1976). Intervenors argue that New Jersey's statute is inherently different from the statutes under review in those cases because there "the plain language of the statutes, which incorporated the word prayer, made apparent their predominantly religious purpose." (Intervenors' Brief p. 14). Given the history and circumstances of the enactment of Bill 1064, I think it is clear that the omission of the word "prayer" is a cosmetic change only, having no substantial effect. Illustrative of the lack of any practical effect is Sayreville's experience. There the town's original enactment provided for a two minute meditation period in order that the students have an opportunity to pray. The subsequent change in language to omit the reference to praying was not intended to result and did not result in any change in what was actually being done in the schools.

Nor do I believe that the recent Supreme Court case of *Marsh v. Chambers,* _____ U.S. _____, 103 S.Ct. 3330, 77 L.Ed.2d 1019 (1983) was intended to modify the law governing State sponsored prayer in public schools. There the Court held that the practice of the Nebraska Legislature of opening each legislative day with a prayer by a chaplain paid by the State did not violate the Establishment Clause of the First Amendment. The Court noted an unbroken history of more than 200 years during which legislators opened their sessions with a prayer but emphasized that in *Marsh* "the individual claiming injury by the practice is an adult, presumably not readily susceptible to 'religious indoctrination'". At _____, _____, 103 S.Ct. at 3335. This later comment, I believe, suggests a clear intent to distinguish legislative prayer by adults which, like the opening of court, is primarily of a traditional ceremonial nature from mandated prayer by school children.

Thus I conclude that Bill 1064 does not have a bona fide secular purpose and, in fact, has a religious purpose.

Turning to the second prong of the test of validity, I conclude that the Bill both advances and inhibits religion.

It advances the religion of some persons by mandating a period when all students and teachers must assume the traditional posture of prayer of some religious groups and during which those who pray in that manner can do so. This is exactly what happened during the time when Bill 1064 was in effect. In Sayreville, continuing past practice, students were instructed to sit, close their eyes, and observe silence. In Hillsborough Township children were directed to sit and be quiet and still. In Roosevelt Junior High School students were instructed to stand up, bow their heads, close their eyes and observe silence.

Thus the State has injected itself into religious matters by designating a time and place when children and teachers may pray if they do so in a particular manner and by mandating conduct by all other children and teachers so that the prayers may proceed uninterrupted in their presence.

While this form of legislation advances the religion of some, it inhibits the religion of others in at least two ways.

First, there are those whose religious practices include silent prayer and meditation but who, as an article of faith, believe that the State should have no part in religious matters. For them mandated prayer is no longer prayer. It is their conviction that if the State requires any form of religious observance the observance is drained of its substance, loses its power and becomes but an empty shell. *Cf.*, Tillich, *Dynamics of Faith*, Ch. III, Symbols of Faith (Harper & Row 1958). Thus the State, seeking to further religion by mandating certain religious observances, in fact weakens religion by draining vitality from these observances.

Examples of this emasculating process can be seen in the cases. When a legislature routinely opens its sessions with prayer, when a court commences each day with "God save the United States and this honorable court," the courts have recognized that the effect is not to establish religion. Rather, the words which are spoken may represent a solemn and traditional ceremony serving a valuable civil function. They are no longer the words of a believer responding to his views of ultimate reality; they are, therefore, no longer prayer either in a religious or constitutional sense. Certain of those who oppose Bill 1064 on religious grounds seek to spare their mode of prayer from such a fate.

Second, by mandating a minute of silence which permits some persons to engage in prayer, Bill 1064 prevents other persons from engaging in their kind of prayer. Justice Brennan noted in his concurring opinion in *Abington*:

> . . . our religious composition makes us a vastly more diverse people than were our forefathers. They knew differences chiefly among Protestant sects. Today the Nation is far more heterogeneous religiously, including as it does substantial minorities not only of Catholics and Jews but as well of those who worship according to no version of the Bible and

those who worship no God at all. . . . In the face of such profound changes, practices which may have been objectionable to no one in the time of Jefferson and Madison may today be highly offensive to many persons, the deeply devout and the nonbelievers alike.

The religious diversity of which Justice Brennan spoke in 1963 is far more pronounced now. Thus religious practices and the concepts of ultimate reality to which these practices point vary ever more widely. While once the prayers of most religious people could be carried on in an environment of silence, now that is no longer the case. The prayers of some persons require movement and sound. Bill 1064, therefore, mandates an environment which allows some to pray but which prevents others from engaging in their form of prayer.

Finally there are those who profess no religion and to whom any form of prayer is offensive. Bill 1064 requires these persons to assume a posture suggestive of particular forms of prayer which are responsive to particular beliefs about ultimate reality. Understandably those who do not share those beliefs do not wish to be required to maintain a pose which suggests that they do. Children holding these views, as illustrated in the present case, are forced either to endure an exercise which runs counter to their beliefs or to face public opprobrium or ridicule by asking to be excused each day.

There is nothing in the language or reasoning of the Supreme Court's opinion in *Mueller v. Allen*, _____ U.S._____, 103 S.Ct. 3062, 77 L.Ed.2d 721 (1983) which affects the conclusion that the effect of Bill 1064 renders it unconstitutional. There the Court upheld a Minnesota statute which permitted taxpayers in computing their state income tax to deduct certain expenses incurred for the education of their children. This result was reached even though most such expenses involved payments on account of students attending private schools and even though it was established that 95% of such students attended sectarian schools. Applying the three point test, the Court concluded the tax deduction satisfied the primary effect inquiry. However, *Mueller* is of very limited utility in the present case. It is but the most recent in a long line of cases dealing with the question of the extent to which state legislation may, directly or indirectly, aid sectarian schools. The facts of those cases and the problems of church and state relations which they raise are quite different from the facts and problems raised by the school prayer cases.

Bill 1064 impermissibly advances the religion of some and inhibits the religion of others.

The third inquiry is whether Bill 1064 fosters an excessive government entanglement with religion. Implementation of the Bill would not involve the State in the kind of continued and pervasive monitoring of sectarian activities which was condemned in *Lemon v. Kurtzman, supra*. It would, however, tend to promote divisiveness among and between religious groups, another form of entanglement. *Gilfillan v. City of Philadelphia, supra,* at 932. A required minute of silence would put children and parents who believe in prayer in the public schools against children and parents who do not. The events in Princeton are illustrative of this consequence. There the school administrators were threatened with disruptive behavior by students who believed the minute of silence constituted enforced prayer contrary to their own convictions. Elsewhere the opposition did not take the form of threatened disruption, but children and parents were forced to decide whether the children should submit to an exercise which violated their beliefs or whether they should separate themselves from their peers.

With no secular purpose being served, this degree of entanglement causes Bill 1064 to fail the third prong of the test of validity.

For the foregoing reasons Bill 1064 violates the First Amendment and plaintiffs are entitled to a judgment granting the declaratory and injunctive relief they seek.[7]

Under 42 U.S.C. § 1988 a prevailing party may in appropriate circumstances be entitled to recover attorneys fees. In the unusual circumstances of this case I do not believe that such an award is warranted.

The named defendants did not contest the action on the merits. They were not responsible for enactment of the legislation under review. There is no reason why they should be required to pay plaintiffs' attorneys fees.

The intervenors did oppose plaintiffs on the merits. However, even though they did not prevail, their participation in the case served a valuable public purpose. Without their participation the facts and the law would not have been developed adequately. In a difficult case such as this in which important public interests are involved, it was essential that the facts be developed and the law fully presented. Since intervenors' role in this case contributed significantly in that regard it would be inappropriate to charge them with attorneys fees.

For the same reason no costs will be allowed to any party.

Plaintiffs' attorneys are requested to prepare a form of order implementing this opinion.

NOTES

1. It would seem that the minute of silence law under review in this case is the eighteenth in a series of school prayer or moment of silence bills introduced in the New Jersey legislature since 1970. Drakeman, Prayer in the Schools: Is New Jersey's Moment of Silence Law Constitutional? 35 Rut.L.Rev. 341 (1983) (*see* footnote 92 at 356 for a listing of the bills).

2. During the pretrial phase of this case plaintiffs sought to fill the gap left by the absence of a legislative record by taking the depositions of individual legislators and otherwise subjecting them to discovery. I concluded that although the legislative privilege contained in the federal constitution is not available to state legislators and although the legislative privilege contained in the State constitution is not available in § 1983 actions asserting deprivation of federal rights, for general policy reasons the law does not permit individual state legislators to be subjected to discovery in civil cases involving the interpretation or validity of state legislation absent very compelling reasons. Such reasons did not exist here. However, I also concluded that the absence of any official record of legislative proceedings and the inability to depose individual legislators created a situation in which it was more likely that otherwise inadmissible sources of information might be admitted into evidence as indicative of legislative intent, *e.g.,* newspaper accounts of proceedings admitted as an exception to the hearsay rule under Evid.R. 803(24).

3. When the moment of silence was implemented in Las Cruces the school children were given notes to take home to their parents so that the family could discuss what the students would do during the silent moment. Dr. Thompson's four children exhibited a diversity of reactions. His teen-age son believed the statute violated his constitutional rights. One daughter wished to use the moment for prayer. Another daughter asked if she could chant. A third daughter did not do much with the moment.

4. Numerous newspaper articles and similar published materials were offered and received in evidence. During the pretrial stages of the case it seemed that perhaps such sources would be the best evidence of the purpose and effect of the legislation under consideration. However, the testimony and other evidence produced by both sides at the trial proved to be far more helpful in this regard. The articles are clearly evidence of the purposes of the legislation and to some extent are supportive of testimony concerning the public's perception of the Bill 1064. However the articles do not form a basis for my findings as to the public's perception. Consequently it is unnecessary to determine the extent to which public perceptions can be gauged from newspaper articles (*see* on this subject the testimony of Professor Jerome L. Aumente of the Rutgers Journalism Institute).

5. The evidence produced at the trial of this case suggests that I spoke prematurely and oversimplified the situation when I concluded at the time plaintiffs applied for a temporary restraining order that "the statute on its face is neutral" and "does not purport by its terms to mandate prayer."

6. Two recent law review articles have surveyed the law and analyzed the constitutional issues raised by moment or minute of silence laws in general. Note: Moments of Silence, 96 Harv.L.Rev. 1874 (1983); Note: Daily Moments of Silence in Public Schools, 58 N.Y.U. L.Rev. 364 (1983). Another recent law review article has analyzed New Jersey's minute of silence law. Drakeman, Prayer in the School, etc. 35 Rut.L.Rev.341 (1983).

7. Helpful amicus briefs were filed on behalf of the following organizations: New Jersey Education Association (by Zazzali, Zazzali & Kroll, James R. Zazzali, Esq. and

Kenneth I. Nowak, Esq., on the brief); New Jersey Council of Churches (by Donald L. Drakeman, Esq.); Anti-Defamation League of B'nai B'irth, American Jewish Committee, Essex County Board of Rabbis, Jewish Federation of Central New Jersey, Jewish Federation of Southern New Jersey, New Jersey Association of Reform Rabbis, New Jersey-West Hudson Valley Council of the Union of American Hebrew Congregations, and United Synagogues of New Jersey (Howard T. Rosen, Esq.; Of Counsel: Justin J. Finger, Jeffrey P. Sinensky, Ruti G. Teitel, Samuel Rabinove, Andrea S. Klausner, James H. Laskey and Alan Goldstein); American Jewish Congress, Jewish Community Federation of Metropolitan New Jersey, Jewish Federation of North Jersey, Jewish Federation of Raritan Valley, Bayonne Jewish Community Council, and National Council of Jewish Women (by Stern, Steiger, Croland & Bornstein, P.A.; Of Counsel: Nathan Z. Dershowitz, Esq. and Marc D. Stern, Esq.; On the brief: Kenneth S. Goldrich, Esq., Marc D. Stern, Esq. and Jar Rubenstein, Esq.).

THE United States Court of Appeals, Eleventh Circuit, declares unconstitutional the "Alabama school prayer statutes," one of which stated: "From henceforth, any teacher or professor in any public educational institution within the State of Alabama, recognizing that the Lord God is one, at the beginning of any homeroom or any class, may lead the willing students in the following prayer to God: 'Almighty God, You alone are our God. We acknowledge You as the Creator and Supreme Judge of the world. May Your justice, Your truth, and Your peace abound this day in the hearts of our countrymen, in the counsels of our government, in the sanctity of our homes and in the classrooms of our schools. In the name of our Lord. Amen.'" In deciding against the state of Alabama, the court said: "The record reveals that passage of the statute was motivated by religious considerations, and its intention to advance religious beliefs. The fact that the prayer is voluntary and non-denominational does not neutralize the State's involvement. The State must remain neutral not only between competing religious sects, but also between believers and non-believers. . . . The practical effect of this neutrality means that State schools should not function to inculcate or suppress religious beliefs or habits of worship."

Jaffree v. *Wallace*, 705 F.2d 1526 (1983)

HATCHETT, Circuit Judge.

We must decide whether the trial court correctly determined that the recitation of prayers in the Mobile County, Alabama, public schools and the implementation of two Alabama statutes permitting religious practices in those public schools do not violate the establishment clause of the first amendment to the Constitution of the United States.[1] We are not called upon to determine whether prayer in public schools is desirable as a matter of policy. Because we find that the trial court was incorrect, we reverse and remand with directions to the trial court to issue and enforce an injunction prohibiting these unconstitutional practices.

Ishmael Jaffree, the appellant, is the father of five minor children, three of whom are enrolled in the Mobile County, Alabama, public schools. Jaffree's original action challenged the right of teachers in the public schools of Mobile County to conduct prayers in their classes, including group recitations of the Lord's Prayer. Before filing this action, Jaffree attempted to have the teachers discontinue prayer activities in those classes which his children attended. Jaffree held conversations with the teachers, wrote letters to the

superintendent of the school board, and made several telephone calls to the superintendent. When these efforts failed to halt the religious practices, Jaffree instituted this action against the appellee, Board of School Commissioners of Mobile County (Board). Jaffree alleged that in addition to the Lord's Prayer, the teachers and students also recited the following three prayers:

(1) God is great, God is good, Let us thank Him for our food, bow our heads we all are fed, Give us Lord our daily bread. Amen.

(2) God is great, God is good Let us thank Him for our food.

(3) For health and strength and daily food we praise Thy name, oh Lord.

Jaffree amended his complaint to include class action allegations, which the district court denied. Jaffree filed a second amended complaint to include as appellees the Governor of Alabama, the attorney general, and other state education authorities. In this amended action, Jaffree challenged the constitutionality of Ala.Code § 16-1-20.1 (1982) and Ala.Code § 16-1-20.2 (former Ala.Act 82-735), which are known as the "Alabama school prayer statutes." Section 16-1-20.1 states that:

At the commencement of the first class of each day in all grades in all public schools, the teacher in charge of the room in which each such class is held may announce that a period of silence not to exceed one minute in duration shall be observed for meditation or voluntary prayer, and during any such period no other activities shall be engaged in.

Section 16-1-20.2 states that:

From henceforth, any teacher or professor in any public educational institution within the State of Alabama, recognizing that the Lord God is one, at the beginning of any homeroom or any class, may lead the willing students in the following prayer to God:

Almighty God, You alone are our God. We acknowledge You as the Creator and Supreme Judge of the world. May Your justice, Your truth, and Your peace abound this day in the hearts of our countrymen, in the counsels of our government, in the sanctity of our homes and in the classrooms of our schools. In the name of our Lord. Amen.

The district court severed Jaffree's complaint into two causes of action: one related to those teachers' activities unmotivated by the statutes, and the other related to the statutes.[2] Following the severance, the court issued a preliminary injunction against the implementation of the Alabama school prayer statutes. *Jaffree By and Through Jaffree v. James*, 544 F.Supp. 727 (S.D.Ala.1982). After trial on the merits, the district court dismissed both actions, thereby dissolving the preliminary injunction. *Jaffree v. Board of School Commissioners of Mobile County*, 554 F.Supp. 1104 (S.D.Ala.1983); *Jaffree v. James*, 554 F.Supp. 1130 (S.D.Ala.1983). Pending appeal, Jaffree filed an emergency motion for stay and injunction in this court; we denied the motion.[3] Jaffree requested Justice Powell, in his capacity as Eleventh Circuit Justice, to stay the trial court's order or reinstate the preliminary injunction previously issued by the district court. In a memorandum opinion, Justice Powell granted the stay and reinstated the injunction pending final disposition of the appeal in this court. In the memorandum opinion, Justice Powell stated:

In *Engel v. Vitale*, 370 U.S. 421 [82 S.Ct. 1261, 8 L.Ed.2d 601] (1962), the Court held that the Establishment Clause of the First Amendment, made applicable to the States by the Fourteenth Amendment, prohibits a State from authorizing prayer in the public schools. The following Term, in *Murray v. Curlett*, decided with *School District of Abington Township v. Schempp*, 374 U.S. 203 [83 S.Ct. 1560, 10 L.Ed.2d 844] (1963), the Court explicitly invalidated a school district's rule providing for the reading of the Lord's Prayer as part of a school's opening exercises, despite the fact that participation in those exercises was voluntary.

Unless and until this Court reconsiders the foregoing decisions, they appear to control this case. In my view, the District Court was obligated to follow them. Similarly, my own authority as Circuit Justice is limited by controlling decisions of the full Court.

Jaffree v. Board of School Commissioners of Mobile County, _____U.S. _____, _____, 103 S.Ct. 842, 843, 74 L.Ed.2d 924, 926 (1983).

The contentions of the state and county officials of Alabama are easily stated. First, the county education officials contend that if prayers are being recited in the Mobile County public schools, this activity is without state action or participation and not pursuant to any policy or statute authorizing or encouraging such activities. Second, the Alabama officials contend that the Supreme Court has misread history regarding the first amendment and has erred by holding that the first amendment is made applicable to the states through the fourteenth amendment. They present failure of the *Blaine* amendment of 1876 to pass Congress as strong evidence in support of these contentions.

The district court accepted the premise that the first amendment to the United States Constitution does not prohibit states from establishing a religion. The district court conceded that its decision was contrary to the entire body of United States Supreme Court and Eleventh Circuit precedent, but declined to follow that precedent because, in its opinion, "the United States Supreme Court has erred in its reading of history." *Board of School Commissioners of Mobile County,* 554 F.Supp. at 1128.

HISTORY

Two views have been expressed regarding the interpretation of the history surrounding the establishment clause. One view is that the word "establishment" should be interpreted narrowly. Proponents of this view contend that the establishment clause prohibits only Congress, not the states, from establishing a religion. R. Cord, *Separation of Church and State: Historical Fact and Current Fiction* (1982); J. McClellan, *The Making and the Unmaking of the Establishment Clause*, A Blueprint for a Judicial Reform (P. McGuigan and R. Rader eds. n.d. 1981); E. Corwin, *The Supreme Court as a National School Board*, 14 Law and Contemporary Problems 3 (1949).

A second view results in a much broader interpretation of the establishment clause. Proponents of this view contend that the establishment clause prohibits any governmental support of religion on the state or federal level. L. Levy, *Judgments: Essays on American Constitutional History* (1972); L. Pfeffer, *Church,*

State, and Freedom, (rev. ed. 1967); R. Dixon, *Religion, Schools and the Open Society,* 13 Journal of Public Law 267, 278 (1964); Katz, *Freedom of Religion and State Neutrality,* 20 U.Chi.L.Rev. 426, 438 (1953). The Supreme Court has supported the broader view. *See Engel v. Vitale,* 370 U.S. 421, 82 S.Ct. 1261, 8 L.Ed.2d 601 (1962); *Everson v. Board of Education,* 330 U.S. 1, 67 S.Ct. 504, 91 L.Ed. 711 (1946); H. Chase & C. Ducat, *Constitutional Interpretation, Cases-Essays-Materials,* 1384 (2d ed. 1979).

The appellees argue that historically the first amendment to the United States Constitution was intended only to prohibit the federal government from establishing a national religion.[4] Appellees, additionally, argue that historical evidence does not support the fourteenth amendment's incorporation of the first amendment. The appellee and the district court rely heavily on the research of historians. These historians believe the Supreme Court misread the history surrounding the establishment clause. They submit that the establishment clause has a dual purpose (1) to guarantee the people of this country that the federal government will not impose a national religion, and (2) to guarantee states the right to define the meaning of religious establishment under their state constitutions and laws.

The Supreme Court, however, has carefully considered these arguments and rejected them. *See, e.g., School District of Abington Township v. Schempp,* 374 U.S. 203, 83 S.Ct. 1560, 10 L.Ed.2d 844 (1963); *Engel,* 370 U.S. 421, 82 S.Ct. 1261, 8 L.Ed.2d 601 (1962); *McGowan v. Maryland,* 366 U.S. 420, 81 S.Ct. 1101, 6 L.Ed.2d 393 (1961); *McCollum v. Board of Education,* 333 U.S. 203, 68 S.Ct. 461, 92 L.Ed. 649 (1948); *Everson,* 330 U.S. 1, 67 S.Ct. 504, 91 L.Ed. 711 (1946). In *Everson,* the Court presented its careful review of the history surrounding the establishment clause. Justice Black wrote:

The "establishment of religion" clause of the First Amendment means at least this: Neither a state nor the Federal Government can set up a church. Neither can pass laws which aid one religion, aid all religions, or prefer one religion over another. . . . In the words of Jefferson, the clause against establishment of religion by law was intended to erect "a wall of separation between Church and State."

Everson, 330 U.S. at 15 16, 67 S.Ct. 511 512. Justice Rutledge, while dissenting on other grounds in *Everson,* observed that:

Not simply an established church, but any law respecting an establishment of religion is forbidden. The Amendment was broadly but not loosely phrased. . . .

The Amendment's purpose was not to strike merely at the official establishment of a single sect, creed or religion, outlawing only a formal relation such as

had prevailed in England and some of the colonies. Necessarily it was to uproot all such relationships. But the object was broader than separating church and state in this narrow sense. It was to create a complete and permanent separation of the spheres of religious activity and civil authority by comprehensively forbidding every form of public aid or support for religion.

"Religion" appears only once in the Amendment. But the word governs two prohibitions and governs them alike. It does not have two meanings, one narrow to forbid "an establishment" and another, much broader, for securing "the free exercise thereof." "Thereof" brings down "religion" with its entire and exact content, no more and no less, from the first into the second guaranty, so that Congress and now the states are as broadly restricted concerning the one as they are regarding the other.

Everson, 330 U.S. at 31–32, 67 S.Ct. at 519. Justice Jackson, while dissenting on other grounds, also noted that:

There is no answer to the proposition . . . that the effect of the religious freedom Amendment to our Constitution was to take every form of propagation of religion out of the realm of things which could . . . be made public business. . . . This [religious] freedom was first in the Bill of Rights because it was first in the forefathers' minds; it was set forth in absolute terms, and its strength is its rigidity.

Everson, 330 U.S. at 26, 67 S.Ct. at 516. Although differing on the outcome of the case, all Justices perceived the history of the establishment clause as prohibiting any government involvement with religion. This unanimity also existed regarding the history of the first amendment's applicability to the states through the fourteenth amendment.

Appellees suggest that no documentary evidence exists supporting the claim that the fourteenth amendment was intended to apply the establishment clause of the first amendment to the states. To illustrate this point, the appellees turn to the rejection of the *"Blaine* amendment."[5] In 1876, Congress considered a resolution for the adoption of a constitutional amendment expressly forbidding a state from making any law relating to religion. The resolution failed in the Senate. *See* 4 Cong.Rec. 5595 (1876). The appellees argue that this refusal to pass the *Blaine* amendment is indicative of Congress's understanding that the fourteenth amendment left undisturbed the state's freedom to establish religion. This argument is the same as that urged and rejected in *McCollum.* 333 U.S. at 211 n.7, 68 S.Ct. at 465 n.7; *McGowan,* 366 U.S. 420, 81 S.Ct. 1101, 6 L.Ed.2d 393 (1961). Chief Justice Warren, writing for the Court, stated: "[T]he First Amendment, in its final form, did not simply bar a congressional enactment *establishing a church;* it forbade all laws *respecting an establishment of religion.* Thus, this Court has given the Amendment a 'broad interpretation . . . in light of its history and the evils it was designed forever to suppress.'" *McGowan,* 366 U.S. at 441–42, 81 S.Ct. at 1113 (emphasis in original). In *Engel v. Vitale,* the Court meticulously re-examined the history surrounding the first and fourteenth amendments and reaffirmed its view. The Court concluded that:

> By the time of the adoption of the Constitution, our history shows that there was a widespread awareness among many Americans of the dangers of a union of Church and State. . . . The First Amendment was added to the Constitution to stand as a guarantee that neither the power nor the prestige of the Federal Government would be used to control, support or influence the kinds of prayer the American people can say—that the people's religions must not be subjected to the pressures of government for change each time a new political administration is elected to office. Under that Amendment's prohibition against governmental establishment of religion, as reinforced by the provisions of the Fourteenth Amendment, government in this country, be it state or federal, is without power to prescribe by law any particular form of prayer which is to be used as an official prayer in carrying on any program of governmentally sponsored religious activity.

Engel, 370 U.S. at 429–30, 82 S.Ct. at 1266. The interplay between the first and fourteenth amendments engages scholars in endless debate. We are urged to remain mindful of the uses of history. History provides enlightenment; it appraises courts of the subtleties and complexities of problems before them. *See* Wofford, J., *The Blinding Light: The Uses of History in Constitutional Interpretation,* 31 Univ. of Chi.L.Rev. 502, 532 (1964). The important point is: *the Supreme Court has considered and decided the historical implications surrounding the establishment clause.* The Supreme Court has concluded that its present interpretation of the first and fourteenth amendments is consistent with the historical evidence.

PRECEDENT

Under our form of government and long established law and custom, the Supreme Court is the ultimate authority on the interpretation of our Constitution and laws; its interpretations may not be disregarded.

Although the district court recognized the importance of precedent, it chose to disregard Supreme Court precedent. The district court attempted to justify its actions by discussing the limited exceptions to the doctrine of stare decisis. The doctrine of stare decisis pertains to the deference a court may give to its

own prior decisions. *See Hertz v. Woodman,* 218 U.S. 205, 212, 30 S.Ct. 621, 622, 54 L.Ed. 1001 (1910). The stare decisis doctrine and its exceptions do not apply where a lower court is compelled to apply the precedent of a higher court. *See* 20 Am.Jur.2d *Courts* § 183 (1965).

Federal district courts and circuit courts are bound to adhere to the controlling decisions of the Supreme Court. *Hutto v. Davis,* 454 U.S. 370, 375, 102 S.Ct. 703, 705–706, 70 L.Ed.2d 556 (1982); *Stell v. Savannah-Chatham County Board of Education,* 333 F.2d 55, 61 (5th Cir.), *cert. denied,* 379 U.S. 933, 85 S.Ct. 332, 13 L.Ed.2d 344 (1964); *Booster Lodge No. 405, Int. Ass'n of M. & A.W. v. NLRB,* 459 F.2d 1143, 1150 n.7 (D.C.Cir.1972). Justice Rehnquist emphasized the importance of precedent when he observed that "unless we wish anarchy to prevail within the federal judicial system, a precedent of this Court must be followed by the lower federal courts no matter how misguided the judges of those courts may think it to be." *Davis,* 454 U.S. at 375, 102 S.Ct. at 706. *See Also, Thurston Motor Lines, Inc. v. Jordan K. Rand, Ltd.,* _____ U.S. _____, 103 S.Ct. 1343, 75 L.Ed.2d 260 (1983) (the Supreme Court, in a per curiam decision, recently stated: "Needless to say, only this Court may overrule one of its precedents."). The old Fifth Circuit articulated these positions when it stated that "no inferior federal court may refrain from acting as required by [a Supreme Court's] decision even if such a court should conclude that the Supreme Court erred as to its facts or to the law." *Stell,* 333 F.2d at 61. Judicial precedence serves as the foundation of our federal judicial system. Adherence to it results in stability and predictability. If the Supreme Court errs, no other court may correct it.

NON-STATUTORY PRAYER ACTIVITIES

The district court did not specifically analyze or discuss in detail the constitutionality of the two Alabama statutes. The court stated: "In light of the reasoning in [the school prayer activities case], the court holds that the claims in this case fail to state any claim for which relief could be granted under the federal statute." *Jaffree,* 554 F.Supp. at 1132. By permitting the Mobile County school prayer activities to survive the first amendment attack, the district court implicitly concluded that the Alabama school prayer statutes were constitutional. 554 F.Supp. at 1132.

The first amendment provides, in pertinent part, that "Congress shall make no law respecting an establishment of religion, or prohibiting the free exercise thereof. . . ." U.S. Const. amend. I. The objective of the first amendment's religious guarantees are twofold: to preclude government interference with the practice of religious faith, and to preclude the establishment of a religion dictated by government. *Larkin v. Grendel,* _____ U.S. _____, 103 S.Ct. 505, 74 L.Ed.2d 297 (1982). This fundamental and enduring concept of separation of church and state was translated by early decisions into a wall "high and impregnable." *See Reynolds v. United States,* 98 U.S. (8 Otto) 145, 164, 25 L.Ed. 244 (1878); *quoting* Reply from Thomas Jefferson to an address by a committee of the Danbury Baptist Association (January 1, 1802), *reprinted in* 8 Works of Thomas Jefferson 113 (Washington ed. 1861). The establishment clause requires that government be neutral in its relations between various religions and between non-believers and believers. *Everson,* 330 U.S. at 18, 67 S.Ct. at 513. Repeatedly, the Supreme Court has struck down the recitation of prayers, Bible readings, and devotional activities in public schools. *Schempp,* 374 U.S. 203, 83 S.Ct. 1560, 10 L.Ed.2d 844 (1963); *Engel,* 370 U.S. 421, 82 S.Ct. 1261, 8 L.Ed.2d 601 (1962). This circuit has also followed the Supreme Court's lead in holding that public school prayer is unconstitutional because it is inherently a religious exercise. *Karen B. v. Treen,* 653 F.2d 897 (5th Cir.1981). Having recalled these well-settled principles of constitutional jurisprudence, we now turn to the Mobile County school prayer activities.

The appellee contends that since the teachers' prayer activities were not motivated by school board policy or by state statute, the establishment clause is not violated. The appellee reasons that since no Board policy existed or no statutory authority motivated the teachers' prayer activities, no state involvement exists. Thus, the establishment clause is inapplicable by virtue of the absence of state action.

Under Alabama law, teachers are appointed, suspended, and removed by the county school boards. *See* Ala.Code § 16-8-23 (1927). The Alabama county school boards are creatures of the state and are controlled by the state. *See* Ala.Code § 16-3-11 (1927); Ala.Code § 16-8-8 (1927); *Lee v. Macon County Board of Education,* 267 F.Supp. 458 (M.D.Ala.1967); *Opinion of the Justices,* 276 Ala. 239, 160 So.2d 648, 650 (Ala.1964). It is clear from the record that the Board members were on notice of the teachers' prayer activities and took no steps to discourage those activities.[6] Evidence exists to indicate that a large number of teachers discussed the prayer activities with the superintendent of schools. On this record, it is easy to find that the Board's actions ratified the teachers' conduct. If a statute authorizing the teachers' activities would be unconstitutional, then the activities, in the absence of a statute, are also unconstitutional. In *Schempp,* Justice Douglas, in his concurring opinion, pointed out the mockery that would be made of the establishment clause if unconstitutional activities could be carried on merely because no statute authorized the activities. 374 U.S. at 230, 83 S.Ct. at 1575–1576.

The Supreme Court has enunciated three standards that a statute must satisfy in order to survive a first amendment attack: first, the statute must have a secular purpose; second, its principal or primary effect must be one that neither advances nor inhibits religion; and finally, the statute must not foster "an excessive government entanglement with religion." *Lemon v. Kurtzman,* 403 U.S. 602, 612–13, 91 S.Ct. 2105, 2111, 29 L.Ed.2d 745; *Committee for Public Education and Religious Liberty v. Nyquist,* 413 U.S. 756, 773, 93 S.Ct. 2955, 2965–2966, 37 L.Ed.2d 948 (1973); *Walz v. Tax Commission,* 397 U.S. 664, 674, 90 S.Ct. 1409, 1414, 25 L.Ed.2d 697 (1970). *See Murray v. Curlett,* 374 U.S. 203, 83 S.Ct. 1560, 10 L.Ed.2d 844 (1963); and *Engel,* 370 U.S. 421, 82 S.Ct. 1261, 8 L.Ed.2d 601 (1962). If a statute does not meet this standard, it must fall to the first amendment's prohibitions. *Stone v. Graham,* 449 U.S. 39, 40–41, 101 S.Ct. 192, 193–194, 66 L.Ed.2d 199 (1980). The objective of these tests is to insure neutrality of government involvement in religious activity. *E.g., Watson v. Jones,* 13 Wall. 679, 728, 20 L.Ed. 666 (1872).

In applying the Supreme Court's *Kurtzman* test, the Eleventh Circuit in the recent case of *American, etc. v. Rabun County Chamber of Commerce,* 678 F.2d 1379 (11th Cir.1982), held that the establishment clause may be violated by actions of state officials where no statute or ordinance authorizes the particular activity. In that case, Judge Tuttle, writing for the court stated:

> In interpreting the Establishment Clause, the Supreme Court has identified three tests to be applied to the challenged *actions* of a state:
>
> (1) Whether the *action* has a secular purpose;
>
> (2) Whether the "principal or primary effect" is one which neither "advances nor inhibits religion;" and
>
> (3) Whether the *action* fosters "'an excessive government entanglement with religion.' *Waltz [v. Tax Commissioners,* 397 U.S. 664, 674, 90 S.Ct. 1409, 1414, 25 L.Ed.2d 697 (1970)]."

678 F.2d at 1389 (emphasis added).

Although prayer activities in public schools may not be statutorily authorized or conducted pursuant to written school board policy, if state action is present and the activities satisfy the statutory test articulated by the Supreme Court as modified by this circuit, the activities may be declared unconstitutional. *See Burton v. Wilmington Parking Auth.,* 365 U.S. 715, 81 S.Ct. 856, 6 L.Ed.2d 45 (1961); *Marsh v. Alabama,* 326 U.S. 501, 66 S.Ct. 276, 90 L.Ed. 265 (1946). The reach of the establishment clause is not limited by the lack of statutory authorization. *See Schempp,* 374 U.S. 203, 83 S.Ct. 1560, 10 L.Ed.2d 844 (1963); *Murray,* 374 U.S. 203, 83 S.Ct. 1560, 10 L.Ed.2d 844 (1963); *Engel,* 370 U.S. 421, 82 S.Ct. 1261, 8 L.Ed.2d 601 (1962).

Here, we are not concerned with the mechanism used to advance a concept, but the evil against which the clause protects. *See Nyquist,* 413 U.S. at 772, 93 S.Ct. at 2965.

This circuit has stated that "prayer is perhaps the quintessential religious practice . . . since prayer is a primary religious activity in itself, its observance in public school classrooms [implies a religious purpose]." *Treen,* 653 F.2d at 901. Recognizing that prayer is the quintessential religious practice implies that no secular purpose can be satisfied. The primary effect of prayer is the advancement of ones religious beliefs. It acknowledges the existence of a Supreme Being. The involvement of the Mobile County school system in such activity involves the state in advancing the affairs of religion. The Supreme Court and this circuit have indicated that such prayer activities cannot be advanced without the implication that the state is violating the establishment clause. *Schempp* and *Treen.* Indeed, the Supreme Court held in *McCollum* that use of a tax-supported building for the advancement of religious activity, in close cooperation with school authorities, violated the establishment clause. *McCollum,* 333 U.S. at 209, 68 S.Ct. at 464; *cf. Zorach v. Clauson,* 343 U.S. 306, 72 S.Ct. 679, 96 L.Ed. 954 (1952) (religious instruction off school grounds implemented by New York school board held constitutional). The record indicates that the teachers' prayer activities were conducted in the classrooms and did not appear to be secularly motivated. We, therefore, conclude that the Mobile County school activities are in violation of the establishment clause.

THE STATUTES

As to the statutes authorizing prayer, both statutes advance and encourage religious activities. The district court recognized this when it stated:

> The enactment of Senate Bill 8 [Alabama Act 82-735] and § 16-1-20.1 is an effort on the part of the State of Alabama to encourage a religious activity. Even though these statutes are permissive in form, it is nevertheless state involvement respecting an establishment of religion. *Engel v. Vitale,* 370 U.S. 421, 430, 82 S.Ct. 1261, 1266, 8 L.Ed.2d 601 (1962). Thus, binding precedent which this Court is under a duty to follow indicates the substantial likelihood plaintiffs will prevail on the merits.

James, 544 F.Supp. at 732. The statutes are specifically the type which the Supreme Court addressed in *Engel.* Aggravating in this case is the existence of a government composed prayer in Ala.Code § 16-1-20.2. In *Engel,* the Supreme Court held unconstitutional the "non-denominational" state prayer approved for public schools. The prayer involved in *Engel* con-

tained considerably fewer religious references than the prayer now before this court. The Supreme Court stated that "the constitutional prohibition against law respecting an establishment of religion must at least mean that in this country it is no part of the business of government to compose official prayers for any group to recite as part of a religious program carried on by government." *Engel,* 370 U.S. at 425, 82 S.Ct. at 1264. Section 16-1-20.2, as its proponents admit, amounts to the establishment of a state religion. The record reveals that passage of the statute was motivated by religious considerations, and its intention to advance religious beliefs. The fact that the prayer is voluntary and non-denominational does not neutralize the state's involvement. The state must remain neutral not only between competing religious sects, but also between believers and non-believers. *See Schempp,* 374 U.S. at 218, 83 S.Ct. at 1569. The practical effect of this neutrality means that state schools should not function to inculcate or suppress religious beliefs or habits of worship. The implications of the district court's opinion firmly recognizes that Alabama is involving itself in the affairs of religion. Section 16-1-20.2 violates the establishment clause of the first amendment and is therefore unconstitutional.

The objective of the meditation or prayer statute (Ala.Code § 16-1-20.1) was also the advancement of religion. This fact was recognized by the district court at the hearing on the motion for preliminary relief where it was established that the intent of the statute was to return prayer to the public schools. *James,* 544 F.Supp. at 731. The existence of this fact and the inclusion of prayer obviously involves the state in religious activities. *Beck v. McElrath,* 548 F.Supp. 1161 (M.D.Tenn.1982). This demonstrates a lack of secular legislative purpose on the part of the Alabama Legislature. Additionally, the statute has the primary effect of advancing religion. We do not imply that simple meditation or silence is barred from the public schools; we hold that the state cannot participate in the advancement of religious activities through any guise, including teacher-led meditation. It is not the activity itself that concerns us; it is the purpose of the activity that we shall scrutinize. Thus, the existence of these elements require that we also hold section 16-1-20.1 in violation of the establishment clause.

CLASS CERTIFICATION

Jaffree sought class certification under rules 23(a) and 23(b)(2) of the Federal Rules of Civil Procedure.[7] The complaint identified as the class, students currently enrolled in the Mobile County public school system. Upon the pleadings, the district court denied Jaffree's class certification.

Under Federal Rule of Civil Procedure 23, a class

action determination is left to the sound discretion of the district court. *Zeidman v. Ray McDermott & Co., Inc.,* 651 F.2d 1030, 1038–39 (5th Cir.1981); 7A C. Wright & A. Miller, Federal Practice and Procedure, § 1785, at 134 (1972). The district court's decision is reversible only when it abuses its discretion. *See Guerine v. J & W Inv., Inc.,* 544 F.2d 863 (5th Cir.1977).

Jaffree contends the court abused its discretion by denying class certification without first holding an evidentiary hearing. He cites *Shepard v. Beaird-Poulan, Inc.,* 617 F.2d 87, 89 (5th Cir.1980), as authority for the requirement of an evidentiary hearing. We disagree with Jaffree's reading of *Shepard.* *Shepard* teaches that a district court must hold a hearing if it denies certification on the ground that the plaintiff would not adequately represent the class interest. *Shepard,* 617 F.2d at 89. In this instance, the court did not deny certification on this ground. We therefore affirm the district court's denial of class certification.

Appellees, state superintendent and state board, argue that no case or controversy exists between them and Jaffree. Appellees argue that the statutes give teachers the discretion of leading prayers, not the Board nor the state superintendent. Thus, they argue, neither the state board nor the state superintendent has the authority to implement or enforce the statutes. We find that a case or controversy exists between Jaffree and the county superintendent and county education board. Therefore, federal jurisdiction exists and the case or controversy question regarding the state board and the state superintendent becomes inconsequential.

CONCLUSION

Supreme Court and Eleventh Circuit precedent regarding prayer in public schools is abundantly clear. No new issues were presented to the district court. In keeping with this precedent, we hold that the Mobile County school prayer activities, Ala.Code § 16-1-20.1 and Ala.Code § 16-1-20.2, are in violation of the establishment clause of the first amendment to the Constitution of the United States. We do not decide today whether prayer in public schools is the proper policy to follow. This court merely applies the principles established by the Supreme Court. While many may disagree on the subject of prayer in public schools, our Constitution provides that the Supreme Court is the final arbiter of constitutional disputes. In this instance, these religious exercises failed to survive the three standards articulated by the Supreme Court. *See Lemon, Nyquist, Engel,* and *Everson.* Consequently, (1) we reverse the district court's dismissal of these actions, (2) affirm the decision denying class certification, (3) reverse the denial of costs to the ap-

pellants, and (4) remand the case to the district court. Upon remand, the district court is directed to award costs to appellant and forthwith issue and enforce an order enjoining the statutes and activities held in this opinion to be unconstitutional.

AFFIRMED IN PART, REVERSED IN PART, and REMANDED WITH DIRECTIONS.

NOTES

1. U.S. Const., amend I, states that:
   Congress shall make no law respecting an establishment of religion, or prohibiting the free exercise thereof; or abridging the freedom of speech, or of the press; or the right of the people peaceably to assemble, and to petition the Government for a redress of grievances.
2. This court ordered consolidation of *Jaffree v. Board of School Commissioners of Mobile County,* 554 F.Supp. 1104 (S.D.Ala.1983), and *Jaffree v. James,* 554 F.Supp. 1130 (S.D.Ala.1983).
3. The following were amicus parties on the appeal: Senator John P. East (North Carolina), Concerned Women for American Educational and Legal Defense Foundation, James Madison Institute—A Project of the North Carolina Conservative Research and Education Institute, Center for Judicial Studies, American Civil Liberties Union, Alabama Civil Liberties Union, American Jewish Congress, and the Anti-Defamation League of B-nai Brith.
4. The intervenors, Douglas T. Smith, et al., (more than 500 teachers and parents) basically offered the same arguments as the appellees.
5. Title 4 Cong.Rec. 5580 (1876) states, in pertinent part, that:
   No State shall make any law respecting an establishment of religion, or prohibiting the free exercise thereof; and no religious test shall ever be required as a qualification for any office of public trust under any State. No public property, and no public revenue of, nor any loan of credit by or under the authority of the United States, or any State . . . shall be appropriated to, or made or used for, the support of any school, educational or other institution, under the control of any religious or anti-religious sect . . . wherein the particular creed or tenets of any religious or anti-religious sect . . . shall be taught; and no such particular creed or tenets shall be read or taught in any school or institution supporting in whole or in part by such revenue or loan of credit; and no such appropriation or loan of credit shall be made to any religious or anti-religious sect . . . to promote its interests or tenets. This article shall not be construed to prohibit the reading of the Bible in any school or institution.
6. The district court found as a fact:
   Finally, Ms. Boyd was made aware of the contents of a letter drafted by Mr. Jaffree, dated May 10, 1982, which had been sent to Superintendent Hammons complaining about the prayer activity in Ms. Boyd's classroom. . . . [*Board of School Commissioners of Mobile County,* 554 F.Supp. at 1107.]
   Upon learning of the plaintiff's concern over prayer

activity in their schools, defendants Reed and Phillips consulted with teachers involved, however, neither defendant advised or instructed the defendant teachers to discontinue the complained of activity. [554 F.Supp. at 1108.]

7. Fed.R.Civ.P. 23(a) and 23(b)(2) reads, in pertinent part:

(a) Prerequisites to a Class Action. One or more members of a class may sue or be sued as representative parties on behalf of all only if (1) the class is so numerous that joinder of all members is impracticable, (2) there are questions of law or fact common to the class, (3) the claims or defenses of the representative parties are typical of the claims or defenses of the class, and (4) the representative parties will fairly and adequately protect the interests of the class.

(b) Class Actions Maintainable. An action may be maintained as a class action if the prerequisites of subdivision (a) are satisfied, and in addition:

(2) the party opposing the class has acted or refused to act on grounds generally applicable to the class, thereby making appropriate final injunctive relief or corresponding declaratory relief with respect to the class as a whole. . . .

THE United States Court of Appeals, Eleventh Circuit, decides against a Georgia county school district which had, among other things, permitted "a Youth For Christ Club or any other religious student group to meet on school premises under faculty supervision," authorized "announcements of church sponsored activities by means of the schools' public address systems and bulletin boards," and permitted "the placing of religious signs on school property." After considering the facts, the Court of Appeals stated: "When the evidence above is evaluated in light of the district's apparent support of religious assemblies, religious signs, and announcements of church sponsored activities via bulletin boards and public address systems . . . , we are unable to conclude that the district court abused its discretion in issuing the preliminary injunction."

Nartowicz v. *Stripling,* 736 F.2d 646 (1984)

PER CURIAM:

The defendant, Clayton County School District, appeals to this court from an order of the District Court for the Northern District of Georgia, granting the plaintiff Nartowicz's motion for a preliminary injunction.

In January of 1983, the plaintiffs commenced an action in federal district court, pursuant to 42 U.S.C. § 1983, alleging that certain of the school district's practices contributed to the establishment of religion, in contravention of the first amendment to the United States Constitution. Specifically, the plaintiffs sought to enjoin the defendants from: (1) permitting a Youth For Christ Club or any other religious student group to meet on school premises under faculty supervision; (2) authorizing announcements of church sponsored activities by means of the schools' public address systems and bulletin boards; (3) permitting the placing of religious signs on school property; and (4) authorizing student assemblies that promote or advance religion. The district court granted the plaintiffs' motion for a preliminary injunction with respect to all four practices at issue, and defendant appeals from the injunction as it applies to the first two practices.[1]

We note at the outset that the scope of our review of a district court's order granting a preliminary injunction is limited:

The grant or denial of a preliminary injunction is a decision within the sound discretion of the district court. [citation omitted]. On appeal from the grant or denial of a preliminary injunction we do not review the intrinsic merits of the case. "It is the function of the trial court to exercise its discretion in deciding upon and delicately balancing the equities of the parties involved." [citations omitted]. We consider the court's decision under the abuse of discretion standard of review.

The court must exercise its discretion in light of the following four prerequisites for a preliminary injunction: "(1) a substantial likelihood that plaintiff will prevail on the merits, (2) a substantial threat that plaintiff will suffer irreparable injury if the injunction is not granted, (3) that the threatened injury to plaintiff outweighs the threatened harm the injunction may do to defendant, and (4) that granting the preliminary injunction will not disserve the public interest." [citation omitted]. Because a preliminary injunction is "an extraordinary and drastic remedy," its grant is the exception rather than the rule, and plaintiff must clearly carry the burden of persuasion. [citation omitted].

United States v. Lambert, 695 F.2d 536, 539 (11th Cir.1983). Neither party questions the district court's conclusion that in the context of this case, the propriety of issuing the preliminary injunction hinges upon the likelihood that plaintiffs will prevail on the merits; if such a likelihood is substantial, the remaining three considerations will favor the plaintiffs, and if success on the merits is unlikely, the plaintiffs have failed to carry their burden of persuasion.

Turning then to the likelihood of plaintiffs' success on the merits, allegations of establishment clause violations are evaluated with reference to a three part test articulated in *Lemon v. Kurtzman:*

1) Does the policy or practice of the state or state entity have a secular (non-religious) purpose?
2) Is the primary effect of the policy or practice one that neither advances nor inhibits religion?
3) Does the policy or practice avoid excessive entanglement with religion?

403 U.S. 602, 612–13, 91 S.Ct. 2105, 2111, 29 L.Ed.2d 745, 755 (1971). If the answer to any one of the above three questions is "no," an establishment clause violation has been made out. *Id.* Here, the plaintiffs assail two of the school district's practices as contravening the establishment clause: permitting a student group called "Youth For Christ" to meet on school property after school hours under faculty supervision; and using the school's public address system and bulletin boards to announce events sponsored by local religious organizations.

The Youth For Christ Group

The affidavits, depositions and pretrial testimony to date reveal that there has been a "Youth For Christ" (YFC) group at North Clayton Junior High School for over eleven years. (T. v.I at 90). Meetings of the YFC are conducted after school hours on school property, and are supervised by a faculty sponsor. (T. v.I at 89). A "devotion" is read at each meeting, and there is "no praying at a majority of the meetings." (T. v.I at 89).

The district court held that permitting the YFC to meet violated the first factor of the *Lemon* test requiring that the state practice have a secular purpose, because the YFC was a non-secular or religious group. The court did not address the two remaining *Lemon* factors. This analysis may construe the secular purpose requirement too strictly. In *Widmar v. Vincent*, the Supreme Court held that permitting a concededly religious group to meet on public university property would not violate the establishment clause. 454 U.S. 263, 102 S.Ct. 269, 70 L.Ed.2d 440 (1981). The Court noted that the secular purpose in allowing such meetings would be to further the university's policy of providing a forum in which students can exchange ideas. *Id.* at 275 n. 10.

Similarly, it has been held that there is a secular purpose in high schools encouraging extracurricular activities, a purpose that is made no less secular by the fact that one of the activities permitted is of a religious nature. *Brandon v. Board of Education of Guilderland Central School District*, 635 F.2d 971, 978 (2d Cir.1980); *Bender v. Williamsport Area School District*, 563 F.Supp. 697, 709 (M.D.Pa.1983); *cf. Lubbock Civil Liberties Union v. Lubbock Independent School District*, 669 F.2d 1038, 1044–45 (5th Cir.1982) (secular purpose requirement violated where the school district expressly authorized students to assemble after school for religious purposes). The meager evidence presently in the record makes it impossible to speculate as to whether the YFC was introduced for the purpose of advancing religion, as opposed to the secular purpose of encouraging extracurricular activity; final resolution of this issue must await further development of relevant facts upon remand.

The second component of the *Lemon* test calls for an inquiry into whether the junior high school's practice of permitting the YFC to meet on school property under faculty supervision has a primary secular effect of accommodating, rather than advancing or promoting religion. There are three pieces of evidence in the record pertaining to the YFC: First, there is an affidavit of the YFC faculty sponsor, indicating that YFC meetings take place after school, that a "devotion" is read at each meeting, that there is no praying at a majority of the meetings, and that there is no preaching or witnessing at any of the meetings. Second, there is an affidavit of the assistant principal at North Clayton Junior High School indicating that the YFC has been in the school for eleven years. Finally, there is the testimony of the assistant principal indicating that, as with other extracurricular clubs at the school, she schedules the meeting times for the clubs, and announces the schedule over the school's public address system.

When the evidence above is evaluated in light of the district's apparent support of religious assemblies, religious signs, and announcements of church sponsored activities via bulletin boards and public address systems (discussed below), we are unable to conclude that the district court abused its discretion in issuing the preliminary injunction.[2] We add, however, that upon submission for final injunctive relief it would be useful to explore more fully several avenues of inquiry in determining the propriety of permanent relief. The ultimate question, of course, is whether the school district merely accommodates, as opposed to endorses, the YFC. In answering that question, it would be helpful to know: 1) to what extent faculty sponsors participate in YFC activities; 2) whether the school district has a policy of accommodating any group desiring space, and would freely extend access to any religious or anti-religious group, or whether before a group may meet on school property, it must first obtain school approval; 3) apart from what the school district has done to accommodate or support the YFC as a matter of fact, how is the school's position perceived by North Clayton Junior High School students, or put another way, to what extent does the impressionability of the students affect their perceptions of the school's actions?

Announcement of Activities Sponsored by Religious Organizations

The superintendent of the school district testified that it was his policy to permit various schools' public address systems and bulletin boards to be used by churches to announce church sponsored secular activities and other messages of "public importance." (T. v.3 at 90–91; T. v.1 at 87). The superintendent further observed that in order to ascertain whether a particular event that is the subject of a prospective announcement is secular in character, or of public importance, it may be necessary to make an inquiry into the nature of the event. The district court found no written guidelines in existence to assist administrators at the various schools in determining which messages could properly be announced (T. v.1 at 192); consistent with that finding is the superintendent's statement in his affidavit that he had no knowledge of what kinds of announcements were in fact being authorized. (T. v.1 at 87).

The district court held that the policy and practice of announcing "secular" activities[3] sponsored by religious organizations created excessive entanglement problems. The court therefore issued a preliminary injunction against announcements of church sponsored activities through school facilities, but specifically exempted from the order secular activities taking place at a particular church, provided that the activities were not church sponsored.

We conclude that the court acted within its discretion in issuing the injunction as to such announcements. The excessive entanglement component of the *Lemon* test has been interpreted to mean that "some governmental activitiy that does not have an imper-

missible religious effect may nevertheless be unconstitutional, if in order to avoid the religious effect government must enter into an arrangement which requires it to monitor the activity." *Americans United for Separation of Church and State v. School District of the City of Grand Rapids,* 718 F.2d 1389, 1400 (6th Cir.1983). Here, the defendants concede that the announcement of church sponsored religious activities would have the impermissible effect of advancing religion. It would appear from the evidence presently available that in order to avoid announcing religious activities school representatives must monitor and occasionally investigate the subject matter of proposed announcements, and sort out those church sponsored activities that are religious from those that are not, without the benefit of written policy guidelines. Under these circumstances, it was not an abuse of discretion to hold that there existed a substantial likelihood of entanglement.

AFFIRMED.

NOTES

1. The school district concedes that it may not authorize religion promoting assemblies, and has discontinued its practice of placing allegedly religious signs on school property.
2. Because of our holding that adequate grounds exist to issue the injunction in light of the secular effect component of the *Lemon* test, we need not address questions of excessive entanglement, the third inquiry under *Lemon.*
3. Both parties agreed that the announcement of "religious" activities would be impermissible.

I_N a 6-3 decision, the United States Supreme Court declares unconstitutional the following Alabama statute: "At the commencement of the first class of each day in all grades in all public schools the teacher in charge of the room in which each class is held may announce that a period of silence not to exceed one minute in duration shall be observed for meditation or voluntary prayer, and during any such period no other activities shall be engaged in." Delivering the opinion of the Court, Justice Stevens wrote: "When the court has been called upon to construe the breadth of the Establishment Clause, it has examined the criteria developed over a period of many years. Thus in *Lemon* v. *Kurtzman* . . . we wrote: 'Every analysis in this area must begin with consideration of the cumulative criteria developed by the court over many years. Three such tests may be gleaned from our cases. First, the statute must have a secular legislative purpose; second, its principal or primary effect must be one that neither advances nor inhibits religion . . . ; finally, the statute must not foster an excessive government entanglement with religion. . . .' It is the first of these three criteria that is most plainly implicated by this case. As the district court correctly recognized, no consideration of the second or third criteria is necessary if a statute does not have a clearly secular purpose. . . . In applying the purpose test, it is appropriate to ask 'whether government's actual purpose is to endorse or disapprove of religion.' In this case, the answer to that question is dispositive. For the record not only provides us with an unambiguous affirmative answer, but it also reveals that the enactment of § 16-1-20.1 was not motivated by any clearly secular purpose—indeed, the statute had *no* secular purpose."

Wallace v. *Jaffree,* 105 S.Ct. 2479 (1985)

Justice STEVENS delivered the opinion of the Court.

At an early stage of this litigation, the constitutionality of three Alabama statutes was questioned: (1) § 16-1-20, enacted in 1978, which authorized a one-minute period of silence in all public schools "for meditation";[1] (2) § 16-1-20.1, enacted in 1981, which authorized a period of silence "for meditation or voluntary prayer";[2] and (3) § 16-1-20.2, enacted in 1982, which authorized teachers to lead "willing students" in a prescribed prayer to "Almighty God . . . the Creator and Supreme Judge of the world."[3]

At the preliminary-injunction stage of this case, the District Court distinguished § 16-1-20 from the other two statutes. It then held that there was "nothing wrong" with § 16-1-20,[4] but that § 16-1-20.1 and §

16-1-20.2 were both invalid because the sole purpose of both was "an effort on the part of the State of Alabama to encourage a religious activity."[5] After the trial on the merits, the District Court did not change its interpretation of these two statutes, but held that they were constitutional because, in its opinion, Alabama has the power to establish a state religion if it chooses to do so.[6]

The Court of Appeals agreed with the District Court's initial interpretation of the purpose of both § § 16-1-20.1 and 16-1-20.2, and held them both unconstitutional.[7] We have already affirmed the Court of Appeals' holding with respect to § 16-1-20.2.[8] Moreover, appellees have not questioned the holding that § 16-1-20 is valid.[9] Thus, the narrow question for decision is whether § 16-1-20.1, which authorizes a period of silence for "meditation or voluntary prayer," is a law respecting the establishment of religion within the meaning of the First Amendment.[10]

I.

Appellee Ishmael Jaffree is a resident of Mobile County, Alabama. On May 28, 1982, he filed a complaint on behalf of three of his minor children; two of them were second-grade students and the third was then in kindergarten. The complaint named members of the Mobile County School Board, various school officials, and the minor plaintiffs' three teachers as defendants.[11] The complaint alleged that the appellees brought the action "seeking principally a declaratory judgment and an injunction restraining the Defendants and each of them from maintaining or allowing the maintenance of regular religious prayer services or other forms of religious observances in the Mobile County Public Schools in violation of the First Amendment as made applicable to states by the Fourteenth Amendment to the United States Constitution."[12] The complaint further alleged that two of the children had been subjected to various acts of religious indoctrination "from the beginning of the school year in September, 1981";[13] that the defendant teachers had "on a daily basis" led their classes in saying certain prayers in unison;[14] that the minor children were exposed to ostracism from their peer group class members if they did not participate;[15] and that Ishmael Jaffree had repeatedly but unsuccessfully requested that the devotional services be stopped. The original complaint made no reference to any Alabama statute.

One June 4, 1982, appellees filed an amended complaint seeking class certification,[16] and on June 30, 1982, they filed a second amended complaint naming the Governor of Alabama and various State officials as additional defendants. In that amendment the appellees challenged the constitutionality of three Alabama statutes: §§ 16-1-20, 16-1-20.1, and 16-1-20.2.[17]

On August 2, 1982, the District Court held an evidentiary hearing on appellees' motion for a preliminary injunction. At that hearing, State Senator Donald G. Holmes testified that he was the "prime sponsor" of the bill that was enacted in 1981 as § 16-1-20.1.[18] He explained that the bill was an "effort to return voluntary prayer to our public schools . . . it is a beginning and a step in the right direction."[19] Apart from the purpose to return voluntary prayer to public school, Senator Holmes unequivocally testified that he had "no other purpose in mind."[20] A week after the hearing, the District Court entered a preliminary injunction.[21] The court held that appellees were likely to prevail on the merits because the enactment of §§ 16-1-20.1 and 16-1-20.2 did not reflect a clearly secular purpose.[22]

In November 1982, the District Court held a four-day trial on the merits. The evidence related primarily to the 1981-1982 academic year—the year after the enactment of § 16-1-20.1 and prior to the enactment of § 16-1-20.2. The District Court found that during that academic year each of the minor plaintiffs' teachers had led classes in prayer activities, even after being informed of appellees' objections to these activities.[23]

In its lengthy conclusions of law, the District Court reviewed a number of opinions of this Court interpreting the Establishment Clause of the First Amendment, and then embarked on a fresh examination of the question whether the First Amendment imposes any barrier to the establishment of an official religion by the State of Alabama. After reviewing at length what it perceived to be newly discovered historical evidence, the District Court concluded that "the establishment clause of the first amendment to the United States Constitution does not prohibit the state from establishing a religion."[24] In a separate opinion, the District Court dismissed appellees' challenge to the three Alabama statutes because of a failure to state any claim for which relief could be granted. The court's dismissal of the challenge was also based on its conclusion that the Establishment Clause did not bar the States from establishing a religion.[25]

The Court of Appeals consolidated the two cases; not surprisingly, it reversed. The Court of Appeals noted that this Court had considered and had rejected the historical arguments that the District Court found persuasive, and that the District Court had misapplied the doctrine of *stare decisis.*[26] The Court of Appeals then held that the teachers' religious activities violated the Establishment Clause of the First Amendment.[27] With respect to § 16-1-20.1 and § 16-1-20.2, the Court of Appeals stated that "both statutes advance and encourage religious activities."[28] The Court of Appeals then quoted with approval the District Court's finding that § 16-1-20.1, and § 16-1-20.2, were efforts "'to encourage a religious activity. Even though these statutes are permissive in form, it is nevertheless state involvement respecting an establishment of religion.'"[29] Thus, the Court of Appeals concluded that both statutes were "specifically the type which the Supreme Court addressed in *Engel* [v. *Vitale,* 370 U.S. 421, 82 S.Ct. 1261, 8 L.Ed.2d 601 (1962)]."[30]

A suggestion for rehearing en banc was denied over the dissent of four judges who expressed the opinion that the full court should reconsider the panel decision insofar as it held § 16-1-20.1 unconstitutional.[31] When this Court noted probable jurisdiction, it limited argument to the question that those four judges thought worthy of reconsideration. The judgment of the Court of Appeals with respect to the other issues presented by the appeals was affirmed. *Wallace v. Jaffree,* 466 U.S. _____, 104 S.Ct. 1704, 80 L.Ed.2d 178 (1984).

II.

Our unanimous affirmance of the Court of Appeals' judgment concerning § 16-1-20.2 makes it unnecessary to comment at length on the District Court's remarkable conclusion that the Federal Constitution imposes no obstacle to Alabama's establishment of a state religion. Before analyzing the precise issue that is presented to us, it is nevertheless appropriate to recall how firmly embedded in our constitutional jurisprudence is the proposition that the several States have no greater power to restrain the individual freedoms protected by the First Amendment than does the Congress of the United States.

As is plain from its text, the First Amendment was adopted to curtail the power of Congress to interfere with the individual's freedom to believe, to worship, and to express himself in accordance with the dictates of his own conscience.[32] Until the Fourteenth Amendment was added to the Constitution, the First Amendment's restraints on the exercise of federal power simply did not apply to the States.[33] But when the Constitution was amended to prohibit any State from depriving any person of liberty without due process of law, that Amendment imposed the same substantive limitations on the States' power to legislate that the First Amendment had always imposed on the Congress' power. This Court has confirmed and endorsed this elementary proposition of law time and time again.[34]

Writing for a unanimous Court in *Cantwell v. Connecticut,* 310 U.S. 296, 303, 60 S.Ct. 900, 903, 84 L.Ed. 1213 (1940), Justice Roberts explained:

" . . . We hold that the statute, as construed and applied to the appellants, deprives them of their liberty without due process of law in contravention of the Fourteenth Amendment. The fundamental concept of liberty embodied in that Amendment embraces the liberties guaranteed by the First Amendment. The First Amendment declares that Congress shall make no law respecting an establishment of religion or prohibiting the free exercise thereof. The Fourteenth Amendment has rendered the legislatures of the states as incompetent as Congress to enact such laws. The constitutional inhibition of legislation on the subject of religion has a double aspect. On the one hand, it forestalls compulsion by law of the acceptance of any creed or the practice of any form of worship. Freedom of conscience and freedom to adhere to such religious organization or form of worship as the individual may choose cannot be restricted by law. On the other hand, it safeguards the free exercise of the

chosen form of religion."

Cantwell, of course, is but one case in which the Court has identified the individual's freedom of conscience as the central liberty that unifies the various clauses in the First Amendment.[35] Enlarging on this theme, THE CHIEF JUSTICE recently wrote:

"We begin with the proposition that the right of freedom of thought protected by the First Amendment against state action includes both the right to speak freely and the right to refrain from speaking at all. See *Board of Education v. Barnette,* 319 U.S. 624, 633–634 [63 S.Ct. 1178, 1182–1183, 87 L.Ed. 1628] (1943); *id.,* at 645 [63 S.Ct., at 1188] (Murphy, J., concurring). A system which secures the right to proselytize religious, political, and ideological causes must also guarantee the concomitant right to decline to foster such concepts. The right to speak and the right to refrain from speaking are complementary components of the broader concept of 'individual freedom of mind.' *Id.,* at 637 [63 S.Ct., at 1185].

* * *

"The Court in *Barnette, supra,* was faced with a state statute which required public school students to participate in daily public ceremonies by honoring the flag both with words and traditional salute gestures. In overruling its prior decision in *Minersville District v. Gobitis,* 310 U.S. 586 [60 S.Ct. 1010, 84 L.Ed. 1375] (1940), the Court held that 'a ceremony so touching matters of opinion and political attitude may [not] be imposed upon the individual by official authority under powers committed to any political organization under our Constitution.' 319 U.S., at 636 [63 S.Ct., at 1184]. Compelling the affirmative act of a flag salute involved a more serious infringement upon personal liberties than the passive act of carrying the state motto on a license plate, but the difference is essentially one of degree. Here, as in *Barnette,* we are faced with a state measure which forces an individual, as part of his daily life— indeed constantly while his automobile is in public view—to be an instrument for fostering public adherence to an ideological point of view he finds unacceptable. In doing so, the State 'invades the sphere of intellect and spirit which it is the purpose of the First Amendment to our Constitution to reserve from all official control.' *Id.,* at 642 [63 S.Ct., at 1187]." *Wooley v. Maynard,* 430 U.S. 705, 714–715, 97 S.Ct. 1428, 1435, 51 L.Ed.2d 752 (1977).

Just as the right to speak and the right to refrain from speaking are complementary components of a broader concept of individual freedom of mind, so also the individual's freedom to choose his own creed is the counterpart of his right to refrain from accepting the creed established by the majority. At one time it was thought that this right merely proscribed the preference of one Christian sect over another, but would not require equal respect for the conscience of the infidel, the atheist, or the adherent of a non-Christian faith such as Mohammedism or Judaism.[36] But when the underlying principle has been examined in the crucible of litigation, the Court has unambiguously concluded that the individual freedom of conscience protected by the First Amendment embraces the right to select any religious faith or none at all.[37] This conclusion derives support not only from the interest in respecting the individual's freedom of conscience, but also from the conviction that religious beliefs worthy of respect are the product of free and voluntary choice by the faithful,[38] and from recognition of the fact that the political interest in forestalling intolerance extends beyond intolerance among Christian sects—or even intolerance among "religions"—to encompass intolerance of the disbeliever and the uncertain.[39] As Justice Jackson eloquently stated in *Board of Education v. Barnette,* 319 U.S. 624, 642, 63 S.Ct. 1178, 1187, 87 L.Ed. 1628 (1943):

> "If there is any fixed star in our constitutional constellation, it is that no official, high or petty, can prescribe what shall be orthodox in politics, nationalism, religion, or other matters of opinion or force citizens to confess by word or act their faith therein."

The State of Alabama, no less than the Congress of the United States, must respect that basic truth.

III.

When the Court has been called upon to construe the breadth of the Establishment Clause, it has examined the criteria developed over a period of many years. Thus, in *Lemon v. Kurtzman,* 403 U.S. 602, 612–613, 91 S.Ct. 2105, 2111, 29 L.Ed.2d 745 (1971), we wrote:

> "Every analysis in this area must begin with consideration of the cumulative criteria developed by the Court over many years. Three such tests may be gleaned from our cases. First, the statute must have a secular legislative purpose; second, its principal or primary effect must be one that neither advances nor inhibits religion, *Board of Education v. Allen,* 392 U.S. 236, 243 [88 S.Ct. 1923, 1926, 20 L.Ed.2d 1060] (1968); finally, the statute must not foster 'an excessive governmental entanglement with religion.' *Walz* [*v. Tax Commission,* 397 U.S. 664, 674 [90 S.Ct. 1409, 1414, 25 L.Ed.2d 697] (1970)]."

It is the first of these three criteria that is most plainly implicated by this case. As the District Court correctly recognized, no consideration of the second or third criteria is necessary if a statute does not have a clearly secular purpose.[40] For even though a statute that is motivated in part by a religious purpose may satisfy

the first criterion, see, *e.g., Abington School Dist. v. Schempp,* 374 U.S. 203, 296–303, 83 S.Ct. 1560, 1610–1614, 10 L.Ed.2d 844 (1963) (BRENNAN, J., concurring), the First Amendment requires that a statute must be invalidated if it is entirely motivated by a purpose to advance religion.[41]

In applying the purpose test, it is appropriate to ask "whether government's actual purpose is to endorse or disapprove of religion."[42] In this case, the answer to that question is dispositive. For the record not only provides us with an unambiguous affirmative answer, but it also reveals that the enactment of § 16-1-20.1 was not motivated by any clearly secular purpose—indeed, the statute had *no* secular purpose.

IV.

The sponsor of the bill that became § 16-1-20.1, Senator Donald Holmes, inserted into the legislative record—apparently without dissent—a statement indicating that the legislation was an "effort to return voluntary prayer" to the public schools.[43] Later Senator Holmes confirmed this purpose before the District Court. In response to the question whether he had any purpose for the legislation other than returning voluntary prayer to public schools, he stated, "No, I did not have no other purpose in mind."[44] The State did not present evidence of *any* secular purpose.[45]

The unrebutted evidence of legislative intent contained in the legislative record and in the testimony of the sponsor of § 16-1-20.1 is confirmed by a consideration of the relationship between this statute and the two other measures that were considered in this case. The District Court found that the 1981 statute and its 1982 sequel had a common, nonsecular purpose. The wholly religious character of the later enactment is plainly evident from its text. When the differences between § 16-1-20.1 and its 1978 predecessor, § 16-1-20, are examined, it is equally clear that the 1981 statute has the same wholly religious character.

There are only three textual differences between § 16-1-20.1 and § 16-1-20: (1) the earlier statute applies only to grades one through six, whereas § 16-1-20.1 applies to all grades; (2) the earlier statute uses the word "shall" whereas § 16-1-20.1 uses the word "may"; (3) the earlier statute refers only to "meditation" whereas § 16-1-20.1 refers to "meditation or voluntary prayer." The first difference is of no relevance in this litigation because the minor appellees were in kindergarten or second grade during the 1981–1982 academic year. The second difference would also have no impact on this legislation because the mandatory language of § 16-1-20 continued to apply to grades one through six.[46] Thus, the only significant textual difference is the addition of the words "or voluntary prayer."

The legislative intent to return prayer to the public

schools is, of course, quite different from merely protecting every student's right to engage in voluntary prayer during an appropriate moment of silence during the school day. The 1978 statute already protected that right, containing nothing that prevented any student from engaging in voluntary prayer during a silent minute of meditation.[47] Appellants have not identified any secular purpose that was not fully served by § 16-1-20 before the enactment of § 16-1-20.1. Thus, only two conclusions are consistent with the text of § 16-1-20.1: (1) the statute was enacted to convey a message of State endorsement and promotion of prayer; or (2) the statute was enacted for no purpose. No one suggests that the statute was nothing but a meaningless or irrational act.[48]

We must, therefore, conclude that the Alabama Legislature intended to change existing law[49] and that it was motivated by the same purpose that the Governor's Answer to the Second Amended Complaint expressly admitted; that the statement inserted in the legislative history revealed; and that Senator Holmes' testimony frankly described. The Legislature enacted § 16-1-20.1 despite the existence of § 16-1-20 for the sole purpose of expressing the State's endorsement of prayer activities for one minute at the beginning of each school day. The addition of "or voluntary prayer" indicates that the State intended to characterize prayer as a favored practice. Such an endorsement is not consistent with the established principle that the Government must pursue a course of complete neutrality toward religion.[50]

The importance of that principle does not permit us to treat this as an inconsequential case involving nothing more than a few words of symbolic speech on behalf of the political majority.[51] For whenever the State itself speaks on a religious subject, one of the questions that we must ask is "whether the Government intends to convey a message of endorsement or disapproval of religion."[52] The well-supported concurrent findings of the District Court and the Court of Appeals —that § 16-1-20.1 was intended to convey a message of State-approval of prayer activities in the public schools—make it unnecessary, and indeed inappropriate, to evaluate the practical significance of the addition of the words "or voluntary prayer" to the statute. Keeping in mind, as we must, "both the fundamental place held by the Establishment Clause in our constitutional scheme and the myriad, subtle ways in which Establishment Clause values can be eroded,"[53] we conclude that § 16-1-20.1 violates the First Amendment.

The judgment of the Court of Appeals is affirmed.

It is so ordered.

NOTES

1. Alabama Code § 16-1-20 (Supp.1984) reads as follows:
   "At the commencement of the first class each day in the first through the sixth grades in all public schools, the teacher in charge of the room in which each such class is held shall announce that a period of silence, not to exceed one minute in duration, shall be observed for meditation, and during any such period silence shall be maintained and no activities engaged in."
   Appellees have abandoned any claim that § 16-1-20 is unconstitutional. See Brief for Appellees 2.

2. Alabama Code § 16-1-20.1 (Supp.1984) provides:
   "At the commencement of the first class of each day in all grades in all public schools the teacher in charge of the room in which each class is held may announce that a period of silence not to exceed one minute in duration shall be observed for meditation or voluntary prayer, and during any such period no other activities shall be engaged in."

3. Alabama Code § 16-1-20.2 (Supp.1984) provides:
   "From henceforth, any teacher or professor in any public educational institution within the state of Alabama, recognizing that the Lord God is one, at the beginning of any homeroom or any class, may pray, may lead willing students in prayer, or may lead the willing students in the following prayer to God:
   "Almighty God, You alone are our God. We acknowledge You as the Creator and Supreme Judge of the world. May Your justice, Your truth, and Your peace abound this day in the hearts of our countrymen, in the counsels of our government, in the sanctity of our homes and in the classrooms of our schools in the name of our Lord. Amen."

4. The court stated that it did not find any potential infirmity in § 16-1-20 because "it is a statute which prescribes nothing more than a child in school shall have the right to meditate in silence and there is nothing wrong with a little meditation and quietness." *Jaffree v. James,* 544 F.Supp. 727, 732 (SD Ala.1982).

5. *Ibid.*

6. *Jaffree v. Board of School Commissioners of Mobile County,* 544 F.Supp. 1104, 1128 (SD Ala.1983).

7. *Jaffree v. Wallace,* 705 F.2d 1526, 1535–1536 (CA11 1983).

8. *Wallace v. Jaffree,* 466 U.S. _____, 104 S.Ct. 1704, 80 L.Ed.2d 178 (1984).

9. See n.1, *supra.*

10. The Establishment Clause of the First Amendment, of course, has long been held applicable to the States. *Everson v. Board of Education,* 330 U.S. 1, 15–16, 67 S.Ct. 504, 511–12, 91 L.Ed. 711 (1947).

11. App. 4-7.

12. *Id.,* at 4.

13. *Id.,* at 7.

14. *Ibid.*

15. *Id.,* at 8–9.

16. *Id.,* at 17.

17. *Id.,* at 21. See nn. 1, 2, and 3, *supra.*

18. *Id.,* at 47–49.

19. *Id.,* at 50.

20. *Id.,* at 52.

21. *Jaffree v. James,* 544 F.Supp. 727 (SD Ala.1982).

22. See *Lemon v. Kurtzman,* 403 U.S. 602, 612–613, 91 S.Ct. 2105, 2111, 29 L.Ed.2d 745 (1971). Insofar as relevant to the issue now before us, the District Court

explained:

"The injury to plaintiffs from the possible establishment of a religion by the State of Alabama contrary to the proscription of the establishment clause outweighs any indirect harm which may occur to defendants as a result of an injunction. Granting an injunction will merely maintain the status quo existing prior to the enactment of the statutes.

*   *   *

"The purpose of Senate Bill 8 [§ 16-1-20.2] as evidenced by its preamble, is to provide for a prayer that may be given in public schools. Senator Holmes testified that his purpose in sponsoring § 16-1-20.1 was to return voluntary prayer to the public schools. He intended to provide children the opportunity of sharing in their spiritual heritage of Alabama and of this country. *See* Alabama Senate Journal 921 (1981). The Fifth Circuit has explained that 'prayer is a primary religious activity in itself. . . .' *Karen B. v. Treen*, 653 F.2d 897, 901 (5th Cir.1981). The state may not employ a religious means in its public schools. *Abington School District v. Schempp*, [374 U.S. 203, 224, 83 S.Ct. 1560, 1572, 10 L.Ed.2d 844] (1963). Since these statutes do not reflect a clearly secular purpose, no consideration of the remaining two-parts of the *Lemon* test is necessary.

"The enactment of Senate Bill 8 [§ 16-1-20.2] and § 16-1-20.1 is an effort on the part of the State of Alabama to encourage a religious activity. Even though these statutes are permissive in form, it is nevertheless state involvement respecting an establishment of religion. *Engel v. Vitale*, [307 U.S. 421, 430, 82 S.Ct. 1261, 1266, 8 L.Ed.2d 601] (1962). Thus, binding precedent which this Court is under a duty to follow indicates the substantial likelihood plaintiffs will prevail on the merits." 544 F.Supp., at 730–732.

23. The District Court wrote:
"Defendant Boyd, as early as September 16, 1981, led her class at E.R. Dickson in singing the following phrase:
"'God is great, God is good,'
"'Let us thank him for our food,
"'bow our heads we all are fed,
"'Give us Lord our daily bread.
"'Amen!'
"The recitation of this phrase continued on a daily basis throughout the 1981–82 school year.

*   *   *

"Defendant Pixie Alexander has led her class at Craighead in reciting the following phrase:
"'God is great, God is good,
"'Let us thank him for our food.'
"Further, defendant Pixie Alexander had her class recite the following, which is known as the Lord's Prayer:
"'Our Father, which are in heaven, hallowed be Thy name. Thy kingdom come. Thy will be done on earth as it is in heaven. Give us this day our daily bread and forgive us our debts as we forgive our debtors. And lead us not into temptation but deliver us from evil for thine is the kingdom and the power and the glory forever. Amen.'
"The recitation of these phrases continued on a daily basis throughout the 1981–82 school year.

*   *   *

"Ms. Green admitted that she frequently leads her class in singing the following song:
"'For health and strength and daily food, we praise Thy name, Oh Lord.'
"This activity continued throughout the school year, despite the fact that Ms. Green had knowledge that plaintiff did not want his child exposed to the abovementioned song." *Jaffree v. Board of School Commissioners of Mobile County*, 554 F.Supp., at 1107–1108.

24. *Id.*, at 1128.

25. *Jaffree v. James*, 554 F.Supp. 1130, 1132 (SD Ala.1983). The District Court's opinion was announced on January 14, 1983. On February 11, 1983, Justice POWELL, in his capacity as Circuit Justice for the Eleventh Circuit, entered a stay which in effect prevented the District Court from dissolving the preliminary injunction that had been entered in August 1982. Justice POWELL accurately summarized the prior proceedings:
"The situation, quite briefly, is as follows: Beginning in the fall of 1981, teachers in the minor applicants' schools conducted prayers in their regular classes, including group recitations of the Lord's Prayer. At the time, an Alabama statute provided for a one-minute period of silence 'for meditation or voluntary prayer' at the commencement of each day's classes in the public elementary schools. Ala.Code § 16-1-20.1 (Supp.1982). In 1982, Alabama enacted a statute permitting public school teachers to lead their classes in prayer. 1982 Ala.Acts 735.
"Applicants, objecting to prayer in the public schools, filed suit to enjoin the activities. They later amended their complaint to challenge the applicable state statutes. After a hearing, the District Court granted a preliminary injunction. *Jaffree v. James*, 544 F.Supp. 727 (1982). It recognized that it was bound by the decisions of this Court, *id.*, at 731, and that under those decisions it was 'obligated to enjoin the enforcement' of the statutes, *id.*, at 733.
"In its subsequent decision on the merits, however, the District Court reached a different conclusion. *Jaffree v. Board of School Commissioners of Mobile County*, 554 F.Supp. 1104 (1983). It again recognized that the prayers at issue, given in public school classes and led by teachers, were violative of the Establishment Clause of the First Amendment as that Clause had been construed by this Court. The District Court nevertheless ruled 'that the United States Supreme Court has erred.' *Id.*, at 1128. It therefore dismissed the complaint and dissolved the injunction.
"There can be little doubt that the District Court was correct in finding that conducting prayers as part of a school program is unconstitutional under this Court's decisions. In *Engel v. Vitale*, 370 U.S. 421, 82 S.Ct. 1261, 8 L.Ed.2d 601 (1962), the Court held that the Establishment Clause of the First Amendment, made applicable to the States by the Fourteenth Amendment, prohibits a State from authorizing prayer in the public schools. The following Term, in *Murray v. Curlett*, decided with *Abington School District v. Schempp*, 374 U.S. 203, 83 S.Ct. 1560, 10 L.Ed.2d 844 (1963), the Court explicitly invalidated a school district's rule providing for the reading of the Lord's Prayer as part of a school's opening exercises, despite the fact that participation in those exercises was

voluntary.

"Unless and until this Court reconsiders the foregoing decisions, they appear to control this case. In my view, the District Court was obligated to follow them." *Jaffree v. Board of School Commissioners of Mobile County,* 459 U.S. 1314, 1314–1316, 103 S.Ct. 842, 842–843, 74 L.Ed.2d 924 (1983).

26. The Court of Appeals wrote:

"The stare decisis doctrine and its exceptions do not apply where a lower court is compelled to apply the precedent of a higher court. *See* 20 Am.Jur.2d *Courts* § 183 (1965).

"Federal district courts and circuit courts are bound to adhere to the controlling decisions of the Supreme Court. *Hutto v. Davis,* [454 U.S. 370, 375, 102 S.Ct. 703, 706, 70 L.Ed.2d 556] (1982). . . . Justice Rehnquist emphasized the importance of precedent when he observed that 'unless we wish anarchy to prevail within the federal judicial system, a precedent of this Court must be followed by the lower federal courts no matter how misguided the judges of those courts may think it to be.' *Davis,* [454 U.S. at 375, 102 S.Ct., at 706]. *See Also, Thurston Motor Lines, Inc. v. Jordan K. Rand, Ltd.,* [460 U.S. 533, 535, 103 S.Ct. 1343, 1344, 75 L.Ed.2d 260] (1983) (the Supreme Court, in a per curiam decision, recently stated: 'Needless to say, only this Court may overrule one of its precedents')." *Jaffree v. Wallace,* 705 F.2d at 1532.

27. *Id.,* at 1533–1534. This Court has denied a petition for a writ of certiorari that presented the question whether the Establishment Clause prohibited the teachers' religious prayer activities. *Board of School Commissioners of Mobile County, Alabama v. Jaffree,* 466 U.S. _____, 104 S.Ct. 1707, 80 L.Ed.2d 181 (1984).

28. 705 F.2d at 1535.

29. *Ibid.*

30. *Ibid.* After noting that the invalidity of § 16-1-20.2 was aggravated by "the existence of a government composed prayer," and that the proponents of the legislation admitted that that section "amounts to the establishment of a state religion," the court added this comment on § 16-1-20.1:

"The objective of the meditation or prayer statute (Ala.Code § 16-1-20.1) was also the advancement of religion. This fact was recognized by the district court at the hearing for preliminary relief where it was established that the intent of the statute was to return prayer to the public schools. *James,* 544 F.Supp. at 731. The existence of this fact and the inclusion of prayer obviously involves the state in religious activities. *Beck v. McElrath,* 548 F.Supp. 1161 (MD Tenn.1982). This demonstrates a lack of secular legislative purpose on the part of the Alabama Legislature. Additionally, the statute has the primary effect of advancing religion. We do not imply that simple meditation or silence is barred from the public schools; we hold that the state cannot participate in the advancement of religious activities through any guise, including teacher-led meditation. It is not the activity itself that concerns us; it is the purpose of the activity that we shall scrutinize. Thus, the existence of these elements require that we also hold section 16-1-20.1 in violation of the establishment clause." *Id.,* at 1535–1536.

31. *Jaffree v. Wallace,* 713 F.2d 614 (CA11 1983) (*per curiam*).

32. The First Amendment provides:

"Congress shall make no law respecting an establishment of religion, or prohibiting the free exercise thereof; or abridging the freedom of speech, or of the press; or the right of the people peaceably to assemble, and to petition the Government for a redress of grievances."

33. See *Permoli v. Municipality No. 1 of the City of New Orleans,* 3 How. 589, 609, 11 L.Ed. 739 (1845).

34. See, *e.g., Wooley v. Maynard,* 430 U.S. 705, 714, 97 S.Ct. 1428, 1435, 51 L.Ed.2d 752 (1977) (right to refuse endorsement of an offensive state motto); *Terminiello v. Chicago,* 337 U.S. 1, 4, 69 S.Ct. 894, 895, 93 L.Ed. 1131 (1949) (right to free speech); *Board of Education v. Barnette,* 319 U.S. 624, 637–638, 63 S.Ct. 1178, 1185, 87 L.Ed. 1628 (1943) (right to refuse to participate in a ceremony that offends one's conscience); *Cantwell v. Connecticut,* 310 U.S. 296, 303, 60 S.Ct. 900, 903, 84 L.Ed. 1213 (1940) (right to proselytize one's religious faith); *Hague v. CIO,* 307 U.S. 496, 519, 59 S.Ct. 954, 965, 83 L.Ed. 1423 (1939) (opinion of Stone, J.) (right to assemble peaceably); *Near v. Minnesota ex rel. Olson,* 283 U.S. 697, 707, 51 S.Ct. 625, 628, 75 L.Ed. 1357 (1931) (right to publish an unpopular newspaper); *Whitney v. California,* 274 U.S. 357, 373, 47 S.Ct. 641, 647, 71 L.Ed. 1095 (Brandeis, J., concurring) (right to advocate the cause of communism); *Gitlow v. New York,* 268 U.S. 652, 672, 45 S.Ct. 625, 632, 69 L.Ed. 1138 (1925) (Holmes, J., dissenting) (right to express an unpopular opinion); cf. *Abington School District v. Schempp,* 374 U.S. 203, 215, n. 7, 83 S.Ct. 1560, 1567, n. 7, 10 L.Ed.2d 844 (1963), where the Court approvingly quoted *Board of Education v. Minor,* 23 Ohio St. 211, 253 (1872), which stated: "The great bulk of human affairs and human interests is left by any free government to individual enterprise and individual action. Religion is eminently one of these interests, lying outside the true and legitimate province of government."

35. For example, in *Prince v. Massachusetts,* 321 U.S. 158, 164, 64 S.Ct. 438, 441, 88 L.Ed. 645 (1944), the Court wrote:

"If by this position appellant seeks for freedom of conscience a broader protection than for freedom of the mind, it may be doubted that any of the great liberties insured by the First Article can be given higher place than the others. All have preferred position in our basic scheme. *Schneider v. State,* 308 U.S. 147, 60 S.Ct. 146, 84 L.Ed. 155; *Cantwell v. Connecticut,* 310 U.S. 296, 60 S.Ct. 900, 84 L.Ed. 1213. All are interwoven there together. Differences there are, in them and in the modes appropriate for their exercise. But they have unity in the charter's prime place because they have unity in their human sources and functionings."
See also *Widmar v. Vincent,* 454 U.S. 263, 269, 102 S.Ct. 269, 274, 70 L.Ed.2d 440 (1981) (stating that religious worship and discussion "are forms of speech and association protected by the First Amendment").

36. Thus Joseph Story wrote:

"Probably at the time of the adoption of the constitution, and of the amendment to it, now under consideration [First Amendment], the general, if not the universal sentiment in America was, that christianity ought to receive encouragement from the state, so far as was not incompatible with the private rights of conscience, and the freedom of religious worship. An attempt to level all religions, and to make it a matter of state policy to hold all in utter indifference, would have created universal disapprobation, if not universal indignation." 2 J. Story, Commentaries on the Constitution of the United States § 1874, p. 593 (1851) (footnote omitted).

In the same volume, Story continued:

"The real object of the amendment was, not to countenance, much less to advance, Mahometanism, or Judaism, or infidelity, by prostrating christianity; *but to exclude all rivalry among christian sects, and to prevent any national ecclesiastical establishment, which should give to a hierarchy the exclusive patronage of the national government. It thus cut off the means of religious persecution (the vice and pest of former ages,) and of the subversion of the rights of conscience in matters of religion,* which had been trampled upon almost from the days of the Apostles to the present age. . . ." *Id.,* § 1877, at 594 (emphasis supplied).

37. Thus, in *Everson v. Board of Education,* 330 U.S., at 15, 67 S.Ct., at 511, the Court stated:

"The 'establishment of religion' clause of the First Amendment means at least this: Neither a state nor the Federal Government can set up a church. Neither can pass laws which aid one religion, aid all religions, or prefer one religion over another."

Id., at 18, 67 S.Ct., at 513 (the First Amendment "requires the state to be a neutral in its relations with groups of religious believers and non-believers"); *Abington School District v. Schempp,* 374 U.S., at 216, 83 S.Ct., at 1568 ("this Court has rejected unequivocally the contention that the Establishment Clause forbids only governmental preference of one religion over another"); *id.,* at 226, 83 S.Ct., at 1573 ("The place of religion in our society is an exalted one, achieved through a long tradition of reliance on the home, the church and the inviolable citadel of the individual heart and mind. We have come to recognize through bitter experience that it is not within the power of the government to invade that citadel, whether its purpose or effect be to aid or oppose, to advance or retard. In the relationship between man and religion, the State is firmly committed to a position of neutrality"); *Torcaso v. Watkins,* 367 U.S. 488, 495, 81 S.Ct. 1680, 1683–84, 6 L.Ed.2d 982 (1961) ("We repeat and again reaffirm that neither a State nor the Federal Government can constitutionally force a person 'to profess a belief or disbelief in any religion.' Neither can constitutionally pass laws or impose requirements which aid all religions as against non-believers, and neither can aid those religions based on a belief in the existence of God as against those religions founded on different beliefs").

38. In his "Memorial and Remonstrance Against Religious Assessments, 1785," James Madison wrote, in part:

"1. Because we hold it for a fundamental and undeniable truth, 'that Religion or the duty which we owe to our Creator and the [Manner of discharging it, can be directed only by reason and] conviction, not by force or violence.' The Religion then of every man must be left to the conviction and conscience of every man; and it is the right of every man to exercise it as these may dictate. This right is in its nature an unalienable right. It is unalienable; because the opinions of men, depending only on the evidence contemplated by their own minds, cannot follow the dictates of other men: It is unalienable also; because what is here a right towards men, is a duty towards the Creator. It is the duty of every man to render to the Creator such homage, and

such only, as he believes to be acceptable to him. . . . We maintain therefore that in matters of Religion, no man's right is abridged by the institution of Civil Society, and that Religion is wholly exempt from its cognizance.

* * *

"3. Because, it is proper to take alarm at the first experiment on our liberties. We hold this prudent jealousy to be the first duty of citizens, and one of [the] noblest characteristics of the late Revolution. The freemen of America did not wait till usurped power had strengthened itself by exercise, and entangled the question in precedents. They saw all the consequences in the principle, and they avoided the consequences by denying the principle. We revere this lesson too much, soon to forget it. Who does not see that the same authority which can establish Christianity, in exclusion of all other Religions, may establish with the same ease any particular sect of Christians, in exclusion of all other Sects?" The Complete Madison 299–301 (S. Padover ed. 1953).

See also *Engel v. Vitale,* 370 U.S. 421, 435, 82 S.Ct. 1261, 1269, 8 L.Ed.2d 601 (1962) ("It is neither sacrilegious nor antireligious to say that each separate government in this country should stay out of the business of writing or sanctioning official prayers and leave that purely religious function to the people themselves and to those the people choose to look for religious guidance").

39. As the *Barnette* opinion explained, it is the teaching of history, rather than any appraisal of the quality of a State's motive, that supports this duty to respect basic freedoms:

"Struggles to coerce uniformity of sentiment in support of some end thought essential to their time and country have been waged by many good as well as by evil men. Nationalism is a relatively recent phenomenon but at other times and places the ends have been racial or territorial security, support of a dynasty or regime, and particular plans for saving souls. As first and moderate methods to attain unity have failed, those bent on its accomplishment must resort to an ever-increasing severity. As governmental pressure toward unity becomes greater, so strife becomes more bitter as to whose unity it shall be. Probably no deeper division of our people could proceed from any provocation than from finding it necessary to choose what doctrine and whose program public educational officials shall compel youth to unite in embracing. Ultimate futility of such attempts to compel coherence is the lesson of every such effort from the Roman drive to stamp out Christianity as a disturber of its pagan unity, the Inquisition, as a means to religious and dynastic unity, the Siberian exiles as a means to Russian unity, down to the fast failing efforts of our present totalitarian enemies. Those who begin coercive elimination of dissent soon find themselves exterminating dissenters. Compulsory unification of opinion achieves only the unanimity of the graveyard." 319 U.S., at 640–641, 63 S.Ct., at 1186–1187.

See also *Engel v. Vitale,* 370 U.S., at 431, 82 S.Ct., at 1267 ("a union of government and religion tends to destroy government and degrade religion").

40. See *supra,* n. 22.

41. See *Lynch v. Donnelly,* 465 U.S. _____, _____, 104 S.Ct. 1355, _____, 79 L.Ed.2d 604 (1984); *id.,* at

_____, 104 S.Ct., at _____ (O'CONNOR, J., concurring); *id.*, at _____, 104 S.Ct., at _____ (BRENNAN, J., joined by MARSHALL, BLACKMUN and STEVENS, JJ., dissenting); *Mueller v. Allen,* 463 U.S. 388, _____ __ _____, 103 S.Ct. 3062, _____, _____, 77 L.Ed.2d 721 (1983); *Widmar v. Vincent,* 454 U.S., at 271, 102 S.Ct., at 275; *Stone v. Graham,* 449 U.S. 39, 40–41, 101 S.Ct. 192, 193–194, 66 L.Ed.2d 199 (1980) (*per curiam*); *Wolman v. Walter,* 433 U.S. 229, 236, 97 S.Ct. 2593, 2599, 53 L.Ed.2d 714 (1977).

42. *Lynch v. Donnelly,* 465 U.S., at _____, 104 S.Ct., at 1368 (O'CONNOR, J., concurring) ("The purpose prong of the *Lemon* test asks whether government's actual purpose is to endorse or disapprove of religion. The effect prong asks whether, irrespective of government's actual purpose, the practice under review in fact conveys a message of endorsement or disapproval. An affirmative answer to either question should render the challenged practice invalid").

43. The statement indicated, in pertinent part: "Gentlemen, by passage of this bill by the Alabama Legislature our children in this state will have the opportunity of sharing in the spiritual heritage of this state and this country. The United States as well as the State of Alabama was founded by people who believe in God. *I believe this effort to return voluntary prayer* to our public schools for its return to us to the original position of the writers of the Constitution, this local philosophies and beliefs hundreds of Alabamians have urged my continuous support for permitting school prayer. Since coming to the Alabama Senate I have worked hard *on this legislation to accomplish the return of voluntary prayer in our public schools and return to the basic moral fiber."* App. 50 (emphasis added).

44. *Id.,* at 52. The District Court and the Court of Appeals agreed that the purpose of § 16-1-20.1 was "an effort on the part of the State of Alabama to encourage a religious activity." *Jaffree v. James,* 544 F.Supp., at 732; *Jaffree v. Wallace,* 705 F.2d, at 1535. The evidence presented to the District Court elaborated on the express admission of the Governor of Alabama (then Fob James) that the enactment of § 16-1-20.1 was intended to "clarify [the State's] intent to have prayer as part of the daily classroom activity," compare Second Amended Complaint ¶ 32(d) (App. 24–25) with Governor's Answer to § 32(d) (App. 40); and that the "expressed legislative purpose in enacting Section 16-1-20.1 (1981) was to 'return voluntary prayer to public schools,'" compare Second Amended Complaint ¶¶ 32(b) and (c)(App. 24) with Governor's Answer to ¶¶32(b) and (c) (App. 40).

45. Appellant Governor George C. Wallace now argues that § 16-1-20.1 "is best understood as a permissible accommodation of religion" and that viewed even in terms of the *Lemon* test, the "statute conforms to acceptable constitutional criteria." Brief for Appellant Wallace 5; see also Brief for Appellants Smith et al. 39 (§ 16-1-20.1 "accommodates the free exercise of the religious beliefs and free exercise of speech and belief of those affected"), *id.,* at 47. These arguments seem to be based on the theory that the free exercise of religion of some of the State's citizens was burdened before the statute was enacted. The United States, appearing as *amicus curiae* in support of the appellants, candidly acknowledges that "it is unlikely that in most contexts a strong Free Exercise claim could be made that time for personal prayer must be set aside during the school

day." Brief for United States as *Amicus Curiae* 10. There is no basis for the suggestion that § 16-1-20.1 "is a means for accommodating the religious and meditative needs of students without in any way diminishing the school's own neutrality or secular atmosphere." *Id.,* at 11. In this case, it is undisputed that at the time of the enactment of § 16-1-20.1 there was no governmental practice impeding students from silently praying for one minute at the beginning of each school day; thus, there was no need to "accommodate" or to exempt individuals from any general governmental requirement because of the dictates of our cases interpreting the Free Exercise Clause. *See, e.g., Thomas v. Review Board, Indiana Employment Security Div.,* 450 U.S. 707, 101 S.Ct. 1425, 67 L.Ed.2d 624 (1981); *Sherbert v. Verner,* 374 U.S. 398, 83 S.Ct. 1790, 10 L.Ed.2d 965 (1963); see also *Abington School District v. Schempp,* 374 U.S., at 226, 83 S.Ct., at 1573 ("While the Free Exercise Clause clearly prohibits the use of state action to deny the rights of free exercise to *anyone,* it has never meant that a majority could use the machinery of the State to practice its beliefs"). What was missing in the appellants' eyes at time of the enactment of § 16-1-20.1—and therefore what is precisely the aspect that makes the statute unconstitutional—was the State's endorsement and promotion of religion and a particular religious practice.

46. See n. 1, *supra.*

47. Indeed, for some persons meditation itself may be a form of prayer. B. Larson, Larson's Book of Cults 62–65 (1982); C. Whittier, Silent Prayer and Meditation in World Religions 1–7 (Cong. Research Service 1982).

48. If the conclusion that the statute had no purpose were tenable, it would remain true that *no purpose* is not a *secular purpose.* But such a conclusion is inconsistent with the common-sense presumption that statutes are usually enacted to change existing law. Appellants do not even suggest that the State had no purpose in enacting § 16-1-20.1.

49. *United States v. Champlin Refining Co.,* 341 U.S. 290, 297, 71 S.Ct. 715, 719, 95 L.Ed. 949 (1951) ("a statute cannot be divorced from the circumstances existing at the time it was passed"); *id.,* at 298, 71 S.Ct., at 720 (refusing to attribute pointless purpose to Congress in the absence of facts to the contrary); *United States v. National City Lines, Inc.,* 337 U.S. 78, 80–81, 69 S.Ct. 955, 956–957, 93 L.Ed.1226 (1949) (rejecting Government's argument that Congress had no desire to change law when enacting legislation).

50. See, *e.g., Stone v. Graham,* 449 U.S., at 42, 101 S.Ct., at 194 (*per curiam*); *Committee for Public Education v. Nyquist,* 413 U.S. 756, 792–793, 93 S.Ct. 2955, 2975–2976, 37 L.Ed.2d 948 (1973) ("A proper respect for both the Free Exercise and the Establishment Clauses compels the State to pursue a course of 'neutrality' toward religion"); *Epperson v. Arkansas,* 393 U.S. 97, 109, 89 S.Ct. 266, 273, 21 L.Ed.2d 228 (1968); *Abington School District v. Schempp,* 374 U.S., at 215–222, 83 S.Ct., at 1567–71; *Engel v. Vitale,* 370 U.S., at 430, 82 S.Ct., at 1266 ("Neither the fact that the prayer may be denominationally neutral nor the fact that its observance on the part of the students is voluntary can serve to free it from the limitations of the Establishment Clause"); *Illinois ex rel. McCollum v. Board of Education,* 333 U.S. 203, 211–212, 68 S.Ct. 461, 465–466 (1948); *Everson v. Board of Education,* 330 U.S., at 18, 67 S.Ct., at 513.

51. As this Court stated in *Engel v. Vitale,* 370 U.S., at 430, 82 S.Ct., at 1267:

"The Establishment Clause, unlike the Free Exercise Clause, does not depend upon any showing of direct governmental compulsion and is violated by the enactment of laws which establish an official religion whether those laws operate directly to coerce nonobserving individuals or not."

Moreover, this Court has noted that "[w]hen the power, prestige and financial support of government is placed behind a particular religious belief, the indirect coercive pressure upon religious minorities to conform to the prevailing officially approved religion is plain." *Id.,* at 431, 82 S.Ct., at 1262. This comment has special force in the public-school context where attendance is mandatory. Justice Frankfurter acknowledged this reality in *McCollum v. Board of Education,* 333 U.S. 203, 227, 68 S.Ct. 461, 473, 92 L.Ed. 649 (1948) (concurring opinion): "That a child is offered an alternative may reduce the constraint, it does not eliminate the operation of influence by the school in matters sacred to conscience and outside the school's domain. The law of imitation operates, and non-conformity is not an outstanding characteristic of children."

See also *Abington School District v. Schempp,* 374 U.S., at 290, 83 S.Ct., at 1607 (BRENNAN, J., concurring); cf. *Marsh v. Chambers,* 463 U.S. 783, 792, 103 S.Ct. 3330, _____, 77 L.Ed.2d 1019 (1983) (distinguishing between adults not susceptible to "religious indoctrination" and children subject to "peer pressure"). Further, this Court has observed:

"That [Boards of Education] are educating the young for citizenship is reason for scrupulous protection of Constitutional freedoms of the individual, if we are not to strangle the free mind at its source and teach youth to discount important principles of our government as mere platitudes." *Board of Education v. Barnette,* 319 U.S., at 637, 63 S.Ct., at 1185.

52. *Lynch v. Donnelly,* 465 U.S., at _____, 104 S.Ct., at 1368 (O'CONNOR, J., concurring) ("The purpose prong of the *Lemon* test requires that a government activity have a secular purpose. . . . The proper inquiry under the purpose prong of *Lemon* . . . is whether the government intends to convey a message of endorsement or disapproval of religion").

53. *Id.,* at _____.

A United States District Court in West Virginia declares unconstitutional the West Virginia "prayer amendment" which read: "Public schools shall provide a designated brief time at the beginning of each school day for any student desiring to exercise their right to personal and private contemplation, meditation or prayer. No student of a public school may be denied their right to personal and private contemplation, meditation or prayer nor shall any student be required or encouraged to engage in any contemplation, meditation or prayer as part of the school curriculum." The court states that it "must determine first, whether the statute has a secular purpose; second, whether its principal or primary effect either advances or inhibits religion; and third, whether the provision fosters 'an excessive government entanglement with religion.'" As to whether the statute has a secular purpose, the court states that it "has determined that the provision here in issue fails to meet the first element of the test in that it clearly does not have a secular purpose, but instead has a religious purpose." Secondly, "the Amendment must likewise fail when examined to determine if its 'principal or primary effect either advances or inhibits religion.'" And lastly, "with respect to the third prong of the test—excessive entanglement—the Court has concluded that the time, manner and place of the activity mandated by the Amendment are sufficient to warrant a finding of excessive entanglement."

Walter v. *West Virginia Bd. of Education,* 610 F.Supp. 1169 (1985)

HALLANAN, District Judge.

Plaintiffs in this class action for declaratory and injunctive relief request that the Court declare Article 3, Section 15-a[1] (hereinafter, "the Amendment") of the West Virginia Constitution, now commonly referred to as the "Prayer Amendment," unconstitutional as violative of their rights as guaranteed by the First and Fourteenth Amendments to the United States Constitution. Plaintiffs further seek to have this Court permanently enjoin implementation of said Amendment in West Virginia's public schools.

This action was brought pursuant to Title 42 United States Code § 1983, Title 28 United States Code § § 2201 and 2202, and directly under the First and Fourteenth Amendments to the United States Constitution.

This Court has jurisdiction over the parties and the subject matter herein falls within the ambit of Title 28 United States Code § 1343(3). Venue is proper by virtue of Title 28 United States Code § 1392(a).

After denying temporary relief on two occasions,[2]

this Court determined that Plaintiffs had met their burden of proof with respect to their application for preliminary injunctive relief and granted a preliminary injunction halting implementation of the Amendment pending resolution of the merits of the issues raised.

Extensive hearings were conducted in this matter, the Court heard testimony of a number of witnesses and the arguments of counsel, and received certain documentary evidence. The Defendants did not present any witnesses nor did any person appear voluntarily to testify in behalf of the Amendment, including any member of the Legislature or representatives of any of the 55 county school systems.

A partial summary of Plaintiffs' evidence is set forth below.

An eleven year-old child of the Jewish faith testified as follows:

"DIRECT EXAMINATION BY MR. ROWE:

Q   I believe you stated before that you were in public school;—

A   Uh-huh.

Q   —is that right?

A   Uh-huh.

Q   Were you in public school last week?

A   Uh-huh.

Q   When was your holiday over?

A   We went back to school on Wednesday.

Q   I'd ask you to speak as loudly as you can so everybody can hear, even the folks way in the back. Your holiday ended on Wednesday of last week?

A   3rd, 2nd.

Q   Okay. Was there any time after you went back to school that you heard announced that there would be a time for meditation, contemplation, or prayer, anything like that?

A   Yes. On Wednesday our teacher started explaining it to us and then on Thurdsday (sic) our principal or guidance counselor read the guidelines for it to us over the intercom.

Q   Okay. Now, was this at a particular time during the day?

A   Uh-huh, during home room, which is fifteen minutes before the beginning of the classes.

Q   Okay. So this is the first thing you do during the day?

A   Uh-huh.

Q   Okay. And are you saying that you go to home room first before you go to any of the classes?

A   Yes.

Q   Okay. What happens at home room usually?

A   Before or after the amendment went into effect?

Q   Well, before the amendment went into effect.

A   We would come in and our teacher would take the roll and then over the intercom we would do the Pledge of Allegiance and then if there were any announcements to be made such as like what was happening after school then the principal or guidance counselor would make them.

Q   Okay. And would roll be taken?

A   Yeah.

Q   Okay. And you say this took about fifteen minutes?

A   Uh-huh, unless there was some reason that they needed more time.

Q   Okay. Now, what happened on Wednesday in home room?

A   On Wednesday our teacher kind of started to explain to us about the guidelines for the amendment for meditation, I guess you'd call it, and he didn't get very far because the bell rang for us to go to first period, so we had to go to first period.

Q   Okay. And then did anything else happen concerning the amendment that day?

A   Not really. He just kind of started telling us about it.

Q   Okay. And then the next day what happened?

A   Well, then the next day our principal or guidance counselor read the whole sheet of guidelines to us. Then we had the moment of silence and I read a book during it.

Q   Okay. Did, what kind of book did you read?

A   Science fiction.

Q   Okay. A fantasy book?

A   Uh-huh.

Q   Do you understand the difference between fantasy and reality?

A   Uh-huh.

Q   Do you like fantasy books?

A   Yep.

Q   Okay. Did anything happen or did anybody say anything to you during home room about that?

A   No.

Q   Okay. How long did the, did the period last?

A   I'm not exactly sure. It may have been a minute, may have been thirty seconds. I don't know.

Q   You say that they read something to you. You referred to the guidelines. Do you remember the substance of any of those, what they did?

A   Well, basically they said, they told us how long it was supposed to be and quite a few times they kept saying, "contemplation, meditation, and prayer," and then towards the end they told us that if we had any religious questions, we would be referred to our parents or to, I think the phrase was "a leader of our faith," but I am not exactly sure about the phrasing.

Q   And then after that what was said?

A   After that, we did the Pledge of Allegiance.

Q   Okay. Did you participate in the Pledge of Allegiance?

A   Yes.

Q   Okay. And were there announcements?

A   I don't think there were very many that day.

Q   Okay. And then what happened after the bell rang?

A   Well, we all went to first period.

Q   Okay. Anything happen to you in first period?

A   No.

Q   Okay. How about second period?

A   Well, in second period, which was science, our teacher left the room to go find something and one of the people who was in my home room turned around and asked me why I had been reading a book during the moment of silence. And I told him that I didn't have to pray then and I didn't want to and then he told me that I should be praying all the time and then he said something to the effect that if I prayed all the time, maybe I could go to heaven with all the Christians when Jesus came for the second time instead of, as he put it, going down with all the other Jews.

Q   Okay. Are you a member of the Jewish faith?

A   Uh-huh.

Q   That's your religion?

A   Uh-huh.

Q Did he know that you were a member of that faith?

A Yes, he did.

Q Okay. And do you know what he meant about going to heaven or going down?

A Well, I think he, from what—

Q What did it mean to you?

A Well, I think it meant that he was saying that certain people were going to all go to heaven. I mean, it didn't make much sense to me because I don't know anything about his faith and that the rest of the people were going to, you know, be stuck someplace if they didn't believe in the right things.

Q Okay. Did he say what the right things were to believe in?

A Uh-huh.

Q What did he say?

A Well, he said that you should believe in Christ basically.

Q Okay. Did you say anything to him?

A I tried to explain to him that I had my own beliefs and that I went by, I followed my beliefs and not his and, you know, when the time came, it was going to be my problem and not his.

Q Did anybody else participate in the conversation?

A Yes. There was another person who, this first boy told another boy that the Jews only used the Old Testament and they didn't use the New Testament and this other boy thought that it was really stupid and then there was some period of another, of more speech, more conversation that I don't remember, but then the second boy said something to the effect that, why was he even trying to talk to me because the Jews weren't worth saving because they had killed Christ and that was about the end of it.

Q Okay. Did you say anything after that or—

A Well, I, not really. I just, I guess I said, I just told him it was my right not to pray and he, I had my rights and he had his.

Q Okay. How did you feel about that?

A Well, I felt, you know, hurt. Then I kind of felt angry because I didn't think it was fair that he should be able to say things like that during school and get away with it. I also felt kind of uncomfortable because it's kind of hard to try and tell somebody that, who keeps on talking that you are not listening to them.

Q Okay. Did you, did you talk with your teacher?

A No, I didn't.

Q Any reason that you didn't or—

A Well, I was afraid that the teacher either wouldn't listen or if the teacher did listen, there would be a big issue made out of it and I would be in the limelight for the wrong reasons and I was afraid that I could have a lot of bad publicity, I guess you'd say, from that.

Q Okay. You mean in your school?

A Uh-huh." (Tr. 19-25).

A Baptist pastor testified that he objects to prayer "in a school setting where everyone else is praying as an act of religious faith and so forth, not because one could do that just because everyone else is doing it, it's something one chooses or affirms for himself or herself."

The pastor said, "It tends to trivialize one's religious devotion and that makes it, well, it sometimes borders on sacrilege."

A 12-year old boy of the Roman Catholic faith testified he is afraid to challenge his teacher's directions to stand and pray each morning because he might receive demerits for "doing wrong or disobeying the teacher." Other witnesses representing the Lutheran, Roman Catholic, Moslem and Jewish faiths and the teaching and psychology professions also testified in opposition to the Amendment.

The parties have exhaustively briefed the issues joined, the record is complete, and the matter is now mature for decision on the merits.

The ultimate issue for decision is a straightforward one. Does *W. Va. Const.* Art. III, § 15-a impermissibly infringe upon Plaintiffs' rights under the "Establishment Clause" of the First Amendment?

United States Constitution Amendment 1 provides: Congress shall make no law respecting the establishment of religion, or prohibiting the free exercise thereof; or abridging the freedom of speech, or of the press; or the right of the people peaceably to assemble, and to petition the Government for a redress of grievances.

There is no challenge raised herein with respect to the Plaintiffs' standing in this matter, nor has a defense been asserted on the matter of the existence of a case or controversy. The Court finds that Plaintiffs do have standing to challenge the constitutionality of the Amendment and that an actual case or controversy is before the Court making declaratory relief appropriate. 28 U.S.C. § 2201.

After a thorough review of the applicable law on the issues raised herein, the Court has concluded that its task from a legal standpoint is a relatively simple one, in view of the ample precedent available to guide the Court's deliberation.

From a personal and moral standpoint, however, the decision herein contained is the most difficult one with which this Court has ever been faced and indeed, is likely as exacting as any which will ever come before it.

Nevertheless, as the Court has noted, the sworn duty imposed upon this Court to uphold the law of these United States must and shall be held inviolate.

It is the duty of this Court to interpret the law of the United States, not to make it. The latter function belongs to the Congress of the United States. It is a fixed star in our form of government that the final arbiter of constitutional questions such as this one is the United States Supreme Court. This Court is duty bound to follow the precedent established by that Court and fully intends to do so in all matters which come before it lest "anarchy (shall) prevail within the federal judicial system." *Hutto v. Davis*, 454 U.S. 370, 375, 102 S.Ct. 703, 706, 70 L.Ed.2d 556 (1982).

Without question, Plaintiffs have established a factual basis for their claims herein through the testimonial and documentary evidence in this record. The question for the Court at this juncture is one of law.

The Supreme Court has examined with meticulous scrutiny the parameters of the "Establishment Clause" on a number of occasions.

In *Everson v. Board of Education of Ewing Tp.*, 330 U.S. 1, 67 S.Ct. 504, 91 L.Ed. 711 (1947), the Court observed:

The 'establishment of religion' clause of the First Amendment means at least this: Neither a state nor the Federal Government can set up a church. Neither can pass laws which aid one religion, aid all religions, or prefer one religion over another. Neither can force nor influence a person to go to or to remain away from church against his will or force him to profess a belief or disbelief in any religion. No person can be punished for entertaining or professing religious beliefs or disbeliefs, for church attendance or non-attendance. No tax in any amount, large or small, can be levied to support any religious activities or institutions, whatever they may be called, or whatever form they may adopt to teach or practice religion. Neither a state nor the Federal Government can, openly or secretly, participate in the affairs of any religious organizations or groups and vice versa. In the words of Jefferson, the clause against establishment of religion by law was intended to erect 'a wall of separation between Church and State.' [Citation omitted].

Id. at 15-16, 67 S.Ct. at 511-512. *See also, School District of Abington Township v. Schempp*, 374 U.S. 203, 83 S.Ct. 1560, 10 L.Ed.2d 844 (1963); *Engel v. Vitale*, 370 U.S. 421, 82 S.Ct. 1261, 8 L.Ed.2d 601 (1962).

Mr. Justice Black eloquently examined the historical basis which underlay inclusion of the "Establishment Clause" in the First Amendment in *Engel*,[3] where the Court struck down a New York law which required prayer in the public schools.

While the United States Supreme Court has not spoken with respect to the application of the "Establishment Clause" to the particulars of provisions such as those with which we are here concerned, it will soon have opportunity to do so.

In *Jaffree v. Wallace*, 705 F.2d 1526 (11th Cir. 1983), *appeal granted*, —U.S.—, 104 S.Ct. 1704, 80 L.Ed.2d 178 (1984), the Court is faced in part with determining the constitutionality of an Alabama law which provides:

At the commencement of the first class of each day in all grades in all public schools, the teacher in charge of the room in which each such class is held may announce that a period of silence is [sic] not to exceed one minute in duration shall be observed for meditation or voluntary prayer, and during any such period no other activities shall be engaged in.

705 F.2d 1526, 1528, Ala.Code § 16-1-20.2. Cf. the West Virginia Constitutional provision at issue here quoted *supra* at n.1.[4]

With respect to that provision, the Eleventh Circuit Court of Appeals opined:

The objective of the meditation or prayer statute (Ala.Code § 16-1-20.1) was also the advancement of religion. This fact was recognized by the district court at the hearing on the motion for preliminary relief where it was established that the intent of the statute was to return prayer to the public schools. . . . The existence of this fact and the inclusion of prayer obviously involves the state in religious activities. . . . This demonstrates a lack of secular legislative purpose on the part of the Alabama Legislature. Additionally, the statute has the primary effect of advancing religion. We do not imply that simple meditation or silence is barred from the public schools; we hold that the state cannot participate in the advancement of religious activities through any guise, including teacher-led meditation.

As stated in *Jaffree*, the test to be employed in ascertaining the constitutional validity of such provisions is well established. The Court must determine first, whether the statute has a secular purpose; second, whether its principal or primary effect either advances or inhibits religion, and third, whether the provision fosters "an excessive government entanglement with religion." *Id.* at 1534, *citing, Lemon v. Kurtzman*, 403 U.S. 602, 612-13, 91 S.Ct 2105, 2111-12, 29 L.Ed.2d 745 (1971); *Committee for Public Education and Religious Liberty v. Nyquist*, 413 U.S. 756, 773, 93 S.Ct. 2955, 2965, 37 L.Ed.2d 948 (1973); *Walz v. Tax Commission*, 397 U.S. 664, 674, 90 S.Ct. 1409, 1414, 25 L.Ed.2d 697 (1970); *Murray v. Curlett*, 374 U.S. 203, 83 S.Ct. 1560, 10 L.Ed.2d 844 (1963); and, *Engel v. Vitale*, 370 U.S. 421, 82 S.Ct. 1261, 8 L.Ed.2d 601 (1962). See also, *Karen B. v. Treen*, 653 F.2d 897, 900 (5th Cir.1981), *aff'd*, 455 U.S. 913, 102 S.Ct. 1267, 71 L.Ed.2d 455 (1982); and, *Stone v. Graham*, 449 U.S. 39, 101 S.Ct. 192, 66 L.Ed.2d 199 (1980).

The test as enunciated above has been applied by a number of district courts to govern their deliberations on this issue. *See, Duffy v. Las Cruces Public Schools*, 557 F.Supp. 1013 (D.N.M.1983), and *May v. Cooper-*

man, 572 F.Supp. 1561 (D.N.J. 1983).

Defendants argue that the recent cases of *Lynch v. Donnelly,* — U.S. —, 104 S.Ct. 1355, 79 L.Ed.2d 604 (1984) and *Marsh v. Chambers,* 463 U.S. 783, 103 S.Ct. 3330, 77 L.Ed.2d 1019 (1983) indicate that "the United States Supreme Court is in a state of flux with regard to the test applicable to Establishment Clause cases. . . ."

The Court cannot agree and does not find the arguments advanced by Defendants persuasive. Accord, *May v. Cooperman,* 572 F.Supp. 1561, 1574 (D.N.J.1983): "[The Court's comments in *Marsh*] suggest a clear intent to distinguish legislative prayer by adults which, like the opening of court, is primarily of a traditional ceremonial nature from mandated prayer by school children." This Court would further comment that such ceremony is meaningful but is participated in by consenting adults.

The authorities cited herein make it abundantly clear that if the law under scrutiny does not meet any of the three elements of the test set forth above, it must fail as violative of the "Establishment Clause."

The West Virginia provision fails to meet any of the three.

With respect to the first element, the legislative history of this particular provision reveals beyond doubt that its purpose was to return prayer to West Virginia's public schools. The Court has scrupulously reviewed all of the available evidence reflecting the legislative history and has concluded that no reasonable individual could reach a contrary conclusion. As one Senator stated during debate on the Amendment, " . . . you cannot do by indirection what you can't do directly." Another stated, " . . . it takes about 20 seconds to say the Lord's Prayer. Two minutes is just too long of a time to have kindergarten, middle school and type students stand in silence." One of the sponsors of the legislation has been publicly quoted as saying. "To me separation of church and state concept is a myth, like evolution."

During House debate, a Delegate quoted with approval from a constituent's letter: "I believe it is time when we should welcome God back into the classrooms and not by just meditation but by prayer and praise also." Numerous other similar comments are a major part of the legislative debate on the Amendment. No attempt was made to hide the clear intent of the legislation, namely that the State through its school system, would sponsor silent prayer.

The inclusion of the word "prayer"[5] is likewise indicative of the lack of a secular purpose, although at least one Court has held a similar statute unconstitutional even absent use of that term.[6]

The Court has determined that the provision here in issue fails to meet the first element of the test in that it clearly does not have a secular purpose, but instead has a religious purpose.

The only argument on this issue advanced by Defendants may be summarized as follows. Quoting a dissenting opinion in *Karen B. v. Treen,* 653 F.2d 897, 903, they argue, "§ 15-a has the primary purpose and effect of promoting not religion, but religious freedom. The promotion of religious freedom is a legitimate secular purpose, consonant with the purpose of the Free Exercise Clause of the First Amendment."

Again, the Court cannot find this argument persuasive, and inasmuch as Defendants cite no authority for this proposition, it is apparent that no other court has relied upon that rationale. As far as this Court can ascertain, the concept advanced is somewhat novel.

In any event, the Court considers the claim advanced by Defendants inherently contradictory and therefore it must be rejected.[7]

The Amendment must likewise fail when examined to determine if its "principal or primary effect either advances or inhibits religion."

The Court has concluded that on this issue, after examining the evidence adduced by Plaintiffs at the hearings conducted in this matter, that the rationale expressed by the Court in *May v. Cooperman,* 572 F.Supp. 1561 (D.N.J.1983) is supported by the facts in the case *sub judice.*

The *May* court stated:

I conclude that the Bill both advances and inhibits religion.

It advances the religion of some persons by mandating a period when all students and teachers must assume the traditional posture of prayer of some religious groups and during which those who pray in that manner can do so.

* * * * *

Thus the State has injected itself into religious matters by designating a time and place when children and teachers may pray if they do so in a particular manner and by mandating conduct by all other children and teachers so that the prayers may proceed uninterrupted in their presence.

While this form of legislation advances the religion of some, it inhibits the religion of others. . . .

First, there are those whose religious practices include silent prayer and meditation but who, as an article of faith, believe that the state should have no part in religious matters. For them, mandated prayer is no longer prayer. It is their conviction that if the State requires any form of religious observance the observance is drained of its substance, loses its power and becomes but an empty shell. . . .

Second, by mandating a minute of silence which permits some persons to engage in prayer, Bill 1064 prevents other persons from engaging in their kind of prayer. . . .

[R]eligious practices and the concepts of ultimate reality to which these practices point vary ever more widely. While once the prayers of most religious people could be carried on in an environment of silence, now that is no longer the case. The prayers of some persons require movement and sound. Bill 1064, therefore, mandates an environment which allows some to pray but which prevents others from engaging in their form of prayer.

Finally, there are those who profess no religion and to whom any form of prayer is offensive.

Id. at 1574, 1575.

The *May* court's rationale is compelling in the instant case and Plaintiffs' factual evidence obviously warrants adoption of that rationale by this Court.

Accordingly the Court finds that the West Virginia provision fails to withstand scrutiny in that its primary effect both advances *and* inhibits religion.

With respect to the third prong of the test—excessive entanglement—the Court has concluded that the time, manner and place of the activity mandated by the Amendment are sufficient to warrant a finding of excessive entanglement.

As stated in *Duffy v. Las Cruces Pub. Schools,* 557 F.Supp. 1013 (D.N.M.1983),

The moment of silence is intended to provide a time, place and atmosphere for prayer. The time chosen is during school hours, and the place is the school grounds. The atmosphere of silence is instilled by the teachers. These facts alone have been found sufficient to constitute excessive entanglement. [Citations omitted].

In sum, the clear weight of authority supports this Court's view that the Amendment here challenged cannot withstand constitutional scrutiny and Plaintiffs are entitled to the relief they seek by virtue of the facts proved herein.

This Court cannot refrain from observing that in its opinion a hoax conceived in political expediency has been perpetrated upon those sincere citizens of West Virginia who voted for this amendment to the West Virginia Constitution in the belief that even if it violated the United States Constitution, "majority rule" would prevail. There is no such provision in the Constitution.

The goals of the many citizens of West Virginia might have been far better served if the Amendment to the West Virginia Constitution had been realistically written within the guidelines of decisions of the Supreme Court of the United States. That Court has, in at least one instance, allowed a program in which students in public schools were released so they could receive religious training at other appropriate locations. *Zorach v. Clauson,* 343 U.S. 306, 772 S.Ct 679, 96 L.Ed. 954 (1952). In *Zorach,* a majority of the Justices found that the early release of students so they could attend religious classes off school property was only accommodating the wishes of those who desired to be free of the state school system in order to receive religious education.

The Court anticipates continuing adverse reaction to its decision but considers its obligation to uphold the United States Constitution to be a duty which cannot in good conscience be shirked because of intimidation.

Finally, the Court observes that nothing in this Order prohibits or impedes the right of any West Virginia citizen, young or old, to pray in his or her own manner, any place, anytime. This Order only prohibits State sponsorship of such prayer.

ORDER

Accordingly, it is hereby ORDERED that Plaintiffs' request for a declaratory judgment is GRANTED, and *W.Va. Const.* Art.III § 15-a is ADJUDGED and DECLARED violative of the First Amendment of the United States Constitution pursuant to 28 U.S.C. § 2201.

It is further ORDERED, by virtue of the provisions of 28 U.S.C. § 2202, that the Defendant class shall be ENJOINED and RESTRAINED from implementation of said Amendment both now and in the future. All members of the Defendant class, their officers, agents and employees, are ORDERED to comply with the terms of this Order immediately and are advised that failure to do so may result in their being held in contempt of this Court.

With respect to Plaintiffs' motion for an award of attorney's fees under the provisions of 42 U.S.C. § 1988, the Court shall withhold ruling on the propriety of such an award and ORDERS that Plaintiffs' counsel shall file a memorandum of law in support of said motion within 10 days of the date of this Order. Counsel for Defendants may file any desired response within 10 days thereafter, at which time the Court shall consider the matter mature for decision and may rule thereon without further notice to the parties. The Court shall retain jurisdiction over this matter until such time as resolution of the above motion has been reached.

The Clerk is directed to mail a certified copy of this Order to all counsel of record, and to each member of the Defendant class FORTHWITH.

NOTES

1. *W.Va. Const.* Art. III, § 15-a provides:
   "Public schools shall provide a designated brief time at the beginning of each school day for any student desiring to exercise their right to personal and private contem-

plation, meditation, or prayer. No student of a public school may be denied their right to personal and private contemplation, meditation or prayer nor shall any student be required or encouraged to engage in any given contemplation, meditation or prayer as a part of the school curriculum."

2. *See*, Orders Entered December 10, 1984, and January 9, 1985. Additionally, the Court Ordered that the hearing on the application for a preliminary injunction be consolidated with the trial on the merits pursuant to Fed.R.Civ.P. 65(a)(2). Further, the Court's Order entered on December 10, 1984, certified the class of Plaintiffs as "all parents and guardians of all infants and persons who presently attend public schools in West Virginia who object to the provisions of Article 3, Section 15-a and are affected thereby." The Defendant class was certified to include "all present county school superintendents and county boards of education located in the State of West Virginia." Fed.R.Civ.P. 23(a) and (b)(3). Notice was properly given through publication in accordance with Fed.R.Civ.P. 23(c)(2). Three persons notified the Court of their desire to opt out of the Plaintiff class, Mr. Jerry Grugin of Farmington, West Virginia, and Mr. and Mrs. Ernest Mitehem of Charlestown, West Virginia. Said individuals are, accordingly, ORDERED excluded from the Plaintiff class.

3. "It is an unfortunate fact of history that when some of the very groups which had most strenuously opposed the established Church of England found themselves sufficiently in control of colonial governments in this country to write their own prayers into laws, they passed laws making their own religion the official religion of their respective colonies. [Footnote omitted]. Indeed, as late as the time of the Revolutionary War, there were established churches in at least eight of the thirteen former colonies and established religions in at least four of the other five. [Footnote omitted]. But the successful Revolution against English political domination was shortly followed by intense opposition to the practice of establishing religion by law. This opposition crystallized rapidly into an effective political force in Virginia where the minority religious groups such as Presbyterians, Lutherans, Quakers and Baptists had gained such strength that the adherents to the established Episcopal Church were actually a minority themselves. In 1785-1786, those opposed to the established Church, led by James Madison and Thomas Jefferson, who, though themselves not members of any of these dissenting religious groups, opposed all religious establishments by law on grounds of principle, obtained the enactment of the famous 'Virginia Bill for Religious Liberty' by which all religious groups were placed on equal footing so far as the State was concerned. . . . By the time of the adoption of the Constitution, our history shows that there was a widespread awareness among many Americans of the dangers of a union of Church and State. These people knew, some of them from bitter personal experience, that one of the greatest dangers to the freedom of the individual to worship in his own way lay in the Government's placing its official stamp of approval upon one particular kind of prayer or one particular form of religious services. They knew the anguish, hardship and bitter strife that could come when zealous religious groups struggled with one another to obtain the Government's stamp of approval from each King, Queen, or Protector that came to temporary power. The Constitution was intended to avert a part of this danger by leaving the government of this country in the hands of the people rather than in the hands of any monarch. But this safeguard was not enough. Our Founders were no more willing to let the content of their prayers and their privilege of praying whenever they pleased be influenced by the ballot box than they were to let these vital matters of personal conscience depend upon the succession of monarchs. The First Amendment was added to the Constitution to stand as a guarantee that neither the power nor the prestige of the Federal Government would be used to control, support or influence the kinds of prayer the American people can say—that the people's religions must not be subjected to the pressures of government for change each time a new political administration is elected to office." 370 U.S. at 427-430, 82 S.Ct. at 1265-1267.

4. West Virginia's provision under scrutiny here mandates ("*shall* provide") the activity provided for, while the Alabama statute merely *permits* ("*may* announce") such activity.

5. "Prayer is perhaps the quintessential religious practice for many of the world's faiths, and it plays a significant role in the devotional lives of most religious people. Indeed, since prayer is a primary religious practice in itself, its observance in public school classrooms has, if anything, a more obviously religious purpose than merely displaying a copy of a religious text in a classroom." *Karen B. v. Treen*, 653 F.2d 897, 901, (5th Cir.1981), *aff'd*, 455 U.S. 913, 102 S.Ct. 1267, 71 L.Ed.2d 455 (1982). *See also, Duffy v. Las Cruces Public Schools*, 557 F.Supp. 1013 (D.N.M.1983).

6. *See, May* v. *Cooperman*, 572 F.Supp. 1561 (D.N.J.1983). The statute there declared unconstitutional provided, "1. Principals and teachers in each public elementary and secondary school of each school district in this State shall permit students to observe a 1 minute period of silence to be used solely at the discretion of the individual student, before the opening exercises of each school day for quiet and private contemplation or introspection." *Id*. at 1562. New Jersey P.L.1982, Ch. 205.

7. Conspicuously absent from Defendants' argument in this regard is enunciation of the concept now advanced in the legislative history of this measure. A rationale developed long after passage of the Amendment in question but asserted in support of its "purpose" is entitled to little probative value.

T HE "Balanced Treatment for Creation-Science and Evolution-Science in Public School Instruction" Act of Louisiana is declared unconstitutional by the United States Court of Appeals, Fifth Circuit. Under the Act no school was "required to give any instruction in the subject of the origin of mankind, but if a school chooses to teach either evolution-science or creation-science, it must teach both, and it must give balanced treatment to each theory." In declaring the act unconstitutional, the court said: "The Act violates the Establishment Clause of the First Amendment because the purpose of the statute is to promote a religious belief."

Aguillard v. *Edwards,* 765 F.2d 1251 (1985)

E. GRADY JOLLY, Circuit Judge:

We consider today a constitutional challenge to the Louisiana law entitled "Balanced Treatment for Creation-Science and Evolution-Science in Public School Instruction" (the Act). The statute in essence requires the teaching of creation-science in Louisiana public schools whenever evolution is taught. The district court struck down the law as unconstitutional, holding that there was no legitimate secular purpose for the Act and that the Act would have the effect of promoting religion. We affirm the district court's judgment. In truth, notwithstanding the supposed complexities of religion-versus-state issues and the lively debates they generate, this particular case is a simple one, subject to a simple disposal: the Act violates the establishment clause of the first amendment because the purpose of the statute is to promote a religious belief.

I.

We approach our decision in this appeal by recognizing that, irrespective of whether it is fully supported by scientific evidence, the theory of creation is a religious belief. Moreover, this case comes to us against a historical background that cannot be denied or ignored. Since the two aged warriors, Clarence Darrow and William Jennings Bryan, put Dayton, Tennessee, on the map of religious history in the celebrated *Scopes* trial in 1927[1] courts have occasionally been involved in the controversy over public school instruction concerning the origin of man. With the igniting of fundamentalist fires in the early part of this century, "anti-evolution" sentiment, such as that in *Scopes,* emerged as a significant force in our society.

As evidenced by this appeal, the place of evolution and the theory of creation in the public schools continues to be the subject of legislative action and a source of critical debate. The subject of this appeal, La.Rev. Stat.Ann. §§ 17:286.1 to .7, was enacted in 1981 when the Louisiana legislature added a provision to Louisiana's general school law applicable to all public secondary and elementary schools.[2] The statute *requires* the public schools to give balanced treatment to creation-science and to evolution-science. Creation-science and evolution-science are similarly defined in the statute as "the scientific evidences for creation (or evolution) and the inferences from those scientific evidences." Under the Act no school is required to give any instruction in the subject of the origin of mankind, but if a school chooses to teach either evolution-science or creation-science, it must teach both, and it must give balanced treatment to each theory. In addition, the statute prohibits discrimination against any teacher "who chooses to be a creation-scientist or to teach scientific data which points to creationism."[3]

The plaintiffs, a group of Louisiana educators, religious leaders and parents of children in the Louisiana public schools, challenged the constitutionality of the Act in district court, seeking an injunction and a declaration that the Act violated the Louisiana Constitution and the first amendment of the United States Constitution. The plaintiffs were joined by the Louisiana Board of Elementary and Secondary Education and the Orleans Parish School Board.[4] The defendants-appellants are the Governor, Attorney General and State Superintendent of Education of Louisiana, in their official capacities, the State Department of Education and the St. Tammany

Parish School Board.

The action was initially stayed pending the resolution of a separate action brought by the Act's sponsor and others for a judgment declaring the Act constitutional and an injunction to enforce the Act. That lawsuit, however, was dismissed on jurisdictional grounds. *Keith v. Louisiana Department of Education*, 553 F.Supp. 295 (M.D.La.1982). Following the *Keith* decision, the district court lifted its stay and held that the Act violated the Louisiana constitution.[5] On appeal, we certified the state constitutional question to the Louisiana Supreme Court which found no violation of the constitution. *Aguillard v. Treen*, 440 So.2d 704 (La.1983). We then remanded to the district court with instructions to address the federal constitutional questions. *Aguillard v. Treen*, 720 F.2d 676 (5th Cir.1983). The plaintiffs moved for summary judgment in district court, contending that the statute violated the establishment clause of the first amendment as a matter of law. The contentions of the parties before the district court were essentially the same as those advanced on appeal. The plaintiffs argue that the Act is simply another effort by fundamentalist Christians to attack the theory of evolution and to incorporate in the public school curricula the Biblical theory of creation described in the Book of Genesis. The state contends that the purpose and effect of the Act *is* to promote academic freedom and thus is a legislative enactment precisely tailored to serve a legitimate secular interest.

The district court granted the plaintiff's summary judgment motion declaring the Act unconstitutional and enjoining its implementation. The district court reasoned that the doctrine of creation-science necessarily entailed teaching the existence of a divine creator and the concept of a creator was an inherently religious tenet. The court thus held that the purpose of the Act was to promote religion and the implementation of the Act would have the effect of establishing religion. The state appeals that judgment.

II.

The sole issue for our resolution is whether the Balanced Treatment Act violates the first amendment of the United States Constitution. Although many affidavits have been filed by the state concerning the Act's purpose and effect, it is not necessary to detail the factual record. Our disposition requires only that we consider one threshold question: whether the Act has a secular legislative purpose.

III.

A.

We take this opportunity to note initially that, as a general proposition, states have the right to prescribe the academic curricula of their public school systems. We therefore exercise great care and restraint when called upon to intervene in the operation of public schools. *Epperson v. Arkansas*, 393 U.S. 97, 104, 89 S.Ct. 266, 270, 21 L.Ed.2d 228 (1968). Courts, however, have not failed to protect against violations of the first amendment, which forbids all laws "respecting an establishment of religion." *See Epperson*, 393 U.S. at 104, 89 S.Ct at 270; *School District of Abington v. Schempp*, 374 U.S. 203, 215, 83 S.Ct. 1560, 1567, 10 L.Ed.2d 844 (1963).[6] This bar includes, of course, laws respecting a particular religious belief. Hence, the state's right to prescribe its public school curriculum is limited to the extent that it may not compel or prohibit the teaching of a theory or doctrine for religious reasons. *Epperson*, 393 U.S. at 107, 89 S.Ct. at 272. The vigilant protection of the First Amendment is nowhere more vital than in American public education. *Id.* at 104, 89 S.Ct. at 270.

Although the establishment clause prohibits the enactment of laws respecting an establishment of religion, it is equally certain that total separation of church and state is not possible in an absolute sense, and "[s]ome relationship between government and religious organizations is inevitable." *Lynch v. Donnelly*, 465 U.S. 668, 104 S.Ct. 1355, 1358, 79 L.Ed.2d 604 (1984) (quoting *Lemon v. Kurtzman*, 403 U.S. 602, 614, 91 S.Ct. 2105, 2112, 29 L.Ed.2d 745 (1971)). Time and again the Supreme Court has recognized that religion is closely identified with our history and government. *See Schempp*, 374 U.S. at 212, 83 S.Ct. at 1566.[7] Indeed, the Court has observed that "nearly everything in our culture worth transmitting, everything that gives meaning to life, is saturated with religious influences. . . ." *McCollum v. Board of Education*, 333 U.S. 203, 235-36, 68 S.Ct. 461, 477, 92 L.Ed. 649 (1948). Thus, the establishment clause clearly does not require the public sector to be insulated from all that may have religious origin or significance. *Stone v. Graham*, 449 U.S. 39, 45, 101 S.Ct. 192, 196, 66 L.Ed.2d 199 (1980)(Rehnquist, J., dissenting).

Acknowledging the problems inherent in this sensitive area, we must set forth a framework for determining whether the Act is unconstitutional. This inquiry calls for line-drawing but no fixed *per se* rule can be expressed or applied in any particular case. *Lynch*, 104 S.Ct. at 1361. Although the Supreme Court has expressed unwillingness to be confined to any single test or criterion, *id.* at 1362, three principal criteria, nevertheless, have emerged to determine whether a state legislative enactment comports with the establishment clause: (1) whether the statute has a secular legislative purpose; (2) whether the principal or primary effect of the statute advances or inhibits religion; and (3) whether the statute fosters an excessive entanglement with religion. *Lemon v. Kurtzman*, 403 U.S. 602, 612–13, 91 S.Ct. 2105, 2111, 29 L.Ed.2d 745 (1971).[8] If a statute fails to satisfy any of these three criteria, it will not survive constitutional scrutiny under the establishment clause. *Stone*, 449 U.S. at 40, 101 S.Ct. at 193; *Karen B. v. Treen*, 653 F.2d 897, 900 (5th Cir.1981). Our decision today requires only that we consider the purpose prong of the *Lemon* test, for as the Supreme Court recently expressed, "[N]o consideration of the second or third criteria is necessary if a statute does not have a clearly secular purpose." *Wallace v. Jaffree*, — U.S. —, —, 105 S.Ct. 2479, 2490, 86 L.Ed.2d 29 (1985). The secular purpose requirement is not satisfied by the mere existence of *some* secular purpose if it is shown that the legislature's action was dominated by religious purposes. *Id.* at —, 105 S.Ct. at 2490; *Lynch*, 104 S.Ct. at 1368 (O'Connor, J., concurring); *Stone*, 449 U.S. at 41, 101 S.Ct. at 194. If the state's actual purpose is to endorse or disapprove of religion, the first prong of the *Lemon* test will not be satisfied. *Wallace*, — U.S. at — & n. 42, — & n. 52, 105 S.Ct. at 2490 & n. 42, 2493 & n. 52; *Lynch*, 104 S.Ct. at 1368 (O'Connor, J., concurring).

B.

With these principles as our foundation, we now examine the Act itself to determine whether it, in reality, establishes a religious belief. Our decision is not made in a vacuum, nor do we write on a clean slate. We must recognize that the theory of creation is a religious belief. We cannot divorce ourselves from the historical fact that the controversy between the proponents of evolution and creationism has religious overtones.[9] We do not, indeed cannot, say that the theory of creation is to all people solely and exclusively a religious tenet. We also do not deny that the underpinnings of creationism may be supported by scientific evidence. It is equally true, however, that the theory of creation is a theory embraced by many religions. Specifically, we must recognize that evolution has historically been offensive to religious fundamentalists because the theory cannot be reconciled with the Biblical account of the origin of man. Nor can we ignore the fact that through the years religious fundamentalists have publicly scorned the theory of evolution and worked to discredit it. *See Epperson*, 393 U.S. at 98, 107, 89 S.Ct. at 267, 272; *Crowley v. Smithsonian Institution*, 636 F.2d 738, 741–43 (D.C.Cir.1980); *McLean v. Arkansas Board of Education*, 529 F.Supp. 1255, 1258–60 (E.D.Ark.1982); *Wright v. Houston Independent School District*, 366 F.Supp. 1208, 1209–11 (S.D.Tex.1972), *aff'd per curiam*, 486 F.2d 137 (5th Cir.1973). It is in the light of the fact that the theory of creation is a religious belief and in the light of its historical setting that we look to the plain language of the Act to determine whether it embodies a secular purpose.

We begin by considering the stated purpose of the statute: to "protect academic freedom." Although we must treat the legislature's statement of purpose with deference[10] we are not absolutely bound by such statements or legislative disclaimers. *Stone*, 449 U.S. at 40–43, 101 S.Ct. at 193–94; *McLean*, 529 F.Supp. at 1263. Nor do the remarks of the sponsor or author of a statute control our determination of legislative purpose. *See Karen B.*, 653 F.2d at 900; *McLean*, 529 F.Supp. at 1263.

Although the record here reflects self-serving statements made in the legislative hearings by the Act's sponsor and supporters, this testimonial avowal of secular purpose is not sufficient, in this case, to avoid conflict with the first amendment. *See Stone*, 449 U.S. at 41, 101 S.Ct. at 193–94. Two Fifth Circuit decisions illustrate this proposition. In *Karen B. v. Treen*, we considered the constitutionality of a Louisiana statute providing for student participation in prayer in the public schools. The district court, relying upon the testimony of two legislative sponsors, found a secular legislative purpose. 653 F.2d at 900. In rejecting the sponsor's testimony, we held that the plain language of the statute made apparent its predominantly religious purpose. We observed:

> [The state does] not explain . . . how the personal asseverations of individual legislators can be more compelling that the expression of secular intent actually embodied in the statute. In fact, the personal testimony of individual proponents, given in court after enactment of the statute, is far less persuasive, since it reflects only the partial perspectives of those legislators and not the collective intention of the entire legislative body. Neither such testimony nor the words of the enactment is sufficient to overcome the obvious religious means employed by the statute. Therefore [the statute] violates the first prong of the [*Lemon*] test.

653 F.2d at 901. In *Lubbock Civil Liberties Union v. Lubbock Independent School District*, 669 F.2d 1038, 1041 (5th Cir.1982), we considered a school policy permitting students to gather on school property before or after school for religious, moral, educational or other similar purposes. In reversing the district court, we analyzed the policy on its face in the context in which it was written and determined "there was no 'preeminent' secular purpose." *Id.* at 1044–45 & n. 13.

As in *Karen B.* and *Lubbock*, a review of the plain language of the Balanced Treatment Act convinces us that it has no secular legislative purpose. Although purporting to promote academic freedom, the Act does not and cannot, in reality, serve that purpose. Academic freedom embodies the principle that individual instructors are at liberty to teach that which they deem to be appropriate in the exercise of their professional judgment. The principle of academic freedom abjures state interference with curriculum or theory as antithetical to the search for truth. The Balanced Treatment Act is contrary to the very concept it avows; it requires, presumably upon risk of *sanction* or *dismissal* for failure to comply, the teaching of creation-science whenever evolution is taught. Although states may prescribe public school curriculum concerning science instruction under ordinary circumstances, the compulsion inherent in the Balanced Treatment Act is, on its face, inconsistent with the idea of academic freedom as it is universally understood. In reaching this conclusion we reject the state's argument that compelled instruction in creation-science is necessary to promote academic freedom because public school teachers believe it illegal to teach creation-science. No court of which we are aware has prohibited voluntary instruction concerning purely scientific evidence that happens, incidentally, to be consistent with a religious doctrine or tenet. It simply does not follow that science instruction violates the Establishment Clause merely because it "happens to coincide or harmonize with the tenets of some or all religions." *McGowan*, 366 U.S. at 442, 81 S.Ct. at 1113; *Crowley*, 636 F.2d at 742.

Not only does the Act fail to promote academic freedom, it fails to promote creation science as a genuine academic interest. If primarily concerned with the advancement of creation-science, the Act, it certainly appears to us, would have required its teaching irrespective of whether evolution was taught. Thus a primary academic interest in creation-science would seem to be gainsaid because the Act requires the teaching of the creation theory only if the theory of evolution is taught.

Finally, this scheme of the statute, focusing on the religious *bete noire* of evolution, as it does, demonstrates the religious purpose of the statute. Indeed, the Act continues the battle William Jennings Bryan carried to his grave. The Act's intended effect is to discredit evolution by counterbalancing its teaching at every turn with the teaching of creationism, a religious belief. The statute therefore is a law respecting a particular religious belief. For these reasons, we hold that the Act fails to satisfy the first prong of the *Lemon* test and thus is unconstitutional.

Nothing in our opinion today should be taken to reflect adversely upon creation-science either as a religious belief or a scientific theory. Nothing in our opinion today should be taken to reflect a hostile attitude toward religion. Rather we seek to give effect to the first amendment requirement that demands

that no law be enacted favoring any particular religious belief or doctrine. We seek simply to keep the government, qua government, neutral with respect to any religious controversy. *See Karen B.* 653 F.2d at 901. The words of Chief Judge Charles Clark have special relevance here: "To say that the Constitution forbids what Louisiana . . . [has] done is only to give effect to [the] special constitutional solicitude for the vitality of religion in American life." *Karen B.*, 653 F.2d at 903. The district court's judgment is AFFIRMED.

APPENDIX

TITLE 17 GENERAL SCHOOL LAW

SUB-PART D-2. BALANCED TREATMENT FOR CREATION-SCIENCE AND EVOLUTION-SCIENCE IN PUBLIC SCHOOL INSTRUCTION

§ 286.1. Short title

This Subpart shall be known as the "Balanced Treatment for Creation-Science and Evolution-Science Act."

§ 286.2. Purpose

This Subpart is enacted for the purposes of protecting academic freedom.

§ 286.3. Definitions

As used in this Subpart, unless otherwise clearly indicated, these terms have the following meanings:

(1) "Balanced treatment" means providing whatever information and instruction in both creation and evolution models the classroom teacher determines is necessary and appropriate to provide insight into both theories in view of the textbooks and other instructional materials available for use in his classroom.

(2) "Creation-science" means the scientific evidences for creation and inferences from those scientific evidences.

(3) "Evolution-science" means the scientific evidences for evolution and inferences from those scientific evidences.

(4) "Public schools" mean public secondary and elementary schools.

§ 286.4. Authorization for balanced treatment; requirement for nondiscrimination.

A. Commencing with the 1982–1983 school year, public schools within this state shall give balanced treatment to creation-science and to evolution-science. Balanced treatment of these two models shall be given in classroom lectures taken as a whole for each course, in textbook materials taken as a whole for each course, in library materials taken as a whole for the sciences and taken as a whole for the humanities, and in other educational programs in public schools, to the extent that such lectures, textbooks, library materials, or educational programs deal in any way with the subject of the origin of man, life, the earth, or the universe. When creation or evolution is taught, each shall be taught as a theory, rather than as proven scientific fact.

B. Public schools within this state and their personnel shall not discriminate by reducing a grade of a student or by singling out and publicly criticizing any student who demonstrates a satisfactory understanding of both evolution-science or creation-science and who accepts or rejects either model in whole or part.

C. No teacher in public elementary or secondary school or instructor in any state-supported university in Louisiana, who chooses to be a creation-scientist or to teach scientific data which points to creationism shall, for that reason, be discriminated against in any way by any school board, college board, or administrator.

§ 286.5. Clarifications

This Subpart does not require any instruction in the subject of origins but simply permits instruction in both scientific models (of evolution-science and creation-science) if public schools choose to teach either. This Subpart does not require each individual textbook or library book to give balanced treatment to the models of evolution-science and creation-science; it does not require any school books to be discarded. This Subpart does not require each individual classroom lecture in a course to give such balanced treatment but simply permits the lectures as a whole to give balanced treatment; it permits some lectures to present evolution-science and other lectures to present creation-science.

§ 286.6. Funding of inservice training and materials acquisition

Any public school that elects to present any model of origins shall use existing teacher inservice training funds to prepare teachers of public school courses presenting any model of origins to give balanced treatment to the creation-science model and the evolution-science model. Existing library acquisition funds shall be used to purchase nonreligious library books as are necessary to give balanced treatment to the creation-science model and the evolution-science model.

§ 286.7. Curriculum Development

A. Each city and parish school board shall de-velop and provide to each public school classroom teacher in the system a curriculum guide on presentation of creation-science.

B. The governor shall designate seven creation-scientists who shall provide resource services in the development of curriculum guides to any city or parish school board upon request. Each such creation-scientist shall be designated from among the full-time faculty members teaching in any college and university in Louisiana. These creation-scientists shall serve at the pleasure of the governor and without compensation.

NOTES

1. *Scopes v. State of Tennessee,* 154 Tenn. 105, 289 S.W. 363 (1927).
2. The full text of La.Rev.Stat.Ann. § § 17:286.1 to .7 is set forth as an appendix to this opinion.
3. The statute does not contain a similar provision prohibiting discrimination against teachers who teach evolution.
4. Upon agreement of the parties, the court permitted counsel for the American Jewish Congress and the Anti-Defamation League of the B'nai B'rith to submit briefs as amicus curiae urging affirmance of the district court's judgment.
5. In an unpublished opinion the district court held that the Act violated the Louisiana constitution, which grants authority over the public school system to the Board of Elementary and Secondary Education.
6. The First Amendment in relevant part provides: "Congress shall make no law respecting an establishment of religion or prohibiting the free exercise thereof . . . ." This prohibition is applicable to the states through the Fourteenth Amendment. *Stone v. Graham,* 449 U.S. 39, 41 n. 2, 101 S.Ct. 192, 193 n. 2, 66 L.Ed.2d 199 (1980); *School District of Abington v. Schempp,* 394 U.S. 203, 215–16, 83 S.Ct. 1560, 1567–68, 10 L.Ed.2d 844 (1963).
7. *See also Engel v. Vitale,* 370 U.S. 421, 434, 82 S.Ct. 1261, 1268, 8 L.Ed.2d 601 (1962). ("[T]he history of man is inseparable from the history of religion"); *Zorach v. Clauson,* 343 U.S. 306, 313, 72 S.Ct. 679, 684, 96 L.Ed. 954 (1952) ("We are a religious people whose institutions presuppose a supreme being").
8. That the *Lemon* test continues to have vitality is evidenced by recent decisions of the Supreme Court. *See Estate of Thornton v. Caldor, Inc.,* __ U.S. __, __, 105 S.Ct. 2914, 2917, 86 L.Ed.2d 557 (1985); *Wallace v. Jaffree,* __ U.S. __, __, 105 S.Ct. 2479, 2490, 86 L.Ed.2d 29 (1985); *Lynch,* 104 S.Ct. at 1365; *Stone,* 449 U.S. at 40, 101 S.Ct. at 193. Justice Brennan dissenting in *Lynch* observed that "the court properly looked for guidance to the settled test announced in *Lemon v. Kurtzman.*" 104 S.Ct. at 1370. He stated that the court's return to the settled analysis of *Lemon* was gratifying but characterized the application of the *Lemon* test in that particular case as "less than vigorous." *Id.* More recently, the Court in *Wallace* applied only the purpose prong of the *Lemon* test to invalidate an Alabama law permitting a period of silence in the

public schools "for meditation or silent prayer." __ U.S. at __, 105 S.Ct. at 2491.

9. In determining legislative purpose, we may consider, among other things, the historical context of the Act and the sequence of events leading to the passage of the Act. *See Village of Arlington Heights v. Metropolitan Housing Corp.*, 429 U.S. 252, 267, 97 S.Ct. 555, 564, 50 L.Ed.2d 450 (1977); *Epperson*, 393 U.S. at 98–105, 89 S.Ct. at 267–70.

10. *See Committee for Public Education & Religious Liberty v. Nyquist*, 413 U.S. 756, 773, 93 S.Ct. 2955, 2965, 37 L.Ed.2d 948 (1973); *McGowan v. Maryland*, 366 U.S. 420, 445, 81 S.Ct. 1101, 1115, 6 L.Ed.2d 393 (1961).

Index